Protecting Children from Violence

Evidence-Based Interventions

Edited by
James Michael Lampinen
University of Arkansas

Kathy Sexton-Radek
Elmhurst College

 Psychology Press
Taylor & Francis Group

NEW YORK AND HOVE

Published in 2010
by Psychology Press
270 Madison Avenue, New York, NY 10016
www.psypress.com

Published in Great Britain
by Psychology Press
27 Church Road, Hove, East Sussex BN3 2FA

Copyright © 2010 by Psychology Press

Psychology Press is an imprint of the Taylor & Francis Group, an Informa business

Typeset by RefineCatch Limited, Bungay, Suffolk, UK
Printed and bound by Sheridan Books, Inc. in the USA on acid-free paper
Cover design by Lisa Dynan

10 9 8 7 6 5 4 3 2 1

Library of Congress Cataloging-in-Publication Data
Lampinen, James M.
  Protecting children from violence : evidence based interventions / James Michael Kathy Sexton-Radek.—1st ed.
    p. cm.
Includes bibliographical references and index.
  ISBN 978-1-84872-840-0 (hardback : alk. paper)—ISBN 978-1-84872-841-7 (pbk. : alk. paper)—ISBN 978-0-203-85292-7 (electronic book)   1. Children and violence—Psychological aspects.   I. Sexton-Radek, Kathy.   II. Title.
HQ784.V55.L36 2010
362.76'6—dc22

                                                                                2009048771

ISBN: 978-1-84872-840-0 (hbk)
ISBN: 978-1-84872-841-7 (pbk)

Protecting Children from Violence

Evidence-Based Interventions

Contents

Preface

Recent headlines in the *Chicago Tribune* listed the newest efforts to address reported violence in the high schools. With much hope, school peace summits and advocacy groups staffed by antiviolence consultants were set up to elicit dialog and then strategies to address the problem of violence in the schools. Also, as this volume gets ready to go to the presses, media accounts describe cases of missing and abducted children, including the recovery of Jaycee Dugard after almost 20 years in captivity. Many other examples of violence against children make up a part of the media landscape: bullying, physical abuse and neglect, sexual abuse, Internet predators, and the list goes on and on.

The need to address the problems of violence against children has been part of both of our research work and Kathy's clinical work for years. Each of us has employed our skills as a scientist and scientist–practitioner to broaden the understanding of the problem of violence against children and the effectiveness of approaches meant to ameliorate that problem. Given our shared interest in these issues, we worked together to host a small conference in Chicago the day before the meeting of the Association for Psychological Science in May 2008. The conference included national, regional, and local social scientists who jointly addressed the issue of how violence against children could be addressed.

With public concern about the problem of violence against children, and the myriad of media accounts of specific acts of violence against children, we hoped that our conference would contribute to the development of a broader view of the problem of violence against children. These problems, which include child abduction by strangers and family members, Internet predators of children while on the computer, violence and bullying at school, sexual exploitation, physical violence, and acts of terrorism, war, and human trafficking, require, we feel, this concerted effort by social scientists to understand the behaviors and to indicate effective interventions that can be enacted by law enforcement, school's faculty and staff, judiciary, and members of the general public. We think that ameliorating the problem of violence against children also requires an evidence-based approach. The important issues require not only the sophisticated theoretical analyses of the root causes of these problems but also the likely consequence and the system variables that can be used to eliminate the problem. We have written this book to provide a volume of solutions to the problem of violence against children and, in particular, the empirical evaluation of proposed solutions.

The group of presenters from the conference was expanded to consider additional topics that our luncheon conversations prompted. The framework of each chapter represents the consensus points that we felt provided the necessary continuity to focus on the messages within each chapter but also between the chapters. Thus, each chapter has a case study and then sections for media portrayals of the issue, public reactions, and policy statements are joined by the scholarly, experienced approach of each chapter author. Together, we think, this volume explores the nature and consequences of violence against children and the effectiveness of approaches that have been proposed to ameliorate these effects. Each chapter was written by experts on the specific topic being addressed within the framework of the common elements. A review of the most recent research on the topic is given by each chapter author and evidence-based recommendations for reducing violence against children are stated.

Each chapter provides the reader with the message of how the concept is viewed and studied, along with suggestions for addressing the issue for constructive change. We begin in the introductory chapter with an explanation of the demographics to provide the baseline census and frequency counts of the problem of violence against children. Our chapter (Chapter 1) addresses topics of the exposure to violence and prevention interventions. Specific descriptions of what can be provided to make a safe home for children and the Internet that they use for school activity are given. Forensic issues of the Juvenile Sex Offender Registry Laws, eye witness memory, and tactics used by law enforcement to find missing children are presented. Important meta-issues of child vulnerability and developmental status (including an evolutionary perspective), along with issues related to domestic violence nationally and internationally as it affects the child, are presented. We conclude our volume with a discussion of the broad international concern for children. With our concluding remarks in Chapter 25 we have provided a listing of websites for the reader. This is followed by a Bibliography. It has been our design to present the varied perspectives on violence against childhood in a way that will provide clear descriptions and realistic implications to this significant problem that children are vulnerable to.

We appreciate the hard work and dedication to detail shown by the authors whose work is represented in this volume. We would like to thank the University of Arkansas's Marie Wilson Howells endowment and Alzada Tipton, Dean of the Faculty at Elmhurst College, for funding the conference on which the book is based. Additional thanks are given to Kate Volpe from the Association for Psychological Science (APS) who helped us in the arrangement of the conference held the day before APS conference. We would like to thank Erin Flahrety and Debra Riegert from

Psychology Press for their help with this manuscript as well as who provided reviews of this book and Wendy Langford for her attention to detail in the production stages of the manuscript.

Jim owes personal thanks to his wife Stephanie, his five dogs (Popo, P-ROC, Chaos, Bear, and Gabbro), and his two cats (Marble and Frotteur) for making life so fun and fulfilling. Kathy thanks Debra Meyer, PhD, of the Elmhurst College Education department for her comments on the policy recommendations in Chapter 4. She also thanks the patience of her husband Matt and three sons Brett, Neal, and Ted as they endured her time away from the family for the planning and writing of this book.

James Michael Lampinen and Kathy Sexton-Radek
December 1, 2009

About the Editors

Jim Lampinen is an Associate Professor of Psychology at the University of Arkansas and director of the Law and Psychology Laboratory. He received his Bachelor degree in psychology from Elmhurst College and his Master and PhD degrees in cognitive psychology from Northwestern University. After a 2-year postdoctoral fellowship at Binghamton University, Dr. Lampinen joined the faculty at the University of Arkansas. Dr. Lampinen lives in Fayetteville, Arkansas, with his wife Stephanie in a little cabin in the woods.

Kathy Sexton-Radek, PhD, is a licensed clinical psychologist in the state of Illinois with practices in Western Springs and Westmont. She has been teaching undergraduate and graduate psychology courses for 20 years and is a Full Professor of Psychology at Elmhurst College and Adjunct Faculty at the Chicago School of Professional Psychology. Dr. Sexton-Radek served as a consultant to both suburban and city schools in the design, implementation, and evaluation of antiviolence programming in school systems. She is the author of four books, the most recent being *Violence in Schools: Issues, Consequences, and Expressions*, and over 60 peer-reviewed book chapters, articles, and presentations. Dr. Sexton-Radek's research areas include violence prevention, health psychology interventions, and sleep medicine. She resides in the suburb of North Riverside with her husband Matt and three sons Brett, Neal, and Ted.

Contributors

Lyndon Abrams, The University of North Carolina at Charlotte, Charlotte, NC, USA

Elizabeth Altshuler Bard, University of Oklahoma, Norman, OK, USA

Jack D. Arnal, McDaniel College, Westminster, MD, USA

Jesse Bering, Queen's University Belfast, Belfast, UK

Mary E. Bodzy, Illinois Institute of Technology, Chicago, IL, USA

Bette L. Bottoms, University of Illinois at Chicago, Chicago, IL, USA

Timothy A. Cavell, University of Arkansas, Fayetteville, AR, USA

Stephen J. Ceci, Cornell University, Ithaca, NY, USA

Crystal M. Cooper, University of Texas at Arlington, Arlington, TX, USA

Amber Culbertson-Faegre, University of Arkansas, Fayetteville, AR, USA

James Galezewski, The Chicago School of Professional Psychology, Chicago, IL, USA

Jennifer Hahn-Holbrook, Queen's University Belfast, Belfast, UK

Colin Holbrook, Queen's University Belfast, Belfast, UK

Robyn E. Holliday, University of Leicester, Leicester, UK

Elizabeth A. Keller, University of Arkansas, Fayetteville, AR, USA

Robin M. Kowalski, Clemson University, Clemson, SC, USA

James M. Lampinen, University of Arkansas, Fayetteville, AR, USA

Kenya T. Malcolm, University of Arkansas, Fayetteville, AR, USA

L. Alvin Malesky, Jr., Western Carolina University at Cullowhee, NC, USA

Paula T. McWhirter, University of Oklahoma, Norman, OK, USA

Cynthia J. Najdowski, University of Illinois at Chicago, Chicago, IL, USA

Rebecca A. Newgent, University of Arkansas, Fayetteville, AR, USA

Timothy N. Odegard, University of Texas at Arlington, Arlington, TX, USA

Christopher S. Peters, University of Arkansas, Fayetteville, AR, USA

Patricia A. Petretic, University of Arkansas, Fayetteville, AR, USA

Sharon G. Portwood, University of North Carolina at Charlotte, Charlotte, NC, USA

Jessica M. Salerno, University of Illinois at Chicago, Chicago, IL, USA

Robert Schleser, Illinois Institute of Technology, Chicago, IL, USA

Rachel A. Doran, University of Illinois at Chicago, Chicago, IL, USA

Amy D. Seay, University of Arkansas, Fayetteville, AR, USA

Kathy Sexton-Radek, Elmhurst College, Elmhurst, IL, USA

Margaret C. Stevenson, University of Evansville, Evansville, IN, USA
Chris E. Stout, Center for Global Initiatives, Kildeer, IL, USA
Lindsey Sweeney, University of Arkansas, Fayetteville, AR, USA
Elizabeth White-Chaisson, University of Arkansas, Fayetteville, AR, USA
Tisha R. A. Wiley, University of Illinois at Chicago, Chicago, IL, USA

Acknowledgments

The authors would like to thank several people and groups who made this volume possible. The volume grew out of a conference held the day before the May 2008 Meeting of the Association for Psychological Science in Chicago, Illinois. Although the conference was not officially part of the APS program, Kate Volpe of APS was a huge help to us. She helped us obtain a conference room at the hotel where APS was being held and also helped us arrange audiovisual equipment and a continental breakfast for speakers and audience members. Funding for the event came partly from the Marie Wilson Howells endowment, which helps fund research in Psychology at the University of Arkansas, and from the Dean's Office at Elmhurst College.

CHAPTER 1

Protecting Children from Violence
Historical Roots and Emerging Trends

James Michael Lampinen and Kathy Sexton-Radek

A couple of years ago, one of us presented a talk about missing children at a local college. Following the talk, a member of the audience came up to the podium to chat. "It's really horrible," she said. "I don't let my kids leave my sight for a minute. Not for a minute. Not for a single minute." Her voice was strident. Her concern was palpable. It was concern not just for her children, but also for the world they were growing up in. It is a concern shared by many.

In the past two decades there has been growing public and professional interest in the problem of violence against children. The authors who have contributed to the present volume have spent much of their professional lives trying to understand this problem and the potential solutions to it. Violence against children is a broad and multifaceted concept. Skinnider (1998) defined violence against children as "deliberate behavior by people against children that is likely to cause physical or psychological harm." So defined, violence against children encompasses a wide range of events and has deep historical roots that continue into the present day and are evidenced worldwide. Children are victims of physical abuse (Abrams & Portwood, Chapter 3; Galezewski, Chapter 2; Haan-Holbrook, Holbrook, & Bering, Chapter 12; McWhirter & Altshuler Bard, Chapter 13; Petretic & White-Chaisson, Chapter 10), sexual abuse (Petretic & White-Chaisson, Chapter 10; Salerno, Stevenson, Wiley, Najdowski, Bottoms, &

Doran, Chapter 9), family and non-family abductions (Haan-Holbrook et al., Chapter 12; Lampinen, Arnal, Culbertson-Faegre, & Sweeney, Chapter 7), bullying and other forms of violence in schools (Galezewski, Chapter 2; Newgent, Seay, Malcolm, Keller, & Cavell, Chapter 5; Peters, Kowalski, & Malesky, Chapter 8; Sexton-Radek, Chapter 4), human trafficking (Lampinen et al., Chapter 7), Internet predators (Peters et al., Chapter 8), and a variety of other forms of violence and mistreatment (Stout, Chapter 14). Perpetrators of violence against children include parents and other relatives, strangers and acquaintances, other children, and societal institutions (e.g., Haan-Holbrook et al., Chapter 12; Lampinen et al., Chapter 7; Stout, Chapter 14). Outcomes of violence against children include serious physical injuries and death, psychological trauma including depression, anxiety disorders, and post-traumatic stress, and damage to the very social fabric of communities (Galezewski, Chapter 2). Some children are more resilient to the damage caused by these types of violence (Petretic & White-Chaisson, Chapter 10; Schleser & Bodzy, Chapter 11), but all child victims are harmed in one way or another. Social scientists have attempted to address these problems by coming to an evidence-based understanding of the causes and consequences of violence against children. Increasingly, social scientists have also begun to test evidence-based solutions. These potential solutions are the focus of the present volume.

Violence Against Children has Deep Historical Roots

Violence against children is not a new phenomenon. Infanticide was common in ancient times and continues in some parts of the world right up until the present day (de Mause, 1974). Under the Roman principle of *pater familias*, the father had absolute power over the lives of his wife and children (Saller, 2001). When children were born, the father could legally decide that he would raise them. He could also legally decide to kill them on the spot. Or if the children broke his rules he could kill them as they got older. It was entirely up to him. In ancient Sparta, children were examined by a committee of elders (Radbill, 1987). If they were judged to be deformed, they were killed by exposure to the elements. In many societies, children were killed if it was suspected that they were illegitimate (Sarl & Biiyiikiinal, 1991). According to de Mause (1998) about half of all children were killed during ancient times. Girls were killed more often than boys (Sarl & Biiyiikiinal, 1991).

In some cultures girls would be buried alive in order to do away with them (Sarl & Biiyiikiinal, 1991).

Infants were sometimes killed in order to appease the gods (de Mause, 1974). These deaths were often cruel and degrading. Children were thrown into dung heaps. They were drowned in rivers and lakes. In the city of Jericho, children were sealed into the foundations of buildings during the city's construction. Every form of death imaginable befell them. In the ruins of ancient Carthage, archeologists uncovered a cemetery containing the bodies of more than 20,000 children killed in ritual sacrifices between 400 and 200 BC (de Mause, 1998). Parents promised the gods that they would sacrifice their children if their prayers (e.g., for a good harvest) were answered. When the parents' prayers were answered, the parents kept their word. In Aztec society, children would be killed in rituals designed to placate a number of different deities (Schwartz-Kenny, McCauley, & Epstein, 2001). According to Schwartz-Kenny et al. (2001), in order to please the god of rain children would be drowned, in order to please the god of fire children would be set on fire, in order to please the god of hunting children would be shot with arrows, and so on. Mayans also engaged in the ritual sacrifice of children (Schwartz-Kenny et al., 2001).

The practice of infanticide was not restricted to ancient times. De Mause (1998) estimates that one-third of all infants born during the Medieval age were victims of infanticide (de Mause, 1998). The practice continued into the industrial age. Dead babies could be found in the streets of London, abandoned like pieces of trash, all the way up until the 1890s (de Mause, 1974). Sarl and Biiyiikiinal (1991) report that in 19th century England parents would sometimes kill their babies, sell the babies' clothing, and use the proceeds of the sale to buy glasses of gin. In 1917 in Chicago, Illinois, 1000 of the 4000–5000 illegitimate children born that year just disappeared (ten Bensel, Rheinberger, & Radbill, 1997). It is no surprise then that de Mause (1974) claimed that, "The history of childhood is a nightmare from which we have only recently begun to awaken." Although not widely acknowledged, evidence indicates that infanticide continues even into the present day in some countries (e.g., Murphy, 1995).

Even when children were not killed, they were often subjected to severe forms of physical abuse and neglect. Physical beatings of children were not uncommon in Ancient Rome (Wiedemann,

1989). Fathers had the legal right to excommunicate misbehaving children or to beat them. And beatings with rods were so commonplace in Roman schools that Roman poets committed it in verse (Wiedemann, 1989). However this does not present a full picture of Roman society. Many ancient Romans disapproved of the physical abuse of children. Indeed, Saller (2001) points out that there was ongoing debate in Roman society. Some ancient authorities argued that physical punishment was needed to maintain the moral fabric of society. Others argued that only slaves should be beaten, and that free children should never be subjected to physical punishment. Indeed, the physical harm of being flogged was seen as less serious than the insult to dignity that was involved in being treated like a slave.

Centuries later St. Augustine explicitly made the argument that children should be physically punished for their sins (de Mause, 1998). His argument was basically that it was better for children to suffer physical blows on Earth than for their souls to burn in Hell. In the Middle Ages, children were considered the property of their parents and were expected to follow their parents' dictates to the letter (ten Bensel et al., 1997). If they failed to do so, severe beatings were considered to be appropriate methods of correction. One source from the Middle Ages stated, "If one beats a child until it bleeds, then it will remember – but if one beats it to death, the law applies" (cited in ten Bensel et al., 1997). In the 1600s to 1700s child labor in mills also led to the mistreatment of children. For instance, children between the ages of 4 and 10 years old working in cotton mills were punished with a device that forced their heads between their knees, causing them to bleed from the nose and ears (ten Bensel et al., 1997).

Severe maltreatment of children was commonplace well into the industrial age and of course continues to this day. Consider the story of Mrs. Etta Wheeler (Shelman & Lazoritz, 2005). In 1873, Mrs. Wheeler was visiting a tenement in New York City as a missionary for St. Lukes Mission. In one of the tenements, she found Mary Ellen Wilson, a 9-year-old girl shackled to her bed. She was physically underdeveloped, appearing to be only 5 or 6 years old. She suffered from malnutrition and showed signs of being beaten. In the tenement, Mrs. Wheeler found a leather whip that had been used on the child. Mrs. Wheeler reported the abuse to local authorities, but they told her there was nothing they could do to help the child. No law prohibited this kind of treatment of children. Finally, in desperation, Mrs. Wheeler appealed to the Association for the Prevention of Cruelty to Animals (ASPCA). She argued that children deserved at least the same protection that animals received. Eventually the ASPCA interceded. Three months later, Mary Ellen was removed from the tenement and placed with a foster family who took good care of her. Think of that. Children were so devalued that organizations existed to protect animals from cruelty, but no organizations existed to protect children from cruelty. Mary Ellen's plight eventually resulted in the creation of the Society for the Prevention of Cruelty to Children, one of the first organizations specifically devoted to protecting children from violence. In 1895 the Society published a report documenting many of the ways children in London were mistreated. Children were hit with "boots, crockery, pans, shovels, straps, ropes, thongs, pokers, fire, and boiling water" (ten Bensel et al., 1997, p. 3). The Society also documented instances of gross neglect that left children "miserable, vermininfested, filthy, shivering, ragged, nigh naked, pale, puny, limp feeble, faint dizzy, famished and dying" (ten Bensel et al., 1997, p. 3).

Childhood sexual abuse also has a long history. It is well known that in ancient Greece pedophilia was considered a perfectly acceptable practice (ten Bensel et al., 1997). Plutarch even wrote an essay advising fathers of the best kind of person to give their sons to for sex (de Mause, 1998). In ancient Rome, sexual abuse of children was illegal (Wiedemann, 1989) if the children were Roman citizens. Nevertheless, Roman aristocrats sometimes engaged in the sexual abuse of children (de Mause, 1998; Wiedemann, 1989). In Eskimo cultures parents would loan their daughters to their house guests as a token of hospitality (Radbill, 1987). Wealthy aristocrats during the Renaissance in Europe would openly seek sexual favors from young children (ten Bensel et al., 1997). In India in the 1920s, when the government tried to prohibit child marriages, there were protests by men and women alike (de Mause, 1998). Mothers feared that if their daughters were not married early they would likely be raped by family members. British doctors in the 19th century regularly found that when a man came in with venereal disease, his daughter usually also had venereal disease (de Mause, 1998). In fact, doctors actually prescribed having sex with young girls as a cure for venereal disease (de Mause, 1998). During much of the 20th century, the sexual exploitation of children was largely swept under the rug (Gordon, 1998). But by the 1970s the problem of child sexual abuse became a major topic of public conversation and of public policy action (Conte, 1998). Although childhood sexual abuse is no longer considered acceptable, the practice continues at alarming rates (Finkelhor, Hotaling, Lewis, & Smith, 1990).

Violence Against Children Continues

The above discussion illustrates that violence against children has deep historical roots. Sadly, violence against children, in diverse forms, still permeates societies worldwide. Consider the following data concerning violence against children in the United States:

- In 2007 approximately 794,000 children were victims of child maltreatment (U.S. Department of Health and Human Services, 2009).
- Approximately 1530 children die every year as a consequence of child abuse and neglect (U.S. Department of Health and Human Services, 2008).
- The prevalence of child sexual abuse of girls has been estimated to be approximately 27%, while the prevalence in boys has been estimated at approximately 16% (Finkelhor et al., 1990).
- Approximately 1.6 million children in grades 6–10 are victims of bullying on a weekly basis (Office of Juvenile Justice and Delinquency Prevention, 2001).
- In one survey, 18% of students reported carrying a weapon at some time in the past month and 6% of students reported carrying a weapon onto school property (U.S. Department of Education, 2008).
- There are close to 200,000 family abductions every year (Flores, 2002) and close to 60,000 non-family abductions every year (Finkelhor, Hammer, & Sedlak, 2002). More than 1.6 million children run away from home or are forced to leave home every year (Flores, 2002).

Nor is the problem of violence against children just a problem for the United States. Rather it is a worldwide problem with worldwide consequences. The United Nations recently issued a report documenting the scope of the problem (Pinheiro, 2006). The results show just how far we have come and how far we still have to go:

No violence against children is justifiable; all violence against children is preventable. Yet the in-depth study on violence against children (the Study) confirms that such violence exists in every country of the world, cutting across culture, class, education, income and ethnic origin. In every region, in contradiction to human rights obligations and children's developmental needs, violence against children is socially approved, and is frequently legal and State-authorized. (Pinheiro, 2006, p. 5)

Consider some of the findings from the report.

- More than 50,000 children are murdered every year around the world.
- Between 80 and 98% of children worldwide are subjected to physical punishment, with about one-third of those children being beaten with objects.
- School bullying occurs worldwide with 20–65% of children indicating that they have been the victims of either verbal or physical bullying in the past month.
- Worldwide, more than 200,000,000 children under the age of 18 years old were victims of child sexual abuse in 2002 alone.
- Approximately 1.2 million children are victims of human trafficking worldwide.

And these are just some of the forms of violence that children are subjected to.

The Internet is also awash with stories about violence against children. In preparing the present chapter we did a search of Google news for the word "child". Figure 1.1 shows the results for the first 100 news stories we sampled. As can be seen, 60% of the stories had to do with some sort of violence against children. The stories included cases of child physical abuse, child sexual abuse, neglect and abandonment, child pornography, suicide, child abduction, human trafficking, corporal punishment, and murder. Of course, the fact that events are covered by the news media is not necessarily indicative of the true incidence of the problem. However, the widespread dissemination of stories concerning violence against children both reflects and perhaps underlies the widespread public concern with these problems.

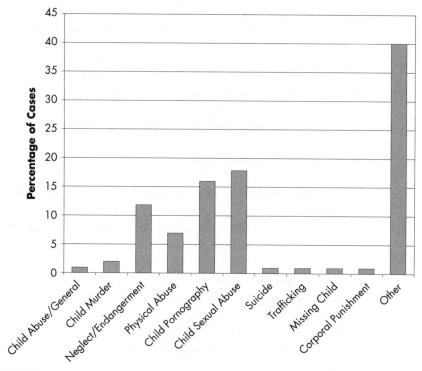

FIGURE 1.1 Results of a Google news search for the term "child", suggesting that most media coverage focuses on acts of violence against children.

Protecting Children from Violence: Major Themes

Violence against children is a major national and international problem. The purpose of the present volume is to pull together research from experts in the field examining the best practices that can be used to help protect children from violence. A number of themes emerge when examining this research. These themes run throughout each of the chapters in the present volume.

Human Stories

One theme that runs throughout the present volume concerns the very real human cost that occurs in these cases. Each chapter presents case studies illustrating different types of abuse and neglect. The purpose of these case studies is to illustrate the key concepts that the chapters address. But even more importantly, these case studies make real the tragic costs involved when violence is directed against children. The stories told throughout this volume are often heart-breaking and are sometimes chilling. They make all too clear how important the problem of violence against children is.

Nature and Scope of the Problem

A second theme that runs throughout the present volume concerns the importance of gaining an adequate, empirically driven estimate of the nature and scope of the problem of violence against children. All of the authors agree that children are subjected to violence. But what type of violence are children most likely to be subjected to? And who is most at risk? This requires carefully conducted research, using strong designs, and carefully developed and applied operational definitions.

Empirical Interventions

A third theme that runs throughout the present volume concerns the importance of testing potential interventions designed to reduce violence. Most people want something to be done to decrease the amount of violence children are subjected to and the harm that results from that violence. But interventions to reduce violence need to be based on solid data. This is true in two major ways. First, approaches to reducing violence and the impact of violence should be grounded in strong theoretical models. As Kurt Lewin (1952, p. 169) famously opined, "There is nothing more practical than a good theory." Theories can be applied at several different levels. Why do people commit violence against children? How do children cope when they are victimized? What can be done to prevent violence in the future or undo the harm caused by violence? Each of these questions can be addressed best by applying empirically established theoretical models. Second, it is important that researchers empirically test the effectiveness of particular interventions in order to see which interventions are most effective. Just because something works in theory does not mean it will work in practice. Examining the effectiveness of approaches used to combat violence requires the use of pilot projects and carefully conducted outcome studies. These approaches to using the scientific method to protect children from violence are at the core of the contributions to the present volume.

Public Perceptions and Public Policy

Another theme that runs throughout the present volume is that public perceptions of the problem of violence against children do not always square well with the reality as reflected in scientific data. This mismatch between public perception and the current state of the scientific data is discussed in many locations throughout the present volume. One issue that arises when public perceptions and scientific data collide is the question of which will inform public policy decisions. Of course, in democratic countries policy-makers are ultimately responsive to the priorities of their constituents. To the extent that public perceptions are systematically distorted, it follows that public policy will tend to be similarly distorted. This does not make children any safer. Social scientists have an important responsibility in helping to inform public policy debates concerning how to best protect children from violence. This does not mean advocating any particular public policy. But, certainly, decisions about governmental policies should clearly be informed by the relevant scientific data and social scientists are in the best position to provide those insights.

Violence Against Children is an International Problem

One final theme of the present volume is that violence against children is not limited to one country or one region, but is a worldwide problem. Chapter 12 by McWhirter and Altshuler Bard, describing international perspectives on domestic violence, and Chapter 13 by Stout, describing the efforts of the Center for Global Initiatives, make explicit the international scope of the problem of violence against children. However, the international scope of the problem is a theme that is implicitly present throughout the present volume. Parents suffer the trauma of having their children go missing for a variety of reasons all over the world. As is clear from the U.N. report cited above, violence and bullying in schools are not limited to one region. Childhood sexual and physical abuse knows no boundaries. Each of these problems exists across national boundaries and has been around for a long time. Moreover, as Chapter 12 by Hahn-Holbrook and colleagues makes clear, basic attempts to adapt to the problem of violence, such as wariness of strangers, may be hard-wired and thus broadly disseminated across peoples.

Conclusions

The problem of violence against children is not a new problem, nor is it a problem of only one country or reason. It is a complex and multifaceted problem with often dire consequences for the children who are victimized. Although violence against children will undoubtedly always be with us, there is much that can be done to reduce the amount of violence that children are subjected to. The present volume presents a state-of-the-art review of some of these approaches and an empirical evaluation of the effectiveness of these approaches.

References

Conte, J. R. (1998). Child sexual abuse: Awareness and backlash. *The Future of Children, 4,* 224–232.

De Mause, L. (1974). Foundations of Psychohistory. In L. de Mause (Ed.), *The history of childhood* (pp. 1–22). New York: Psychohistory Press.

De Mause, L. (1998). The history of child abuse. *Journal of Psychohistory, 25,* 216–236.

Finkelhor, D., Hammer, H., & Sedlak, A. J. (2002). *Nonfamily abducted children; national estimates and characteristics. Incidence studies of missing, abducted, runaway and throwaway children.* Washington, DC: U.S. Department of Justice.

Finkelhor, D., Hotaling, G., Lewis, I. A., & Smith, C. (1990). Sexual abuse in a national survey of adult men and women: Prevalence, characteristics, and risk factors. *Child Abuse and Neglect, 14,* 19–28.

Flores, J. R. (2002). *Highlights from the NISMART Bulletins. National incidence studies of missing, abducted, runaway and throwaway children.* Washington, DC: U.S. Department of Justice.

Gordon, L. (1998). The politics of child sexual abuse: Notes from American history. *Feminist Review, 28,* 56–64.

Lewin, K. (1952). *Field theory in social science: Selected theoretical papers by Kurt Lewin.* London: Tavistock.

Murphy, P. (1995, May 21). Killing baby girls routine in India. *San Francisco Examiner,* C12.

Office of Juvenile Justice and Delinquency Prevention (2001). *Addressing the problem of juvenile bullying.* Washington, DC: U.S. Department of Justice.

Pinheiro, S. (2006). *The U.N. study on violence against children.* Official Report presented to the 61st UN General Assembly. http://www.violencestudy.org/IMG/pdf/English-2-2.pdf

Radbill, S. X. (1987). Children in a world of violence: A history of child abuse. In R. E. Helfer & R. S. Kempe (Eds.), *The battered child* (pp. 3–41). Chicago: University of Chicago Press.

Saller, R. (2001). Family values in Ancient Rome. *Fathom archive,* University of Chicago. http://fathom.lib.uchicago.edu/1/777777121908/

Sarl, N., & Biiyiikiinal, S. N. C. (1991). A study of the history of child abuse. *Pediatric Surgery International, 6,* 401–406.

Schwartz-Kenny, B. M., McCauley, M., & Epstein, M. A. (2001). *Child abuse: A global perspective.* Santa Barbara, CA: Greenwood.

Shelman, E. A., & Lazoritz, S. (2005). *The Mary Ellen Wilson case and the beginning of children's rights in 19th century America.* Jefferson, NC: MacFarland.

Skinnider, E. (1998). Violence against children: International criminal justice norms and strategies. Presented at the 3rd Annual Conference of the International Association of Prosecutors "Secret Crimes – Focus on Crimes Against Children", Dublin.

Ten Bensel, R. W., Rehinberger, M. M., & Radbill, S. X. (1997). Children in a world of violence: The roots of child maltreatment. In R. E. Helfer, R. S. Kempe, & R. D. Krugman (Eds.), *The battered child* (pp. 3–28). University of Chicago: Chicago Press.

U.S. Department of Education (2008). *Indicators of school crime and safety.* Washington, DC: National Center for Education Statistics.

U.S. Department of Health and Human Services (2008). *Child abuse and neglect fatalities: Statistics and interventions.* Washington, DC: U.S. Government Printing Office.

U.S. Department of Health and Human Services (2009). *Child maltreatment 2007.* Washington, DC: U.S. Government Printing Office.

Wiedemann, T. (1989). *Adults and children in the Roman Empire.* London: Routledge.

CHAPTER **2**

Exposure to Violence
Who is Most Affected and Why?

James Galezewski

Case Illustration

In numerous doctor's and therapist's offices, in community child welfare agencies, hospitals, typical and therapeutic schools, and other treatment sites there are countless files of at-risk, aggressive, and delinquent children and adolescents that may have lines like the following in them:

> G____lived with his parents until he was placed in a treatment center. His father reportedly used drugs and alcohol and was physically abusive to him and his mother. He had difficulties in school from the second grade and had problems making friends. At 14, G____joined a gang and was caught in a robbery attempt.

> W____reported that he has enjoyed watching horror films since he was 6 years old (he is now 16), and preferred to ~¹ video games where he could shoot or stab ¹· said that he especially liked the ⸀ out the vanquished enemy's spine ar. he treated the people he bullied ⸀ enemies.

> S____said that she witnessed her ₁ abused by a series of boyfriends as a reportedly chronically depressed and

S____and her siblings. She reported that she is in a relationship where she and her boyfriend "seem to be always fighting."

Overview of the Issues

While these cases are quite different, they all have one thing
in common: They reported prolonged exposure to violence. This
exposure, combined with other familial, environmental, and
personal factors, has led to their adopting aggressive thoughts,
attributions, and behaviors as late adolescents and young adults.

There are many studies that point to the fact that violence in
its many shapes and types impacts and changes a child: psychologically, socially, intellectually, emotionally, and even neurologic-
ally. This chapter will serve as a focused review of research
literature that seeks to answer some questions: What types of
violence most affect children and adolescents? In what ways are
children impacted by violence? How is research sometimes at
odds with popular perceptions of how violence affects children?
What recommendations, programs, and interventions are being
developed for violence prevention or to lessen its impact?

Types of Violence

From birth, children exist in a world full of violence and are
vulnerable to all of its forms. Most children will either be a victim
of, or a witness to, violence of one kind or another. Osofsky (1995)
suggested that violence in all of its forms is becoming so prevalent
that it has become a "public health epidemic."

Of all the different types of violence, research suggests that
three major types of violence tend most to interface with children
and adolescents: family violence in the form of direct or vicarious
domestic violence; media such as television, movies, music, and
video games; and community and school-based violence.

Media Violence

Of all of the forms of violence that children are exposed to,
none has been researched as thoroughly as that of media violence.
Since the 1950s over 3500 studies have examined the possible association between exposure to media violence and violent
behavior in children and adolescents. Donald Cook (2000), in
testimony before the U.S. Congress, stated that all but 18 of
studies suggested a positive correlation between media

exposure and violent behavior. In 1998, the American Psychiatric Association study concluded that a child watched 28 hours of television a week and that by age 18 an average child saw 16,000 simulated murders and 200,000 acts of violence (Cook, 2000). With increased use of both the Internet and video games, Perry (2001) wrote that children are "bathed in violent images."

Research evidence is clear that television, which contains so much violent content, has a great influence on the subsequent aggressive behavior of viewers (Huesmann, Moise, & Podolski, 1997; Sanson & diMuccio, 1993; Wood, Wong, & Chachere, 1991). In one longitudinal study, children's preferences for violent television shows at age 8 were related to the seriousness of criminal convictions by age 30 (Huesmann, 1986). Other evidence suggests that the observation of media violence can lead to a greater readiness to act aggressively and to insensitivity to the suffering of victims of aggression (Bushman & Geen, 1990; Gadow & Sprafkin, 1993; Paik & Comstock, 1994). The American Academy of Pediatrics (AAP) suggested that exposure to media violence was a factor in 50% of homicides involving youth.

What is it about exposure to violent media that impacts the child and in what way? Albert Bandura (1983; Bandura, Ross, & Ross, 1963), a major proponent of Social Learning Theory, emphasized that aggression evolves from social and environmental influences. In short, aggression is a learned behavior, stemming from both modeling and reinforcement from aggressive role models they interact with. In 1963, Leonard Eron suggested that television provided aggressive role models. He studied third grade children's viewing habits and aggressive behavior and concluded that there was a positive relationship between violence witnessed on TV and levels of aggressive behavior. He specifically concluded that aggressive behavior was more due to the content of the programming than the time spent watching (Eron, 1963). In 1974, Drabman and Thomas studied third and fourth graders' exposure to media violence and found that such exposure desensitized them to the aggressive behavior of other children. In 1980, the National Institute for Mental Health (NIMH) issued a two-volume report on the impact of television. In a 15-year longitudinal study that compared TV viewing at ages 6 and 10 and compared it with young adult aggressive behavior, Heusmann, Moise-Titus, Podolski, and Eron (2003) suggested that, after chronic exposure to violent media, children tended to identify with aggressive characters and also tended to perceive that media violence is realistic.

This effect transcended gender, socioeconomic status and family structure. The researchers in this study noted that violent media had its greatest negative impact when violence was paired with reward or glory for the violent perpetrator.

Family Violence

Domestic violence is widespread and crosses socioeconomic and cultural boundaries (Osofsky, 1999). In some areas of the United States, more than 50% of the calls for police assistance are for domestic disturbances. Many children and adolescents are exposed to actual violence from an early age. Margolin and Vickerman (2007) estimate that abuse occurs in approximately 30% of two-parent families. Sources vary widely as to the estimate of children in the United States who either are the victim of, or witness to, physical and verbal abuse – from approximately 6 million children in 1998 (NCIPC, 1998) to 15.5 million in 2006 (McDonald, Jouriles, Ramisetty-Miller, Caetano, & Green, 2006). The percentage estimate is about 5–10% of all children (Pagelow, 1984; as cited in Osofsky, 1999, p. 34; also see Margolin & Vickerman, 2007).

In any discussion on violence and child development, it is important to include family dynamics, as family relations influence the capacity for self-regulation of emotions and behavior (Ehrensaft, Cohen, Brown, Smailes, Chen, & Johnson, 2003). Children who witnessed episodes of domestic violence had physical, emotional, and psychological effects, especially dissociative behaviors and angry outbursts both at home and in the larger community (Chemtob & Carlson, 2004). This same study suggested that there were high rates of posttraumatic stress disorder (about 40%) among the children who had direct or witnessed exposure to violence.

Domestic violence also affects the parent–child relationship. Children whose parents show uninvolved parenting styles (especially that of the mother) tend to develop externalizing behavior problems. They tend to act dependent, moody, and hostile, showing lower levels of social skills and self-control (Baumrind, 1971, 1980; Feldman, 1998). Yet, maternal warmth and support may help to prevent the development of these symptoms (Skopp, McDonald, Jouriles, & Rosenfeld, 2007). However, mothers who have been the victim of, or exposed to, domestic violence demonstrate high levels of parenting stress and lower psychological functioning (Chemtob & Carlson, 2004; Levandosky, Huth-Bocks,

Shapiro, & Semel, 2003). Abused mothers tend to struggle with powerlessness and compromised skills and abilities, although a study by Levandosky et al. (2003) suggested that some mothers' parenting skills are increased as they attempt to compensate for the violence in the home. However, no matter what the level of parenting skills, mothers who are the victim of, or witness to, abuse exhibit high levels of depression, anger, and dissociation. They tend to be more physically and emotionally distant and reactive, are more behaviorally impulsive, tend to evaluate their child's behavior more negatively, and underestimate their child's distress. In short, it may be difficult for an abused and traumatized mother to provide "a sufficient context of safety" (Chemtob & Carlson, 2004; Owen, Thompson, & Kaslow, 2006). The lack of such a context leaves children with a chronic sense of danger and uncertainty and a less secure parent–child attachment bond (Margolin & Vickerman, 2007).

Physical aggression on the part of parents is known to be positively associated with how children regulate their emotions and adjust to social situations outside the home (Halperin, Newcorn, Matier, Bedi, Hall, & Sharma, 1995; Loeber et al., 1993; Martin & Clements, 2002). Several studies found that early experiences of personal maltreatment and rejection by parents will lead a child to develop hostile attribution biases, social problem-solving deficits, and proneness to anticipate rejection at the hands of others, as well as a tendency to display reactive violence (Dodge, 1991; Ehrensaft et al., 2003; Owen et al., 2006). Child aggression is also correlated with marital discord, parenting stress, erratic and inconsistent use of punishment, and ineffective parental monitoring (Patterson, 1982).

There are additional family variables besides exposure to violence that go into whether a child is chronically aggressive. These variables go back to a child's infancy. If parents react to a child with "difficult" and demanding temperament by showing anger and inconsistency, then the child is more likely to experience behavior problems. On the other hand, parents who display warmth and consistency are more likely to have children who have fewer problems (Belsky, Fish, & Isabella, 1991; Teerikangas & Aronen, 1998).

Socioeconomic status (SES) may also have an impact on patterns of aggression in children and adolescents. Aggressive and conduct-disordered behavior is associated with family SES (Szaymari, Boyle, & Offord, 1989). The impact of poverty on the family tends to increase parental hostility and child–parent conflict (Paternite, Loney, & Langhorne, 1976).

Community and School Violence

Children are particularly impacted by "chronic community violence," which is usually random and involving the use of guns and knives, in low-income or recently economically depressed areas (Osofsky, 1999). One survey conducted at a public hospital in a large urban area found that 1 in 10 children under the age of 6 reported witnessing a shooting or stabbing. Other studies suggest that one-third of children in some urban areas have seen a homicide and that two-thirds have seen a serious assault (Farver & Frosch, 1996; Groves, Zuckerman, Marans, & Cohen, 1993; Osofsky, 1995). The impact of witnessing chronic violence in one's immediate community may lead to a child learning to withdraw from his/her immediate environment in fear or to live in a victim's stance. Or he/she may learn that violence and aggression are adaptive and even admirable ways of thriving in the world. Through the modeling and tutelage of peers and aggressive adolescents and adults, violent behaviors may be reinforced and victims/enemies dehumanized (Goldsmith, 2005). An interesting theory, Lorenz' frustration–aggression theory (as cited in Goldsmith, 2005), may provide an answer to how communities with chronic and random violence may frustrate and overcome those who try to escape or transcend the violence. In this theory, the interruption of a goal by the external environment increases the possibility of aggressive behavior. If the goal-directed behavior (in this case, escaping and transcending violence) is very motivated, the possibility of aggressive behavior increases as the inability to escape also increases, causing frustration, pain, and hopelessness.

A good deal of exposure to violence occurs in the schools, as children act out aggressively upon other children ("bullying") who take that behavior to their school environment. About 15% of students bully others at one time or another. About half of bullies come from abusive homes. They tend to watch more television containing violence and they misbehave more at school and home than non-bullies. When they get into trouble, bullies tend to blame others and try to lie their way out of consequences. They show little remorse for their actions (Garrity, Jens, & Porter, 1996; Kaltiala-Heino, Rimpela, Marttunen, Rimpela, & Rantanen, 1999).

Bullies and victims both use aggression as ways of coping with social and emotional discomfort. Recent studies suggest that bullies utilized both reactive and proactive aggression, while victims tended only to use reactive aggression (Camodeca, Goosens, Meerum Terwogt, & Schnengel, 2002). In short, victims tended to act out in frustration, possibly due to feelings of powerlessness and helplessness. While bullies also tended to act out aggressively when feeling out of control, their aggression was also fueled at times by rewards, such as peer approval or bolstering their sense of self.

How does the experience of bullying impact the child who is the object of violence? How do the victims of bullying cope? The victims of bullies share several characteristics. Most often they are loners who are fairly passive. They tend to lack the social skills that might otherwise defuse a bully. Their coping styles tend to vary according to the type of aggression they experience and their age. In a study by Roecker Phelps (2001), it was found that child victims of bullying used more internalizing strategies, such as to take the aggressive behaviors against them in silence or to cry easily, for coping with relational aggression (such as peer rejection and social isolation) and more externalizing strategies, such as returning violence with violence, for coping with overt verbal or physical aggression. Adolescent victims of bullying reported more use of externalizing and less use of internalizing strategies than children. After a time of silently being the victim of bullying, the victim may "snap," acting out in verbal aggression and physical violence. Profiles of such victims who turn aggressive are described as having a low sense of self, feeling unpopular, and disconnected from their peers. These violent victims are described as finding identity and reconnection with others via violent retaliation (Pollack, 1998).

The Consequences of Violence: How it Impacts a Child

The chronic experience of violence involves many transactional processes between the child and his or her environment. Responses to violence and trauma are made that ultimately impact not only how the environment changes the child, but also how the child impacts his/her environment. Many children who are at highest risk have social, emotional, and behavioral problems that appear early and are predictive of adaptive difficulties in adolescence and early adult life. These vulnerabilities include genetic, neuropsychological, temperamental, cognitive, perceptual, and social factors. Inasmuch as these factors often are highly correlated, it is not clear whether they contribute independently or additively in predicting risk. Nonetheless, it is important to examine each factor and the impacts that are made on the child.

Biological and Neurological Impacts

Perry (2001) described how certain patterns of brain activation related to the "fight–flight" response can alter brain growth and development. In turn, these alterations result in changes to physiological, emotional, cognitive, and social functioning. Occasional and moderate stress can actually be helpful for children, as it allows for the development of healthy and successful responses to stress (a sort of stress inoculation). Yet, unpredictable and chronic stress results in the child becoming overwhelmed, which in turn results in vulnerability to future stress, deficits in the ability to tolerate stress, and the child's ability to clearly interpret and respond to threat in an adaptive and socially acceptable way.

According to Perry (2001), if a child is exposed to fear and violence for long enough, his/her neurobiology will adapt to the chronic violence, resulting not only in changes of brain structure but also of behavior. The child's brain is in a chronic alarm state, which can alter cortical and subcortical development, which would in turn alter the level of efficiency and accuracy of the brain. In turn, the brain and body are activated less efficiently and how the brain takes in, interprets, and responds to the environment is also less efficient. The two major types of behavior patterns that emerge from chronic violence are hyperarousal and dissociative types. Symptoms and behaviors related to hyperarousal include increased startle response, higher resting heart rate, hypervigilance and irritability, problems with control of arousal, motor movement, and reactive behavior (Davis, 1992; Perry, 1994, 2001; Perry, Pollard, Blakely, Baker, & Vigilante, 1995). Children with this behavior type are more likely to be violent in and beyond childhood (Halperin et al., 1995; Loeber et al., 1993). The dissociative type tends to disengage from what he/she experiences, reacting with passivity, distraction, and escape into daydreaming, fantasy, derealization, and depersonalization (Perry, 2001). The pattern of behaviors that both types tend to share includes defensive misreading of verbal and non-verbal cues, less mature problem solving (many times using aggression and violence as a tool), and impulsive responses without reflection on the consequences of those responses. Given these behavior patterns, it is not surprising that many children who are exposed to violence and have developed hyperarousal are given diagnoses of posttraumatic stress disorder (PTSD), attention deficit hyperactivity disorder (ADHD), and conduct disorder (CD), and those children who have developed dissociative-type behaviors are diagnosed with anxiety, depression, and somatic complaints.

Neurobiological changes alone do not account for the development of a violent child or adolescent personality. Even those children and adolescents who are at low risk for aggression due to biological or neuropsychological factors may be more likely to act with chronic aggression if some of the following risk factors are present: a neglectful or conflict-ridden environment, the experience of frequent random and/or intense violence, and the availability of few resiliency factors. Resilience factors include such things as relationships with dependable adults, safe havens, and positive peer groups. Perry (2001) suggested that the children who are at highest risk are the "ones who are safe nowhere," and who live with a pervasive sense of threat.

Cognitive Impacts

Biological and neuropsychological factors, however, do not act independently of other factors, such as learned and developed patterns of thoughts and feelings and one's social environment. Some psychologists suggest that a combination of neurophysiological changes and learned behavior resulting from exposure to violence may lead to various maladaptive patterns in their cognitive functioning. There tends to be a slower rate of information processing and decision making in children who have been chronically exposed to violence, possibly due to decreased attention and concentration. This may lead to the child not perceiving and putting together all of the information she/he needs to make a good decision or not understanding all of the nuances of the situation before him/her (Rossman & Ho, 2000).

Such a pattern of processing, combined with high emotional arousal, the flooding of affect (see next subsection), and reliance on past ways of dealing with others, increases the chance that the child or adolescent will develop aggression as a product of their social information processing patterns and will develop attributions regarding the social interactions they encounter daily. These information processing patterns and attributions include: overestimations of danger, overinterpretations of ambiguous cues as aggression, a sense of preoccupied worry, and intrusive thoughts about the safety of oneself or of loved ones (Briere, 1992). These processing patterns and attributions act as proximal mechanisms for aggression, because such a pattern makes a child more prone to developing a "hostile attributional bias," interpreting benign actions as being hostile (Dodge, Murphy, & Buchsbaum, 1984; Dodge & Newman, 1981).

Subsequently, in deciding how to respond to the intentions of another child or adolescent, a young person with a hostile attributional bias tends to respond with reactive, aggressive behavior to what they see as a negative interpretation of another's behavior, although it may be an inaccurate interpretation (Dodge, 1991; Dodge & Crick, 1990; Dodge, Price, Bachorowski, & Newman, 1990; Nasby, Hayden, & dePaulo, 1979; Slaby & Guerra, 1988). Children who see others' behavior as aggressively motivated also tend to show less empathy, have trouble recognizing appropriate emotions in others, and have difficulty taking another person's perspective (Schonfeld, Schaffer, O'Connor, & Portnoy, 1988).

Another factor in the development of aggressive attitudes and attributions is the role of a violent parent as a model. The way a child or adolescent perceives and interprets the intentions and conflict resolution styles and behaviors of their parents also tends to drive how they evaluate effectiveness and outcomes (responses) to those intentions and behaviors. Researchers found that children who have experienced violence in their household were more likely than their peers to choose aggressive strategies for solving problems and were more likely to evaluate those outcomes favorably (Crick & Ladd, 1990; Ehrensaft et al., 2003; Perry, Perry, & Rasmussen, 1986).

Hostile attributions and aggressive outcomes have a significant impact on the level of social acceptance a child or adolescent has. Studies suggest that the way in which children understand the causes of another child's behavior and how they anticipate and evaluate the outcomes of their social problem-solving strategies determines their level of social acceptance and the amount of successful social interaction they have (Crick & Ladd, 1990). Further studies (Crick & Dodge, 1996; Dodge, Pettit, McClaskey, & Brown, 1986; Dodge et al., 1990; Milich & Dodge, 1984; Slaby & Guerra, 1988) suggest that reactively and proactively aggressive children show deficits in social information processing, both in early and later stages, and, consequently, experience problems relating to and being accepted by peers.

Emotional and Behavioral Impacts

Not only are thoughts, attitudes, and attributions learned, but emotions and their expressions are also learned to a great extent. Patterns of feeling as well as thinking come into play when examining the impact of exposure to violence.

Hopf, Huber, and Weiss (2008), in a 2-year international longitudinal study, concluded that children exposed to chronic media violence (films, TV, and video games) develop "long-term aggressive emotions" such as frustration, rage, humiliation, blame, sadistic pleasure, and hate early on in their development. Feelings of inadequacy, shame, and powerlessness emerge for males who are the victims of or witnesses to chronic violence (Pollack, 1998). Children who repeatedly witness violence in their home and/or community tend to exhibit the emotional profile of PTSD, which includes nightmares, clinginess to parents, fear of natural exploring beyond their immediate environment, the numbing of emotions, distractibility, intrusive thoughts, and feelings of not belonging (Widom, 1989). These symptoms may occur as early as infancy and toddlerhood and last well into early adolescence (Osofsky, 1999).

Studies of posttraumatic stress in children and adolescents exposed to family violence (Margolin & Vickerman, 2007; van der Kolk, 2005) found that these children tended to be flooded with negative affect. This flooding may make the child more susceptible to intense affective and physiological reactions (such as increased arousal), leading to inappropriate displays of emotion, difficulties with emotional control, and impulse control problems. They also tended to have less self-efficacy and self-esteem compared to their peers and problems with making and keeping friends.

Public Perceptions

Often public perceptions of violence against children do not quite square well with what research tells us. This section will address a few important misconceptions about child-related violence.

Many assume that violence exposure only impacts older children, as younger children are believed to be too small to grasp or recall the violence they were exposed to. In fact, studies suggest that exposure to violence is linked to the development of negative behaviors in children, regardless of age (Osofsky, 1999). Some studies (Cicchetti & Toth, 1995; Perry, 2001) have concluded that infants and toddlers who are the direct victims of violence or witnesses of violence in their homes and/or community show increased irritability and overarousal, immature behavior, sleep disturbances, emotional distress, fears of being alone, and regression in toileting and language. Psychosocial developmental theorists, especially Erik Erikson (1950), suggest that exposure to trauma interferes with a child's development of trust and later behaviors that lead to the building of autonomy and independence in childhood and of identity in adolescence.

As with infants and toddlers, elementary-age children are more likely to have sleep disturbances (nightmares), will be less likely to explore or play freely, have less range of emotion, and have less attention and concentration. They will also have greater possibility of exhibiting internalizing behaviors, aggressive and acting-out behaviors, poor social competence, and poor school performance (Osofsky, 1999).

Many also assume that children "will get over it" – that is, that most responses to exposure to violence, while difficult in the short run, will lessen or disappear. Yet, age and chronicity of exposure to violence tend to have an impact on the degree to which the impact is short term or long term. Longitudinal studies of the impact of violent media on behavior concluded that not only was childhood exposure related to adult aggression in both males and females, but the earlier the child was exposed, the more likely the impact on behavior was to be long term (Hopf et al., 2008; Huesmann et al., 2003). The authors of this research called for awareness that media exposure to violence is much more likely to bring about a long-term effect the earlier such exposure begins.

Policy Recommendations

Media Violence

Many policy recommendations have come from research on children and violence, yet many have also come from the work on resilience and resiliency factors. Commenting on the NIMH report on the impact of television on children, Rubenstein (1983) recommended that the entertainment industry should lead with their creativity to develop media products that were not violent, rather than follow the market for violent products. He also recommended that parents be deliberate in teaching viewing skills, such as application of values to choice of media product.

This parental strategy would involve taking an active interest in what their children watched, perhaps co-viewing with comment and discussion. The American Association of Pediatrics (AAP), in a testimony made by Cook before the U.S. Senate Commerce Committee, recommended that parents need to "ensure that their children are thoughtful critical consumers of media" (Cook, 2000). Parents were encouraged to set media content, set time limits on media use, monitor and discuss the media the children use, and take TVs and video games out of their children's bedrooms (Cook, 2000). The AAP also called on the entertainment industry to work with health professionals to establish programs that would lead to children becoming "media literate," learning to read and critically examine the messages in the media for what they are rather than passively accepting them. Other researchers recommended parental co-viewing with comment and feedback (Huesmann et al., 2003; Nathanson, 1999), suggesting that such involvement would reduce their children's identification with the perpetrator, reduce the perception of the violence as real, and reduce the possibility that the child will rehearse the behavior in fantasy or play after the observation.

The American Psychological Association (APA), after a detailed review of the research on video games, passed the Resolution on Violence in Video Games and Interactive Media in 2005. In this resolution, the APA called for programs that would educate both young people and parents on media literacy, support research on the effects of interactive media violence, engage the entertainment/game developers to address the issue of violent games and aggressive behaviors, and establish a content-based rating system for video games (American Psychological Association, 2005).

In short, both researchers and policy-makers call for prevention programs to reduce violent media exposure, increase parent involvement and monitoring, and encourage an environment where the industry drives the market (and the content of video games) rather than the other way around.

Family Violence

The Chentob and Carlson study (2004) stated that about 50% of mothers and 40% of children who are the victims of or witnesses to domestic violence fit the profile of someone with PTSD. Of those mothers, 91% had not obtained psychiatric help for their children. Such a study points to the need for programs that would encourage mothers in homes with domestic violence to get mental health interventions for themselves and their children.

Parent training and education may help to reduce aggressive behavior, both in children and in their parental role models. Pollack (1998) recommended that parents stay truly involved and connected with their children and notice what they are up to. It is what the parent does and how the parent behaves that is most important. He posits that parents are the primary models in modeling such things as perspective taking and empathy, anger management, emotional expression, and behavior within relationships. According to Pollack, forms of treatment that specialize in providing opportunities to talk to their children and adolescents are paramount to the prevention of aggression. A popular program geared for parents and all adults who work with children is the ACT Against Violence Program (Silva, Sterne, & Anderson, 2000), which will be explained in detail at the end of this section.

Finally, family therapy has proven effective for a range of child and adolescent problems. When family members are involved, changes are more likely to be maintained because the family system, with parents and siblings, and not just the child, is being transformed.

Community and School Violence

School-related violence is a real problem for children and adolescents. Without sustained intervention, it will not go away. Many types of home-, school-, and therapy-based interventions have been designed to counter school-related violence. Therapeutic interventions can provide significant and relatively lasting improvements for a range of child and adolescent problems, with a multisystemic approach working best (Strauss, 1994). These interventions focus on the way a child or adolescent feels (emotion), thinks (cognitions), and acts (behavior). More than 230 different treatment techniques are currently in use for children and adolescents (Kazdin, 1993).

Among individual therapy approaches, perspective taking, or knowing the cycle of violence, is a way of positively empowering the perpetrator, victim, and witness of violence to think about violence and to respond in a different way. This form of cognitive-behavioral therapy consists of training the youth to identify triggers (such as events, people, interactions) of violence and to identify what feelings (especially self-blame and discomfort) arise and what thinking distortions power the violent reaction. Then skill training in generating alternative ways to respond and in employing new and creative solutions to their problems is taught. This type of therapy aids children in controlling the meaning of a situation and in containing powerful disruptive emotions.

Many programs created to address school-related violence for perpetrator, victim and witness are group focused, focusing on primary prevention. These programs tend to address three different skill areas in which both bullies and victims usually have deficiencies: interpersonal skills, problem-solving skills, and cognitive-coping skills (Strauss, 1994). Some school-based programs deal with violence by what they call "bully proofing." The students are trained on what behaviors make a bully and what behaviors make students attractive targets for bullies. Students then acquire skills in defusing situations in which bullies approach them. This program also attempts to redirect bully energy into positive activities, such as appointing them the "guardian" of victims (Pollack, 1998). Another popular program used in schools is the Second Step Program (Frey, Hirschstein, & Guzzo, 2001), which is a primary prevention program designed to deter aggression by promoting social competence in the areas of empathy, problem solving, and anger management. When unpopular children completed social competency programs, they tended to interact more with their peers, hold more conversations, develop higher self-esteem, and were more accepted by their peers (Asher & Rose, 1997; Bierman & Furman, 1984). Children in similar programs became more adept at accurately reading facial expressions, increased their sensitivity to others' emotions, and became better at making friends (Nowicki & Oxenford, 1989).

Garrity, Jens, and Porter (1996) suggest that victims and witnesses of violence can also be taught skills to help them cope and to decrease the possibility of their becoming aggressive. These skills may include leaving situations where violence occurs, increasing their tolerance, understanding that they need not get upset, and realizing that they are not to blame.

The ACT Against Violence Training Program

The ACT Against Violence Training Program developed as the result of a joint initiative between the American Psychological Association (APA) and the National Association for the Education of Young Children (Guttman, Mowder, & Yasik, 2006). The program is based on a few basic tenets. The first is that the time from birth through to age 8 is a critical time for a child to learn the basic skills that they will need for a lifetime. The second tenet is that "what a child learns about violence, a child learns for life."

While ACT is targeted toward children, the actual focus of training is on those adults that work with and raise children. There are training modules for both professionals and parents, with the goal of teaching research-based interventions so that adults can teach and model positive ways to deal with conflict, anger, and aggression in the context of social relationships. There are four modules to ACT that are geared to violence prevention: Anger Management, Social Problem Solving, Discipline, and Media Violence (Silva & Randall, 2005).

The module on Anger Management is for the adults in the program to learn to teach children the skills to express anger adaptively and constructively. Topics in the module include helping children and adults to manage and appropriately express their anger, using anger management to prevent violence, issues in child development, and the development of anger management skills (Silva et al., 2000).

The Social Problem Solving module is designed not only to instruct professionals in teaching social skills to children, but also to help families teach social skills in the context of the home. Topics include how important it is to teach social skills, the development of social skills in children, the role of families, and targeted social skill-teaching activities (Silva et al., 2000).

The Discipline module purports to teach the relationship between discipline and violence prevention, the importance of discipline on child development, the difference between discipline and punishment, and specific strategies for responding to behavior that is challenging (Silva et al., 2000).

Teaching in the Media Violence module stresses the impact of media violence on children's development and on their behavior, as well as giving targeted strategies for adults to teach and model responsible media consumerism (Silva et al., 2000).

An evaluation of the ACT Against Violence Training Program showed that the program was quite effective in teaching adults both knowledge and technique. The researchers/evaluators suggested that not only are the teachers better informed and equipped, but they can use their new knowledge and technique for regulating their own behavior as well as that of the children they care for (Guttman et al., 2006). The researchers also noted that ACT addresses and bolsters six primary characteristics of parenting: bonding, discipline, education, general welfare and protection, responsivity, and sensitivity. The program, then, can bring about behavioral change not only in the child but in the parent as well.

References

American Psychological Association (2005). *Resolution on violence in video games and interactive media.* Retrieved June 10, 2009 from http://www.apa.org/releases/resolutionvideoviolence.pdf

Asher, S. R., & Rose, A. J. (1997). Promoting children's social and emotional adjustment with peers. In P. Salovey & D. J. Sluyter (Eds.), *Emotional development and emotional intelligence: Educational implications* (pp. 196–230). New York: Basic Books.

Bandura, A. (1983). Psychological mechanisms of aggression. In R. Geen & E. Donnerstein (Eds.), *Aggression: Theoretical and empirical reviews, Vol.1. Theoretical and methodological reviews* (pp. 1–40). New York: Academic Press.

Bandura, A., Ross, D., & Ross, S. (1963). Vicarious extinction of avoidance behavior. *Journal of Personality and Social Psychology, 49*, 521–532.

Baumrind, D. (1971). Current patterns of parental authority. *Developmental Psychology Monographs, 4* (1, part 2).

Baumrind, D. (1980). New directions in socialization research. *Psychological Bulletin, 35*, 638–652.

Belsky, J., Fish, M., & Isabella, R. (1991). Continuity and discontinuity in infant negative and positive emotionality: Family antecedents and attachment consequences. *Developmental Psychology, 27*, 421–431.

Bierman, K. L., & Furman, W. (1984). The effects of social skills training and peer involvement on the social adjustment of preadolescents. *Child Development, 55*, 151–162.

Briere, J. N. (1992). *Child abuse trauma.* Newbury Park, CA: Sage.

Bushman, B. J., & Geen, R. G. (1990). Role of cognitive-emotional mediators and individual differences in the effects of media violence on aggression. *Journal of Personality and Social Psychology, 58*, 156–163.

Camodeca, M., Goosens, F. A., Meerum Terwogt, M., & Schnengel, C. (2002). Bullying and victimization among school-age children: Stability and links to proactive and reactive aggression. *Social Development, 11*, 332–345.

Chentob, C. M., & Carlson, J. G. (2004). Psychological effects of domestic violence on children and their mothers. *International Journal of Stress Management, 11*(3), 209–226.

Cicchetti, D., & Toth, S. L. (1995). A developmental perspective on child abuse and neglect. *Journal of the American Academy of Child and Adolescent Psychiatry, 34*, 541–565.

Cook, D. E. (2000, September). *Testimony of the American Academy of Pediatrics on media violence before the US Senate Commerce Committee*, Washington, DC. Retrieved from the American Academy of Pediatrics website: www.aap.org/advocacy/

Crick, N. R., & Dodge, K. A. (1996). Social information-processing mechanisms in reactive and proactive aggression. *Child Development*, *67*, 993–1002.

Crick, N. R., & Ladd, G. W. (1990). Children's perceptions of the outcomes of social strategies: Do the ends justify being mean? *Developmental Psychology*, *26*, 612–620.

Davis, M. (1992). The role of the amygdala in conditioned fear. In J. P. Aggleton (Ed.), *The amygdala: Neurobiological aspects of emotion, memory, and mental dysfunction* (pp. 255–306). New York: Wiley-Liss.

Dodge, K. A. (1991). The structure and function of reactive and proactive aggression. In D. J. Pepler & K. H. Rubin (Eds.), *The development and treatment of childhood aggression* (pp. 201–218). Hillsdale, NJ: Lawrence Erlbaum Associates, Inc.

Dodge, K. A., & Crick, N. R. (1990). Social information-processing bases of aggressive behavior in children. *Personality and Social Psychology Bulletin*, *16*, 8–22.

Dodge, K. A., Murphy, R. R., & Buchsbaum, K. (1984). The assessment of intention-cue detection skills in children: Implications for developmental psychopathology. *Child Development*, *55*, 163–173.

Dodge, K. A., & Newman, J. P. (1981). Biased decision-making processes in aggressive boys. *Journal of Abnormal Psychology*, *90*, 375–379.

Dodge, K. A., Pettit, G. S., McClaskey C. L., & Brown, M. (1986). Social competence in children. *Monographs of the Society for Research in Child Development*, *44* (2, Serial No. 213).

Dodge, K. A., Price, J. M., Bachorowski, J., & Newman, J. M. (1990). Hostile attributional biases in severely aggressive adolescents. *Journal of Abnormal Psychology*, *99*, 385–392.

Drabman, R. S., & Thomas, M. H. (1974). Does media violence increase children's toleration of real life aggression? *Developmental Psychology*, *10*, 418–421.

Ehrensaft, M. K., Cohen, P., Brown, J., Smailes, E., Chen, H., & Johnson, J. G. (2003). Intergeneration transmission of partner violence: A 20 year prospective study. *Journal of Consulting and Clinical Psychology*, *71*, 741–753.

Erikson, E. (1950). *Childhood and society*. New York: W. W. Norton.

Eron, L. D. (1963). Relationship of TV viewing habits and aggressive behavior in children. *Journal of Abnormal and Social Psychology*, *67*, 193–196.

Farver, J. A. M., & Frosch, D. L. (1996). L.A. stories: Aggression in preschoolers' spontaneous narratives after the riots of 1992. *Child Development*, *67*, 19–32.

Feldman, R. S. (1998). *Child development*. Upper Saddle River, NJ: Prentice Hall.

Frey, K. S., Hirschstein, M. K., & Guzzo, B. A. (2001). Second step: Preventing aggression by promoting social competence. In H. M. Walker & M. H. Epstein (Eds.), *Making schools safer and violence free: Critical issues, solutions and recommended practices* (pp. 88–98). Austin, TX: Pro-Ed, Inc.

Gadow, K. D., & Sprafkin, J. (1993). Television "violence" and children with emotional and behavioral disorders. *Journal of Emotional and Behavioral Disorders, 1,* 54–63.

Garrity, C., Jens, K., & Porter, W. W. (1996). *Bully–victim problems in the school setting*. Paper presented at the annual meeting of the American Psychological Association, Toronto, Canada.

Goldsmith, C. E. (2005). Psychoanalytic/developmental theories related to adolescence and aggression. In K. Sexton-Radek (Ed.), *Violence in schools: Issues, consequences and expressions* (pp. 35–47). Westport, CT: Praeger.

Groves, B., Zuckerman, B., Marans, S., & Cohen, D. (1993). Silent victims: Children who witness violence. *Journal of the American Medical Association, 269,* 262–264.

Guttman, M., Mowder, B. A., & Yasik, A. E. (2006). The ACT Against Violence Training Program: A preliminary investigation of knowledge gained by early childhood professionals. *Professional Psychology: Research and Practice, 37,* 717–723.

Halperin, J. M., Newcorn, J. H., Matier, K., Bedi, G., Hall, S., & Sharma, V. (1995). Impulsivity and the initiation of fights in children with disruptive behavior disorders. *Journal of Child Psychology and Psychiatry, 36,* 1199–1211.

Hopf, W. H., Huber, G. L., & Weiss, R. H. (2008). Media violence and youth violence: A 2-year longitudinal study. *Journal of Media Psychology, 20,* 79–96.

Huesmann, L. R. (1986). Psychological processes promoting the relations between exposure to media violence and aggressive behavior by the viewer. *Journal of Social Issues, 42,* 125–139.

Huesmann, L. R., Moise, J. F., & Podolski, C. (1997). The effects of media violence on the development of antisocial behavior. In D. M. Stoff, J. Brieling, & J. D. Maser (Eds.), *Handbook of antisocial behavior* (pp. 181–193). New York: John Wiley & Sons.

Huesmann, L. R., Moise-Titus, J., Podolski, C., & Eron, L. D. (2003). Longitudinal relations between children's exposure to TV violence and their aggressive and violent behavior in young adulthood: 1977–1992. *Developmental Psychology, 39,* 201–221.

Kaltiala-Heino, R., Rimpela, M., Marttunen, M., Rimpela, A., & Rantanen, P. (1999). Bullying, depression and suicidal ideation in Finnish adolescents: School survey. *British Medical Journal, 329,* 348–351.

Kazdin, A. E. (1993). Adolescent mental health: Prevention and treatment. *American Psychologist, 48*, 127–141.

Levandosky, A. A., Huth-Bocks, A. C., Shapiro, D. L., & Semel, M. A. (2003). The impact of domestic violence on the maternal–child relationship and preschool-age children's functioning. *Journal of Family Psychology, 17*, 275–287.

Loeber, R., Wung, P., Keenan, K., Giroux, B., Stouthamer-Loeber, M., Van Kammen, W. B., & Maughan, B. (1993). Developmental pathways in disruptive child behavior. *Development and Psychopathology, 5*, 103–133.

Margolin, G., & Vickerman, K. A. (2007). Posttraumatic stress in children and adolescents exposed to family violence I: Overviews and issues. *Professional Psychology: Research and Practice, 38*, 613–619.

Martin, S. E., & Clements, S. L. (2002). Young children's responding to interparental conflict: Associates with marital aggression and child adjustment. *Journal of Child and Family Studies, 11*, 231–244.

McDonald, R., Jouriles, E. N., Ramisetty-Miller, S., Caetano, R., & Green, C. E. (2006). Estimating the number of American children living in partner violent families. *Journal of Family Psychology, 20*, 137–142.

Milich, R., & Dodge, K. A. (1984). Social information processing in child psychiatry populations. *Journal of Abnormal Child Psychology, 12*, 471–489.

Nasby, W., Hayden, B., & dePaulo, B. M. (1979). Attributional bias among aggressive boys to interpret unambiguous social stimuli as displays of hostility. *Journal of Abnormal Psychology, 89*, 459–468.

Nathanson, A. I. (1999). Identifying and explaining the relationship between parental mediation and children's aggression. *Communication Research, 26*, 124–143.

NCIPC (National Center for Injury Prevention and Control), Division of Violence Prevention, Family and Intimate Violence (1998). *Fact sheet on dating violence.* Atlanta, GA: U.S. Department of Health and Human Services, NCIPC, Centers for Disease Control and Prevention.

Nowicki, S., & Oxenford, C. (1989). The relation of hostile nonverbal communication styles to popularity in preadolescent children. *Journal of Genetic Psychology, 150*, 39–44.

Osofsky, J. D. (1995). Children who witness domestic violence: The invisible victims. *Social Policy Report, 9*, 1–18.

Osofsky, J. D. (1997). The effects of exposure to violence on young children. *American Psychologist, 50*, 782–788.

Osofsky, J. D. (1999). The impact of violence on children. *The Future of Children: Domestic Violence and Children, 9*, 33–49.

Owen, A. E., Thompson, M. P., & Kaslow, N. J. (2006). The mediating role of parenting stress in the relation between intimate partner violence and child adjustment. *Journal of Family Psychology, 20*, 505–513.

Pagelow, M. D. (1984). *Family violence.* New York: Praeger.

Paik, H., & Comstock, G. (1994). The effects of television violence on antisocial behavior: A meta-analysis. *Community Resources, 21,* 516–546.

Paternite, C. E., Loney, J., & Langhorne, J. E. (1976). Relationships between symptomatology and SES-related factors in hyperkinetic/MBD boys. *American Journal of Orthopsychiatry, 46,* 291–301.

Patterson, G. R. (1982). *Coercive family processes.* Eugene, OR: Castalia.

Perry, B. D. (1994). Neurobiological sequalae of childhood trauma: Post-traumatic stress disorders in children. In M. Murberg (Ed.), *Catecholamines in post-traumatic stress disorder: Emerging concepts* (pp. 253–276). Washington, DC: American Psychiatric Press.

Perry, B. D. (2001). The neurodevelopmental impact of violence in childhood. In D. Schetky & E. P. Benedeck (Eds.), *Textbook of child and adolescent psychiatry* (pp. 221–238). Washington, DC: American Psychiatric Press.

Perry, D. G., Perry, L. C., & Rasmussen, P. (1986). Cognitive social learning mediators of aggression. *Child Development, 57,* 700–711.

Perry, B. D., Pollard, R., Blakely, T., Baker, W. L., & Vigilante, D. (1995). Childhood trauma, the neurobiology of adaptation and "use-dependent" development of the brain: How "states" become "traits". *Infant Mental Health Journal, 16,* 271–291.

Pollack, W. (1998). *Real boys.* New York: Henry Holt.

Roecker Phelps, C. E. (2001). Children's responses to overt and relational aggression. *Journal of Clinical and Adolescent Psychology, 30,* 240–252.

Rossman, B. B. R., & Ho, J. (2000). Posttraumatic response and children exposed to parental violence. *Journal of Aggression, Maltreatment and Trauma, 3,* 85–106.

Rubenstein, E. A. (1983). Television and behavior: Research conclusions of the 1982 NIMH report and their policy implications. *American Psychologist, 38,* 820–825.

Sanson, A., & diMuccio, C. (1993). The influence of aggressive and neutral cartoons and toys on the behavior of preschool children. *Australian Psychologist, 28,* 93–99.

Schonfeld, I. S., Schaffer, D., O'Connor, P., & Portnoy, S. (1988). Conduct disorder and cognitive functioning: Testing three causal hypotheses. *Child Development, 59,* 993–1007.

Silva, J., & Randall, A. (2005). Giving psychology away: Educating adults to ACT against early childhood violence. *Journal of Early Childhood and Infant Psychology, 1,* 37–44.

Silva, J., Sterne, M. L., & Anderson, M. P. (2000). *ACT Against Violence Training Program manual.* Washington, DC: American Psychological Association and National Association for the Education of Young Children.

Skopp, N. A., McDonald, R., Jouriles, E. N., & Rosenfeld, D. (2007). Partner aggression and children's externalizing problems: Maternal and partner warmth as protective factors. *Journal of Family Psychology, 21,* 459–467.

Slaby, R. G., & Guerra, N. G. (1988). Cognitive mediators of aggression in adolescent offenders: I. Assessment. *Developmental Psychology, 24,* 580–588.

Strauss, M. B. (1994). *Violence in the lives of adolescents.* New York: W. W. Norton.

Szatmari, P., Boyle, M., & Offord, D. R. (1989). ADDH and conduct disorder: Degree of diagnostic overlap and difference among correlates. *Journal of the American Academy of Child and Adolescent Psychiatry, 30,* 219–230.

Teerikangas, O. M., & Aronen, E. T. (1998). Effect of infant temperament and early intervention on the psychiatric symptoms of adolescents. *Adolescent Psychiatry, 37,* 1070–1077.

Van der Kolk, B. A. (2005). Developmental trauma disorder. *Psychiatric Annals, 35,* 401–408.

Widom, K. (1989). Does violence beget violence? A critical examination of the literature. *Psychological Bulletin, 106,* 3–28.

Wood, W., Wong, F. Y., & Chachere, J. G. (1991). Effects of media violence on viewers' aggression in unconstrained social interaction. *Psychological Bulletin, 109,* 371–383.

CHAPTER 3

Protecting Children in their Homes

Effective Prevention Programs and Policies

Lyndon Abrams and Sharon G. Portwood

Case Illustration

Margaret is a member of an interagency group of social and community service providers, the Pinedale Interagency Organization for Child and Family Advocacy (PIOC). PIOC was established to coordinate a more seamless, less redundant human services network by marshalling the efforts of both public and private agencies and organizations in the Pinedale community. PIOC has also been charged with facilitating forward-focused public policy on behalf of children and families. The organization is comprised of representatives from a variety of local service providers, including a children's hospital, the Department of Social Services, law enforcement, a community research group from a regional state university, and parenting and family support providers affiliated with the school district.

Pinedale, a city of 800,000, is located in a southeastern state where the textile industry had been a central element in the city and regional economic infrastructure. However, recent "off-shoring" and changes in trade policy have led to diminished textile profitability and the subsequent closing of the three largest textile operations in the region. The loss of support industries followed. Recent failures in the savings and loan industry have also damaged Pinedale's economic infrastructure. Two of the nation's larger savings and loan banks had been headquartered in the local community until both companies lost profitability amidst a falling housing market. These two organizations were taken over by larger banking organizations headquartered in other regions of the country. As a result, local unemployment rates have risen substantially, and it appears that the operations in Pinedale will be scaled back even further in the coming months.

Recently, researchers at Pinedale State University have identified another disturbing trend – local child protective services data show a steady increase in reports and substantiated cases of physical child abuse in recent months. These trends run counter to declining national child maltreatment rates. Local concern over the apparent increase in child abuse has intensified following the recent deaths of four preschool children in their homes. In response to escalating public outrage, even amidst declining state and local budgets, as well as lowered philanthropic giving, local elected officials have asked PIOC to lead efforts to identify an evidence-based response to the apparent increase in child abuse. Margaret has been designated as the project coordinator by PIOC.

Overview of the Issues

An unacceptably high rate of child maltreatment is not a problem unique to the fictional community presented in the introductory case study. To the contrary, in 2006, child protection agencies across the United States received approximately 3,300,000 allegations of child maltreatment, involving 6,000,000 children (U.S. Department of Health and Human Services, 2008). Despite these disturbing numbers, other recent data have pointed to some encouraging trends. More specifically, Finkelhor and Jones (2006) documented a significant decline in the rates of physical abuse and sexual abuse over the past two decades. The downward trend for physical abuse began in 1996, reaching a record 48% decrease by 2006. A similar decrease was noted in sexual abuse cases, which declined 53% between 1992 and 2006.

Unfortunately, data further suggest that prevailing environmental factors threaten to stop or even to reverse this positive trend. As Finkelhor (2008) observed, during the period of declining physical and sexual abuse rates, the country experienced sustained economic growth, improvements in child protective services and law enforcement, improved public awareness of child maltreatment, advances in family and psychiatric medicine, and improvements in mental health services. Clearly, not only are current economic conditions in direct contrast to the economic prosperity that characterized the period of reductions in child maltreatment rates, but today's economic environment cannot sustain the other conditions that contributed to the positive trend. In fact, as exemplified in the case study, many communities have already begun to manifest the effects of a troubling economy in their child welfare systems. Often drastic reductions in the resources available to support child welfare typically result not only in a reduction in intervention services, but also in the virtual elimination of prevention programs as service providers and policy-makers struggle to make difficult decisions around the allocation of scarce resources. Perhaps most troubling is the fact that at the same time resources are declining at an alarming rate, additional resources are desperately needed to support increased need. The implications for current efforts to protect children are profound. Now, more than ever, it is essential that professionals such as Margaret select prevention programs carefully to ensure that they employ strategies that are best suited to their community's goals, both in terms of the population and the outcomes they will target. Likewise, efforts to affect supportive public policy are essential.

This chapter will examine key considerations in formulating a community-based strategy for preventing child maltreatment that includes both program and policy elements. The focus is on the prevention of the physical abuse of children.

Child Abuse Prevention Programming

General Considerations

Programs aimed at preventing child abuse vary along multiple dimensions. At the outset, those seeking to implement a prevention strategy must identify their overarching goal and, consequently, the scope of the program they will need to employ. Indicated (or tertiary) prevention programs are the most narrow in scope in that they target families with a history of maltreatment and seek to prevent the re-occurrence of abuse. More broad in scope are selective (or secondary) prevention programs that target populations deemed to be at risk for abuse. Universal (or primary) prevention programs, which perhaps most closely align with general conceptions of "prevention," are directed at the general population and aim to reduce the overall occurrence of abuse

(Rae-Grant, 1994). Despite the obvious appeal of programs that seek to prevent abuse *before* it occurs, relatively few programs have taken a universal approach to prevention, no doubt due, in part, to the difficulty in documenting positive outcomes among such a large and diverse target group. Instead, the majority of prevention programs can be classified as selective prevention programs.

Along with their scope and general prevention goals, programs may be categorized according to their theoretical orientation. In the case of child maltreatment, a number of theories have evolved that offer a casual explanation for abuse. Initial models focused on parental pathology as the singular root cause of physical child abuse. It was generally believed that resolving the psychological problems of the parent would diminish his or her risk for abusive behavior. Later causal models expanded their focus to patterns of interaction between parents/caregivers and children. Some models incorporate family systems theory to postulate that systemic interactions within the family lie at the root of violence against children in the home. For example, a non-attentive parent may withhold attention from a child who, in turn, escalates her attention-seeking behavior. The parent may then become annoyed by this behavior and react harshly toward the child. This response inadvertently reinforces the child's negative behavior to create an interlocking pattern of behavior between parent and child that can intensify and eventually result in abusive behavior by the parent aimed at stopping the child's attention-seeking behavior. Focusing solely on either the child or the parent in an effort to prevent maltreatment would ignore half of the context and thus be ineffective. The most recent theories of child maltreatment have expanded the focus even further, incorporating aspects of individual models, family systems models, and broader social impact factors (Belsky, 1993).

While, overall, conceptualizations of child physical abuse have become more global and complex, as noted, prevention efforts have nonetheless remained primarily focused on individual and family systems. Such programs may be further categorized along five theoretical dimensions that reflect the program's specific approach to effecting change through (1) behavioral, (2) multimodal, (3) behavioral humanistic, (4) cognitive-behavioral, or (5) rational emotive intervention methods (Barlow, Coren, & Stewart-Brown, 2005; Bunting, 2004). The selection of a particular theoretical modality can be informed by the demographic characteristics or capacity of the target group. For example, behaviorally oriented programs may be more effective for younger parents, who tend to be more pragmatic (i.e., more directly focused on behavioral outcomes) in their approach to parenting.

Along with general theoretical orientation, available scientific research evidence on the risk factors associated with child maltreatment may prove valuable in selecting effective prevention programming strategies. While these risks are complex, they can be delineated as factors related to the child, the parent or caregiver, the family system, and the community or broader social environment. Individual child risk factors include the child's age, the presence of behavioral problems, and having a disability. Children under age 4 have consistently been recognized as being at higher risk for physical abuse, particularly severe injury or death, than are older children (Cicchetti & Toth, 2000; Graham-Bermann, 2002). It is widely believed that child age may be linked to the level and appropriateness of parental expectations. Similarly, because parent expectations and child behavior are reciprocally related, it is often difficult to disentangle which is the preceding cause of abuse. Moreover, the particular needs of children who have behavioral or other disabilities may contribute to a level of stress that exceeds the coping ability of their parents (Belsky, 1993; Urquiza & McNeil, 1996). As illustrated by these observations, risk factors seldom occur in isolation. Instead, child characteristics may operate in concert with other factors to intensify the risk of maltreatment (Belsky, 1993; Cicchetti & Toth, 2000).

Parental risk factors are equally complex. Among the potential risk factors supported by research are a lack of knowledge of child development, single parenting, and a history of being physically abused as a child (Sedlak, 1997). For example, a parent whose knowledge of child development is limited may view a 2-year-old's attempts at individuation as disrespectful acts of defiance. This attribution may, in turn, prompt the parent to attempt to discipline the child, who is simply working through an appropriate developmental sequence of learning to think and to act independently. Parents who are parenting without a partner typically have less support along multiple dimensions, resulting in increased susceptibility to the stress related to childrearing. Some suggest that this risk is compounded further by financial stress and social isolation (Goldman, Salus, Wolcott, & Kennedy, 2003; Hecht & Hansen, 2001). Consistent with "cycle of violence" theories, abusive parents tend to report experiencing more family violence during their own childhood than do parents who have not abused their children. Nonetheless, most parents who were abused themselves as children (about 70%) are not abusive (Miller-Perrin & Perrin, 1999).

Both parent and child factors are embedded within the family system. It is generally believed that there is a circular relationship between individual and family risk and resiliency. Black, Heyman, and Slep (2001) noted significant relationships between maltreatment and elevated family stress, rigid family structure, and low familial contact. Other family environmental factors that have been shown to be related to child physical abuse include domestic violence, illness, death of a family member, and monetary stress (Miller-Perrin & Perrin, 1999; Milner, 1998).

Family factors must, in turn, be considered in the context of the relationship between the family and the larger community. There is a statistical link between child maltreatment and social connectedness (Thompson, 1994). Child maltreatment rates are low even in high poverty communities where there is a greater sense of connection among residents (e.g., where neighbors know each other and and where individuals feel at ease to ask for support from others) (Emery & Laumann-Billings, 1998).

The constructs identified by Barlow, Coren, and Stewart-Brown (2006) in their review of parent training programs adhere to four general categories: parental stress and anxiety, social skills and support, parental skill, and functionality of the parental dyad. This framework is consistent with the larger body of research on risk factors summarized in the preceding paragraphs and thus may serve to inform the identification of appropriate and effective prevention programs.

Program Outcomes

Despite the widespread use of parent education programs, only a small number have been evaluated for the specific purpose of determining whether they have an impact on child maltreatment (Daro & McCurdy, 1994). The limited data available demonstrate some positive gains in overall parenting skill, positive parent–child interactions, leveraging social supports, reduced corporal punishment, self-esteem, and personal functioning; for teenage mothers, there is also some evidence of fewer subsequent births, higher employment rates, and less welfare dependency (Daro & Cohn, 1988; Daro & Connelly, 2002). However, positive outcomes have not been reliably demonstrated across programs (Gomby, Culross, & Behrman, 1999).

In an analysis of 24 program evaluation studies, Medway (1989) found that individuals who participated in parenting programs experienced gains on the evaluative measures that were about 62% greater than those of control group members. A meta-analysis by Zepeda and Morales (2001) suggested that the greater the intervention, the more dramatic the improvement on outcome measures; however, embedded programs made it difficult to isolate the effects of the primary program and selection of participants tended to favor individuals who were more desirous of change, perhaps artificially inflating positive results.

Available Programs

The most common approaches to child abuse prevention involve providing education and/or support to parents (Gomby et al., 1999). Such programs are comprised of public education and awareness efforts; home visitation programs; and parenting education and support services directed to at-risk parents (Daro & Connelly, 2002). All tend to be based on the general proposition that lack of knowledge about child development and inadequate parenting skills are principal causes of abuse (Cowen, 2001; Wolfe, 1985). In order to build parent's resources, coping skills, and parenting competencies, programs typically focus on teaching parents new skills that expand or may even need to replace those learned during their own childhood (Reppucci, Britner, & Woolard, 1997).

The two most well-known and perhaps best-researched parent education programs – the Olds' model, operationalized as the Nurse Family Partnership, and the Healthy Families model – are both built around a home visitation component. However, the Nurse Family Partnership employs trained nurses to conduct home visits (Holden, Willis, & Corcoran, 1992), whereas the Healthy Families model relies on paraprofessional home visitors. Other essential elements of both the Nurse Family Partnership and Healthy Families include embedding services within the context of a therapeutic and supportive relationship, an established curriculum, opportunities to model effective parenting, and linking families to appropriate community resources. Although the selection criteria used to identify families differ, both programs target first-time mothers who are perceived to be high risk, and thus constitute indicated prevention programs. Research has demonstrated positive outcomes associated with both the Olds' model (e.g., Kitzman et al., 1997, 2000) and Healthy

Families (Duggan et al., 1999), including parenting attitudes and behavior and reports of child maltreatment. However, these findings have been limited to the effects on reducing the abuse of younger children; the impact on older children has not been established.

Among the expansive array of child abuse prevention programs currently available, as noted, relatively few are supported by scientifically sound data. In an effort to disseminate high quality programs, the National Registry of Evidence-based Programs and Practices (NREPP), administered through the Substance Abuse and Mental Health Services Administration (SAMHSA) of the U.S. Department of Health and Human Services, provides public information on parenting education programs. This information is available in print or may be searched using the Internet. Accordingly, individuals such as Margaret, who are interested in identifying potential strategies for their community, may review program data, including the program's history of use with various populations and its scientifically established outcomes.

At present, fewer than 25 parenting education programs are included in the NREPP. However, for those programs that are included, NREPP offers the additional advantage of indicating whether the program is recognized as a promising, effective, or model program. Programs that have demonstrated some treatment efficacy, but have not been evaluated thoroughly enough to meet the effective program standard, are deemed to be promising programs. Effective programs have met SAMHSA's high standards for research, but have not yet been widely disseminated. Those programs that have achieved SAMHSA's designation as a "model program" have been rigorously evaluated, shown to be effective, and are ready for widespread dissemination, with technical support available from the program developers.

Among the model parenting programs recognized by SAMHSA is Olds' Nurse Family Partnership. In addition, Incredible Years, Parenting Wisely, and the Triple-P Positive Parenting Program have been designated as model programs. Incredible Years is comprised of a comprehensive set of curricula aimed at children between the ages of 2 and 12 years, their teachers, and parents. While primarily focused on preventing behavioral and emotional problems in children, the parent training component of the intervention may also serve to prevent child maltreatment by enhancing parenting competencies. In fact, among the outcomes documented for Incredible Years are an increase in positive and nurturing parenting and a decrease in harsh, coercive, and negative parenting (Webster-Stratton, 1994; Webster-Stratton & Hammond, 1997: Webster-Stratton, Reid, & Hammond, 2004). Similarly, there is some suggestion that the Parenting Wisely program may serve a preventive function, despite its targeting goals other than reducing child abuse. Parenting Wisely consists of a series of self-administered, interactive CD-ROM programs that can be offered as an alternative or complement to other family services. Originally designed for low-income, single-parent families (Gordon & Stanar, 2003), Parenting Wisely has demonstrated a positive impact on parents' knowledge and use of effective parenting skills, problem solving, and ability to establish clear expectations (Cefai, Smith, & Pushak, 2005; Kacir & Gordon, 1999; Lagges & Gordon, 1999).

The Triple-P Positive Parenting Program, developed by Sanders and colleagues in Australia, uses a combined parenting education and family support strategy to prevent severe behavioral, emotional, and developmental problems and child maltreatment (Sanders, Cann, & Markie-Dadds, 2003). The multilevel Triple-P system is designed to enhance protective factors and to reduce risk factors among parents, children, and their environment. The primary focus is on developing parents' capacity and giving them the skills necessary to be independent problem-solvers, to ensure a positive environment for their child, to discipline appropriately, to have appropriate expectations of their child, and to care for themselves as parents. Notably, the Triple-P Program comports with the increasing recognition that community-based models that incorporate multiple intervention components should be pursued as a promising strategy for preventing child maltreatment. Another program that employs a community-based approach to prevention is Strong Communities, which Melton and colleagues are currently evaluating in South Carolina (www.clemson.edu/strongcommunities). The goal of this program is to strengthen neighborhoods, to enhance parent leadership, and to engage a variety of community partners in activities (e.g., pediatric well-child visits, community policing, school-based programs) that make child protection a central feature of daily life.

Like SAMHSA, the Centers for Disease Control and Prevention (CDC), also of the U.S. Department of Health and Human Services, has been involved in efforts to assist in identifying effective, evidence-based programs for the prevention of child maltreatment. Recently, the CDC has specifically sought to support research to identify effective universal child maltreatment prevention programs (National Center for Injury Prevention and Control, 2004). Among the efforts currently supported by the CDC is a study by the authors of this chapter to examine the impact of the ACT Parents Raising Safe Kids Program (ACT). Like the majority of prevention programs aimed at reducing violence against children, ACT targets parents and other primary caregivers. However, ACT is unique in its universal approach to prevention. The program is designed such that it can be implemented in diverse settings (e.g., schools, community agencies) and integrated into the broader community framework of services for parents (e.g., Head Start, Healthy Families, GED courses), regardless of their level of risk. In fact, one of the strengths of ACT is its ability to be administered to *all* groups of parents in an efficient and cost-effective manner (the program materials are available through the American Psychological Association at a cost of $50 and training workshops are offered free of charge), such that the prevention of violence against children becomes an important piece of a public health approach to violence within the community.

As originally conceived, ACT integrates two major strategies: a national media campaign and a training program. Both components provide complementary messages through media outlets (e.g., public service announcements for radio and newspapers, billboards, a website, and a toll-free number) and workshops, training sessions, and presentations. Partnering with the National Association for the Education of Young Children (NAEYC), the American Psychological Association (APA) developed the ACT program materials based on empirical research on child development, aggression, and violence prevention. Since the introduction of the Adults and Children Together Against Violence initiative in 2000, the APA and its numerous partners have trained more than 600 professionals working with children and adults, who, in turn have now introduced ACT to more than 15,000 adults (primarily parents) across the country. In order to increase the fidelity of program replication and adoption and to proceed with an outcome/impact evaluation, as well as to position ACT to meet increasing demand for the program in Latino communities, in 2005 the APA redesigned the program intervention model, refined the materials, and created the ACT Parents Raising Safe Kids program. Based on the original ACT program materials, the Parents Raising Safe Kids curriculum, which is available in English and Spanish versions, organizes the program into eight, 2-hour sessions for parents and other adults raising young children. Program content includes understanding your child's behavior, children and violence, adults dealing with their anger, dealing with children's anger, resolving conflicts in a positive way, positive discipline, reducing the influence of media on children, and parents' role in raising safe kids.

The current outcome evaluation of the ACT Parents Raising Safe Kids Program is designed to examine whether ACT produces positive outcomes for parents who have not already perpetrated child maltreatment. In regard to the significance of this study, it is important to note that ACT was not developed to be a "competitor" to existing parenting programs that target parents identified as being at high risk for child maltreatment (e.g., parents of children with behavioral disorders); rather, ACT was designed to complement these empirically based programs, many of which were created by prominent psychologists and members of the APA. Importantly, there are three distinctive features to ACT: (1) it was designed to benefit all parents, regardless of risk level, by providing education on basic principles of child development, parenting, conflict management, and violence prevention; (2) it was designed to be incorporated into the broader community framework of programming for children and families in order to establish a "foothold" for violence prevention (and, in some cases, may serve as a gateway program to more intensive services); and (3) it can be provided at a low cost and thus widely disseminated. Each of these program characteristics make ACT a unique and important potential contributor to a national effort to prevent child maltreatment. Using an experimental design with random assignment to groups, the current study will examine program impact on participating parents' knowledge, behavior, and attitudes compared to those of a comparison group of parents receiving standard community-based support services. It is hypothesized that ACT will benefit all participants equally across all program delivery formats. In addition to investigating program outcomes, the costs of implementing ACT across communities will be examined, including the cost-effectiveness of the program as a function of community, agency, and participant characteristics.

Another well-known parent education program currently being evaluated for its impact on preventing child physical abuse is Project Safe Care (Gershater-Molko, Lutzker, & Sherman, 2002).

Project Safe Care delivers a structured, skill-based protocol focused on parent–child interaction training, home safety, and child health to parents in the home setting. Families with parenting risk factors and at least one co-morbid problem, such as substance abuse, are currently participating in a randomized trial of Project Safe Care in Oklahoma that promises to produce sound evaluation data.

Best Practices in Child Abuse Prevention

Despite the relatively limited research evidencing the effectiveness of any particular program, there is a growing body of literature (e.g., Bethea, 1999; Daro, 1996; Guterman, 1997; MacLeod & Nelson, 2000) that points to a number of best practices that child maltreatment prevention programs should encompass. More specifically, research (Portwood, 2008) indicates that:

- Programs should identify, validate, and build on family strengths.
- Program instruction should be appropriate to the developmental level of the children whose parents are the target of the program.
- Programs should afford an opportunity for reciprocal demonstration of targeted skills.
- Programs should encourage the development and utilization of social support networks.
- Programming needs to include a continuum of services that allows for easy transition for individuals requiring more or less intensive services.
- Programs need to be implemented in a manner that recognizes and respects cultural diversity in family structure and behavior, while identifying problematic behaviors in a manner that is not ethnocentric or monoculturally biased against the culturally diverse.
- Program implementation must be consistent with the program's design and theoretical underpinnings.
- Evaluation of program process and outcomes should be an essential feature of programming efforts.

In recognition of the multifaceted nature of child maltreatment, prevention efforts should be adapted and customized to the distinct population to whom they are directed. As suggested by Daro and Connelly (2002), prevention activities should be tailored to the particular needs, cultural makeup, resources, and strengths of the target population. However, this presents particular challenges to those who, like Margaret, are seeking to implement a prevention program in their home community despite the fact that there is little research on whether the effectiveness of established programs will generalize to audiences with characteristics other than those of the group(s) to whom the program has already been offered. In fact, existing research and practices emphasize the need for fidelity to existing program models, which were most likely developed – and evaluated – with a population that differs in some important respect from the population now to be served.

While, as indicated above, some very good programs are available, most have not been disseminated with diverse populations. In their review of prevention programs, Zepeda and Morales (2001) noted that (1) there were limited programs focused on parents with children from birth through age 5 and (2) an examination of the applicability of the program across culturally differing groups was missing in most studies. Moreover, the high attrition rates of 30–50% in most programs may reflect a poor fit between what the program offers and what the service population needs (Daro & Connelly, 2002).

Prevention Programming Challenges and Recommendations

In summary, while Margaret can easily access information on available child abuse prevention programs, she will be faced with numerous challenges in meeting her goal of identifying and implementing an effective program to reduce child abuse in Pineville. At the outset, Margaret will need to determine the scope of the program that the community and available resources will support. A number of promising universal prevention programs are currently being evaluated, some of which, such as ACT, may be implemented at a relatively low cost. Moreover, such programs rely heavily on community collaboration, a resource that appears to be available to Margaret through the PIOC.

There is considerably more research support for the effectiveness of indicated or secondary prevention programs that target children, parents, and/or families deemed to be at a heightened level of risk for child maltreatment. However, such programs tend to require more resources to implement – resources that may not be available in Margaret's current environment. Ideally, Margaret's community could implement a multilevel prevention strategy, providing universal prevention programs on a community-wide basis and indicated prevention programs in pockets where the incidence of maltreatment is high. More general universal prevention programs may further serve as a vehicle for identifying those families in need of more intense services, beyond basic parenting information.

Public Perceptions

The fact that the general public tends to view child abuse as a heinous and, typically, criminal act may actually have the paradoxical effect of challenging rather than facilitating prevention efforts. Rather than viewing the prevention of child maltreatment as a community responsibility, and one for which each individual has an obligation, the tendency appears to be for the public to view child maltreatment as "someone else's problem." This difficulty is compounded by the sensitivity that parents typically exhibit around others' examining – and judging – their parenting ability.

While it is understandable that most parents avoid acknowledging their potential for abusive behavior toward their children, child maltreatment rates provide clear evidence of the fact that many parents *do* commit abusive acts. Thus, the challenge is how to remove the stigma associated with parents who seek help in building their parenting capacity and to engage all parents in activities that promote the protection of children from violence in the home.

Clearly, individuals such as Margaret, who are faced with the task of engaging parents, will encounter difficulties in registering participants for "a child abuse prevention program," and, most likely, even a "parenting program" given prevailing public perceptions. In the experience of these authors, organizations that provide such services to parents frequently couch their child abuse prevention efforts in broader terms and market these programs in a manner that does not call excessive attention to the abuse prevention component. A program that is marketed toward improving family relationships or building on family strengths may have broader appeal.

Despite these challenges, Finkelhor (2008) noted that improved public understanding of child maltreatment was a contributing factor to the reductions in physical and sexual abuse observed over the past two decades. It follows that a more accurate public perception of child maltreatment, including a recognition of the fact that all parents, regardless of their demographic characteristics, can benefit from parent education and support, might lead to program participation being viewed as socially desirable rather than as an admission of being a poor parent. Recent conceptualizations pose that there are two dimensions to social desirability: self-deception and impression management. Self-deception allows the individual to maintain a distorted view of self wherein he or she sees himself or herself as more closely aligned with the ideal or socially desirable way of being. For example, a parent or caregiver might view physical abuse as unacceptable, but fail to acknowledge his or her own behavior as abusive. The individual employs impression management to alter his or her presentation to conform to the prevailing social standard. Thus, a parent may strive to refrain from behavior that could be construed as abusive (e.g., spanking) in public, only to revert to this behavior in private, when there is no risk of observation or evaluation. Put simply, while increased public perception, attention to, and rejection of child maltreatment may generally be viewed as positive, increased attention may inadvertently operate to drive potentially abusive behavior out of the public view, making it more difficult to identify and to address.

Further complicating the relationship between public perception and prevention efforts is the difficulty in determining exactly what constitutes "abuse." Research demonstrates not only that there is wide variation in whether particular acts are viewed as abusive (Portwood, 1998), but also that characteristics and experiences of the individual making that decision frequently enter into his or her assessment (Portwood, 1999). It follows that individuals will typically do a poor job in assessing whether or not they can benefit from prevention services. In addition, there is racial bias in the reporting and assessment of child maltreatment (Berger, McDaniel, & Paxson, 2005). Clearly, such bias may have the effect of further isolating historically marginalized subpopulations such that they are reluctant or simply refuse to access those services that might prove effective in promoting positive parenting behaviors. Taken together, this body of research emphasizes the need for universal prevention efforts that do not limit their target audience; at the same time, however, it is clear that any such mass appeals must be crafted with an appreciation and respect for diverse cultural values and perspectives.

Policy Recommendations

Child Abuse Prevention Policy

Implementing sound programs and services is only one part of the equation for effective child maltreatment prevention. In addition, communities must ensure that the necessary policies are in place to support their programmatic framework. Although declarations of profound concern for the well-being and safety of children are regularly at the forefront of public discourse on child and family policy, these expressions of concern have not always translated into meaningful policy and consequent action to protect children (Portwood & Dodgen, 2005). In fact, frequent public testaments to the importance of children may have created the illusion that there has been more progress on policy related to child maltreatment than is, in fact, the case. For example, the Child Abuse Prevention and Treatment Act (CAPTA), originally enacted in 1974, remains the sole federal policy aimed specifically at child abuse prevention. The major prevention component of CAPTA is the Community-Based Family Resource and Support (CBFRS) program, which provides funding for a variety of community-based family support programs aimed at preventing child abuse, including parenting classes, substance abuse treatment, mental health services, respite care, and domestic violence services. Notably, however, in the more than 30 years since its original passage, CAPTA has yet to be fully funded – even in those years when the country was not facing economic difficulties (Portwood, 2006).

In recent years, the clear trend has been toward moving responsibility for child-related programs to the states. Unfortunately, the severe financial crisis in which many states find themselves inevitably means that funding for children will be reduced, placing increased responsibility on local communities for supporting child abuse prevention programs. The emerging scenario is one in which championing the causes of children and families will be left largely to local organizations, many of which are challenged by limited funding and meager sociopolitical power (Portwood & Dodgen, 2005). In Margaret's case, the existing collaboration in her community offers a vehicle through which to combine policy efforts and, hopefully, leverage political capital. While Margaret's situation is undeniably a challenging one, there may nonetheless be opportunities to advance child abuse prevention policies by supporting policies that cut across multiple issues to promote the well-being of children.

Recent initiatives in child physical abuse policy have revolved around three primary concerns: providing victims with quality physical and mental health services, providing additional educational support for individuals affected by violence in the home, and renewing attention to the goal of preventing violence against children in the home (Bethea, 1999). By supporting other child- and family-related policies, however, advocates may indirectly achieve child abuse prevention goals. For example, welfare policy aimed at keeping children out of poverty and providing affordable, quality childcare would clearly contribute to the prevention of physical abuse (Hay & Jones, 1994). Nonetheless, few efforts have been directed at preventing child abuse by helping families to avoid the stresses associated with poverty, which may, in some instances, lead to abusive parenting (Garbarino, 1999). Like those programs that encourage teen parents to complete or to obtain additional education, thus enhancing their self-sufficiency, policies that support programs and other activities designed to assist all parents in achieving financial stability may ultimately serve to prevent child maltreatment. By combining parent support and education efforts with economic supports, Margaret and others might well succeed in employing a universal prevention approach.

It is also important to note that the individuals who are statistically at greater risk for perpetrating child maltreatment are the same individuals who tend to be underserved by mental health and preventive medical services. By supporting policy efforts to link parents with these other needed services, Margaret and others could further advance their child abuse prevention agenda.

A valuable, but often underutilized partner in advocating for prevention policy and promoting positive parenting is the media. There is an abundance of ready-made public service materials that community providers such as Margaret can easily access; however, before distribution, it is important to ensure that materials are well-suited to the specific characteristics and needs of the local community. The success of media efforts to educate parents on the dangers of shaking a baby serves as a prominent example of how this powerful tool can be leveraged (Showers, 1992). Mandell (2000) provides another salient example, chronicling efforts by the Mayor's Office for Children and Youth and the Baltimore City Commission for Children and Youth. Following a community effort that included televised public service announcements aired before and after report card distribution, combined with informational inserts in the cards themselves, there was a reduction in observed incidents of child abuse associated with receiving a bad report card.

Dodgen (2000) suggested that individuals charged with the task of policy making should develop collaborative relationships with individuals who have knowledge and expertise in the area of child maltreatment (e.g., psychologists, social workers, counselors). While policy-makers are skilled at navigating the policy-making process, they often lack the contextual understanding that can best be provided by human service professionals. Partnerships between policy-makers and child maltreatment professionals (including researchers) allow for greater communication and exchange between those who more fully understand the issue and those who are empowered actually to change or to effect the policy. Portwood and Dodgen (2005) advise that human service professionals need to understand the process of policy making, to be knowledgeable on pertinent policies at all levels (federal, state, and local), and to establish effective ways of communicating with policy-makers.

Conclusions and Recommendations

Supportive public policies are the cornerstone for implementing and sustaining effective child abuse prevention programs and services. Accordingly, it is essential that human service professionals such as Margaret develop a sophisticated understanding of the nature and complexities of the policy-making process. It is also important for such child advocates to develop the collaborative relationships necessary to establish the bilateral communication that will ensure that community providers are aware of the prevailing opportunities and challenges and that they are positioned to bring their relevant expertise to bear on policy decisions.

References

Barlow, J., Coren, E., & Stewart-Brown, S. S. B. (2006). Parent training programmes for improving maternal psychosocial health. *The Cochrane Collaboration, 3,* (no page number). Retrieved October 31, 2006, from http://gateway.ut.ovid.com?gw1/ovidweb.cgi

Belsky, J. (1993). Etiology of child maltreatment: A developmental-ecological analysis. *Psychological Bulletin, 114,* 413–434.

Berger, L. M., McDaniel, M., & Paxson, C. (2005). Assessing parenting behaviors across racial groups: Implications for the child welfare system. *Social Service Review, 79*, 653–688.

Bethea, L. (1999). Primary prevention of child abuse. *American Family Physician, 59*, 1577–1579.

Black, D. A., Heyman, R. E., & Slep, A. M. (2001). Risk factors for child physical abuse. *Aggression and Violent Behavior, 6*, 121–188.

Bunting, L. (2004). Parenting programmes: The best available evidence. *Child Care in Practice, 10*, 327–343.

Cefai, J., Smith, D., & Pushak, R. E. (2005). The Parenting Wisely Parent Training Program: An evaluation with an Australian sample. Unpublished manuscript, Royal Melbourne Institute of Technology.

Cicchetti, D., & Toth, S. L. (2000). Developmental processes in maltreated children. In D. J. Hansen (Ed.), *Motivation and child maltreatment: Volume 46 of the Nebraska Symposium on Motivation* (pp. 85–160). Lincoln, NE: University of Nebraska Press.

Cowen, P. S. (2001). Effectiveness of a parent education intervention for at-risk families. *Journal for Specialists in Pediatric Nursing, 6*, 73–82.

Daro, D. (1996). Preventing child abuse and neglect. In J. Briere, L. Berliner, J. A. Bulkley, C. Jenny, & T. Reid, (Eds.), *The APSAC handbook on child maltreatment* (pp. 343–358). Thousand Oaks, CA: Sage.

Daro, D., & Cohn, A. H. (1988). Child maltreatment efforts: What have we learned? In G. T. Hotaling, D. Finkelhor, J. T. Kirkpatrick, & M. A. Straus (Eds.), *Coping with family violence: Research and policy perspectives* (pp. 275–287). Thousand Oaks, CA: Sage Publications.

Daro, D., & Connelly, A. C. (2002). Child abuse prevention: Accomplishments and challenges. In J. E. B. Meyers, L. Berliner, J. Briere, C. T. Hendrix, C. Jenny, & T. A. Reid (Eds.), *The APSAC handbook on child maltreatment* (2nd ed., pp. 431–448). Thousand Oaks, CA: Sage Publications.

Daro D., & McCurdy, K. (1994). Preventing child abuse and neglect: Programmatic interventions. *Child Welfare, 73*, 405–430.

Dodgen, D. (2000). Public policy and intimate violence: Making the case for prevention and services. *University of Missouri Kansas City Law Review, 69*, 127–137.

Duggan, A. K., McFarlane, E. C., Windham, A. M., Rohde, C. A., Salkever, D. S., Fuddy, L., et al. (1999). Evaluation of Hawaii's healthy start program. *The Future of Children, 9*, 66–90.

Emery, R. E., & Laumann-Billings, L. (1998). An overview of the nature, causes, and consequences of abusive family relationships: Toward differentiating maltreatment and violence. *American Psychologist, 44*, 121–135.

Finkelhor, D. (2008). *Child victimization: Violence, crime, and abuse in the lives of young people.* New York: Oxford University Press.

Finkelhor, D., & Jones, L. (2006). Why have child maltreatment and child victimization declined? *Journal of Social Issues, 62,* 685–716.

Garbarino, J. (1999). What children can tell us about living with violence. In M. Sugar (Ed.). *Trauma and adolescence* (pp. 165–181). Madison, CT: International Universities Press.

Gershater-Molko, R. M., Lutzker, J. R., & Sherman, J. A. (2002). Intervention in child neglect: An applied behavioral perspective. *Aggression and Violent Behavior, 7,* 103–124.

Goldman, J. Salus, M. K., Wolcott, D., & Kennedy, K. Y. (2003). *A coordinated response to child abuse and neglect: The foundation for practice.* Washington, DC: U.S. Department of Health & Human Services, Office on Child Abuse and Neglect. Available online at http://www.childwelfare.gov/pubs/usermanuals/foundation.

Gomby, D., Culross, P., & Behrman, R. (1999). Home visiting: Recent program evaluations–analysis and recommendations. *The Future of Children, 9,* 4–26.

Graham-Bermann, S. A. (2002). Child abuse in the context of domestic violence. In J. E. B. Myers, L. Berliner, J. Briere, C. T. Hendrix, C. Jenny, & T. A. Reid (Eds.), *The APSAC handbook on child maltreatment* (2nd ed., pp. 21–54). Thousand Oaks, CA: Sage Publications.

Guterman, N. (1997). Early prevention of child physical abuse and neglect: Existing evidence and future directions. *Child Maltreatment, 2,* 12–34.

Hay, T., & Jones, L. (1994). Societal interventions to prevent child abuse and neglect. *Child Welfare Journal, 73,* 379–403.

Hecht, D. B., & Hansen, D. J. (2001). The environment of child maltreatment: Contextual factors and the development of psychopathology. *Aggression and Violent Behavior, 6,* 433–457.

Holden, E. W., Willis, D. J., & Corcoran, M. M. (1992). Preventing child maltreatment during the prenatal/perinatal period. In D. J. Willis, E. W. Holden, & M. S. Rosenberg (Eds.), *Prevention of child maltreatment: Developmental and ecological perspectives* (pp. 17–46). Oxford, UK: Wiley.

Kacir, C., & Gordon, D. (1999). Parenting adolescents wisely: The effectiveness of an interactive videodisk parent training program in Appalachia. *Child and Family Behavior Therapy, 21,* 19–37.

Kitzman, H., Olds, D. L., Henderson Jr., C. R., Hanks, C., Cole, R., Tatelbaum, R., et al. (1997). Effect of prenatal and infancy home visitation by nurses on pregnancy outcomes, childhood injuries, and repeated childbearing: A randomized controlled trial. *Journal of the American Medical Association, 278,* 644–652.

Kitzman, H., Olds, D. L., Henderson Jr., C. R., Hanks, C., Cole, R., et al. (2000). Enduring effects of nurse home visitation on maternal life course. A 3-year follow-up of a randomized trial. *Journal of the American Medical Association, 283,* 1983–1989.

Lagges, A., & Gordon, D. (1999). Use of an interactive laserdisc parent training program with teenage parents. *Child and Family Behavior Therapy, 21,* 19–37.

MacLeod, J., & Nelson, G. (2000). Programs for the promotion of family wellness and the prevention of child maltreatment: A meta-analytic review. *Child Abuse and Neglect, 24,* 1127–1149.

Mandell, S. (2000). Child abuse prevention at report card time. *Journal of Community Psychology, 28,* 687–690.

Medway, F. J. (1989). Measuring the effectiveness of parent education. In M. J. Fine (Ed.), *The second handbook on parent education: Contemporary perspectives* (pp. 237–255). San Diego, CA: Academic Press.

Miller-Perrin, C., & Perrin, R. (1999). *Child maltreatment: An introduction.* Thousand Oaks, CA: Sage Publications.

Milner, J. S. (1998). Individual and family characteristics associated with intafamilial child physical and sexual abuse. In P. K. Trickett & C. J. Schellenbach (Eds.), *Violence against children in the family and the community* (pp. 141–170). Washington, DC: American Psychological Association.

National Center for Injury Prevention and Control (2004). *Using evidence-based parenting programs to advance CDC efforts in child maltreatment prevention.* Atlanta, GA: Centers for Disease Control and Prevention.

Portwood, S. G. (1998). Factors influencing individuals' definitions of child maltreatment. *Child Abuse and Neglect, 22,* 437–452.

Portwood, S. G. (1999). The impact of individuals' characteristics and experiences on their definitions of child maltreatment. *Child Maltreatment, 4,* 56–68.

Portwood, S. G. (2006). What we know – and don't know – about preventing child maltreatment. *Journal of Aggression, Maltreatment, and Trauma, 12,* 55–80.

Portwood, S. G. (2008). Physical abuse in childhood (ages 5–13). In T. P. Gullotta and G. M. Blau (Eds.), *Family influences on childhood behavior and development* (pp. 267–292). New York: Routledge.

Portwood, S. G., & Dodgen, D. W. (2005). Influencing policy making for maltreated children and their families. *Journal of Clincial Child and Adolescent Psychology, 34,* 628–637.

Rae-Grant, N. I. (1994). Preventive interventions of child sexual abuse victimization: Where we are now and how far have we come? *Canadian Journal of Community Mental Health, 13,* 17–36.

Reppucci, N. D., Britner, P. A., & Woolard, J. L. (1997). *Preventing child abuse and neglect through parent education.* Baltimore: Paul H. Brooks.

Sanders, M. R., Cann, W., & Markie-Dadds, C. (2003). The triple P-positive parenting programme: A universal population-level approach to the prevention of child abuse. *Child Abuse Review, 12,* 155–171.

Sedlak, A. J. (1997). Risk factors for the occurrence of child abuse and neglects. *Journal of Aggression, Maltreatment, and Trauma, 1,* 149–187.

Showers, J. (1992). "Don't shake the baby": The effectiveness of a prevention program. *Child Abuse and Neglect, 16,* 11–18.

Thompson, R. A. (1994). Social support and the prevention of child maltreatment. In: G. B. Melton, & F. D. Barry (Eds.), *Protecting children from abuse and neglect: Foundations for a new strategy* (pp. 40–130). New York: Guilford Press.

Urquiza, A. J., & McNeil, C. B. (1996). Parent–child interaction therapy: An intensive dyadic intervention for physically abusive families. *Child Maltreatment, 1,* 134–144.

U.S. Department of Health and Human Services, Administration on Children, Youth and Families (2008). *Child maltreatment 2006.* Washington, DC: U.S. Government Printing Office.

Webster-Stratton, C. (1994). Advancing videotape parent training: A comparison study. *Journal of Consulting and Clinical Psychology, 62,* 583–593.

Webster-Stratton, C., & Hammond, M. (1997). Treating children with early-onset conduct problems: A comparison of child and parent training interventions. *Journal of Consulting and Clinical Psychology, 65,* 93–109.

Webster-Stratton, C., Reid, M. J., & Hammond, M. (2004). Treating children with early onset conduct disorder: Intervention outcomes for parent, child, and teacher training. *Journal of Clinical Child and Adolescent Psychology, 33,* 105–124.

Wolfe, D. A. (1985). Child-abusive parents: An empirical review and analysis. *Psychological Bulletin, 97,* 462–482.

Zepeda, M., & Morales, A. (2001). Supporting parents through parent education. In N. Halfon, E. Shulman, & M. Hochstein (Eds.), *Building community services for young children.* Los Angeles, CA: UCLA Center for Healthier Children.

CHAPTER 4

Empirically-Based Violence Prevention Interventions

Kathy Sexton-Radek

The increasing volume of children involved in violence in our society is alarming. The manner in which the violence meets the child varies, but it is consistently detrimental to the child's welfare. The sources of violence that are individually based, such as from another child or from an adult, have a vast effect on a child's development. The unpredictable nature and uncertain extent of violence presents a unique challenge to the prevention. This chapter will examine the issues of scope of violence, school-based prevention programs, and the evaluation of such programs. Venerable constellations of programs to prevent violence have been designed. The means to measure their effects and thereby to improve them is less common.

The American Psychological Association reported that school-associated violent deaths represent less than 1% of all homicides and suicides that occur among school-aged children. Further, 40% of youth are reported to have been concerned about a potentially violent classmate (American Psychological Association Help Center, 2008) and young adults between the ages of 12 and 24 are at the greatest risk of being a victim of violence, with 1 in 12 high school students threatened or injured with a weapon each year (American Psychological Association Help Center, 2008).

The Chicago Violence Prevention Strategic Plan has identified the following factors as contributing to youth violence: societal disenfranchisement, limited economic opportunities, lack of access to youth-focused community institutions, lack of positive role models, lack of caregiver presence, school failure, gang involvement, violent peers, weapon possession, direct exposure to violence, personal substance use, excessive violence in the media, lack of future orientation, propensity to take risks. Therefore, interventions have been designed in categories to address the prominent issues. Emotion-based interventions focus on anger management and anger/discomfort triggers leading to violence. The cognition-based approaches focus on the development of problem-solving skills and perspective taking. The behavior-based approaches are skill based to train to identify triggers and engage in alternate, non-violent behaviors. The majority of interventions in this area are psychoeducational. The therapeutic models focus on group and individual counseling interventions with students meeting some or all of the psychiatric symptom diagnostic patterns of conduct disorder, oppositional defiant disorder, depression, and learning disorders, particularly information processing and behavioral disorders. Here, experiential and impulse behaviors are replaced by purposeful acts of behavior.

The focus of intervention is at the primary level where mentoring, dispute resolution, peer mediation, and social skill training are conducted. Specialized survey instruments are utilized as a pre-intervention measure and to detect outcome.

Case Illustration

It is a 4th grade classroom in Chicago's west side on the morning of a winter day. The popular, overworked young man teaching the class is in front of 47 seats of 4th graders, writing decimal equations and numbers on the blackboard. The room is at a moderate roar and some eight or nine students are looking to the board. The majority of students are turned about talking to their neighbor, vying for attention with loud talk and actions. Observing further, one sees four students, one small-framed boy and three girls – two are heavyset and tall for their age, traveling from desk to desk to see what the other students have in their book bag or what instruments they are using to take notes with. One child grabs an object while the other grabs it from a different direction and then another piece of student property is grabbed, accompanied by a loud, "let me see that!" This behavior is accompanied by loud bantering and aggressive body posturing (leaning and towering over each child). As the teacher turns around, they bow into a pseudo-sitting posture facing forward and emit a mocking comment of an empty question about decimals to the teacher. He then turns around to continue writing. A small slight-sized boy seated in the middle row, a few seats from the back of the classroom, has fashioned an igloo-like surround to his desk using his book bag, the jacket on the back of his chair, a pile of books on his desk, and an enormous three-ring binder. His darting looks of fear were quickly hidden with insincere complacence. The other students watched.

It is not always the terrorism of a gun-wielding, maladjusted aggressor in our schools but the everyday, subtle effects of bullying that affect our children's safety. It is this complicated challenge of how the classroom teacher can manage overcrowded classrooms, how the classroom teacher can teach to those so distracted by life strains, and the challenge of what life skills we can give through training to our children to combat bullying of all sorts (social, personal, coercive to join a gang or buy drugs or to supply answers on a test or give up prepared homework). The issues of this case study are complicated, but to start let us consider:

- Social bullying, the power of the aggressor.
- Personal bullying, the victimization by personality type.
- Social/community, to join a gang, to buy or sell drugs to otherwise support a gang member in some social situation.
- The bullied teacher with too much work, too many students in a class, aggressive students, and parents threatening for a grade.
- The classroom community overwrought with opportunity for the aggressor.

Overview of the Issues

A casual look at the newspaper will reveal staggering statistics related to violence in our schools. One of the most common forms of violence is that between individuals. There seems to be an increase in the number of aggressive acts in our society: teachers being attacked by students, students being threatened by another student, students being attacked by another student, parents threatening teachers and students. The past two decades have seen an increase in violent crime in the United States. The general rate of violent youths adjudicated in courts has risen by 31%

(Davis, 1991). In 1994, some 100,000 forcible rapes were reported to law enforcement, along with an estimated one million assaults. Some 25% of the increase in violent crime is attributed to youths/juveniles. Some authorities report that these figures are an underestimation, given the increased number of incarcerated youths (American Psychological Association Help Center, 2008).

A developmental pathway is often cited to explain these increased crime rates and detentions of our youths. Most logical models explain, that without intervention aggressive behaviors escalate and merge to form the characteristic patterns seen in our youths. Loeber and Stouthamer-Loeber (1998) concluded that there is substantial evidence that the development of violence takes place in an orderly rather than a random fashion. The absence of learning sufficient self-regulation and moderation skills funnels the behavior of stressed youths to such patterns. Patterson, Forgatch, Yoefger, and Stoolmiller (1998) stated that antisocial behavior seen at grade 4 is predictive of later aggressive behavior. It seems that as early as grade 4 information may be processed reflecting a self-view that one must react (often seemingly to the world) (Huesman, 1988; Patterson et al., 1998). Family factors such as inconsistent and harsh parenting, victims of abuse, and socially inept parents/parenting, together with school-based warnings such as teacher ratings of aggression, reported negative peer interactions, and low levels of academic-involved time compared with non-aggressive peers, add to this skewed developmental pattern, leading to the outcome of using aggression, manipulation, and coercion instead of appropriate learning skills.

This emotional deregulation is problematic when intense emotions of frustration and anger mount in youths. It seems that the skill-based approach common to the development of cognitive and perceptual mediation of emotion is lacking in youths who engage in aggression. This starts as an immaturity or stunted social growth pattern that evolves to problematic proportions with aggressive behaviors. In the absence of alternative problem solving to moderate this emotion, the immaturities and improper behaviors become habitual reactions to the hostile world some have experienced. Research in this area has identified, when intelligence is controlled, that there is a measured statistically significant difference between aggressive youths in terms of cognitive actions (i.e., fantasy and imagination; Huesman, 1988) due to the psychosocial development of retaining a mistrustful worldview as a consequence of early learning and thwarted social encounters.

Additionally, violent youth seem unable to learn from violent behaviors, in that they are considered unable to cognitively conceptualize the situation and its consequences. While cognitive arousal is evident and higher in aggressive youths compared with same-aged peers, it is diffuse, unhandled excitement. This narrow bandwidth of emotional expression, the limited cognitive ability to detect and understand consequences of aggressive behavior, and the concrete and limited perceptual ability (which in turn impairs moral thinking) present considerable difficulties in modulating emotional expression. Psychophysiological measures of violent youths indicate higher levels that curiously become cued to very specific stimuli (e.g., social derogation, negative attention). From a clinical perspective, violent youths are often male and view their destructiveness as necessary and one of a limited number of reactions afforded to them. In its most deviant form, the aggressive act is the only way to make contact. In effect, these factors of psychopathy, anger expression deregulation, cognitive and perceptual production deficits, parenting styles/modeling and chronic stress become markers to center the necessary intervention programming.

How does the child at risk – who suffers from disability, or poverty, or paternal mental illness – manage to meet development tasks with some success? A review of the literature by Masten and Coatsworth (1998) resulted in a list of the qualities of the child and environment that are associated in many studies with good outcomes under adverse conditions. What is important to note here is that resilience is not a trait, not solely an attribute of the person. Rather it is the outcome of an interaction between personal characteristics and the environment, which supports the fact that developmental tasks are made more difficult by risk factors. Of course, a history of negotiation of these developmental challenges may leave the person with many characteristics (e.g., skills, attitudes, and coping mechanisms) of proven success that are carried into new situations (Sexton-Radek, 2005).

The school has the role of providing safety and preventing violence. However, not all children have developmental experiences that are formative to prepare them for socializing appropriately in a school. Additionally, not all children are able to attach and commit to a school environment. Children who manage to bond to the schools (i.e., who develop a commitment to learning and an attachment to the school community, to teachers, and to other students) will be more successful academically and will be less likely to engage in serious crime, including violent behavior (Hawkins, Pepler, & Craig, 2001; Sexton-Radek, 2005).

Bonding is likely to occur when the school offers: opportunities for active involvement in the education process (appropriate to the child's level of skills, in order to motivate engagement in learning); the development of skills or competencies (the exercise of which makes the opportunities for involvement satisfying); sanctions (reinforcements, rewards, recognition) for skillful involvement. This is the skills–opportunities–sanctions model. What must a school do to create the conditions for commitment and attachment?

It has been suggested that the development of a sense of caring may call for the following:

■ Creating one-on-one time with students; an appropriate amount of self-disclosure from the teacher; networking with family members, friends, and neighbors of students; using rituals and traditions to build a sense of community within the classroom; providing emotional as well as academic support.

■ Thematic, experiential, comprehensive curricula provide opportunities for involvement, as do programs that employ cooperative learning activities.

■ Programs that allow students to be resources for each other help to build a sense of involvement, achievement, and community.

■ High expectations can be expressed in a mastery orientation that stresses self-improvement, disciplined effort, and task mastery rather than competition.

■ The progress of each student would need to be closely monitored and corrective instruction and tutoring provided to ensure that the designated skills were being acquired.

■ The opportunity structure within the classroom and school must value a wide diversity of talents, skills, and learning styles, and recognition should not be limited to a few top-ranking students in any endeavor (Sexton-Radek, 2005).

This is a version of the social development model that seeks to build a relationship that fosters academic achievement through involvement and high standards and seeks to build an emotional attachment that heightens the salience of a message of non-violence. In this context the whole school constitutes the prevention program. Given the knowledge that experiences affect rates of learning, a powerful intervention comes in the form of promoting academic achievement. Spivack (2001) explained that there are many strategies that teachers can use to make sure instructors and assigned tasks are not frustrating the student, particularly those with low skills.

Samples and Aber (1998) have presented an approach where violence prevention programs should target the conceptual readiness of the student at his or her developmental level of competence. The student's environment, which is critically important for successful developmental success, changes with the tasks at each stage.

Yoshikawa (1994) reviewed violence prevention programs in light of this social developmental model and concluded from several long-term studies of early childhood programs that combined preschool programs and family support and education services have shown not only short-term improvements in self-regulation but also long-term reductions in antisocial behaviors, including those serious enough to warrant involvement in the criminal justice system. Intellectual and social competence is taught in skill-based programming. Additionally, programs that include parent training increase the effectiveness of the violence prevention programs. At the middle school level, violence prevention programs focus on skill development across three general approaches: (1) the teaching of cognitive, social, and emotional skills thought to aid in non-violent conflict management (e.g., active listening, perspective taking, negotiating, anger management); (2) the promotion of prosaical attitudes and values; and (3) instruction in the risk factors or triggers that can lead to violence.

Muffit (1993) categorized the functions that violence serves to the adolescent: an impression management function for achieving and maintaining a high-status role; a materialism, status, and social identity function, where the adolescent may obtain pleasure from taking a possession from another; a power function wherein the dominance of others directly or following humiliation of opponents occurs; a rough justice, social control, and self-help function where illegal or preemptive violence has a deterrent value; and a defiance of authority function as an expression of unfairness of the social order. Violence prevention programs, when designed to develop affective identification and expression, address these important issues. The American Psychological Association Zero Tolerance Task Force (2008) policies have reviewed the nationwide use of this policy. It seems that the removal of disruptive students did not work and data were found to indicate that strict adherence to zero tolerance policies leads to a poorer school climate and higher rates of suspensions and expulsions.

Halpern, Baxter, and Mollard (2000) defined good programs of violence prevention to attend to a multiple set of developmental goals (e.g., identity, affiliation, mastery, autonomy):

- Challenges and activities that are "real" in the sense of being consequential and valued by their communities rather than manufactured to entertain, occupy, or contain the adolescents (McLaughlin & Irby, 1994).
- Opportunities to develop and demonstrate status-conferring skills and accomplishments, with tests of physical endurance and power being especially important for inner-city males (Chaiken, 1998).
- A group identity and organization of traditions (Chaiken, 1998).
- Opportunities to exercise some autonomy, within the context of organization rules that are clear.
- Family-like environments in which individuals are valued (McLaughlin & Irby, 1994).
- Adults that communicate caring, personal interest, and commitment.

The primary aim of prevention is to provide violence prevention strategies, effective academic instruction, and schoolwide behavior in an effort to limit the emergence of violent behavior. Secondary prevention serves at-risk children for problem behavior in an effort to reverse the harm of exposure to risk factors, whereas tertiary prevention aims to reduce the harm of behavior problems for students already identified with behavioral problems. Thus, the schools that provide primary intervention as the overall goal will provide a positive environment to their students.

Antiviolence Programming

The necessity for psychoeducational programming becomes evident with a review of the facts and statistics related to violence exposure and our children. A review of the literature reveals that program design and evaluation of antiviolence programming in this area is varied (Sexton-Radek, 2005). Despite the staggering numbers and percentages, some obvious factors need attention in this area. First, the roles of the administration, the community, the direct line teacher, and the parent are not always taken into account in the formation of programming in this area. Consequently, stand-alone programs that are distinct in their success and ability to promote change in this challenging area are not as visible as their merits. Second, the logical focus on the emotional, cognitive, and behavioral categorization of programs promotes diverse psychoeducational interventions with measured success. The problem, however, arises with the generalization of these findings outside of the weekly meetings. Furthermore, additional clarity is needed for the implementation of these interventions beyond the research program. Thus, when effectiveness is evidenced the programming is short term and may contain elements of clinically/educably relevant programs in that they are too short to effect change.

Elementary Schools

Psychoeducational programming is frequently conducted at the elementary-grade levels. This type of intervention is typically integrated within the curriculum, thus facilitating the collection of data as part of classroom procedure. It is admirable that the research is conducted, but design weaknesses in terms of reliance on single-group studies, small sample sizes, little or no follow-up data, lack of control group, and small random assignments to groups or matching and other basic elements severely limit the ability to demonstrate effectiveness (Sexton-Radek, 2005). Gerrity and DeLucia-Waack (2007) stated from meta-analytic findings that communication, anger management, aggression control, empathy development, and problem-solving skills were the most common psychoeducational focus in schools. For example, externalizing and anger assessments improved after a psychoeducational school-based intervention that focused on anger intervention (Bennet & Williams, 2002). Kaufman (2005) explained that the success of a program is linked to the degree of teacher acceptance and student response. In a multimethod design using formative and summative data collection of cognitive, affective, and behavioral responses to a violence prevention program focused at the emotional development of the students, Kaufman (2005) reported that preprogram teacher preparation and teacher perception of developmental appropriateness accounted for the amount of success with the program. In "Project Blue" Giancola and Bear (2003) measured some 20,000 students across 20 states who received services and intervention assistance (at their school building) based on federal funding with the "Safe Schools/ Healthy Students" grant initiative. A myriad of activities and services, from family crisis social workers, to school safety liaisons, to interventions specialists who provided mediation and social skills training to the students, were provided. A lack of fidelity of these services was reported, based on the need to have more clarity in leadership roles and investment in the programming from the teachers in the schools.

Runyon, Deblinger, Ryan, and Thakkar-Kolar (2004) reported on the utility of a parent-only cognitive-behavioral treatment intervention that ran concurrently with school-based support groups for children. This integrated intervention reported gains in relieving depression symptoms in the children and increasing the parent's use of child management techniques rather than physical punishment, thus engendering a safe situation for the child. Further research is needed in this area of comprehensive models of parent–child interaction. Cunningham, Henggeler, Limber, Melton, and Nation (2000) reported that the Youth Risk Behavior Surveillance System monitors categories of health-risk behavior among youths and young adults, including violence. Survey results from 10–24-year-olds indicated that 17.1% had carried a weapon and 33.0% of high school students had been in a physical fight (Grunbaum et al., 2003). The National Institute of Mental Health provides materials such as "What Community Members Can Do" that specify topics and means of discussion of violent community/world acts with children. Specific curricula by grade level are available. Evaluation data of these methods were not found.

High School

The federal program "Safe Schools/Healthy Students" that was implemented in California took on historic proportions because it was unique to have this cluster of comprehensive services (Elizondo, Feske, Edgull, & Walsh, 2003). Decreases in school crime, increased participation in parenting programs, and decreased truancy at several schools were reported outcomes of this project. Also, the increased funding of this program provided additional officers that were able to locate parole violators, thus deterring criminal activity on campus and reducing the risk for violence on campus. Brokenbrough, Cornell, and Loper (2002) reported on the association of aggressive attitudes with carrying weapons, using alcohol, engaging in physical fights at schools, and harboring aggressive attitudes toward others. This valuable information helped to detect these at-risk behaviors in the intervention programs and thereby reduce the opportunities for repeated victimization. The Olweus Bullying Prevention Program involved the training of staff for a discussion group format with high school students (e.g., school rules about bullying) in addition to classroom-level skill training, weekly parental meetings, and the development of individual intervention plans (Olweus & Limber, 1999).

Bosworth, Espelage, and DuBay (1998) presented the unique computer-based violence prevention intervention for young adolescents, called "Smart Talk". This program entailed the students completing pre- and post-test materials and four 40-minute modules on antiviolence. Knowledge of alternative behaviors was frequently reported as a gain from the program by the participants (Bosworth, Espelage, & DuBay, 1998). Paul, Sexton-Radek, Adickas, and Fousek (1999) reported significant differences in reporting and discussion about violence from participants of a six-session antiviolence program. The intervention was implemented by two leaders and college students with training in the area, thus increasing the impact of the antiviolence messaging. Friedman, Terras, and Glassman (2002) conducted a prevention/early intervention project with a control group of drug abusers. The intervention included modules on the social learning model for controlling tendencies toward violence and in the directing of one's emotions and energies along socially and personally acceptable lines. Composite scores of pre- and post-classroom intervention reflected a significant difference in the targeted group (Friedman, Terras, & Glassman, 2002). A program evaluation using cost–benefit analysis was conducted by Kerns and Printz (2002) on violence prevention programming. Developmental issues and intervention fidelity were highlighted issues for future study in this area.

Paige, Kitzis, and Wolfe (2003) identified the need to build elements of developing resiliency into violence prevention programs. In their rural community, Paige et al. (2003) explained that a public health approach to violence prevention was most effective with adolescents. School-based interventions were combined with identification of at-risk youths and detainment of acting-out youths, as well as active involvement from law enforcement and health care, in this program called "Rural Underpinnings for Resiliency and Linkages". Results from school climate surveys indicated improvements (Paige et al., 2003).

College

Hamburg (1998) reported on the whole-school violence prevention program and university public school collaboration. The goals of the psychoeducative intervention were to educate students for personal enrichment and productive membership in society. Social workers lead the team implementation (college students or peer trainers) in the administration of social skill training for prosocial behaviors. Data are being collected in this longitudinal study of incidents of violence, rates of truancy, and school retention (Haymes, Howe, & Peck, 2003). Banyard, Plante, and Moynihan (2004) implemented a bystander education project to decrease sexual violence. Approximately 2.8% of women experience the most serious forms of sexual violence, rape, or attempted rape during the college academic year (Fisher, Cullen, & Turner, 2000). The hope is to widen community change with the use of the bystander model. Participants in this bystander program were taught skills to detect and ask for assistance in role-playing situations. Conceptual explanations are provided by these researchers, with data-based measurements to follow (Banyard, Plante, & Moynihan, 2004). In a rigorous review, the American Psychological Association Zero Tolerance Task Force (2008) chose three effective zero tolerance programs: "Bullying Prevention" (Olweus & Limber, 1999); "Threat Assessment" (Cornell, Sheras, & Cole, 2006); and "Restorative Justice" (Karp & Breslin, 2001). The "Safe and Responsive Schools" program was regarded as having probable efficacy (American Psychological Association Zero Tolerance Task Force, 2008; Skiba, Ritter, Simmons, Peterson, & Miller, 2006).

Public Perceptions

The public harbor fear and annoyance with the present circumstances of violence in schools. To make school safe means that parents and their perceptions have to be considered and that community perceptions of the problem have to be addressed. For many, there is a fundamental misunderstanding of the risk of devastating terrorist/mass murders at schools. The heightened attention by the media places an inordinate amount of attention on the issue. There is a case for following up with fiscal support via taxes for public school programming. Some parents attribute violent behaviors as reflecting moral training and thus under the purview of the parents and church/synagogue/mosque. Also, the issue of cultural blindness endures where prejudice identifies certain groupings as the source and site of the problem behaviors. Lastly, there is the complicated issue of violent behavior being combined with or considered as part of mental illness.

Eidelson and Eidelson (2003) identified five core beliefs associated with conflict and aggression. Each belief, they propose, operates on both an individual and a group level. Eidelson and Eidelson (2003) stated that superiority (belief that one's culture is superior to all other cultures in every possible way), injustice (the belief that one, either as an individual or a group, has a legitimate grievance against another individual), vulnerability (the belief that one is subject to annihilation at the hands of aggressive others), and distrust (the belief that another individual or group will not honor their commitments) lead to aggression.

Our cultural blindness may also propel public perceptions about violence. Cota-Robles and Gamble (2006) investigated the role of family relationships to violent behavior in different cultural groups. The role and importance of family members are defined differently in different cultures and thus not considering these factors may also account for the features of violence that the general population expounds. Mother–adolescent attachment was related to reduced risk of delinquency for boys and but this was less apparent for girls from families of Mexican-American heritage (Cota-Robles & Gamble, 2006).

Borowsky and Ireland (2004) measured the number of non-fatal injuries resulting from violence. Given that non-fatal violence precedes fatal violence in youths (Luckenbill, 1977), findings of increases in the number of non-fatal violence are alarming. Moreover, witnessing or being involved in non-fatal violence co-occurs with higher rates of diagnosed depression in teenage girls. Thus, non-fatal injuries are not just another teenage "risky behavior" but part of a complicated trigger factor leading to increased violence. With new antiviolence prevention programs, the shared life perspectives (Reese, Vera, & Hasbrook, 2003) will direct the interventions that will promote life choices. Violence prevention programming will be advanced if the interventions are culturally meaningful, which would include methods of verbal expression that are appropriate and contextually meaningful for the cultural group (Reese, Vera, & Caldwell, 2006).

Popular public perceptions of violence include superpredator, quarantining the contagious, corrective surgery, man as computer, vaccine, and chronic disease, according to Dodge, Petit, and Bates (2001). The annual cost of crime to American society is over $1 trillion (Anderson, 1999). In general the public is skeptical about the effectiveness of antiviolence programming, despite some evidence to the contrary. This, taken together with programs largely designed in quasi-experimental terms (Sexton-Radek, 2005), means that the strong message of program effectiveness traditionally coming from policy-makers influenced by evidence-based science and traditional designs is never formulated. Whether the current perceptions are accurate or new more inspirational metaphors to youth violence can be obtained remains to be seen; however, the objective – to make schools safe – is commonly understood and, to date, not obtained universally.

Policy Recommendations

Policy recommendations are to be specific to the field in which ongoing measurement is taking place. In an effort to provide prevention that works, emphasis is to be placed on procedural training for safety. In teaching safety in the classroom, a culture within the classroom community that mirrors safety is to be done. Equally important is how we heal after direct and indirect assaults. A commitment of resources in terms of personnel, materials, and designated budgeting has become a line item in a budget rather than a one-time expense. Actions large and small are needed, in terms of changing a dress code to prohibit the clothing expression of a gang's allegiance or general disrespectful/provocative dress, on a large scale such as regular assemblies.

The means by which data are collected and surveyed impacts policy change. The arrest records indicate the results of longstanding problems that culminate into a behavior. For prevention to work, school records of injuries and youth self-reports of violence and experiences, in essence, need to precede the end-stage violent acts documented in police records. Ongoing review of these pre-existing records can facilitate preventative programming based on recent events and surveillance.

Strong efforts are needed to reduce or neutralize incidents where social rejection or social isolation and lack of social support have become areas of concern. Again, here, small efforts such as hall monitoring, security at entrance and exit points, and tracking of all individuals in the student community will not only provide a deterrent to potential crime but also induce a sense of safety.

With regard to the literature in this area and public policy, evidence-based evaluation efforts have to be made. The gold standard in the evaluation of laboratory-designed intervention has been the true experiment. However, the immediate need for programming and design implementation while maximizing resources to provide the highest quality of measured intervention has led to a preponderance of non-experimental design approaches. While research-based evaluations of antiviolence programming measure moderate success, the applied means of implementation (i.e., quasi-experimental designs targetted at specific types of group to provide services) have superseded the randomization procedures found in experimentation.

The next factor in this research issue is the fidelity of the intervention. Meeting the criteria for consistency in training is essential for intervention fidelity. Consistently defined variables of both the intervention and the outcome are essential. The ability to demonstrate effectiveness will dictate the ongoing use of the programming. However, real-life issues such as varying teaching philosophies may moderate the content and degree to which areas are addressed in the interventions.

An economic evaluation provides information with regard to the allocation of fiscal resources. For example, healthcare costs in Pennsylvania were found to be escalated due to violence acts (Health Services Research, 2000). The partition of monetary units of caring for individuals as reflected from their association with violence can be calculated and clearly represented in reports of the literal "cost" of unsafe schools. Such financial projection data collected with monitoring approaches and treatment outcome studies provide a complete picture of violence in schools and the savings for safe schools (model or design here). Astor, Meyer, Benbenishty, Marachi, and Rosemond (2005) advocate surveillance mapping within microcommunities such as schools, along with more empiricism in program measurement and local involvement at the locations where children are to engender a "safe" local morality. Armstrong (1983) reported that grant writing, program and resource coordination, clinical services, program evaluation, staff training, parent advocacy, and steering committee membership are the policy-funded resources to maintain safe schools. The overall framework constitutes more focus on intervention planning, implementation, and maintenance to provide safe schools with contextual factors to substantiate this setup.

In conclusion, one single factor emerges from the literature to combat the violence threat – the construction of cultures in settings for children that are incompatible with violence. "Peace power" training materials that parallel targeted skill-based efforts of violence prevention suggest a series of interlocking processes that lead to this culture of non-violence. Appendix 1 lists general policy statements that reflect this commitment to changing the culture of the school community to one that is incompatible with violence. Finally, Appendix 2 lists some useful resources for program development.

In revisiting the case illustration, some resolution was provided to this student with his self-made "igloo of protection" by a 7-week violence prevention program followed by 1-, 3- and 6-month follow-up booster sessions. The roving bullying group was disbanded as a result of the program, with one student dropping out of school and one student "morphing" into a constructive leadership role in the classroom. The student earned above-average grades in this course and the courses to follow. The school implemented schoolwide policies of weekly assemblies for dialog and community building and mandatory uniforms, and outreach to parents was commenced.

References

Alogozzine, B. (2002). Building effective prevention practices. In P. Kay (Ed.), *Preventing problem behaviors: A handbook of successful prevention strategies* (pp. 220–234). Thousand Oaks, CA: Corwin Press.

American Psychological Association Help Center (2008). *Facts and statistics: Youth violence.* Retrieved May 13, 2008, from http://apahelpcenter.org/articles/topic.php?id=6

American Psychological Association Zero Tolerance Task Force (2008). Are zero tolerance policies effective in the schools? *American Psychologist, 63*(9), 852–862.

Anderson, D. A. (1999). The aggregate burden of crime. *Journal of Law and Economics, 42,* 611–642.

Armstrong, K. A. (1983). Economic analysis of a child abuse and neglect treatment program. *Child Welfare, 62,* 3–13.

Astor, R. A., Meyer, A., Benbenishty, R., Marachi, R., & Rosemond, M. (2005). School safety interventions: Best practices and programs. *Children and Schools, 27*(1), 17–32.

Banyard, V. L., Plante, E. G., & Moynihan, M. M. (2004). Bystander education: Bringing a broader community perspective to sexual violence prevention. *Journal of Community Psychology*, *32*(1), 61–79.

Bennet, L., & Williams, O. (2002). *Controversies and recent studies of batterer intervention program effectiveness.* Retrieved September 28, 2002, from http://www.mincava.umn.edu/vawnet/ar_bip.htm

Borowsky, I. W., & Ireland, M. (2004). Predictors of future fight-related injury among adolescents. *Pediatrics*, *113*(3), 530–536.

Bosworth, K., Espelage, D., & DuBay, T. (1998). A computer-based violence prevention intervention for young adolescents: Pilot study. *Adolescence*, *33*(132), 785–795.

Brockenbrough, K. K., Cornell, D. G., & Loper, A. B. (2002). Aggressive attitudes among victims of violence at school. *Education and Treatment of Children*, *25*(3), 273–287.

Chaiken, M. (1998). Tailoring established after school programs to meet urban realities. In D. Elliott, B. Hamburg, & K. Williams (Eds.), *Violence in American schools: A new perspective* (pp. 348–375). New York: Cambridge University Press.

Cornell, D. G., Sheras, P. L., & Cole, J. C. M. (2006). Assessment of bullying. In S. R. Jimerson & M. Furlong (Eds.), *Handbook of school violence and school safety: From research of practice* (pp. 191–209). Mahwah, NJ: Lawrence Erlbaum Associates, Inc.

Cota-Robles, S., & Gamble, W. (2006). Parent–adolescent processes and reduced risk for delinquency: The effect of gender for Mexican-American adolescents. *Youth and Society*, *37*(4), 375–392.

Cunningham, P. B., Henggeler, S., Limber, S. P., Melton, G. B., & Nation, M. A. (2000). Patterns and correlates of gun ownership among non-metropolitan and rural middle school students. *Journal of Clinical Child Psychology*, *29*(3), 432–442.

Davis, D. (1991). *Interventions with aggressive and resistant youth.* Wisconsin: Medical Educational Services.

Dodge, K. A., Petit, G. S., & Bates, J. E. (2001). Mechanisms in the cycle of violence. *Science*, *250*, 1678–1683.

Eidelson, R. J., & Eidelson, J. I. (2003). Dangerous ideas: Five beliefs that propel groups toward conflict. *American Psychologist*, *58*(3), 182–192.

Elizondo, F., Feske, K., Edgull, D., & Walsh, K. (2003). Creating synergy through collaboration with Safe Schools/Healthy Students in Salinas, California. *Psychology in the Schools*, *40*(5), 503–513.

Fisher, B. S., Cullen, F. R., & Turner, M. G. (2000). *The sexual victimization of college women: Findings from two national-level studies.* Washington, DC: National Institute of Justice and Bureau of Justice Statistics.

Friedman, A. S., Terras, A., & Glassman, K. (2002). Multimodal substance use intervention program for male delinquents. *Journal of Child and Adolescent Substance Abuse*, *11*(4), 43–65.

Gerrity, A., & DeLucia-Waack, J. L. (2007). Effectiveness of groups in schools. *Journal of Specialists in Group Work, 31*(1), 97–106.

Giancola, S. P., & Bear, G. G. (2003). Face fidelity: Perspectives from a local evaluation of the Safe Schools/Healthy Students Initiative. *Psychology in the Schools, 40*(5), 515–529.

Grunbaum, J., Kann, L., Kinshen, S., Ross, J., Hawkins, J., Lowry, R., et al. (2003). Youth risk behavior surveillance – United States, 2003. *Morbidity and Mortality Weekly Report, 53*(SS-2), 1–94.

Halpern, R., Baxter, G., & Mollard, W. (2000). Youth programs as alternative spaces to be: A study of neighborhood youth programs in Chicago's West Town. *Youth and Society, 31*, 489–506.

Hamburg, M. A. (1998). Youth violence is a public health concern. In D. S. Elliot, B. A. Hamburg, & K. R. William (Eds.), *Violence in American schools* (pp. 31–54). New York: Cambridge University Press.

Hawkins, D. L., Pepler, D. J., & Craig, W. M. (2001). Naturalistic observations of peer interventions in bullying. *Social Development, 10*, 512–527.

Haymes, E. B., Howe, E., & Peck, L. (2003). Whole-school violence prevention program a university public school collaboration. *Children and Schools, 25*(2), 121–127.

Health Services Research (2000). *Health care costs associated with violence in Pennsylvania.* Camp Hill, PA: Highmark.

Huesman, L. R. (1988). An information processing model for the development of aggression. *Aggressive Behavior, 14*, 13–24.

Karp, D. R., & Breslin, B. (2001). Restorative justice in school communities. *Youth and Society, 11*, 465–484.

Kaufman, R. (2005). The process of experiencing mediated learning as a result of peer collaboration between young adults with severe learning disabilities. *Journal of Cognitive Education and Psychology, 5*(2), 215–216.

Kerns, S. E., & Printz, R. J. (2002). Critical issues in the prevention of violence-related behavior in youth. *Clinical Child and Family Psychology Review, 5*(2), 133–160.

Loeber, R., & Stouthamer-Loeber, M. (1998). Development of juvenile aggression and violence. *American Psychologist, 38*, 242–259.

Luckenbill, D. F. (1977). Criminal homicide as a situated transaction. *Social Problems, 25*, 176–186.

Masten, A., & Coatsworth, J. (1998). The development of competence in favorable and unfavorable environments: Lessons from research on successful children [Special Issue: Applications for Developmental Science]. *American Psychologist, 53*, 205–220.

McLaughlin, M. W., & Irby, M. A. (1994). Neighborhood organizations that keep hope alive. *Phi Delta Kappan, 76*, 300–306.

Muffit, T. E. (1993). Adolescence-limited and life-course-persistent antisocial behavior: A developmental taxonomy. *Psychological Review, 100*, 674–701.

Olweus, D., & Limber, S. (1999). Bullying prevention program. In D. S. Elliott (Ed.), *Blueprints for violence prevention*. Boulder, CO: Venture Publishing.

Paige, L. Z., Kitzis, S. N., & Wolfe, J. (2003). Rural underpinnings for resiliency and linkages (RURAL): A Safe Schools/Healthy Students Project. *Psychology in the Schools, 40*(5), 531–546.

Patterson, G. R., Forgatch, M. S., Yoefger, K. L., & Stoolmiller, M. (1998). Variables that initiate and maintain an early-onset trajectory for juvenile offending. *Development and Psychopathology, 10,* 531–547.

Paul, P., Sexton-Radek, K., Adickas, J., & Fousek, B. (1999). The use of service learning to promote understanding of gang-related issues faced by adolescents. *National Society for Experiential Education,* pp. 3–7.

Reese, L. E., Vera, E. M., & Hasbrook, L. (2003). Examining the impact of violence on ethnic minority youth, their families and communities: Issues for prevention practice and science. In G. Bernal, J. E. Trimble, A. K. Burlow, & F. T. L. Leong (Eds.), *Handbook of racial and ethnic minority psychology* (pp. 465–484). Thousand Oaks, CA: Sage.

Runyon, M. K., Deblinger, E., Ryan, E. E., & Thakkar-Kolar, R. (2004). An overview of child physical abuse: Developing an integrated parent–child cognitive-behavioral treatment approach. *Trauma, Violence, and Abuse, 5,* 1–65.

Samples, F., & Aber, L. (1998). Evaluations of school-based violence prevention programs. In D. Elliott, B. Hamburg, & K. Williams (Eds.), *Violence in American schools* (pp. 217–252). New York: Cambridge University Press.

Sexton-Radek, K. (2005). *Violence in schools: Issues, consequences and expressions.* New York: Praeger Press.

Skiba, R. J., Ritter, S., Simmons, A., Peterson, R., & Miller, C. (2006). The Safe and Responsive Schools Project: A school reform model for implementing best practices in violence prevention. In S. R. Jimerson & M. J. Furlong (Eds.), *Handbook of school violence and safety: From research to practices* (pp. 631–650). New York: Routledge.

Spivack, H. (2001). The need to address bullying – An important component of violence prevention. *Journal of American Medical Association, 28*(16), 2131–2132.

Thomas, A. & Grimes, J. (2002). *Best practices in school psychology IV* (Vols. 1–2). Bethesda, MD: National Association of School Psychologists.

Yoshikawa, H. (1994). Prevention as cumulative protections: Effects of early family support and education on chronic delinquency and its risks. *Psychological Bulletin, 115,* 28–54.

Appendix 1: Policy Recommendations

In order to develop a program, factors that distinguish it as safe, that are well run, and function well to educate children share the following qualities (Alogozzine, 2002):

1. Strong academic and behavioral goals are in place and school personnel are committed to carrying out these goals and helping students to succeed.
2. Positive relationships are in place between students and school officials.
3. The school actively involves parent and the community at large.
4. Possess an attitude that all students can achieve success and behave in a socially responsible manner.
5. Make parents feel welcome at the school, address barriers to parental involvement, and positively engage families in education.
6. Develop strong links to the community through support services, community police, and faith-based communities.
7. Demand respect in the relationships between staff and students, along with trust, honesty, and openness.
8. Teach children about safety and the consequences for behaviors that are inappropriate.
9. Have a system in place where students can feel safe reporting potential violence that they have knowledge of.
10. Provide a safe environment for students to express fears and concerns.
11. Have a referral system and protocol in place for child abuse victims.
12. Have before and after school programs that provide a wide range of activities.
13. Reinforce good citizenship in the school community.
14. Identify problems and monitor progress.
15. Provide support services to help students transition into adult life, such as mentoring, internship, and apprenticeship programs.

Appendix 2: Resources

- The American Psychological Association has produced many useful antiviolence program materials. While dated, the 1996 MTV video is quite excellent and the "Strategies to Prevent Youth Violence: Social-Cognitive Strategy" is very detailed (http://www.apa.org).

■ An Internet search will likely yield consultants in your area who provide School Violence Prevention. The services vary from staff training to geographic/topological studies, parent and visitors to school management, and vulnerability to violence analyses. One very good source to start with is Leadership Excellence Behavioral Risk Management (http://www.pwiusa.com/new).

■ Other resources obtained from the Internet will provide sources of materials and presentation of prominent issues. Some very good sites are the following:

Indiana Prevention Resource Center (http://www.drugs. indiana.edu)

Mendez Foundation (http://www.mendezfoundation.org)

Harvard Youth Violence Prevention Center (http:// www.hsph.harvard.edu)

Sunburst Visual media (http://www.sunburstvm.com)

■ "What Community Members Can Do", from the National Institute of Mental Health. (http://www.nimh.nih.gov).

CHAPTER 5

Identifying Children Potentially at Risk for Serious Maladjustment due to Peer Victimization

A New Model using Receiver Operating Characteristics (ROC) Analysis

Rebecca A. Newgent, Amy D. Seay, Kenya T. Malcolm, Elizabeth A. Keller, and Timothy A. Cavell

Case Illustration

Lu is an 11-year-old Korean-American 5th grader at an affluent private school. Lu excels in all of his classes, but is particularly skilled in literature and writing. The private school setup allows each student to have a 1-hour "special course" block each day where they can choose to enroll in an athletic specialty class, band/music, art/design, or an advanced communication course. Lu is excited by the rigor of the advanced communication elective, although he is the only boy in the 5th grade not pursuing an athletic specialty elective.

The lunch schedule is staggered so that all 5th graders eat lunch at the same time. Each day in the lunchroom, other 5th grade boys, all of whom are considerably larger in stature, taunt Lu. While standing in the lunch line, Lu is often bumped into the wall and then cornered by the other boys. When teachers walk over to the commotion, all the boys except Lu begin laughing. The interaction leaves the teachers to think that the boys are having fun. Sometimes the physical taunting causes Lu to fear eating lunch in the lunchroom. In these cases, Lu goes back to a classroom to prepare for the next class block, often without the teacher's awareness that he has left the lunchroom. If Lu does make it through the lunch line without further victimization, he sits at a table in the corner of the lunchroom (next to the exit) so that he can avoid further taunting by escaping quickly when the bell rings.

One day during lunch, Mr. Clark, the advanced communication teacher, noticed Lu sitting alone in a classroom. On this particular day, Lu had been cornered by the other 5th grade boys and shoved until he fell down. Once he was knocked to the ground, Lu was then laughed at while the boys messed up his hair and ripped the collar of his shirt. Mr. Clark, who usually sees Lu as an excited and engaged student, saw Lu sitting at the desk with his head down. Mr. Clark asked Lu why he was not eating lunch, to which Lu replied, "I am not hungry today."

Lu continued to experience bullying by his peers during each lunch period throughout the remainder of the semester. Mr. Clark began to see a decrease in Lu's enthusiasm during his advanced communication class, a heightened level of anxiety prior to lunchtime, and a generally irritable nature toward his peers in the hallway. Concerned about this noticeable shift in Lu's behavior, Mr. Clark decided to speak to the school counselor.

The school counselor asked Mr. Clark to complete a peer victimization measure and the Teacher's Report Form on Lu. Results showed that Lu was higher than average on peer victimization and had clinically elevated scores on internalizing and externalizing problems. The overall rating scores were indicative of emergent psychopathology. The school counselor and Mr. Clark decided to schedule a meeting with Lu and his parents to discuss intervention options.

There are several questions one might ask: "Is Lu truly in need of help?" Is he appropriate for preventative services? What criteria are we to use to make such decisions? Should we use a single criterion or multiple criteria? Can it be harmful if we help a child who does not believe that a problem exists?

Overview of the Issues

One of the first steps in preventing violence against children or lessening its impact is to properly identify children who are at risk because of their exposure to violence while at school. More specifically, we need a way to identify children who are potentially at risk because of peer victimization (i.e., bullying). Typically, schools use a universal approach to mental health prevention, one designed "to reduce the incidence, or number of new cases during a period of time" (Conyne, 2003, p. 331). Universal prevention does not specifically identify children at risk for a negative developmental trajectory (Cuijpers, 2003). Conversely, selective prevention is "meant to decrease the prevalence, or number and duration, of cases that have already occurred" (Conyne, 2003, p. 331). Developing and implementing a selective prevention program requires a method for accurately identifying those children whose risk status justifies intervention.

Peer Victimization

Borrowing from prior research (Gazelle & Ladd, 2002; Hawker & Boulton, 2000; Juvonen & Graham, 2001; Olweus, 1993), we define *peer victimization* as repeated exposure to peer interactions that (1) convey harmful intent, (2) produce harmful effects, and (3) are sanctioned by peers. This definition emphasizes the chronicity and impact of bully behavior as well as its intent (Kochenderfer-Ladd & Wardrop, 2001). Also recognized is the tendency for power differences to extend beyond the bully–victim dyad to peer groups, where the norm is typically one of non-intervention (Salmivalli & Voeten, 2004). Prevalence rates for peer victimization vary depending on the definition, the informant, the measure, and the child's developmental level (Ladd & Kochenderfer-Ladd, 2002; Nicolaides, Toda, & Smith, 2002; Snell, MacKenzie, & Frey, 2002).

Scholars routinely assess three types of peer victimization in elementary school children: direct physical aggression, direct verbal aggression, and indirect relational aggression (Bjorkqvist, Lagerspertz, & Kaukiainen, 1992; Ladd & Kochenderfer-Ladd, 2002). Bullying is said to affect 15–20% of students at some point (Batsche & Knoff, 1994). Pepler (2006) contends that such estimates obscure the fact that a smaller proportion of children "experience frequent and prolonged victimization at the hands of their peers" (p. 16). Further obscuring the needs of bullied children are reports that schoolwide antibullying campaigns can lead to substantial drops (e.g., 50%) in bullying behavior (e.g., Olweus, 1993). Particularly lacking is research examining strategies for identifying individual students who are repeatedly bullied and are at risk for developmental difficulties. Typically, research in the area of peer victimization focuses on universal interventions that target aggressive children (Espelage & Swearer, 2003; Gazelle & Ladd, 2002; Graham & Juvonen, 2001; Pepler, 2006). Chronically bullied children are generally not the focus, despite being at risk for later maladjustment (Pepler, 2006). We propose a methodology for identifying children who are potentially at risk for adjustment problems due to chronic peer victimization.

Consequences of Peer Victimization

Chronic peer victimization has been linked with a number of negative outcomes, including social isolation, feelings of loneliness, low self-esteem, and disrupted academic performance or school attendance (Espelage & Swearer, 2003; Gazelle & Ladd, 2002; Hawker & Boulton, 2000; Ladd & Ladd, 2001; Snell et al., 2002; Storch & Ledley, 2005). Compared to non-victims, bullied children report more physical and psychosomatic complaints (Fekkes, Pijpers, Fredriks, Vogels, & Verloove-Vanhorick, 2006; Nishina, Juvonen, & Witkow, 2005), are more likely to exhibit heightened levels of internalizing and externalizing symptoms (Hawker & Boulton, 2000), and are more apt to have a psychiatric disorder (Kumpulainen, Rasanen, & Puura, 2001). As adults, chronically bullied children are at risk for depression, self-criticism, and suicidal behavior (Olweus, 1993; Rigby & Slee, 1999).

Kumpulainen et al. (2001) found that only 24% of victimized children were referred to a mental health professional, which is roughly half the rate at which bullies were treated. Many children move in and out of the victim role, with serious risk most evident in those who persist as targets (Hanish & Guerra, 2004; Pepler, 2006). This group is overrepresented by boys and by children who are both bullies and victims, or bully–victims (Goldbaum, Craig, Pepler, & Connolly, 2003; Hanish & Guerra, 2004; Unnever, 2005). Bully–victims, known also as aggressive victims (Schwartz, 2000; Schwartz, Dodge, Pettit, & Bates, 1997), engage in more frequent adolescent risk taking, suicidal ideation, and substance use than their less aggressive counterparts (Ireland & Monaghan, 2006; Kaltiala-Heino, Rimpela, Rantanen, & Laippala, 2001; Viljoen, O'Neill, & Sidhu, 2005).

Many children will experience peer harassment but few are chronically bullied. It is important for researchers to identify correctly those victims who may develop later maladjustment problems. A screening tool is needed that can efficiently categorize potential at-risk victims, a goal that goes beyond the more traditional goal of assessing the overall incidence of school bullying and victimization.

Descriptive studies indicate that bullying, relational aggression, and other forms of peer victimization occur frequently in the elementary school grades, particularly when incidence levels are based solely on children's self-reports (Ladd & Kochenderfer-Ladd, 2002; Olweus, 1993). As a whole, peer victimization has been noted by researchers as being a common experience for children at some time or another within schools (Ladd & Ladd, 2001). However, not all children who are bullied suffer significant ill effects. As stated earlier, serious risk is evident most often in children who persist as targets of peer victimization (Hanish & Guerra, 2004; Pepler, 2006). It is when peer victimization persists or goes untreated that it is often accompanied by a number of psychosocial difficulties, including low self-esteem, loneliness, greater risk of substance use, and symptoms of anxiety and depression. Thus, a child who is chronically victimized and exhibits symptoms of emotional or behavioral problems is a child at risk and in need of preventative intervention.

There is a need to take into account victimized children who are at risk for developing and sustaining later psychopathology (Pepler, 2006). Quick and easy screening done on a schoolwide level that can classify a group for further assessment, a group of potential at-risk victims (PARVs), could save time and money and have universal policy implications. Methods by which to determine who, after screening, might need further assessment can be formulated by employing analyses that select potential at-risk victims from those whose levels of victimization are not associated with excessive psychosocial difficulties.

Prior Strategies for Identifying Potentially At-Risk Victims

Ideally, strategies for identifying bullied children who are potentially at risk for maladjustment would rely on a full range of assessment devices, including self- and peer reports, behavioral observations, and interviews with adult observers such as parents and teachers (Pellegrini, 2001; Stassen Berger, 2007). Real-world application of decision theory, however, often has to take into consideration external constraints and ethical and practical concerns. Cillessen and Bukowski (2000) noted the difficulty in time and costs of obtaining data on large, representative samples from multiple sources with consent from all of these sources. In other words, the most accurate tool for identifying bullied children may not be the most feasibly implemented.

Researchers have developed a number of measures for assessing peer victimization. There are few screening tools, however, that have been validated for the identification of peer victimization (Lyznicki, McCaffree, & Robinowitz, 2004). Rating scales and abbreviated clinical interviews have been used as screeners for potential maladjustment (Lyznicki et al., 2004). Typically, a variety of assessment methods, including self-report, peer nominations, teacher reports, and behavioral observations, are used to estimate the prevalence of bullying and to identify potential bullies and bullied children (Espelage & Swearer, 2003). There are also several rating scales and abbreviated clinical interviews that can be used to screen for potential maladjustment (Lyznicki et al., 2004). There are costs and benefits associated with each method or combination of methods. Little consensus among researchers exists as to what constitutes the most reliable and valid strategy for assessing peer victimization and for further assessment of those victimized children who are at risk for maladjustment.

Self-report scales are the most common method of assessment because they are inexpensive and less obtrusive (Espelage & Swearer, 2003). Because teachers and parents can underestimate instances of peer victimization, self-report is important to obtain (Goldbaum, Craig, Pepler, & Connolly, 2007). Kochenderfer and Ladd (1997) validated their self-report of peer victimization using observational ratings of children's exposure to peer aggression and concluded that the self-report measure yielded sufficiently reliable and valid data for the identification of bullied children. Besides issues of expense and ease of administration, other methodological concerns include the subjectivity of labeling and the dilemma of poor agreement among informants (Theriot, Dulmus, Sowers, & Johnson, 2005). Researchers have compared those who labeled themselves as bullied to those who had reached the threshold for inclusion in the bullied children category but did not label themselves or identify as bullied children. For example, Theriot et al. (2005) found that of those that met the criteria for being bullied only 21.9% indicated that they had been bullied, providing further evidence for the subjectivity involved in self-report of victimization and the need for collateral data.

Self-report methods are advantageous for a number of reasons. They are useful for gathering information about attitudes or behavior from a large group of individuals (Espelage & Swearer,

2003). Self-reports can provide an index for the frequency of bullying experiences, whereas peer reports assess the degree of consensus among peers that an individual is involved in peer harassment (Gazelle & Ladd, 2002). Salmivalli (2001) noted that some measures are more sensitive than others and commented that self-reports of bullying "seem to be the most easy to decrease through intervention work" (p. 276). Ladd and Kochenderfer-Ladd (2002) compared single versus multiple informant measures and found that no single informant measure was better at estimating adjustment. Single-measure assessment strategies may not provide a complete picture. Furthermore, self-reports can be distorted and may not accurately ascertain information about functioning within the peer group (Lemerise & Arsenio, 2000), therefore reports from others should be considered. Although obtaining an individual child's perception of being bullied is the most feasible, it is not always sufficient as an assessment method and additional corroborating reports are often needed, especially to assess potential problems of maladjustment.

Self-report measures alone may not sufficiently capture all aspects of the bullying problem. Juvonen, Graham, and Schuster (2003) note that because researchers typically rely on self-report measures to assess adjustment and identify bullies and victims there is less variability in the picture of the problems presented. That is, self-report may not provide a thorough or adequate assessment of the situation. There is an overwhelming lack of information about the reliability and validity of self-report measures to assess bullying and victimization (Cornell, Sheras, & Cole, 2006). Furthermore, there is a lot of variability in how peer victimization is defined and conceptualized. Even when bullying prevention programs discuss their survey measures, reliability and validity statistics of these measures are often not included (Cornell et al., 2006).

Peer data are particularly valuable when assessing children's involvement with school bullying and their overall level of adjustment (Juvonen et al., 2003). Peers can potentially provide a more accurate assessment of who is involved and have more opportunities to observe peer behavior (Juvonen et al., 2003). Peer nominations have shown predictive value for a number of developmental outcomes and are reliable over time (Morison & Masten, 1991; Perry, Kusel, & Perry, 1988). Typically, children are presented a class roster and asked to nominate peers who fit certain descriptors, such as who bullies and who is bullied (Espelage

& Swearer, 2003). Graham and Juvonen (1998) reported that within their study nominations were then summed for each student and standardized within a class. The authors noted that they used cutoff values that were indicated from prior research to classify children as victims. Specifically, children with victim nomination scores half a standard deviation above the sample mean and bully nomination scores below the mean were identified as victims (Graham & Juvonen, 1998). Further, Espelage and Swearer (2003) suggest that peer and teacher nominations are best for identifying children who might be engaging in bullying behaviors most often. This may also hold true for identifying children who are at risk for maladjustment due to victimization. Pellegrini (2002) compared peer nominations with self-report rating scales and found that peer nominations correlated significantly with self-report scales, students' diary accounts of bullying experiences, and direct observational reports. Peer nomination methods and self-report appear complementary and can be used to assess different constructs (e.g., social reputation, self-perceptions); thus, both are often recommended (Juvonen, Nishina, & Graham, 2001).

It is also important to note that in the examination of the accuracy of teacher, self-, and peer ratings of victimization, Paulk, Swearer, Song, and Tam Carey (1999) found that teachers and peers identified fewer bullied children. Teachers identified 10% of self-rated victims and peers identified 7% of self-rated victims (Paulk et al., 1999). This discrepancy may be due to teachers' beliefs that children's self-reports are overly inclusive in their identification of what is bullying. Peers are not always involved in all peer groups and may not have first-hand knowledge about the extent of bullying. Additionally, a potential bias with teacher- and peer-reporting assessment methods involves stereotyping of behaviors, including gender bias (Hymel, Wagner, & Butler, 1990; Paulk et al., 1999), which may affect the accuracy of the identification strategy.

Although behavioral observation techniques are less commonly used, some researchers believe that they are ideal for obtaining information about the frequency of bullying behaviors and the role of students within the natural school setting (Craig & Pepler, 1997). Observational data can involve direct observation of behaviors as they unfold or can also be obtained using video and coded for information about bullying behavior (Craig & Pepler, 1997). According to Pepler, Jiang, Craig, and Connolly (2007), information obtained by behavioral observation can help to garner a better understanding of the effectiveness of intervention and provide another perspective in addition to student reports. Advantages of using observational measures center on the ability to capture behaviors as they unfold and the ability to integrate these data with survey assessments (Espelage & Swearer, 2003). For example, Kochenderfer and Ladd (1997) used the observational ratings of children's exposure to peer aggression to validate the self-report of peer victimization. In their study, observers noted the rate at which children were the recipients of aggressive behaviors from peers. These ratings were averaged across three time points and analyses yielded a modest association ($r = .27$) with self-report scores (Kochenderfer & Ladd, 1997). There are, however, ethical and methodological challenges associated with observational techniques. Observational assessment can be impractical and there can be state, federal, or school restrictions in place that restrict the collection of behavioral observations in the school setting (Espelage & Swearer, 2003). This can include informed consent. Multiple assessment strategies have been used when identifying bullied children for intervention, research, and prevalence estimation purposes. Because there are pros and cons to each method of assessment and mixed reports of concordance among informants, it is difficult to ascertain which method is most accurate (Stassen Berger, 2007).

Our Contribution to Selective Identification

Prior studies have provided some initial strategies in the identification of potentially at-risk children (Elledge, Newgent, & Cavell, 2008; Hughes, Cavell, & Willson, 2001). Each of these studies utilizes a form of selective identification that serves to inform researchers as to potential strategies for further research and/or selective identification. See Table 5.1 for an overview of these studies.

PrimeTime

In a study by Hughes et al. (2001), 2nd and 3rd grade teachers from 13 public elementary schools in two school districts in a small city in the Southwest were asked to nominate children whom they perceive as matching a behavioral description of an aggressive child. Of the 356 nominated children, parental consent to screen was obtained for 281 (79%), of whom 212 (75%) met the

TABLE 5.1 Overview of Our Selective Identification Studies

Study	Grades	Instruments Used for Selective Identification	Selective Identification Cut Scores	Intervention
Hughes, Cavell, & Willson (2001)	2–3	Teacher Report Form (Aggressive Behavior subscale)	≥ 70T	PrimeTime condition (community-based mentoring with child-focused skills training and consultation for parents)
		Peer-Nominated Overt or Relational Aggression	≥ 2 SD classroom mean	Lunch Buddy condition (a stand-alone, school-based mentoring program that involves lunchtime visits and a different mentor each semester)
Elledge, Newgent, & Cavell (2008)	5	Self-Report of Victimization (The Way Kids Are) Teacher Report of Victimization	Top 33% of summed self and teacher reports of victimization	Lunch Buddy Mentoring (a stand-alone, school-based mentoring program that involves bi-weekly lunchtime visits)
Newgent, Seay, Malcolm, Keller, & Cavell (presented in this chapter)	4–5	Self-Report of Victimization (The Way Kids Are) Teacher Report of Victimization Teacher Report Form	≥ .50 SD of the mean at two points in time on self teacher, or peer reports of victimization ≥ 60T	Results used as a screener to identify children who may be potentially at risk for future psychopathology who need further assessment
		Self–Teacher Sum Score of Victimization	Determined by receiver operating characteristic (ROC)	

following criteria for inclusion in the study: (1) a score at or above 60*T* on the Aggressive Behavior subscale of the Teacher Report Form and a score at or above the classroom mean on peer-nominated overt or relational aggression; or (2) a score at or above 70*T* on the Aggressive Behavior subscale of the Teacher Report Form or score at or above two standard deviations above the classroom mean on peer nominations of overt or relational aggression. Of the 212 eligible children, parental consent for participation in the intervention was obtained for 174 (82%). Parents were told their child would be in one of two mentoring programs. Children with consent were blocked by school and randomly assigned to intervention conditions. Of the 174 recruited children, 89 were assigned to the PrimeTime condition (a combination of community-based mentoring with child-focused skills training and consultation for parents and teachers) and 85 were assigned to the Lunch Buddy condition (a stand-alone, school-based mentoring program that involves lunchtime visits and a different mentor each semester). Children in both conditions showed significant improvement at post-treatment and at the 1- and 2-year follow-up on parent and teacher ratings of externalizing problems and on teacher ratings of behavioral and scholastic competence (Hughes et al., 2001). Results suggest that the selective prevention strategy employed in this study targeted children who benefited from the intervention.

Lunch Buddy Mentoring

Elledge et al. (2008) selected a subset of 5th graders from a larger study (*N* = 343) that examined correlates of peer victimization. Children were identified based on their score on a screening tool assessing peer victimization. The screening measure was derived from child and teacher reports of victimization at one point in time. Scores from a 9-item self-report measure and a 3-item teacher measure were summed for each child. Ratings were made on a 3-point scale (*1 = none, 2 = sometime, 3 = a lot*). Scores could range from 12 to 36, with higher ratings indicative of greater victimization. Children who scored in the top 33% of a composite measure of victimization were eligible for Lunch Buddy mentoring. Peer ratings of victimization were also utilized in the outcome analyses. Twelve children (all who had summed scores ≥ 19) were selected for participation in this study. Elledge et al. (2008) also identified two groups of matched control children. Children were identified as matches based on the following parameters: (1) score on the child–teacher sum victimization index (within 1 SEM), (2) ethnicity, and (3) gender. A distinction between match controls attending the same school as the mentored child (SAME controls, $n = 12$) and those attending a different school (DIFFERENT controls, $n = 12$) was done. Using ANCOVAs to control for fall victimization scores, the three groups were compared on their level of child-, peer-, and teacher-rated victimization. Mentored children were rated by peers as significantly less bullied than DIFFERENT controls, $F(1, 32) = 32.66$, $p < .0001$. However, Lunch Buddy children did not differ significantly from SAME controls. It is possible that contamination effects explain these findings in that SAME controls might have benefited indirectly from mentors' lunchtime visits. Differences among conditions on self- or teacher-reported victimization measures were not significant (Elledge et al., 2008). The method of selective identification in this study resulted in some positive gains for the victimized children. Selective identification appears to have benefits to those children who are most in need of prevention and intervention.

The Need for Selective Identification and Prevention Strategies

Most antibullying interventions involve changes in schoolwide structures (e.g., rules, supervision, consequences) that decrease opportunities and rewards for school bullying (Olweus, 1993). Such programs, if faithfully implemented and continually supported, can lead to significant reductions in peer victimization (Olweus, 1993; Smith, Ananiadou, & Cowie, 2003; Stassen Berger, 2007). However, replicating a successful antibullying program is not easy (e.g., Salmivalli, Kaukiainen, & Voeten, 2005) and negative outcomes have been reported (e.g., Brockenbrough, 2001; Price & Jones, 2001; Stevens, Van Oost, & de Bourdeaudhuij, 2000). Because intervention researchers tend to rely on anonymous surveys to assess changes in the incidence of bullying and victimization (Chan, Myron, & Crawshaw, 2005; Stassen Berger, 2007), it is unclear whether schoolwide programs can significantly alter the risk trajectory of individual children who are chronically bullied. Heavy emphasis on universal, antibullying interventions has prompted some scholars (Nation, 2007; Pepler, 2006) to call for interventions that provide "focused support" (Pepler, 2006, p. 16) to bullied children. Researchers seldom consider the value of selective intervention programs for this population (Gazelle & Ladd, 2002; Nation, 2007).

Current research leaves unanswered key questions about how

school personnel should proceed when seeking to help the chronically bullied child. Schools are unlikely to implement a universal intervention program each time it encounters such cases (Newman-Carlson & Horne, 2004), and those that do launch schoolwide programs cannot sustain them indefinitely (Fekkes et al., 2006; Hirschstein & Frey, 2006). Craig and Pepler (2003) estimate the percentage of children needing selective or indicated interventions to be 10–15% and 5–10%, respectively. Recognizing the paucity of research addressing the identification of children who are bullied and potentially at risk for maladjustment, identifying the obstacles to identification, and developing an accurate identification method are needed.

Identifying Victims: An Obstacle for Selective Interventions

The task of identifying bullied children for selective interventions carries with it certain risks, including the misidentification of victims, the inadvertent stigmatization of labeling children as bullied, and the exacerbation of conditions contributing to peer victimization. There are four additional concerns associated with selective interventions for bullied children that are noteworthy. As Juvonen and Graham (2001) highlight, even well-intentioned efforts can fail (see also Stassen Berger, 2007). The first concern relates to the programs themselves and the insufficient implementation of an intervention program. Worse than ineffective interventions are interventions that are "incomplete, inadequate, or sporadic" in their implementation, which can potentially lead to greater problems for bullied children (Whitted & Dupper, 2005, p. 169).

The second concern relates to the costs associated with identifying bullied children for intervention. Such costs include increased reinforcement of victimization status (DeRosier, Cillessen, Coie, & Dodge, 1994) and increased stigma and self-blame by the victim (Smith et al., 2003; Spivak & Prothrow-Stith, 2001). These risks are highlighted by research suggesting that, once labeled with a social classification, individuals' roles may be difficult to change if they remain with the same group of peers (Hymel et al., 1990). According to Spivak and Prothrow-Stith (2001), labeling children as bullies or victims may increase their sense of self-blame and further stigmatize them. The risk of overinclusion, or designating victim status for those who are not at risk, carries with it the cost of potentially harming children by labeling them as bullied children (Glew, Rivara, & Feudtner, 2000; Spivak & Prothrow-Stith, 2001).

Third, efforts to identify potential at-risk victims must be examined in light of the costs and benefits associated with false positives versus false negatives. A drawback of a cut score that overly identifies bullied children involves unnecessary attention or labels for children who may not be at risk for maladjustment. It is important to avoid stereotyping children as bullies or victims (Glew et al., 2000; Spivak & Prothrow-Stith, 2001). Spivak (2003) warned that identification of a bullied child might be perceived as placing blame on the victim. Drawing added attention to victims of peer harassment could lead to more intense and/or covert victimization experiences. This is not only a concern but also a necessary step in identification.

Lastly, one practical concern that should be taken into consideration when identifying children for selective intervention is that children may not want to report bullying experiences. Researchers have found that older children are less likely to report victimization (Menesini et al., 1997), and those who are bullied more frequently report bullying more often (Fekkes, Pijpers, & Verloove-Vanhorick, 2005). Fekkes et al. (2005) note that of those who report being bullied, approximately half (53%) indicated that they told their teacher about it and 67% indicated that they told their parents. The remainder of children chose not to report as either they did not expect adults to intervene or they did not want adults to intervene.

It is also important to consider the intended purpose of the assessment and how the identification results are to be used. The purpose of a screener would be to identify bullied children who are at risk for developing significant problems and thus warrant selective intervention. A screening tool would allow for quick, efficient, and low cost assessment of peer victimization to identify those bullied children who are potentially at risk for later maladjustment. Cross-informant measures could provide a slightly more diverse picture of the bullying experience than a single self-report measure and should be considered for initial identification of those potentially at risk and in need of further assessment. Self-report of peer victimization is a standard, quick, and easy method of assessment (Ladd & Kochenderfer-Ladd, 2002) that can be augmented relatively easily with data provided by teachers. Teacher reports could potentially refine and qualify distinctions in behavior reported by children themselves (Coie & Dodge, 1988; Ladd & Profilet, 1996) and can provide a more informative initial assessment of risk potential than self-report alone. Using self- and teacher reports of victimization as a screening strategy would appear to offer the following advantage: reliance on multiple informants who provide different but complementary perspectives obtained at relatively low costs and with less potential for harm.

Process for Development of the Proposed Selective Identification Screening Model

We have established that there is value in developing methods for detecting PARVs. The utility of newly developed screening measures is enhanced when statistical methods are used to help maximize the proportion of correct predictions. Based on these statistical procedures, cut scores can be established to maximize the efficiency of the screening tool for correct classification and selection of those who need further assessment.

In order to determine which individuals to target for selective intervention, the ability to discern who is experiencing transient peer victimization from those who are chronically bullied is needed. That is, those bullied children who are at risk for later maladjustment are likely to be those children who are chronically bullied. Based on receiver operating characteristic (ROC) analyses, optimal cut points can be established to maximize the efficiency of the screening for correct classification and selection of those who warrant further assessment. Hill, Lochman, Coie, Greenberg, and the Conduct Problems Prevention Research Group (2004) have used logistic regression and ROC analyses to investigate multi-rater and multitimepoint procedures and accuracy of methods for screening for externalizing problems. Screening tools can be used to identify children and place them into two groups, those who will receive intervention and those who will not or who will get more assessment. Screening tools can also be used in a multiple-gating approach (Hill et al., 2004) for the identification of those who necessitate further, more time intensive assessment in order to address the potential harm factor. What is needed is an efficient process of selecting children whose levels of victimization and risk for later psychopathology are significant enough to outweigh the potential costs of effective prevention efforts.

We propose that a two-step selection process is warranted. See Table 5.1 for an overview of this study. In the first step, prevention programmers would identify children for whom peer victimization was considered a legitimate concern – children whose self-reports of peer victimization were consistent over time or children whose peers or teachers also identified them as victims. This is consistent with prior research (e.g., Ladd & Kochenderfer-Ladd, 2002). Then, taking into consideration what prevention programmers would need to know, we would assess the degree to which children are showing signs of emergent psychopathology or other indications of maladjustment. This can be designated by elevated levels ($T \geq 60$) of internalizing or externalizing problems (Achenbach, 1991) on the Teacher Report Form (TRF; Achenbach, 2001) in relation to some combination of self-, peer, or teacher victimization score. Identification of a potential at-risk victim involves relying on assessment information obtained from self-, peer, and teacher reports of victimization at two points in time. The PARV status criterion is based on self-, teacher, or peer reports of victimization greater than .5 SD above the class mean and at two or more time points.

Multiple combinations of factors that could make up the potential at-risk victims, indices would then be examined through chi-square analysis. Next, the extent to which these at-risk victims, indices (a quick and easy screening) could be used to identify children who are potentially at risk for peer victimization and who were also rated as having elevated levels of internalizing or externalizing problems would be examined. Logistical regression analyses can then be used to assess the degree to which these indices adequately identify (1) potentially at-risk victims and (2) children who exceed our designated cutoffs on the Achenbach scales. The next step involves logistical regression analyses to assess the degree to which the proposed screener, a more easily obtained self- and teacher report of victimization at a single time point, can significantly predict PARV status. Self- and teacher-reported victimization scores can be summed across the self-report items and teacher report items to create a Self-Teacher Sum Score.

In the second step, sensitivity and specificity of the indices will be examined in relation to whether or not these scores were related to elevated TRF scores (binary coded for clinically elevated or not clinically elevated) using ROC analysis. Those positively identified as at risk among those who are actually at risk determine the sensitivity of the measure. Sensitivity of a measure refers to its ability to detect positive cases among positive cases. Specificity refers to the proportion of those who are determined to be not at risk among those that are not at risk, in other words, a true negative. Taking into consideration both the basic measure of the success of the screening tool, sensitivity, and its negative predictive power, specificity, ROC analysis results will be used to derive a cut score to categorize children as having either negative or positive at-risk status.

Lastly, ROC analyses will be used to examine the degree to which the screening tool correctly classifies PARVs. ROC analyses, based on signal detection theory, are often used to identify optimal cut scores for potential screening instruments. When used in conjunction with logistic regression, ROC analyses provide a way of assessing the predictive value of a test and the value of adjusting cut points for specific intervention purposes (Hudziak, Copeland, Stanger, & Wadsworth, 2004). Classification accuracy is measured by the size of the area under the ROC curve. An area of 1 represents a perfect test and an area of .5 indicates that the test does no better than chance.

ROC curves are constructed from corresponding values of sensitivity and 1 − specificity for various cut scores on the predictor variable. The percent of correctly identified PARVs reflects the sensitivity of the screener: that is, its ability to detect positive cases among positive cases. Specificity refers to the proportion of correctly identified non-PARVs: the true negative. Taking into consideration the accuracy of the screening tool, as well as its sensitivity, negative predictive power, and specificity, ROC analysis results will also be used to derive a range of cut scores that can be used to estimate the proportion of children who warrant further assessment or intervention.

To test our screening model we utilized a sample of 379 children in the 4th ($n = 189$) and 5th ($n = 197$) grades at four public elementary schools that were initially part of a larger project examining the correlates of peer victimization. A subset of these participants was used to test our screening model. Reports of peer victimization were obtained from teachers, children, and peers at two time points. A 12-item version of *The Way Kids Are* (Ladd & Kochenderfer-Ladd, 2002) was used to assess children's self-rated experiences with verbal, physical, or relational victimization. Peer reports of victimization were derived from a modified version of the *Class Play* (Masten, Morrison, & Pelligrini, 1985). Teachers were given a 3-item teacher rating of peer victimization. Additionally, TRF (Achenbach, 2001) and the Child Behavior Checklist (Achenbach, 2001) were given to the teachers and parents, respectively, at the end of the academic year. Peer-rejected status, a subscale on the *Class Play* (Masten et al., 1985), was used to assess peer-rejected status.

After the collection of data, we employed our two-step identification process. We found that children who score at or above .50 *SD* of the mean on child-, peer-, or teacher-reported victimization at two time points carry significant risk. Specifically, these children were more likely to have clinically elevated levels of internalizing or externalizing problems as reported by teachers and parents, and to be peer rejected. In our sample, 18% of children fell into this group of PARVs. Having identified a valid external criterion by which to identify PARVs, we next examined the utility of a simple screening measure that did not require collecting data from three different informants at two time points. Our screener sums scores from the child report and the teacher report administered at a single point in time. Logistic regression analyses showed that scores in this child–teacher sum score significantly predicted PARV status: $\beta = 0.48$, $\chi^2(1) = 27.37$, $p < .0001$. ROC analysis indicates that our simple screening tool provided a fair fit to the area under the curve ($AUC = 0.72$).

The benefit of a selection process or detection of potential at-risk victims is that the group selected is not the group that is necessarily placed in an intervention recipient category. The advantage is that children identified initially are further assessed. This selective identification screening model addresses the needs of Lu, presented in the case study earlier. Our model helps to identify who we select, how we select, and what could happen if we over- or underidentify. This process has the benefit of screening in some students and not others, while helping to identify when a more intensive intervention is warranted, rather than school administrators making guesses. Future considerations regarding this model should include adjustments to mean cutoff scores (i.e., = .50, .75, and 1.0) and inclusion of additional measures (i.e., Harter Global Self-Worth Scale, Peer Rejection, Poor Teacher–Student Relationship, Low Reciprocated Friends).

Public Perceptions

Public perceptions about bullying and selective prevention and intervention vary as much as the definition of bullying. We purport that selective prevention and intervention is necessary in order to reduce current incidents of bullying and later psychopathology. One unfortunate local incident that supports our contention was brought to our attention by the national media. This incident involved a high school sophomore who filed a lawsuit against a number of students he claimed had repeatedly bullied him over several years. According to Barry (2008) and Davis and Tracy (2008), these allegations were, in part, supported by school discipline records. It was also alleged that school officials did not respond in a manner consistent with school policy or with what the student or his mother deemed necessary. Public perceptions to this news article were posted on Willyates.blogspot.com and focus mostly on putting the best interest of the children first. The following are excerpts from the blog:

. . . but he cannot grow and thrive in his current school.

Winning a lawsuit, or fighting for what's right in your school district is not the best thing for Billy. Save Billy first, and then continue to volunteer your time to work on bullying in the Fayetteville schools. Most parents who have read about your situation believe that you have a case, but don't use your son's experience to prove this to the school district.

Does it really matter what the kid said, or if he stirs up trouble? These other kids are pounding him!

. . . children need to be protected at school, by laws and staff, or, go old school and the parents of the bullies should be whipping their kids . . .

The Fayetteville School District has a very strong antibullying campaign that has worked very well in the past several years. Sure, it's possible that Mr. Wolfe was bullied without cause, but it's almost impossible to implement a perfect system to ensure the safety of every single student in our school.

A child should have a civil right to go to the school without being called names or being assaulted. It disgusts me how some schools force the VICTIM to change: "don't look at the bully," change classes, walk a separate way home. Why isn't the ATTACKER the one to make the changes?

In yet another incident, a 15-year-old middle school student was shot in a classroom after being harassed about his sexual orientation by some classmates (LA Times, 2008). In this incident, several public officials commented. State Senator Sheila Kuehl (Santa Monica) said, "educators must act immediately to stop the first aggressive acts. Allowing this behavior to go unchallenged creates an environment in which it is seen as acceptable, allowing it to escalate." Bullying is "a life-changing event" according to Ralph Wegis, an attorney representing students in cases against school districts. "We're all familiar with the damage that can be done by physical assault or rape, but these school bullying cases are very much akin to those kinds of damages."

As seen in the above two incidents, there is a diverse spectrum of public responses that emphasize the belief that further education, selective intervention, and awareness of the impact of bullying is needed. When given appropriate outlets, parents as well as other stakeholders can offer suggestions for change that can have a potentially positive impact on students.

Policy Recommendations

According to the Family Equality Council (2008), nine states and Washington (DC) prohibit bullying and harassment in schools based on sexual orientation and gender identity and four states prohibit bullying and harassment in schools based on sexual orientation. Twenty-four states have antibullying and harassment laws that do not list categories. Additionally, Bully Police USA, a watch-dog organization that advocates for bullied children and reports on state antibullying laws, grades states on their antibullying efforts. For example, the state of Maine received an "A–," the state of California received a "B," and the state of Arkansas received an "A–" (Bully Police USA, n.d.). These grades are based upon the consistency with which the states report enforcement of their own antibullying laws. According to PROMO (2008), districts do need more tools to combat bullying, and they need more effective policy.

Because government policy for schoolwide antibullying campaigns often mandates that all groups, not just selective populations, be included in intervention programs, assessment is usually done *en masse*. Typically, real-world application of decision-making theory often has to take into consideration external constraints. It is often presupposed that clinical decision-makers are free to adopt policy and implement decision making that maximizes hit frequency. Social implications also make it such that determining potential at-risk victims using a more developed battery for assessment is imperative. The non-identification of students at risk for maladjustment is not socially acceptable.

Public policy needs to address this issue while being mindful that the assessment of all children may not be possible.

References

Achenbach, T. M. (2001). *Teacher's Report Form for ages 6–18*. Burlington, VT: ASEBA.

Barry, D. (2008, March 24). *A boy the bullies love to beat up, repeatedly*. Retrieved on November 21, 2008, from http://www.nytimes.com/

Batsche, G., & Knoff, H. (1994). Bullies and their victims: Understanding a pervasive problem in the schools. *School Psychology Review, 23*(2), 165–174.

Bjorkqvist, K., Lagerspertz, K., & Kaukiainen, A. (1992). Do girls manipulate and boys fight? Developmental trends in regard to direct and indirect aggression. *Aggressive Behavior, 18*(2), 117–127.

Brockenbrough, K. (2001). Peer victimization and bullying prevention among middle school students. *Dissertation Abstracts International, 62*(1-B), 538. (UMI No. AA13000186)

Bully Police USA (n.d.). *Does your state have an anti-bullying law?* Retrieved October 15, 2008, from www.bullypolice.org/

Chan, J. H. F., Myron, R., & Crawshaw, M. (2005). The efficacy of non-anonymous measures of bullying. *School Psychology International, 26*(4), 443–458.

Cillessen, A. H. M., & Bukowski, W. M. (2000). *Recent advances in the measure of acceptance and rejection in the peer system*. San Francisco, CA: Jossey-Bass.

Coie, J. D., & Dodge, K. A. (1988). Multiple sources of data on social behavior and social status in the school: A cross-age comparison. *Child Development, 59*, 815–829.

Conyne, R. K. (2003). Two critical issues in primary prevention: What it is and how to do it. *Personnel and Guidance Journal, 61*(6), 331–334.

Cornell, D. G., Sheras, P. L., & Cole, J. C. M. (2006). Assessment of bullying. In S. R. Jimerson & M. J. Furlong (Eds.), *Handbook of school violence and school safety: From research to practice* (pp. 191–209). Mahwah, NJ: Lawrence Erlbaum Associates, Inc.

Craig, W. M., & Pepler, D. J. (1997). Observations of bullying and victimization in the school yard. *Canadian Journal of School Psychology, 13*(2), 41–60.

Craig, W. M., & Pepler, D. J. (2003). Identifying and targeting risk for involvement in bullying and victimization. *Canadian Journal of Psychiatry, 48*(9), 577–582.

Cuijpers, P. (2003). Three decades of drug prevention research. *Drugs: Education, Prevention, and Policy, 10*(1), 7–20.

Davis, S. F., & Tracy, D. (2008, April 3). *Who's the bully?: Police, school records raise questions about claims made by Fayetteville High student*. Retrieved on October 16, 2008, from nwanews.com/nwat/News/63772/

DeRosier, M. E., Cillessen, A. H. N., Coie, J. D., & Dodge, K. A. (1994). Group social context and children's aggressive behavior. *Child Development, 65,* 1068–1079.

Elledge, L. C., Newgent, R. A., & Cavell, T. A. (2008). Lunch buddy mentoring as selective prevention for bullied children. Unpublished manuscript.

Espelage, D., & Swearer, S. (2003). Research on school bullying and victimization: What have we learned and where do we go from here? *School Psychology Review, 32*(3), 365–383.

Family Equality Council (2008). *State-by-state: Anti-bullying laws in the U.S.* Retrieved October 15, 2008, from www.familyequality.org

Fekkes, M., Pijpers, F., Fredriks, A. M., Vogels, T., & Verloove-Vanhorick, S. (2006). Do bullied children get ill, or do ill children get bullied? A prospective cohort study on the relationship between bullying and health-related symptoms. *Pediatrics, 117*(5), 1568–1574.

Fekkes, M., Pijpers, F. I. M., & Verloove-Vanhorick, S. P. (2005). Bullying: Who does what, when, and where? Involvement of children, teachers, and parents in bullying behavior. *Health Education Research, 20*(1), 81–91.

Gazelle, H., & Ladd, G. (2002). Interventions for children victimized by peers. In P. Schewe (Ed.), *Preventing violence in relationships: Interventions across the life span* (pp. 55–78). Washington, DC: American Psychological Association.

Glew, G., Rivara, F., & Feudtner, C. (2000). Bullying: Children hurting children. *Pediatric Review, 21,* 186.

Goldbaum, S., Craig, W., Pepler, D., & Connolly, J. (2003). Developmental trajectories of victimization: Identifying risk and protective factors. *Journal of Applied School Psychology, 19*(2), 139–156.

Goldbaum, S., Craig, W. M., Pepler, D., & Connolly, J. (2007). Developmental trajectories of victimization: Identifying risk and protective factors. In J. Zins, M. Elias, & C. Maher (Eds.), *Bullying, victimization, and peer harassment* (pp. 143–160). New York: Haworth Press.

Graham, S., & Juvonen, J. (1998). Self-blame and peer victimization in the middle school: An attributional analyses. *Developmental Psychology, 34,* 587–599.

Graham, S., & Juvonen, J. (2001). An attributional approach to peer victimization. In J. Juvonen & S. Graham (Eds.), *Peer harassment in school: The plight of the vulnerable and victimized* (pp. 49–72). New York: Guilford Press.

Hanish, L., & Guerra, N. (2004). Aggressive victims, passive victims, and bullies: Developmental continuity or developmental change? *Merrill-Palmer Quarterly, 50*(1), 17–38.

Hawker, D., & Boulton, M. (2000). Twenty years' research on peer victimization and psychosocial maladjustment: A meta-analytic review of cross-sectional studies. *Journal of Child Psychology and Psychiatry, 41*(4), 441–455.

Hill, L. G., Lochman, J. E., Coie, J. D., Greenberg, M. T., & the Conduct Problems Prevention Research Group (2004). Effectiveness of early screening for externalizing problems: Issues of screening accuracy and utility in predicting to fourth and fifth grade outcomes in a high-risk population. *Journal of Clinical and Consulting Psychology, 72,* 809–820.

Hirschstein, M., & Frey, K. (2006). Promoting behavior and beliefs that reduce bullying: The steps to respect program. In S. R. Jimerson, & M. Furlong (Eds.), *Handbook of school violence and school safety: From research to practice* (pp. 309–323). Mahwah, NJ: Lawrence Erlbaum Associates, Inc.

Hudziak, J. J., Copeland, W., Stanger, C., & Wadsworth, M. (2004). Screening for DSM-IV externalizing disorders with the Child Behavior Checklist: A receiver-operating characteristic analysis. *Journal of Child Psychology and Psychiatry, 45*(7), 1299–1307.

Hughes, J., Cavell, T., & Willson, V. (2001). Further support for the developmental significance of the quality of teacher–student relationship. *Journal of School Psychology, 39*(4), 289–301.

Hymel, S., Wagner, E., & Butler, L. (1990). Reputational bias: View from the peer group. In S. R. Asher & J. D. Coie (Eds.), *Peer rejection in childhood* (pp. 156–186). Cambridge, UK: Cambridge University Press.

Ireland, J., & Monaghan, R. (2006). Behaviors indicative of bullying among young and juvenile male offenders: A study of perpetrator and victim characteristics. *Aggressive Behavior, 32*(2), 172–180.

Juvonen, J., & Graham, S. (2001). *Peer harassment in school: The plight of the vulnerable and victimized.* New York: Guilford Press.

Juvonen, J., Graham, S., & Schuster, M. A. (2003). Bullying among young adolescents: The strong, the weak, and troubled. *Pediatrics, 112,* 1231–1237.

Juvonen, J., Nishina, A., & Graham, S. (2001). Self views versus peer perceptions of victims status among early adolescents. In J. Juvonen & S. Graham (Eds.), *Peer harassment in school: The plight of the vulnerable and victimized* (pp. 105–124). New York: Guilford Press.

Kaltiala-Heino, R., Rimpela, M., Rantanen, P., & Laippala, P. (2001). Adolescent depression: The role of discontinuities in life course and social support. *Journal of Affective Disorders, 64*(2), 155–166.

Kochenderfer, B., & Ladd, G. (1997). Peer victimization: Cause or consequence of children's school adjustment difficulties? *Child Development, 67,* 1293–1305.

Kochenderfer-Ladd, B., & Wardrop, J. (2001). Chronicity and instability of children's peer victimization experiences as predictors of loneliness and social satisfaction trajectories. *Child Development, 72*(1), 134–151.

Kumpulainen, K., Rasanen, E., & Puura, K. (2001). Psychiatric disorders and the use of mental health services among children involved in bullying. *Aggressive Behavior, 27*(2), 102–110.

Ladd, G., & Kochenderfer-Ladd, B. (2002). Identifying victims of peer aggression from early to middle childhood: Analysis of cross-informant data for concordance, estimation of relational adjustment, prevalence of victimization, and characteristics of identified victims. *Psychological Assessment, 14*(1), 74–96.

Ladd, B., & Ladd, G. (2001). Variations in peer victimization: Relations to children's maladjustment. In J. Juvonen & S. Graham (Eds.), *Peer harassment in school: The plight of the vulnerable and victimized* (pp. 25–48). New York: Guilford Press.

Ladd, G. W., & Profilet, S. M. (1996). The Child Behavior Scale: A teacher-report measure of young children's aggressive, withdrawn, and prosocial behaviors. *Developmental Psychology, 32*, 1008–1024.

LA Times (2008, March 8). *Meaner bullying is leading schools to find new tactics.* Retrieved October 16, 2008, from articles.latimes.com/2008/mar/07/local/me-bullying7

Lemerise, E. A., & Arsenio, W. F. (2000). An integrated model of emotion processes and cognition in social information processing. *Child Development, 71*, 107–118.

Lyznicki, J. M., McCaffree, M. A., & Robinowitz, C. B. (2004). Childhood bullying: Implications for physicians. *American Family Physician, 70*, 1723–1730.

Masten, A., Morrison, P., & Pelligrini, D. (1985). A revised class play method of peer assessment. *Developmental Psychology, 21*, 523–533.

Menesini, E., Eslea, M., Genta, M. L., Gianetti, E., Fonzi, A., Costabile, A., et al. (1997). A cross-national comparison of children's attitudes towards bully/victim problems in school. *Aggressive Behaviour, 23*, 245–257.

Morison, P., & Masten, A. (1991). Peer reputation in middle childhood as a predictor of adaptation in adolescence: A seven-year follow-up. *Child Development, 62*, 991–1007.

Nation, M. (2007). Empowering the victim: Interventions for children victimized by bullies. In J. E. Zins, M. J. Elias, & C. A. Maher (Eds.), *Bullying, victimization, and peer harassment: A handbook of prevention and intervention* (pp. 239–255). New York: Haworth Press.

Newman-Carlson, D., & Horne, A. M. (2004). Bully busters: A psychoeducational intervention for reducing bullying behavior in middle school students. *Journal of Counseling and Development, 82*, 259–267.

Nicolaides, S., Toda, Y., & Smith, P. K. (2002). Knowledge and attitudes about school bullying in trainee teachers. *Journal of Educational Psychology, 72*, 105–118.

Nishina, A., Juvonen, J., & Witkow, M. (2005). Sticks and stones may break my bones but names will make me feel sick: The psychosocial, somatic, and scholastic consequences of peer harassment. *Journal of Clinical Child and Adolescent Psychology, 34*(1), 37–48.

Olweus, D. (1993). *Bullying at school: What we know and what we can do.* Cambridge, MA: Blackwell Publishers.

Paulk, D. L., Swearer, S. M., Song, S., & Tam Carey, M. A. (1999, August). *Teacher, peer, and self-nominations of bullies and victims of bullying.* Presented at the American Psychological Association's 107th Annual Convention, Boston, MA.

Pellegrini, A. D. (2001). A longitudinal study of heterosexual relationships, aggression, and sexual harassment during the transition from primary school through middle school. *Journal of Applied Developmental Psychology, 22*(2), 119–133.

Pellegrini, A. D. (2002). Bullying, victimization, and sexual harassment during the transition to middle school. *Educational Psychologist, 37*(3), 151–164.

Pepler, D. (2006). Bullying interventions: A binocular perspective. *Journal of the Canadian Academy of Child and Adolescent Psychiatry, 15*(1), 16–20.

Pepler, D., Jiang, D., Craig, W., & Connolly, J. (2007). Developmental trajectories of bullying and associated factors. *Child Development, 78*(6), 1870–1871.

Perry, D. G., Kusel, S., J., & Perry, L. C. (1988). Victims of peer aggression. *Developmental Psychology, 24*, 807–814.

Price, S., & Jones, R. (2001). Reflections on anti-bullying peer counseling in a comprehensive school. *Educational Psychology in Practice, 17*(1), 35–40.

PROMO (2008). *PROMO gives the Missouri legislature an "F" on anti-bullying efforts.* Retrieved October 15, 2008, from promoonline.org

Rigby, K., & Slee, P. (1999). Suicidal ideation among adolescent school children involvement in bully-victim problems, and perceived social support. *Suicide and Life-Threatening Behavior, 29*(2), 119–130.

Salmivalli, C. (2001). Peer-led intervention campaign against school bullying: Who considered it useful, who benefited? *Educational Research, 43*(3), 263–278.

Salmivalli, C., Kaukiainen, A., & Voeten, M. (2005). Anti-bullying intervention: Implementation and outcome. *British Journal of Educational Psychology, 75*(3), 465–487.

Salmivalli, C., & Voeten, M. (2004). Connections between attitudes, group norms, and behaviour in bullying situations. *International Journal of Behavioral Development, 28*(3), 246–258.

Schwartz, D. (2000). Subtypes of victims and aggressors in children's peer groups. *Journal of Abnormal Child Psychology, 28*(2), 181–192.

Schwartz, D., Dodge, K., Pettit, G., & Bates, J. (1997). The early socialization of aggressive victims of bullying. *Child Development, 68*(4), 665–675.

Smith, P., Ananiadou, K., & Cowie, H. (2003). Interventions to reduce school bullying. *Canadian Journal of Psychiatry, 48*(9), 591–599.

Snell, J., MacKenzie, E., & Frey, K. (2002). Bullying prevention in elementary schools: The importance of adult leadership, peer group support, and student social-emotional skills. In M. R. Shinn, H. M. Walker, & G. Stoner (Eds.), *Interventions for academic and behavior problems II: Preventive and remedial approaches* (pp. 351–372). Washington, DC: National Association of School Psychologists.

Spivak, H. (2003). Bullying: Why all the fuss? *Pediatrics, 112*, 1421–1422.

Spivak, H., & Prothrow-Stith, D. (2001). The need to address bullying: An important component of violence prevention. *Journal of the American Medical Association, 285*, 2131–2132.

Stassen Berger, K. (2007). Update on bullying at school: Science forgotten? *Developmental Review, 27*(1), 90–126.

Stevens, V., Van Oost, P., & de Bourdeaudhuij, I. (2000). The effects of an anti-bullying intervention programme on peers' attitudes and behaviour. *Journal of Adolescence, 23*(1), 21–34.

Storch, E. A., & Ledley, D. R. (2005). Peer victimization and psychosocial adjustment in children: Current knowledge and future directions. *Clinical Pediatrics, 44*(1), 29–38.

Theriot, M. T., Dulmus, C. N., Sowers, K. M., & Johnson, T. K. (2005). Factors relating to self-identification among bullied victims. *Children and Youth Services Review, 27*, 979–994.

Unnever, J. (2005). Bullies, aggressive victims, and victims: Are they distinct groups? *Aggressive Behavior, 31*(2), 153–171.

Viljoen, J., O'Neill, M., & Sidhu, A. (2005). Bullying behaviors in female and male adolescent offenders: Prevalence, types, and association with psychosocial adjustment. *Aggressive Behavior, 31*(6), 521–536.

Whitted, K., & Dupper, D. (2005). Best practices for preventing or reducing bullying in schools. *Children and Schools, 27*(3), 167–174.

CHAPTER 6

Interviewing Child Victims

Advances in the Scientific Understanding of Child Eyewitness Memory

Timothy N. Odegard, Crystal M. Cooper, Robyn E. Holliday, and Stephen J. Ceci

Case Illustration

Margaret Kelly Michaels was a 26-year-old nursery school teacher when convicted of sexually abusing children at Wee Care Nursery School in Maplewood, New Jersey (Ceci & Bruck, 1995; *State* v. *Michaels*, 1988). Allegedly she had "licked peanut butter off children's genitals, played the piano while nude, made children drink her urine and eat her feces, and raped and assaulted these children with knives, forks, spoons and Lego blocks" (Ceci & Bruck, 1995, p. 12). Yet, none of the parents had any suspicions that their children were being abused nor were any signs of any such abuse reported at the time these events supposedly occurred.

Suspicion first arose when a 4-year-old child reported to a nurse who was taking his temperature rectally, "That's what my teacher does to me at school," referring to Kelly Michaels. When asked he further explained "her takes my temperature." While being questioned by Child Protective Services, the child indicated on an anatomical doll that his teacher had inserted two fingers into his rectum and he also reported that this had happened to two other children as well. Neither of these children reported any such events when questioned. However, one of them reported Michaels to have touched his penis. Events escalated to the point of a letter being sent to all of the parents with children at the nursery school. The letter was followed by 2 months of the children at the daycare facility being interviewed by professionals, such as investigators from the Division of Youth and Family Services. Yet, many of the children did not report any abuse until after having been interviewed multiple times.

Three grand juries reviewed the evidence and decided that the case should be tried. During the time leading up to the trial, the children involved were interviewed numerous times and a therapist treated 13 of the 20 children in group therapy sessions. At the conclusion of the trial, Kelly Michaels was convicted of 115 counts of sexual abuse against 20 children ranging in age from 3 to 5 years old and she was sentenced to 47 years in prison. After serving 5 years, an appeals court reversed the sentence and ruled that if a retrial of Michaels were to take place, a pretrial taint hearing would have to be held to determine the reliability and admissibility of the testimony provided by the children, given the improper methods used to obtain them (*State* v. *Michaels*, 1993). The prosecution eventually dropped all charges against Michaels in 1994.

Overview of the Issues

Children are subjected to many forms of violence, one of which is child abuse and neglect, which in the United States is defined as, "any recent act or failure to act on the part of a parent or caretaker which results in death, serious physical or emotional harm, sexual abuse or exploitation; or an act or failure to act which presents an imminent risk of serious harm" (p. xiii, U.S. Department of Health and Human Services, 2008). In 2006 alone, 905,000 children were victimized, and 1530 children died as a result of abuse and neglect (U.S. Department of Health and Human Services, 2008). Even though these numbers likely grossly underestimate the actual instances of abuse that occur in the United States (Ceci & Bruck, 1995), they still highlight the importance of protecting children from such violence, and an important aspect of doing so is to ensure that the individuals who commit such crimes are brought to justice. Eyewitness accounts provided by the victims can at times greatly facilitate such efforts, and such accounts are particularly valuable in instances such as sexual abuse cases, for which corroborating evidence is commonly unavailable (Roberts & Powell, 2001).

Yet, the Michaels case illustrates the great care that must be taken when interviewing child witnesses and the dire consequences that can result from not doing so. There are two possible states of affairs regarding the Michaels case. First, it is possible that Kelly Michaels was innocent. Second it is possible that she was guilty. If she was innocent, then the suggestive witnessing techniques that were used led to a miscarriage of justice that resulted in Kelly Michaels unjustly losing 5 years of her life. If she was guilty, then a guilty person escaped punishment because poorly conducted interviews led to the judge overturning the conviction. For both of these reasons it is important for investigative interviews to be well conducted. In the following sections we highlight three key aspects of interviewing child witnesses. First, we discuss age-related differences in the ability of children to accurately report past events. Then, we describe several factors that influence the veracity of their memory reports. Finally, we describe a structured forensic interviewing protocol that has been developed for use with children to help maximize accurate information and to help minimize inaccurate information.

Age-Related Differences in the Accuracy of Children's Eyewitness Memory

As illustrated in Figure 6.1, the prevalence of abuse declines as children age, with 80% of abused and neglected children being less than 12 years old. Such data raise a fundamental question. Are there age differences in the ability of children to remember the past and, if so, how might such differences influence the ability of children of different ages to provide testimony? In the Michaels case, the children involved were between the ages of 3 and 5 years old. What do we know about the ability of children in this age range to remember the past? Ideally research aimed at investigating age-related changes in the ability of children to provide eyewitness testimony would assess their ability to remember forensically relevant events. Yet, doing so presents researchers with a unique challenge. Such events are stressful and are charged with a myriad of complex emotions. These characteristics make it difficult to simulate comparable events in a laboratory setting and simulating events comparable to child abuse is unethical.

In an attempt to overcome these obstacles, researchers have questioned children about events that occur in their lives. Such research demonstrated that, in general, young children can remember past real-life events (Farrar & Goodman, 1990; Fivush,

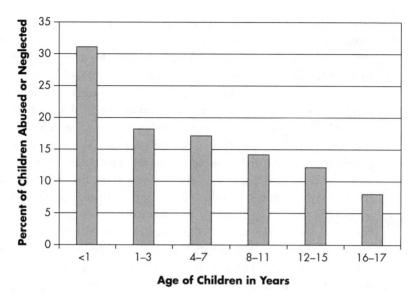

Age of Children in Years

FIGURE 6.1 Percentage of children from different age groups abused and neglected in the United States during 2006 (U.S. Department of Health and Human Services, 2008).

1984; Hudson, 1990; Hudson & Fivush, 1991; Hudson, Fivush, & Kuebli, 1992). For example, 2–6 months after hurricane Andrew, 3- and 4-year-old children remembered a considerable amount of information about the events that took place leading up to, during, and following the hurricane (Bahrick, Parker, Fivush, & Levitt, 1998; Fivush, McDermott Sales, Goldberg, Bahrick, & Parker, 2004). In addition, children, as young as 2 years old are capable of remembering having experienced a fire drill at their preschool and can provide information about its occurrence 2 weeks later (Pillemer, 1992). Moreover, children were still able to remember aspects of this event 7 years later. However, children who were 4 years old at the time of the event provided more detailed accounts than the younger children (Pillemer, Picariello, & Pruett, 1994). Additionally, even 2-year-old children can remember a medical emergency (Peterson & Bell, 1996; Peterson & Rideout, 1998) and can do so even after a considerable amount of time has passed (Peterson, 1999; Peterson & Whalen, 2001). Such data demonstrate that even very young children are capable of remembering past events and of providing details about their occurrence. However, in general, older children provide more detailed reports than younger children (Peterson & Bell, 1996).

Research investigating naturally occurring events in children's

lives has provided a great deal of information about the characteristics of children's memories for stressful real-life events, but a
drawback to using events such as hurricanes and other traumatic
events is that it is often difficult, if not impossible, to ascertain the
accuracy of the memory reports provided by the children. Given
that accuracy is paramount in legal settings, there are limitations
to the applicability of such research. To overcome this obstacle
researchers have had children experience scripted events in controlled settings. Children are later questioned about what took
place during these events in order to test the accuracy of their
memories for these events. Preschool-aged children have been
observed to accurately remember past events when such techniques are used. However, older children provide more details and
the details provided are generally more accurate (Baker-Ward,
Gordon, Ornstein, Larus, & Clubb, 1993; Ornstein, Baker-Ward,
Gordon, Pelphrey, Tyler, & Gramsow, 2006; Ornstein, Merritt,
Baker-Ward, Furtado, Gordon, & Principe, 1998; Quas,
Goodman, Bidrose, Pipe, & Craw, 1999). For example, Baker-
Ward and her colleagues (1993) tested the ability of children
between the ages of 3 and 7 years old to remember a scripted
medical checkup for which the events that transpired were known
by the experimenter. Children in all of the age groups tested
remembered an impressive number of events that took place during the medical examination. For instance, the 3-year-old children
remembered roughly 80% of the events that took place when
tested immediately after the medical exam. However, older children remember a greater number of events than did younger children even when children were initially tested after the medical
exam. Additionally, older children reported more events when
asked open-ended questions (e.g., Tell me what happened when
you went to the doctor's office?), whereas younger children
required more cues to remember the past events (e.g., Did the
doctor shine a light in your eye?) and forgot more information as
time passed than did the older children.

These general findings are similar in nature to others that
have been reported when children were interviewed concerning
medical procedures (Ornstein, Gordon, & Larus, 1992; Ornstein
et al., 1998, 2006; Peters, 1987; Quas et al., 1999; Saywitz,
Goodman, Nicholas, & Moan, 1991). Older children have better
memory for the events and provide more information to open-
ended questions than younger children. Although they report
less than the older children, young children do remember a

considerable amount of information. Yet, the question remains as to the extent to which children of different ages are more prone to report false information when questioned about life experiences. In this regard, an advantage of using real-life events, such as medical examinations, is that they can evoke anxiety in children, while at the same time affording researchers with the luxury of knowing exactly what transpired. This allows researchers to question children about events that did not take place during the examination.

Of these events that did not take place, some were often typical of going to the doctor (e.g., Did the doctor give you a shot?), whereas other events that children are questioned about would likely not have happened at a doctor's office (e.g., Did the doctor cut your hair?). Baker-Ward and her colleagues observed 5-year-old children to falsely indicate having experienced roughly 10–25% of both types of events when tested immediately after the medical examination, and these rates remained relatively constant across the 6-week period of questioning. In contrast, older children correctly rejected both types of items when interviewed immediately after the medical exam. Yet, the false acceptance of the typical events increased over the 6-week period, but the same was not true of the events that were not likely to have occurred in that setting. These findings demonstrate that younger and older children commit memory errors, but important systematic differences are observed between the types of errors committed by children of different ages. Younger children falsely accept both typical and atypical events immediately after having completed the medical exam and continue to do so over a delay. Whereas the older children correctly rejected both typical and atypical events that had not occurred when tested immediately, but falsely accepted a greater number of typical events that had not occurred after a delay.

Several important age-related patterns of memory emerge from the extant literature. First, it is clear that both younger and older children can remember past events and when open-ended questions are used the information provided can be highly accurate. However, older children provide more information to open-ended questions than do younger children, whereas young children require more cues and prompting in order to remember past events (Bahrich et al., 1998; Hudson et al., 1992; Peterson & Bell, 1996; Peterson & Rideout, 1998). Second, when asked pointed questions about events that did not occur, younger children are more prone to errors than older children. In addition, young children do not constrain their answers to events that are likely to have happened. Rather, they appear to be biased to indicate that even events that are unlikely to have occurred actually took place. They also are just as likely to do so when interviewed immediately after the events in question transpired as they are when questioned after a considerable amount of time has passed. However, older children are not inclined to accept events that likely would not have occurred. Rather, when errors are made by these children, they tend to falsely indicate events that likely would have occurred as having taken place (Baker-Ward et al., 1993; Ornstein et al., 1998, 2006).

Such age-related differences in the ability of children to remember past events are critically important to eyewitness memory. In forensic settings the individuals conducting the interview do not know what happened, and an individual might be inclined to probe a child's memory with specific cues (Ceci & Bruck, 1995; Lamb, Sternberg, Orbach, Hershkowitz, Horowitz, & Esplin, 2002; Poole & Lamb, 1998). However, doing so increases the tendency for children of all ages to make errors, especially after time has passed and memories get fuzzier. As illustrated by the Michaels case, reports of abuse provided by younger and older children may not always be accurate and in extreme instances such inaccuracies can have dire consequences. A balance must be achieved when probing a witness. In the instance of the Michaels case, it was eventually determined that unreliable techniques were used to obtain testimony from children. Thus, the consequences of unreliable interviewing techniques are potentially twofold. First, they can result in the wrongful prosecution of an individual based on inaccurate information. Second, they can result in the testimony of a victim being judged as inadmissible even in instances when the information provided might be largely accurate. In the Michaels case the appellate court ruled that improper methods had been used and compromised the testimony of the children. In the next section, we consider what factors specific to the Michaels case might have influenced the reliability of the memories provided by the children involved in that case that are also relevant in recent cases.

Factors that Influence Child Eyewitness Accuracy

There are several aspects of the Michaels case that are disconcerting. First, the children were interviewed using anatomical dolls.

The use of anatomical dolls is thought by many to help interviewers to obtain information from children, but there also is evidence to suggest that they increase the tendency of children to report events that did not occur (Bruck, Ceci, Francoeur, & Renick, 1995; Saywitz et al., 1991; Thierry, Lamb, Orbach, & Pipe, 2005). Second, the children were interviewed about what took place on multiple occasions. Such practices can negatively impact the reliability of the memory reports provided by children, by increasing the amount of false information mistakenly reported (Bruck, Ceci, & Hembrooke, 2002; Ceci, Loftus, Leichtman, & Bruck, 1994). Moreover, children can come to believe that they must somehow be mistaken because it is not typical for someone to continually ask a person about the same thing after an answer has been given. They might also feel that they are not mistaken, but nonetheless feel that they are expected to comply and provide the answer that the interviewer expects to hear (Bruck et al., 2002). Such feelings can be exacerbated by the power imbalance inherent to the social structure of the setting in which forensic interviews take place, which brings us to our third factor (i.e., social factors). Children view adults as authority figures and are typically taught to obey them. This can result in children feeling compelled to please the adult and tell them what they want to hear, which can intensify the negative effects of children being interviewed multiple times (Bruck et al., 2002; Ceci, Ross & Toglia, 1987; Holliday, 2003a, 2003b; Lampinen & Smith, 1995; Toglia, Ross, Ceci, & Hembrooke, 1992).

Anatomical Dolls

As previously mentioned, suspicion first arose in the Michaels case when a 4-year-old child reported to a nurse who was taking his temperature rectally, "That's what my teacher does to me at school," and when questioned further he explained "her takes my temperature." He was later interviewed by Child Protective Services with the use of an anatomical doll. While being questioned the child inserted two fingers into the rectum of the doll and indicated that this had happened to him and two other children. Anatomical dolls are used when interviewing children because they are thought to help overcome barriers that might prevent them from reporting abuse (Everson & Boat, 1994, 2002). Specifically, they are thought to help children to express themselves non-verbally, helping them to overcome their language barriers (Vivard & Tranter, 1988). Additionally, they are also thought to aid children in remembering past abuse by making retrieval cues explicitly available (Davies, 1991).

However, the use of anatomical dolls is also highly controversial because their use has been observed to increase the rate at which children falsely report information suggestive of abuse in field studies (Lamb, Hershkowitz, Sternberg, Boat, & Everson, 1996; Leventhal, Hamilton, Rededal, Tebano-Micci, & Eyster, 1989; Thierry et al., 2005) as well as laboratory studies (Bruck et al., 1995; Bruck, Ceci, & Franceur, 2000; Goodman & Aman, 1990; Saywitz et al., 1991). In addition, children who have not been abused or inappropriately handled will perform sexually provocative or violent acts with the dolls when being questioned about innocuous events from their past (Bruck et al., 1995; Saywitz et al., 1991). For example, in one study children completed a routine medical examination and were later questioned, with the aid of an anatomical doll, about whether the doctor had touched them. More than half the children gave inaccurate descriptions of their examinations. In addition, many of the children indicated having been touched on the genital and anal regions, which did not occur. In addition, 60% of the children used the dolls in a sexualized or aggressive manner.

Repeated Interviews and Questions

Another aspect of the Michaels case that raises concern is the fact that the children involved in the case were repeatedly questioned on multiple occasions by their parents, therapists, Child Protective Services agents and prosecuting attorneys. While it is not uncommon for children to be interviewed numerous times by different legal professionals and family members before a case goes to trial, such practices can negatively impact the accuracy of the information provided by child witnesses. Past research suggests that repeated requests for information within an interview may signal to a child that their earlier answer was incorrect. Young children in particular are apt to change their answers when questioned repeatedly and often feel compelled to provide an answer rather than saying "I don't know" (Holliday, 2003a, 2003b). This reluctance is particularly prominent when *yes/no* questions are asked (Bruck et al., 1995; Peterson & Biggs, 1997; Peterson, Dowden, & Tobin, 1999; Poole & White, 1993).

Yet, there are both positive and negative consequences of repeated interviews. On the postitive side, repeated interviews may produce hypermnesia. Hypermnesia is a phenomenon by which individuals actually remember seemingly forgotten information by repeated interviews or tests. However, it is critical that repeated interview questions be open ended (Peterson, Moores, & White, 2001; Reyna & Titcomb, 1997). When open-ended questions are not used and children are asked leading questions, the rate at which they report inaccurate information over a series of interviews increases (Bruck et al., 2002; Ceci et al., 1994; Powell, Jones, & Campbell, 2003).

For example, over a series of five interviews 4- to 5-year-old children were interviewed about a series of events, half of which were false (Bruck et al., 2002). During the initial interview children were simply asked unbiased questions (e.g., Did you ever see a man come into the daycare and steal something?). However, children were presented with biased questions about the events in the subsequent interviews. Initially children correctly remember events that actually occurred an overwhelming majority of the time (82%). Moreover, they were relatively good at correctly rejecting events that had not occurred, having done so 22% of the time. Yet, the false acceptance rate ballooned to 63%, 91%, 88%, and 78% during the remaining four interviews, which included different forms of bias questions. The findings demonstrate the negative impact that interviewing children multiple times can have on their tendency to report events that had not occurred. It must also be stressed, however, that the 4- to 5-year-old children in the study were relatively good at correctly rejecting events that had not occurred when questioned about them once using non-biased questioning.

Social Factors

The impact of biased questioning is exacerbated by the power structure inherent to interviews. Children are very knowledgeable of the status held by adults generally and authority figures in particular (e.g., parents, police officers, and lawyers). Given the power dynamics that can be present when children are questioned, they can at times feel compelled to question their own memories of the past and defer to what they may perceive as the greater knowledge of what actually took place that is held by the person conducting the interview (Ceci et al., 1987; Holliday, 2003a, 2003b; Lampinen & Smith, 1995; Toglia et al., 1992). Furthermore, children may simply feel compelled to tell the authority figure what they think he or she wants to hear.

For example, Ceci, Ross, and Toglia (1987) investigated the

ability of children between 3 and 12 years old to remember a series of events that took place during a story that was read to them about a girl named Loren. During an initial memory interview some of the children in each age group were asked a series of unbiased questions about the events that took place in the story. Other children in each age group were asked a series of questions that contained biased information that presupposed details not present in the story to have taken place. The 3- to 4-year-old children who were asked biased questions were the most likely to falsely indicate these items as having occurred during the story when questioned for the last time, doing so roughly 65% of the time. In contrast, the youngest children were just as capable of correctly rejecting events that were not present in the story when interviewed with unbiased questions. These data present a mixed story. They clearly indicate the preschool-aged children to be more susceptible to biased forms of questioning relative to older children. However, when unbiased questions were used, the youngest children were very capable of remembering the details included in the story. These results are somewhat perplexing and raise an interesting question. What is causing the preschool-aged children to have seemingly worse memories for the story when asked biased questions in the initial memory interview?

One possible explanation is that the youngest children are the most susceptible to social pressures. Thus, when the interviewer implies that Loren had a headache as opposed to a stomachache during the initial interview, the youngest children defer to the information provided by the interviewer. When later asked, the children then report Loren to have had a headache as opposed to a stomachache. To test this hypothesis, these researchers conducted another study in which 3- to 4-year-old children were presented with biased questions during the first memory interview by either an adult interviewer or by a 7-year-old child. Presumably, if the children are deferring to the adult as an authority figure, then they might be less likely to falsely report the misinformation when it is introduced by a source that is perceived to be a peer. Indeed this was the principal finding. Children interviewed by the 7-year-old child falsely reported the misinformation included in the biased questions 20% less often than did the children interviewed by the adult. These findings were later replicated and extended by Lampinen and Smith (1995). These researchers observed 3- to 5-year-old children to have been less likely to falsely report misinformation introduced by another child or a *silly* adult than misinformation introduced by a *normal* adult. Such data suggest that even young children are quite adept at picking up on social cues of credibility and defer to credible sources when later reporting what took place in the past.

Based on the current review of previous research, it appears that there are important age-related differences in the ability of children to remember the past. Moreover, it also seems apparent that such differences are exacerbated by factors that can be introduced during the interview process. When care is taken to interview children with open-ended questions, past research seems to suggest that age-related differences in memory can be minimized. Such findings are promising and provide hope that structured interviewing techniques might be able to help ensure the credibility of the information obtained from even very young children.

Structured Forensic Interviewing Techniques

Given that there is often little if any corroborating evidence and that there are often no other witnesses to child abuse and child sexual abuse in particular, the victim will likely be questioned about what took place during the alleged instances of abuse (Ceci & Bruck, 1995). Thus, steps must be taken to ensure the accuracy of the eyewitness account. The manner in which a witness is interviewed is crucial for criminal investigations and successful prosecutions, and several structured interviewing techniques have been developed to achieve this. Among these is the National Institute of Child Health and Human Development (NICHD) forensic interviewing protocol, which was developed for use with children based on principles identified by individuals working in the field as well as researchers investigating child memory in the laboratory setting (Lamb et al., 2002; Orbach, Hershkowitz, Lamb, Sternberg, Esplin, & Horowitz, 2000; Poole & Lamb, 1998). These principles include: outlining the roles and purpose of the interview, clearly stating the ground rules, structuring the protocol to minimize the amount of information introduced by the interviewer, encouraging the child witness to provide as much information as possible, and organizing the order of questioning to maximize open-ended questions (i.e., free and cued recall) and to minimize *yes/no* questions (i.e., recognition).

The interview begins with rapport building, which is crucial because, as previously mentioned, children perceive adults to know more than they do. Thus, it must be made clear to a child that the interviewer was not present during the event in question and that the child witness is the person most knowledgeable about what took place. To facilitate this, the child is asked to demonstrate that he or she can distinguish the truth from a lie and is informed that during the interview he or she is to only report truths. The child is also asked to demonstrate an understanding that the interviewer is to be corrected if he or she says something inaccurate. The child is also informed that if she does not know the answer to a question, he or she should say, "I don't know." Next, the child is asked to describe some aspects of his or her life, allowing him or her to interact with the interviewer and grow accustomed to the format of the interview. Afterwards, the child is asked to describe a recent event from her life. For example, a child might be asked to describe how he or she celebrated a recent holiday. Doing so acquaints the child with the format of the questions that will be asked during the substantive section of the interview. Finally, the interviewer asks the child about the events of interest, progressing from open-ended free recall to cued recall, and resorting to *yes/no* recognition questioning as a last resort.

To date, several promising trends have been observed in research testing the efficacy of the NICHD protocol in real-life settings (Lamb, Orbach, Hershkowitz, Esplin, & Horowitz, 2007). First, individuals trained in using this protocol ask three times as many open-ended questions and half as many leading questions, such as *yes/no* recognition-style questions, as do individuals not trained in the NICHD protocol. As highlighted previously, answers to open-ended questions tend to be more accurate than leading questions, and these findings are quite encouraging. Second, child witnesses report roughly half of the forensically relevant information in response to open-ended questions regardless of age. Moreover, the majority of the instances of sexual abuse reported by preschoolers are provided in response to recall questions.

Although ecologically valid, testing the protocol in the field greatly reduces the ability to verify that the information provided by child witnesses is accurate because corroborating evidence is commonly unavailable. To address this shortcoming a controlled study that investigated the ability of children to provide detailed reports of real-life events when interviewed with the NICHD protocol was conducted (Odegard, Cooper, Lampinen, Reyna, & Brainerd, 2009). In this study, children attended birthday parties celebrating the birthdays of fictional characters from the

SpongeBob cartoon and the Harry Potter series of children's books and movies, both of which children should have prior knowledge of. Each party lasted approximately an hour and a half. During the parties, the children played two games, were offered two snacks, made two crafts, and heard two stories. Of the events that occurred at the parties, half were consistent with the theme of the party and the other half were generic events that could have occurred at any birthday party (i.e., eating a magic wand pretzel and a smiley face cookie). After attending all four parties, each child's memory for the events at the parties was tested using the NICHD protocol.

Importantly, 73% of the children in the study did not provide any inaccurate responses to open-ended questions. Yet, younger children were more prone to report events that had not occurred than were older children when responding to open-ended questions. In particular, 45% of the 5- to 6-year-old children reported at least one event that had not occurred in response to open-ended questions, as compared to only 20% of the 7- to 9-year-olds and 20% of the 10- to 12-year-olds. As stated previously, given that when the NICHD protocol is used in real-life settings witnesses report half of the forensically relevant information in response to open-ended questions, the low rate of intrusions is encouraging. Yet, when a child does not provide adequate levels of information to open-ended questions, interviewers are trained to proceed to more recognition-style questions. As seen in previous research, younger children recalled fewer events than did older children. Thus, interviewers would be most likely to have to resort to the use of recognition-style questions when interviewing younger children, and these children were the most likely to falsely recognize distractors presented during recognition-style questioning.

In addition, older children accurately recalled more thematic as opposed to generic events in response to free and cued recall questions than did younger children. Moreover, older children provided more accurate source judgments than did younger children, replicating past research. However, both younger and older children were more accurate when determining the source of thematic as opposed to generic events, suggesting that they used the themes of the parties to help guide their source memory judgments. Yet, the implementation of these themes could also lead children to make more source errors that are based on the theme. Indeed, older children committed more thematic source errors than younger children. Such findings suggest that older children use the themes of episodes to guide their source memory judgments more so than younger children.

As was true of the Kelly Michaels case, children may be required to provide eyewitness accounts of what happened during episodes from their lives. When questioned about events of a target episode, children must distinguish between the events that actually occurred during the target episode from those that were introduced during questioning of the episode (Zaragoza & Lane, 1994), during conversations with their parents (Poole & Lindsay, 2001, 2002), during similar episodes from their lives (Powell, Roberts, Ceci, & Hembrooke, 1999), and through television or other media sources. Moreover, abused children are typically subjected to multiple incidents of abuse (Roberts & Powell, 2001). Thus, a fundamental question is the accuracy of children's memory for repeated similar episodes, where the details of an isolated episode can become intertwined with details of other similar episodes. In this regard, older children in this study were observed to be better than younger children at identifying during which episode an event took place. Another important question is the extent to which best-practice forensic interviewing techniques minimize age-related differences in the ability of children to remember past events. In this regard, age-related differences were still observed even when using best-practice interviewing techniques such as that of the NICHD protocol. However, it must again be stressed that 73% of the children in the study did not provide any inaccurate responses to open-ended questions.

All in all, the results replicate and extend past research in several important ways. First, the results demonstrated older children to be better able than younger children at using the theme of a past episode to remember real-life events. Additionally, the present data demonstrated older children to use the theme when trying to determine during which episode an event occurred. Moreover, age-related differences were observed even with the use of the NICHD protocol. Yet, the study also demonstrates a very counterintuitive finding. In this study, older as opposed to younger children were more likely to commit memory errors that were consistent with the theme of the parties. This finding has extremely important implications for forensic interviewing. First and foremost, it suggests that under certain conditions older children might be more likely than younger children to commit memory errors. Second, it highlights that when older children commit memory errors the errors will likely be compelling, in that they will fit an overall theme.

Public Perceptions

Eyewitness testimony provided by children is viewed with skepticism. Jurors perceive young children as being sincere but lacking the cognitive resources needed to provide eyewitness accounts that are as accurate as those provided by older children and adults (Ross, Dunning, Toglia, & Ceci, 1990; Ross, Jurden, Lindsay, & Keeney, 2003). Even legal professionals are skeptical of the ability of young children to provide reliable eyewitness testimony, perceiving them as being less accurate and more suggestible than older children and adults (Brigham & Spier, 1992; Everson, Boat, Sherries, & Robertson, 1996; Melinder, Goodman, Eilersten, & Magnussen, 2004). Yet, as illustrated in Figure 6.1, the prevalence of abuse declines as children age, with 80% of abused and neglected children being less than 12 years old. Such dramatic age differences are forensically very important because those children with the greatest risk of being abused or neglected are those children perceived as providing the most unreliable eyewitness accounts.

In juxtaposition to one another, these two points highlight an obstacle to protecting children from violence. The very individuals who would be best able to testify to the violence being perpetrated against them are not perceived as being capable of providing reliable accounts of the abuse. A straightforward approach to alleviating this obstacle would be for the reliability of each child witness to be taken into consideration. For example, it would be ideal to simply review the testimony provided by a child and evaluate its overall accuracy. Unfortunately, individuals do not judge the accuracy of the testimony provided by children very well (Connolly, Prince, Lavoie, & Gordon, 2008). Individuals are no better at detecting when a child is reporting events that actually occurred in the past versus events that did not actually occur.

Thus, young children are the most likely to be victims of abuse and neglect, but the eyewitness accounts of such violence are perceived as being more suspect, even when the eyewitness accounts under consideration are accurate. However, the reality seems to be that the blame, as opposed to being laid on the memory of the child in many instances, should be placed on the manner in which the interviews are conducted. Although young children may not provide as much information as older children, they do provide information that can be highly accurate when appropriate methods are used.

Policy Recommendations

Protecting children from violence requires the efforts of individuals from many different disciplines. For example, children are protected from violence time and time again by the *direct* efforts of individuals working in the field. In a more *indirect* way, children are protected from violence *in part* by the efforts of individuals in the scientific community who strive to better understand the problems faced by individuals working in the field and to provide them with practical recommendations on how to better achieve their goal of protecting children from violence. In this chapter we outlined some of the advances that have been made in better understanding age-related differences in the reliability of children's memory, factors that influence their reliability, and means that have been developed to preserve eyewitness accounts obtained from children. Moreover, several points were addressed in our review.

Point 1: Characteristics of Child Abuse

Abused children, one of the largest groups of child witnesses, are typically not subjected to an isolated episode of abuse, but rather are subjected to multiple occurrences. Such violence can continue until the perpetrator of the crime is brought to justice. Thus, every effort should be made within the constraints of the law to bring those individuals who perpetrated such violence to justice and, by doing so, help to ensure that they will not continue to subject the child to additional violence. In instances, such as sexual abuse cases, corroborating evidence is commonly unavailable and the victim is the only witness to the crime. In such instances, the eyewitness account provided by the victim is extremely important in convicting the perpetrator.

Point 2: Preservation of Eyewitness Memory

Given that there is often little, if any, corroborating evidence and that there are often no other witnesses, victims of child abuse and child sexual abuse in particular will likely be questioned about what took place during the alleged instances of abuse. Thus, steps must be taken to ensure the accuracy of the eyewitness account.

However, several factors were highlighted that negatively impact the reliability of eyewitness accounts provided by children, such as the use of anatomical dolls, repeated interviews and questions, and social factors. Yet, the use of structured forensic interviewing techniques, such as the NICHD protocol, can reduce the negative impact of these factors on the overall accuracy of testimony provided by child witnesses.

Point 3: Accuracy and Reliability of Eyewitness Testimony

Two things must be stressed about the accuracy and reliability of eyewitness accounts. First, under ideal circumstances eyewitness accounts provided by *even* young children can be very accurate and reliable. Second, the manner in which eyewitnesses are interviewed can drastically reduce the accuracy and reliability of their testimony. In addition, non-optimal interviewing practices impact the accuracy and reliability of eyewitness accounts provided by young children more so than older children and adults.

Concluding Remarks

In conclusion, there are three extremely important points to take away from the research that has been conducted on the reliability of eyewitness accounts provided by children:

1. Eyewitness accounts provided by even young children (2–3 years old) can be very accurate and reliable.
2. Non-optimal interviewing practices, such as the use of anatomical dolls and repeated biased questioning about an event, reduce the accuracy and reliability of eyewitness accounts provided by children of all ages, as well as adults.
3. The reliability of the testimony provided by young children is influenced more by non-optimal interviewing practices than is the reliability of testimony provided by older children and adults. Yet, when techniques such as the NICHD protocol are used the reports provided by children can be highly accurate.

References

Bahrick, L. E., Parker, J. F., Fivush, R., & Levitt, M. (1998). The effects of stress on young children's memory for a natural disaster. *Journal of Experimental Psychology: Applied, 4*, 308–331.

Baker-Ward, L., Gordon, B. N., Ornstein, P. A., Larus, D. M., & Clubb, P. A. (1993). Young children's long-term retention of a pediatric examination. *Child Development, 64,* 1519–1533.

Brigham, J. C., & Spier, S. A. (1992). Opinions held by professionals who work with child witnesses. In H. R. Dent and R. Flin (Eds.), *Children as witnesses* (pp. 93–111). Chichester, UK: Wiley.

Bruck, M., Ceci, S. J., & Franceur, E. (2000). Children's use of anatomically detailed dolls to report genital touching in a medical examination: Developmental and gender comparisons. *Journal of Experimental Psychology: Applied, 6,* 74–83.

Bruck, M., Ceci, S. J., Francoeur, E., & Renick, A. (1995) Anatomically detailed dolls do not facilitate preschoolers' reports of a pediatric examination involving genital touching. *Journal of Experimental Psychology: Applied, 1,* 95–109.

Bruck, M., Ceci, S. J., & Hembrooke, H. (2002). The nature of children's true and false narratives. *Developmental Review, 22,* 520–554.

Ceci, S. J., & Bruck, M. (1995). *Jeopardy in the courtroom: A scientific analysis of children's testimony.* Washington, DC: American Psychological Association.

Ceci, S. J., Loftus, E. F., Leichtman, M., & Bruck, M. (1994). The possible role of source misattributions in the creation of false beliefs among preschoolers. *International Journal of Clinical and Experimental Hypnosis, 42,* 304–320.

Ceci, S. J., Ross, D. F., & Toglia, M. P. (1987). Suggestibility of children's memory: Psycholegal implications. *Journal of Experimental Psychology: General, 116,* 38–49.

Connolly, D. A., Price, H. L., Lavoie, J. A. A., & Gordon, H. M. (2008). Perceptions and predictors of children's credibility of a unique event and an instance of a repeated event. *Law and Human Behavior, 32,* 92–112.

Davies, G. B. (1991). Research on children's testimony: Implications for interview practice. In C.R. Hollin & K. Howells (Eds.), *Clinical approaches to sex offenders and their victims* (pp. 93–115). Chichester, UK: Wiley.

Everson, M. D., & Boat, B. W. (1994). Putting the anatomical doll controversy in perspective: An examination of major doll uses and related criticisms. *Child Abuse and Neglect, 18,* 113–129.

Everson, M. D., & Boat, B. W. (2002). The utility of anatomical dolls and drawing in child forensic interviews. In M. L. Eisen, J. A. Quas, & G. S. Goodman (Eds.), *Memory and suggestibility in the forensic interview* (pp. 383–408). Mahwah, NJ: Lawrence Erlbaum Associates, Inc.

Everson, M. D., Boat, B. W., Sherries, B., & Robertson, K. R. (1996). Beliefs among professionals about rates of false allegation of child sexual abuse. *Journal of Interpersonal Violence, 4,* 541–553.

Farrar, M. J., & Goodman, G. S. (1990). Developmental differences in the relation between scripts and episodic memory: Do they exist? In R. Fivush & J. A. Hudson (Eds.), *Knowing and remembering in young children* (pp. 30–64). New York: Cambridge University Press.

Fivush, R. (1984). Learning about school: The development of kindergartners' school trips. *Child Development, 55,* 1697–1709.

Fivush, R., McDermott Sales, J., Goldberg, A., Bahrick, L., & Parker, J. (2004). Weathering the storm: Children's long-term recall of Hurricane Andrew. *Memory, 12,* 104–118.

Goodman, G. S., & Aman, C. (1990). Children's use of anatomically detailed dolls to recount an event. *Child Development, 61,* 1859–1871.

Holliday, R. E. (2003a). The effect of a prior cognitive interview on children's acceptance of misinformation. *Applied Cognitive Psychology, 17,* 443–457.

Holliday, R. E. (2003b). Reducing misinformation effects in children with cognitive interviews: Dissociating recollection and familiarity. *Child Development, 74,* 728–751.

Hudson, J. A. (1990). Constructive processing in children's event memory. *Developmental Psychology, 26,* 180–187.

Hudson, J. A., & Fivush, R. (1991). As time goes by: Sixth graders remember a kindergarten experience. *Applied Cognitive Psychology, 5,* 347–360.

Hudson, J. A., Fivush, R., & Kuebli, J. (1992). Scripts and episodes: the development of event memory. *Applied Cognitive Psychology, 6,* 483–505.

Lamb, M. E., Hershkowitz, I., Sternberg, K. J., Boat, B., & Everson, M. D. (1996). Investigative interviews of alleged sexual abuse victims with and without anatomical dolls. *Child Abuse and Neglect, 20,* 1251–1259.

Lamb, M. E., Orbach, Y., Hershkowitz, I., Esplin, P. W., & Horowitz, D. (2007). A structured forensic interview protocol improves the quality and informativeness of investigative interviews with children: A review of research using the NICHD Investigative Interview Protocol. *Child Abuse and Neglect, 31,* 1201–1231.

Lamb, M. E., Sternberg, K. J., Orbach, Y., Hershkowitz, I., Horowitz, D., & Esplin, P. W. (2002). The effects of intensive training and ongoing supervision on the quality of investigative interviews with alleged sex abuse victims. *Applied Developmental Science, 6,* 114–125.

Lampinen, J. M., & Smith, V. L. (1995). The incredible (and sometimes incredulous) child witness: Child eyewitness' sensitivity to source credibility cues. *Journal of Applied Psychology, 80,* 621–627.

Leventhal, J. M., Hamilton, J., Rededal, S., Tebano-Micci, A., & Eyster, C. (1989). Anatomically correct dolls used in interviews of young children suspected of having been sexually abused. *Pediatrics, 84,* 900–906.

Melinder, A., Goodman, G. S., Eilersten, D. E., & Magnussen, S.

(2004). Beliefs about child witnesses: A survey of professionals. *Psychology, Crime, and Law, 10,* 347–365.

Odegard, T. N., Cooper, C. M., Lampinen, J. M., Reyna, V. F., & Brainerd, C. J. (2009). Children's eyewitness memory for multiple real life events. *Child Development, 80,* 1877–1890.

Orbach, Y., Hershkowitz, I., Lamb, M. E., Sternberg, K. J., Esplin, P. W., & Horowitz, D. (2000). Assessing the value of structured protocols for forensic interview of alleged child abuse victims. *Child Abuse and Neglect, 24,* 733–752.

Ornstein, P. A., Baker-Ward, L., Gordon, B. N., Pelphrey, K. A., Tyler, C. S., & Gramsow, E. (2006). The influence of prior knowledge and repeated questioning on children's long-term retention of the details of a pediatric examination. *Developmental Psychology, 42,* 332–344.

Ornstein, P. A., Gordon, B., & Larus, D. M. (1992). Children's memory for a personally experienced event: Implications for testimony. *Applied Cognitive Psychology, 6,* 49–60.

Ornstein, P. A., Merritt, K. A., Baker-Ward, L., Furtado, E., Gordon, B., & Principe, G. (1998). Children's knowledge, expectation, and long-term retention. *Applied Cognitive Psychology, 12,* 387–405.

Peters, D. P. (1987). The impact of naturally occurring stress on children's memory. In S. J. Ceci, M. P. Toglia, & D. F. Ross (Eds.), *Children's eyewitness memory* (pp. 1–23). New York: Springer-Verlag.

Peterson, C. (1999). Children's memory for medical emergencies: 2 years later. *Developmental Psychology, 35,* 1493–1506.

Peterson C., & Bell, M. (1996). Children's memory for traumatic injury. *Child Development, 67,* 3045–3070.

Peterson, C., & Biggs, M. (1997). Interviewing children about trauma: Problems with 'specific' questions. *Journal of Traumatic Stress, 10,* 279–290.

Peterson, C., Dowden, C., & Tobin, J. (1999). Interviewing preschoolers: Comparisons of yes/no and wh-questions. *Journal of Law and Human Behavior, 23,* 539–555.

Peterson, C., Moores, L., & White, G. (2001). Recounting the same events again and again: Children's consistency across multiple interviews. *Applied Cognitive Psychology, 15,* 353–371.

Peterson, C., & Rideout, R. (1998). Memory for medical emergencies experienced by 1- and 2-year olds. *Developmental Psychology, 34,* 1059–1072.

Peterson, C., & Whalen, N. (2001). Five years later: Children's memory for medical emergencies. *Applied Cognitive Psychology, 15,* S7–S24.

Pillemer, D. B. (1992). Preschool children's memories of personal circumstances: The fire alarm study. In E. Winograd and U. Neisser (Eds.), *Affect and accuracy in recall: Studies of 'flashbulb' memories.* New York: Cambridge University Press.

Pillemer, D. B., Picariello, M. L., & Pruett, J. C. (1994). Very long-term memories of a salient preschool event. *Applied Cognitive Psychology*, *8*, 95–106.

Poole, D. A., & Lamb, M. E. (1998). *Investigative interviews of children: A guide for helping professionals*. Washington, DC: American Psychological Association Press.

Poole, D. A., & Lindsay, S. D. (2001). Children's eyewitness reports after exposure to misinformation from parents. *Journal of Experimental Psychology: Applied*, *7*, 27–50.

Poole, D. A., & Lindsay, S. D. (2002). Reducing child witnesses' false reports of misinformation from parents. *Journal of Experimental Child Psychology*, *81*, 117–140.

Poole, D. A., & White, L. T. (1993). Two years later: Effects of question repetition and retention interval on the eyewitness testimony of children and adults. *Developmental Psychology*, *29*, 844–853.

Powell, M. B., Jones, C. H., & Campbell, C. (2003). A comparison of preschoolers' recall of experienced versus non-experienced events across multiple interviews. *Applied Cognitive Psychology*, *17*, 935–952.

Powell, M. B., Roberts, K. P., Ceci, S. J., & Hembrooke, H. (1999). The effects of repeated experience on children's suggestibility. *Developmental Psychology*, *35*, 1462–1477.

Quas, J. A., Goodman, G. S., Bidrose, S., Pipe, M., & Craw, S. (1999). Emotion and memory: Children's long-term remembering, forgetting, and suggestibility. *Journal of Experimental Child Psychology*, *72*, 235–270.

Reyna, V. F., & Titcomb, A. L. (1997). Constraints on the suggestibility of eyewitness testimony: A fuzzy-trace analysis. In D. G. Payne & F. G. Conrad (Eds), *A synthesis of basic and applied approaches to human memory* (pp. 157–174). Hillsdale, NJ: Lawrence Erlbaum Associates, Inc.

Roberts, K. P., & Powell, M. B. (2001). Describing individual incidents of sexual abuse: A review of research on the effects of multiple sources of information on children's reports. *Child Abuse and Neglect*, *25*, 1643–1659.

Ross, D. F., Dunning, D., Toglia, M. P., & Ceci, S. J. (1990). The child in the eyes of the jury. *Law and Human Behavior*, *14*, 5–23.

Ross, D. F., Jurden, F. H., Lindsay, R. C. L., & Keeney, J. M. (2003). Replications and limitations of a two-factor model of child witness credibility. *Journal of Applied Social Psychology*, *33*, 418–431.

Saywitz, K. J., Goodman, G. S., Nicholas, E., & Moan, S. F. (1991). Children's memories of a physical examination involving genital touch: Implications for reports of child sexual abuse. *Journal of Consulting and Clinical Psychology*, *59*, 682–691.

State v. *Michaels* (1988). Superior Court, Essex County, New Jersey.

State v. *Michaels* (1993). 264 N.J. Super 579, 625 A.D. 2d 489.

Thierry, K. L., Lamb, M. E., Orbach, Y., & Pipe, M. (2005). Developmental differences in the function and use of anatomical dolls during interviews with alleged sexual abuse victims. *Journal of Counseling and Clinical Psychology, 73,* 1125–1134.

Toglia, M. P., Ross, D. F., Ceci, S. J., & Hembrooke, H. (1992). The suggestibility of children's memory: A social-psychological and cognitive interpretation. In M. L. Howe, C. J. Brainerd, & V. F. Reyna (Eds), *Development of long-term retention* (pp. 217–241). New York: Springer-Verlag.

U.S. Department of Health and Human Services (2008). *Child maltreatment 2006.* Washington, DC: Government Printing Office.

Vivard, E., & Tranter, M. (1988). Helping young children to describe experiences of child sexual abuse: General issue. In A. Bentovim, A. Elton, J. Hildebrand, M. Tranter, & E. Vizard (Eds.), *Child sexual abuse within the family: Assessment and treatment* (pp. 84–104). Bristol, UK: John Wright.

Zaragoza, M. S., & Lane, S. M. (1994). Source misattributions and the suggestibility of eyewitness memory. *Journal of Experimental Psychology: Learning, Memory, and Cognition, 20,* 1–12.

CHAPTER 7

Missing and Abducted Children

James Michael Lampinen, Jack D. Arnal,
Amber Culbertson-Faegre, and Lindsey Sweeney

Case Illustration

In the summer of 1995 a Little League baseball game was being played in Alma Arkansas. A 6-year-old child, Morgan Nick, came to the game with her mother. Morgan was playing with friends. They were all catching lightening bugs. Morgan walked up to her mother's car and began to empty sand from her shoes. And then she was gone. It has now been more than 10 years. In the years that have passed, Morgan's mother formed the Morgan Nick Foundation to help publicize her daughter's case and to raise awareness about the problem of missing and abducted children. The FBI has received thousands of leads. A reward of $60,000 has been offered for information in the case. Forensic artists have been called in to produce a composite sketch of the suspect. Morgan's picture has been age progressed to provide an estimate of her current appearance. These pictures have been widely circulated. As of the writing of this chapter, Morgan has still not been found (Morgan Nick Foundation, 2009).

Overview of the Issues

The story of Morgan Nick, and other children like her, has been told countless times through media reports on television, in print, and on the radio. The stories are heart-breaking. They are devastating to families and entire communities. They frustrate law enforcement. And they represent just the tip of the iceberg. We came to the problem of missing children as cognitive psychologists interested in human memory and face recognition. We sought to apply that knowledge to the question of how people recognize children that they have been asked to be on the lookout for. In the process we have become interested in the problem of missing persons more generally.

In what follows we will discuss three major issues. First, we will discuss the scope of the problem of missing children and abducted children. Cases like Morgan Nick's are important but, as we will see, cases like hers represent only a small portion of a much broader problem. Children go missing under a wide range of circumstances, for a variety of reasons, and with a variety of outcomes. Second, we will discuss the harm caused to children, parents, and communities when children go missing. This discussion will include both psychological harm caused to children and parents as well as risk of serious physical injury and death. Third, we will discuss empirical research on the effectiveness of approaches currently used to help find missing children. In particular, we will discuss the effectiveness of campaigns that involve putting up posters of missing children in supermarkets and the effectiveness of computerized age progressions. We will conclude that these approaches are laudable, but that much remains to be done to maximize the effectiveness of these approaches.

Scope of the Problem

In the early 1980s there were a series of highly publicized child abductions that resulted in the assault or murder of the victims. These cases led to fear and alarm among the general populace that an epidemic of child snatchings was occurring. This fear was fed by estimates that as many as 50,000 children were being abducted every year (Gentry, 1988). Because of the growing concern regarding missing children, Congress passed the Missing Children's Assistance Act in 1984. Among its other provisions, the Missing Children's Assistance Act required the Department of Justice to track the incidence of missing children in the United States. The Department of Justice responded to this mandate by funding two large-scale studies known as the National Incidence Studies of Missing, Abducted, Runaway and Throwaway Children (Sedlak, Finkelhor, Hammer, & Schultz, 2002). The studies occurred

10 years apart and are known as NISMART-1 and NISMART-2. The NISMART studies are the most comprehensive set of reports on the incidence of missing children available and should be thoroughly read by anyone interested in this problem (Sedlak et al., 2002). Because it is the more recent of the two sets of studies, the data we will be referring to in this section are based primarily on NISMART-2.

The NISMART studies provide basic data on the incidence of missing children in the United States, but even more importantly the studies provided conceptual clarity by distinguishing among several different types of case. For instance, NISMART draws an important distinction between children who are *abducted* and children who are *missing* (Sedlak et al., 2002). Not all missing children have been abducted. For instance, a child who runs away from home or is lost is missing but has not been abducted. Similarly, not all abducted children are missing. For instance, when an estranged spouse abducts a child, the custodial parent may well know where the child is, but may not have access to the child. Thus missing children and abducted children are best characterized as related and partly overlapping categories.

Another distinction made in the NISMART studies is between cases it labels as *caretaker missing* and cases it labels as *reported missing* (Finkelhor, Hammer, & Sedlak, 2002). *Caretaker missing* refers to any case where the caregivers indicate to the researchers that the child has been or is missing. *Reported missing* is a smaller category and refers only to those cases where the caregiver reported the case to authorities. Of course, not all caretaker missing cases result in reports being made to authorities. Parents often refrain from reporting the incident if it only lasts for a short period of time or involves a child running away. Similarly, when a child is abducted by a family member, it may not result in a police report if the primary caregiver does not believe the child is in any danger.

Even when an incident is reported to the police, a response cannot always be expected. Guidelines have been set that urge law enforcement agencies to respond to every missing child case as if it had the potential to be a life-threatening situation. However, police do not always do so (Hammer, Finkelhor, Ormrod, Sedlak, & Bruce, 2008). Of parents in the National Household Survey of Adult Caregivers survey who reported a child missing to the police, only 68% reported even being interviewed by an officer (Hammer et al., 2008). Our own research has found that 63% of family members report being "extremely dissatisfied" with the police response when a loved one is reported missing (Lampinen, Peters, Petretic, Sweeney, & Culbertson-Faegre, in prep).

NISMART-2 covers incidents that occurred within the 1999 calendar year (Flores, 2002). Some of the summary statistics from NISMART-2 are reported in Table 7.1. In 1999 approximately 1,315,600 children went missing (caretaker missing) and 797,500 children were involved in cases that were reported to the authorities (reported missing). Runaways and throwaways made up 48% of the cases. Benign cases, for example a son returning home late because of a misunderstood curfew, make up 28% of the cases. Children who were lost or injured made up about 15% of the cases. About 9% of all missing children were the result of a family abduction and 3% were non-family abductions.[1] In what follows, we describe basic data on the different categories of missing children cases reported in the NISMART studies.

Runaways and Throwaways

Runaways and throwaways are children who leave home (i.e., runaways) or are asked to leave home by their caregivers (i.e., throwaways) for at least one night if they are under 15 or two nights if they are between 15 and 17 (Sedlak et al., 2002). NISMART-1 tried to collect separate data on runaways and throwaways, but this proved difficult (Hammer, Finkelhor, & Sedlak, 2002a). In many cases it was not possible to determine if a particular case was a runaway incident or a throwaway incident. Consequently NISMART-2 used a single category that included both runaways and throwaways (Hammer et al., 2002a). In what follows, we will use the term *runaway* to refer to both types of cases.

Runaways are very common in the United States. However, not every runaway can be characterized as being a "missing child." The NISMART-2 study estimated that 1,682,900 children ran away in 1999. However, in 63% of these cases the caregiver knew the location of the child (Flores, 2002). In our archival study of the cases listed on the website of the National Center for Missing and Exploited Children, runaways accounted for 36.02% of all cases (Lampinen, Arnal, Courtney, & Adams, 2009a). Runaways represent the oldest group of children who are missing, typically being between the ages of 15 and 17 (Flores, 2002), and are as likely to be male as female (Hammer et al., 2002a). Children are about twice as likely to run away during the summer as during any other season. Most runaways stay relatively close to home. Less

TABLE 7.1 Summary of the Results from NISMART–2 Studies

	Missing: Involuntary, Lost, or Injured	Missing: Benign Explanation	Runaway/ Throwaway	Family Abductions	Non-Family Abductions	Stereotypical Kidnappings
Total cases	204,500	374,700	1,682,900	203,900	58,200	115
Caretaker missing	204,500	374,700	628,900	117,200	33,000	90
Reported missing	68,100	340,500	357,600	56,500	12,100	90
% Female	30	39	50	51	65	69
% Male	70	61	50	49	35	31
% < 12 years old	35	36	4	79	19	45
% ≥ 12 years old	65	64	96	21	81	55
% Resolved < 1 day	93	87	18	23	90	91
% Caucasian	77	57	57	59	35	72
% African-American	7	18	17	12	42	19
% Hispanic	10	18	15	20	23	8
Other/no Information	6	7	11	9	0	1
Percentage of total cases	8.10	14.84	66.67	8.08	2.31	0.005
Percentage of caretaker missing	15.06	27.59	46.30	8.63	2.43	0.007
Percentage of reported	8.16	40.79	42.84	6.77	1.45	0.011

Note: The data reported above are compiled from the NISMART–2 studies (references cited in text). Note that percentages in some cells may be unreliable because of the small number of observations. Note also that stereotypical kidnappings are a subset of non-family abductions, not a separate category.

than a quarter of runaways go more than 50 miles from home and less than 10% of runaways leave the state. The vast majority of runaways (93%) return home in less than one month.

Missing for Benign Reasons

Of the children who went missing in 1999, 374,700 (28%) can be characterized as missing for benign reasons (Sedlak, Finkelhor, & Hammer, 2005). For example, a child in the NISMART-2 study believed his curfew did not apply because the next day was not a school night. His father, however, was expecting him home at the regular time. When the son failed to arrive home at the expected time, the father called the police. Of the 374,700 cases categorized as missing for benign reasons in 1999, 340,500 cases were reported to the authorities. About 60% of the cases involve boys. These cases are, of course, typically resolved relatively quickly: 85% of the cases are resolved within 6 hours and 95% of cases are resolved in under a day. Interestingly the cases appear to be more common in the Midwest than other regions of the country. These cases are, of course, frightening to parents when they occur, but thankfully represent simple misunderstandings or mis-communication between parents and their children.

Missing: Involuntary, Lost, or Injured

An estimated 198,300 children, 15% of all missing children, went missing in 1999 because of an injury to the child or because the child was lost or unable to make contact (Sedlak et al., 2002). These disappearances are more likely to occur to male children (about 70% of cases), and often involve children who were playing in secluded or wooded areas (Sedlak et al., 2005). About 65% of the cases involve children who are 12 years old or older. Caucasian children were involved in 77% of all cases categorized as Missing: Involuntary, Lost, or Injured. When NISMART-1 and NISMART-2 are compared there is some evidence of a decrease in the number of these cases (Hammer, Finkelhor, Sedlak, & Porcellini, 2004). Increasing access to wireless com-munication could explain this decrease (Hammer et al., 2004). The NISMART-1 data were collected in 1988, before cellular phones were regularly available. By 1999, when the second study was completed, many children and parents had access to cellular phones. This may indicate that a continued decrease is occurring now, as cellular phones become even more common. Most of these cases are resolved quickly, with 85% of cases being resolved in less than 6 hours and 93% of cases being resolved in less than 1 day.

Family Abductions

Abductions only make up a fraction of all the *caretaker missing* incidents of the NISMART-2 studies and most of those abductions are family abductions (Sedlak et al., 2002). In our archival study of cases listed on the website of the National Center for Missing and Exploited Children, family abductions accounted for 13.5% of all cases (Lampinen et al., 2009a). To qualify as a family abduction the child had to be taken or held by a parent, domestic partner, or other family member who did not have the legal right to take or hold the child. It is estimated that there were 203,900 family abductions in 1999 (Sedlak et al., 2002). Of these there were 117,200 (57%) cases in which the caregiver did not know the child's location (Hammer, Finkelhor, & Sedlak, 2002b).

The children who are victims of family abductions are taken by their biological fathers 52% of the time and by their biological mothers 25% of the time (Flores, 2002). The remaining abductions involve grandparents, extended family members, or the romantic partners of parents. This diversity in perpetrators may reflect the changing face of the American family. Unlike most missing children cases, where victims are most likely to be adolescents between the ages of 12 and 17, family abductions involved younger children. A total of 44% of the victims of family abductions are under 6 years old (Flores, 2002). This may partly reflect the dynamics of separation and divorce, which often happen when couples have young children who then become caught in the middle of contentious custody disputes (Furstenberg, Peterson, Nord, & Zill, 1983). Indeed, children are 2.75 times more likely to become a victim of a family abduction if their parents have been separated in the last year (Finkelhor, Hotaling, & Sedlak, 1991; Plass, Finkelhor, & Hotaling, 1997).

The NISMART studies make a distinction between what they term *broadscope abductions* and *policy-focal abductions* (Finkelhor et al., 1991). *Broadscope abductions* are any case where a child is abducted by a family member who does not have legal custody of the child or who is violating a court-ordered agreement with the other parent. *Policy-focal abductions* are those that involve concealment of the child or transportation of the child over state lines. Policy-focal abductions are much more serious and typically involve an attempt by the non-custodial parent to obtain de facto custody of the child. There was a significant drop in the number of broadscope family abductions between NISMART-1 and NISMART-2 (Hammer et al., 2004). This may be because of increased interaction of the court system within custody battles upon divorce. Some research has been done searching for risk factors that are associated with family abductions, in hopes of finding a preventative measure to help these families (Johnston, Girdner, & Sagatun-Edwards, 1999). Children are more likely to experience a family abduction when their parents are of a low socioeconomic status and when their parents have not been legally married. Children are also at risk when their parents suspect that the other parent may be neglectful, or when they suspect sexual abuse. Family abductions are also common when parents will not seek help from law enforcement or the court system to retain custody of the child.

The NISMART studies also make a distinction between cases that involve *takings* and cases that involve *keepings* (Finkelhor et al., 1991). *Takings* occur when a family member takes a child who is legally under another caretaker's authority. *Keepings* occur when a family member fails to return a child at the end of a visitation period. Abductions where the child is kept are more likely to happen during the summer months and during holidays, when increased visitations lead to increased opportunities. Police involvement was significantly more likely with the children who are taken, compared to episodes where the child is kept (Plass, Finkelhor, & Hotaling, 1995). It is also important to note that both custodial and non-custodial parents may be guilty of family abductions. For instance, if the non-custodial parent has court-ordered visitation rights and the custodial parent refuses to allow the visitation, it would qualify as a broadscope family abduction by the custodial parent.

The typical outcome in a family abduction case is for the child to be returned. This occurs in 91% of the cases. In another 6% of the cases, the child is not returned but is at least located. Most children are recovered in less than a month, but for a substantial number of cases (more than 20%) it takes more than a month before it is resolved. This is especially problematic in that it has been found that the degree of psychological harm suffered by children is related to the duration of the abduction incident (Plass et al., 1995).

Non-family Abductions

In the public mind, missing children cases involve a complete stranger abducting a young child and keeping them for significant periods of time (Sedlak et al., 2002). Although such events occur, and are dangerous, the NISMART studies show that these events represent a small fraction of all missing children cases. NISMART-2 indicated that an estimated 58,200 non-family abductions occurred in 1999 out of a total of 1.3 million missing child cases (Finkelhor et al., 2002). Non-family abductions are carefully defined within NISMART-2 as any occurrence where a child is moved through the use or threat of violence, or detained for at least 1 hour (Sedlak et al., 2002). If the child is under 15 (or mentally incompetent) then force is not necessary if an attempt is made to conceal the child, demand ransom, or permanently detain the child (Sedlak et al., 2002).

Teenagers between the ages of 12 and 17 make up a disproportionate number of non-family abductions (Finkelhor et al., 2002; Flores, 2002): 81% of all non-family abductions involved children who were at least 12 years old. Females are twice as likely to be victims of these abductions. Fifty-three percent of child victims reported that they knew the perpetrator, and 38% reported knowing them as a friend or close acquaintance (Finkelhor et al., 2002; Flores, 2002). Seventy-seven percent of children were abducted from a location besides a residential home (Finkelhor et al., 2002). Most non-family abductions are resolved in less than 24 hours (91% of cases).

A subgroup of non-family abductions is known as *stereotypical kidnappings*. Stereotypical kidnappings are those non-family abductions that conform to the public's errant but earnest perception of what a typical non-family abduction is like. In these cases the child is "detained overnight, transported 50 miles, held for ransom, held with the intention of permanence, or killed" (Sedlak et al., 2002). NISMART-2 found that 115 cases qualified as a stereotypical kidnapping. This amounts to about 1/100th of 1% of all missing child cases reported to police. Females were twice as likely to be victims in these crimes, and 58% of the victims were at least 12 years old. As we will discuss later, although such kidnappings are rare they are extremely dangerous.

Our archival study of the website of the National Center for Missing and Exploited Children (NCMEC) found that about 10% of all the cases listed involved non-family abductions. This compares to about 3% of cases in the NISMART-2 studies. The reason for this discrepancy appears to be that the NCMEC database includes a large number of long-term unresolved non-family abduction cases. The average non-family abduction case in the NCMEC database involves someone who has been missing for more than 20 years. Thus non-family abductions may sometimes result in very long-term missing person cases. One lesson to draw from this may be that although non-family abductions make up only a small proportion of all missing children, they may represent an especially serious type of crime that requires special attention from authorities. Indeed, as we will see in the next section, non-family abductions can occur in the context of another crime, most often sexual assault. So although they are less common than some other categories, they are very serious events that demand our attention and the attention of policy-makers.

Harm Caused when Children go Missing

An important contribution of the NISMART approach has been to clarify the nature and extent of the problem of missing children. Each of the categories of missing children described above is unique in terms of the characteristics of the perpetrators, characteristics of the victims, and extent of the underlying problem. Each of the above categories of missing children results in clearly demonstrable harm to the victimized child, the families of the child, and the community as a whole. These harms are magnified the longer the child remains missing, making the problem of long-term missing children especially serious (Plass et al., 1995). In the section that follows we outline some of the known harms that occur when a child goes missing.

As mentioned above, children who run away from home or who are forced out of the home by caretakers (i.e., throwaway children) represent one of the largest categories of missing children (Finkelhor et al., 1991). The problem of runaway children is sometimes dismissed because the children are seen as being "voluntarily missing" (Hammer et al., 2002a), however this characterization is misleading. NISMART-2 categorized 71% of runaways as endangered runaways because of exposure to drugs, criminal activity, or physical or sexual abuse (Flores, 2002). Sadler (1986) indicates that runaways risk becoming involved in pornography, prostitution, drug dealing, and other potentially harmful activities. Of 600 homeless youths interviewed, 22% had committed theft,

30% sold drugs (85% of those more than once), and 14% committed burglary (Whitbeck & Hoyt, 1999). In addition, a survey of 50 street youths in New York City found that 60% admitted to crimes such as shoplifting, boosting (i.e., stealing something from one store and then selling it to another), and engaging in scams (Finkelstein, 2005). Among runaway and homeless children, the prevalence of HIV is higher than that of children in any other setting (Booth & Zhang, 1997). This is likely to be due to high-risk drug use and sexual behavior. Up to one-third of runaways have had sex in exchange for food or shelter (Klain, 1999). Runaway children may suffer from depression, dissociation, and posttraumatic shock as a result of their experiences (Silbert & Pines, 1982). Homeless children are more likely to have clinical depression and are twice as likely to have a serious mental health problem. In addition, they are almost twice as likely to attempt suicide or to have tried to commit suicide (Klain, 1999). Clearly, quickly finding runaways remains an important and critical law enforcement goal.

A substantial proportion of children also go missing because they are abducted by family members. Although most family abductions are resolved quickly, many cases take more than a month to be resolved (Hammer et al., 2002b). Approximately 40% of family abductions are serious enough that they require the intervention of law enforcement (Plass et al., 1995). Sadler (1986) argued that when children are abducted by family members they are traumatized emotionally and may experience grief and rage as a consequence of the abduction. This is especially true in policy-focal abductions. Parents estimated that psychological harm occurred in 40% of broadscope abductions and 52% of policy-focal abductions. (Finkelhor et al., 1991). Schetky and Haller (1983) found that victims of family abductions suffered from bedwetting, difficulty sleeping, and clinging behavior. Senior, Gladstone, and Nurcombe (1982) provided evidence that family abductions can result in depressive symptoms. Researchers have found that the risk of physical or emotional harm is greater the longer the episode lasts (Plass et al., 1995).

Non-family abductions also produce considerable harm to the children who are victimized. As noted above, it is important to distinguish between the stereotypical stranger abductions that involve of the order of 100 children per year and broadscope abductions that involve thousands of children per year (Asdigian, Finkelhor, & Hotaling, 1995). Non-family abductions are worrisome partly because they often occur in the context of other crimes. Nearly half of all non-family abductions involve sexual assault and many involve physical assaults (Finkelhor et al., 2002). A smaller proportion of non-family abductions occur in the context of other crimes, including robberies, car-jackings, acts of retribution against a parent, intimidation, and dating violence (Asdigian et al., 1995).

Non-family abductions may also occur in the context of human trafficking crimes. Human trafficking involves a kind of modern-day slavery in which people are forced to work for the enrichment of others (Acosta, 2003; Bales & Robins, 2001; De Baca & Tisi, 2002; Logan, Walker, & Hunt, 2009). This involves both labor trafficking, in which people are forced to work in factories, farms, sweatshops, and other locations (Chaiyarachta, 1996; Liao, 1996; Su, 1998; Taran & Geronimi, 2002), and sex trafficking, in which people are forced to work as prostitutes, in the pornography industry, and so on (Farr, 2005; Nelson, 2002; Raymond & Hughes, 2001). The Department of Justice estimates that between 14,000 and 18,000 people are victims of human trafficking in the United States every year (Picarelli & Johnson, 2008). Although labor trafficking cases typically involve male victims in their twenties, sex trafficking predominantly targets female victims often under the age of 18 years old (Farrell, McDevitt, & Fahy, 2008).

Stereotypical kidnappings, although rare, are an extremely important problem for law enforcement because of the extreme danger they represent to the abducted child. The very definition of stereotypical kidnapping provided by NISMART denotes a very serious crime, in which the child is abducted by a stranger, kept overnight or longer, transported 50 miles or more, and in which the motive may include homicide, ransom, or keeping the child permanently (Finkelhor, Hotaling, & Sedlak, 1992). Stereotypical kidnappings also often involve physical assaults, use of a weapon, and robbery. Sexual assault occurs in approximately 50% of stereotypical kidnappings (Finkelhor et al., 2002). In 40% of stereotypical kidnappings the child is killed. In another 4% of stereotypical kidnappings the child is not found. There are approximately 40–150 child abduction murders that occur nationwide each year (Brown & Keppel, 2007). In 44% of those murders the child is killed within 1 hour of the abduction, in 74% of cases the child is killed within 3 hours, and in 99% of cases the child is killed within 7 days. In only 22% of cases was the child alive by the time they were reported missing.

Children are not the only victims in these crimes. Feik and

Glover (1998) have argued that families, in particular, are traumatized when a child goes missing. This is especially true in cases where the child is missing for a long period of time. In these cases, loved ones are left wondering about the child's whereabouts and well-being. Holidays and birthdays are experienced as especially poignant. Feik and Glover (1998) report that parents suffer additional harm when they encounter news reports indicating that a missing body has been found and they experience the anxiety of wondering whether it is their child. There is even some evidence that parents of missing children may experience greater and longer lasting distress than parents of murdered children (DeYoung & Buzzi, 2003). Recognizing the potential trauma that parents experience, the Missing Persons Unit of New South Wales in Australia provides psychological counseling services for families of missing children (Attorney General's Office NSW, 2005).

Our research team has recently begun a longitudinal study of families of missing persons to examine the psychological consequences of having a family member go missing, as well as potential moderator variables that may ameliorate the harm done (Lampinen, Peters, Petretic, Sweeney, & Culbertson-Faegre, in prep). The participants are 27 family members who have had a loved one go missing. They were recruited through internet postings. Participants completed a series of questions designed to measure their psychological well-being, coping methods, and social support. To measure psychological well-being we used the Trauma Symptom Inventory (TSI) developed by Briere (1995). The questionnaire includes 100 items designed to measure symptoms commonly associated with traumatic events and results in 10 clinical subscales. For each subscale, the participant receives a T score indicating how they compared to a normed reference group. T scores are standardized scores. In the norm group the mean T score is set to 50 with a standard deviation of 10. T scores of 65 or greater are typically considered clinically significant and occur less than 7% of the time in the group that the norms are based on (Roberts & Ilardi, 2003).

Figure 7.1 shows the proportion of participants with clinically significant scores ($T \geq 65$) on each of the 10 subscales. As can be seen, on 7 out of the 10 subscales a substantial proportion of our participants showed clinically significant scores. Close to 50% of the participants in the survey showed evidence of clinically significant levels of depression and dissociation symptoms. More than one-third of the participants in the survey showed evidence

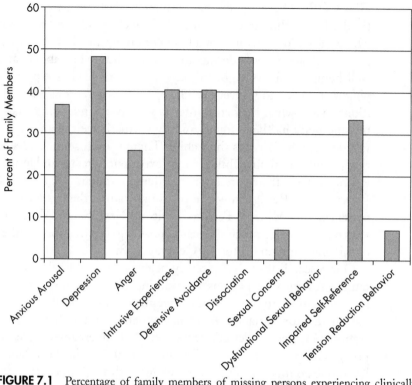

FIGURE 7.1 Percentage of family members of missing persons experiencing clinically significant ($T \geq 65$) levels of symptoms on the TSI.

of clinically significant levels of anxiety-related symptoms, intrusive experiences, defensive avoidance, and impaired self-reference.

Not only did many of the participants in this study show individual symptoms, but many of the participants showed multiple symptoms. Indeed, close to 50% of the participants showed clinically significant scores on four or more of the subscales. The symptoms experienced by these family members are similar to those experienced by other trauma victims and suggest that having a loved one go missing can produce substantial psychological consequences.

Although many of our participants showed symptoms, it is noteworthy that about 22% of participants had no evidence of clinically significant symptom levels. This finding suggests that there may be either individual differences that predict outcomes or particular coping strategies that may be effective. One initial finding is that resiliency as measured by the Connor-Davidson scale (Connor & Davidson, 2003) was negatively correlated with symptoms. Resiliency refers to an individual's ability to bounce back from stressors and continue to function at a high level (see Chapter 10 of this volume for a discussion). To some extent, resiliency may be a stable individual difference variable. Some people may just be better at it than others. However, other research has suggested that people high in resiliency show problem-focused coping strategies rather than emotion-focused coping strategies (Markstrom, Marshall, & Tryon, 2000). A long-term goal of our research is to develop better methods for helping family members of missing persons cope with the trauma of having a loved one go missing.

Because stereotypical kidnappings receive a great deal of media attention, Finkelhor et al. (1992) have argued that these cases can traumatize entire communities, not just the individuals directly involved. Indeed, the thought of one's child being abducted by a complete stranger frightens and preoccupies parents all over the country (Finkelhor, Hotaling, & Asdigian, 1995). "Because of their horrifying nature, these crimes [stereotypical stranger abductions] have traumatizing effects on communities beyond the scope of their numbers" (Finkelhor et al., 1992, p. 240).

Approaches to Solving the Problem

The focus of our own research has been to examine efforts that have been used to help find missing children. A number of approaches have been used, but most of them focus on publicizing the identity of the missing child in hopes that a member of the public will spot the child and contact authorities. This strategy has had some successes and some notable recoveries and our aim has been to use basic research in perception, attention, and memory to help improve the success rate. The success of this strategy depends on (1) the number of people who are exposed to the publicity regarding the missing child, (2) the probability that those people will actively attend to and process the picture of the missing child, (3) the probability that these individuals will actually encounter the child, (4) the probability that upon encountering the child they will recognize the child from the publicity, and (5) the probability that upon recognizing the child they will take the appropriate action.

Each of these factors impacts the probability of a recovery and provides a potential avenue for improving the recovery of missing children. For instance, recovery of a missing child crucially depends on widely disseminating the child's photograph. That way, even if there is only a 5% chance of the child being recognized by any individual member of the public, if enough people have an opportunity to make the identification then the odds that someone will do so goes up. Our own work in recent years has focused on how well people attend to pictures of missing children, as well as both their prospective and retrospective memory for those children.

It is also noteworthy that when it comes to encountering the child there will be some people who have encountered the child prior to seeing the publicity and other people who encounter the child after seeing the publicity. The situation of seeing the publicity after encountering the child can be thought of as a standard retrospective person memory task (i.e., "Have you seen this child?"). The situation of encountering the child subsequent to seeing the publicity can be thought of as a prospective person memory task (i.e., "If you see this child, contact authorities"). Each of these aspects of the problem can and should be examined and provide potential avenues for increasing recovery rates.

Supermarket Campaigns

Perhaps the best known approach to finding missing children involves publicizing the appearance of those children on bulletin boards at local supermarkets (Walmart Foundation, 2001). In recent research, we have examined how effective these campaigns are likely to be by conducting surveys of customers as they leave local supermarkets. In the first study (Lampinen, Arnal, & Hicks, 2009b, 2009c), posters of eight missing children were placed on bulletin boards at the exit of a local grocery store. These posters were modeled after those used in national missing children's campaigns and were placed in exit locations that were similar to the locations used in those campaigns. The posters were put up in the store about a week before the start of the survey and remained up during the entire course of the survey. When customers left the store, they were approached by a member of our survey research team and were asked to complete a two-page questionnaire. The first page of the questionnaire included questions about the participant, such as how old they were, how many children they had, if any, their gender, and so on. The questionnaire also asked them how important they thought the problem of missing children was and the extent to which they looked at the posters of the missing children as they exited the grocery store.

The good news was that the vast majority of customers indicated that they thought the problem of missing children was important. That has been true in all of our studies. The bad news was that only about 30% of the customers indicated that they looked at the posters at all and most of those indicated that they looked only briefly. This result is shown in the two bars on the left side of Figure 7.2. On the second page of the survey, we included pictures of 16 children. Eight of the pictures were of the children who had been depicted on the posters inside the supermarket and eight of the pictures were of children who had not been on the posters. Participants were simply asked to circle those pictures that had been shown in the grocery store and to guess if necessary. The results of this experiment are shown in the first two bars on the left side of Figure 7.3. The black bar shows the proportion of true positives (i.e, correctly circling a picture of a child who really had been shown) and the gray bar shows the proportion of false positives (i.e., incorrectly circling a picture of a child who had not been shown). As can be seen, in this first study, the rate of true positives and false positives did not differ significantly. Memory

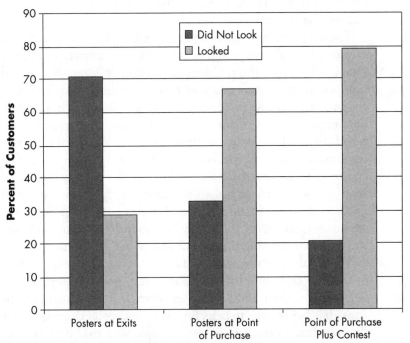

FIGURE 7.2 Self-reported looking time at posters of missing children as a function of manner of display.

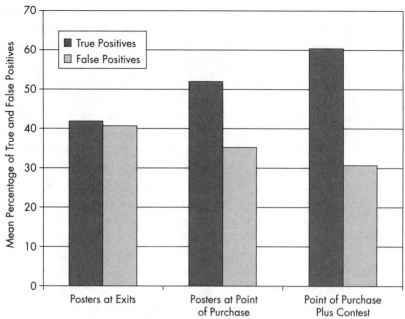

FIGURE 7.3 Memory for posters of missing children as a function of manner of display.

for these children's faces was at chance levels just minutes after passing the posters.

These results have been replicated a couple of different times now and have always produced the same basic pattern of findings. People care about the problem of missing children, but they do not look at the posters and they do not remember the pictures. If customers think the problem of missing children is important, a reasonable question to ask is why they do not take proactive steps to actually look at posters of those children. We asked a group of customers that very question in a follow-up study. The most common reason cited for not looking at the posters was simply that they were busy or rushed or had other things on their mind. That is, although customers care about missing children, as they are busily going about their daily lives they do not think to look at the posters of missing children displayed at grocery stores.

The results of these initial studies were disconcerting. Families of missing children obviously want every possible step taken to help recover their child. Families often feel frustrated that not enough is being done to help. Supermarket poster campaigns have the potential to reach millions of people who may have seen the child. Yet these campaigns can only be effective if customers actually look at the posters. So what can be done? We have recently had some success in increasing the attention that customers pay to posters of missing children (Lampinen, Peters, Hicks, & Arnal, submitted) by making use of a type of marketing called point of purchase advertising. Point of purchase advertising, as the name implies, involves putting advertisements up at or near the location of the sale. In a supermarket the point of purchase is the cash register. Point of purchase advertising has advantages over placing ads at other locations in that it takes advantage of the "captive audience" effect (Bennett, 1998). That is, while customers are waiting at a cash register for their orders to be rung up, they are literally stuck there. There is nothing much for them to do but to look around their environment as they wait. Advertising placed prominently at this location is thus likely to receive additional attention. Indeed, studies in marketing psychology have found that point of purchase advertising results in better memory for product information (Bennett, 1998) and more sales than advertising placed at other locations (Woodside & Waddle, 1975).

We sought to apply these principles from marketing psychology to the problem of finding missing children. If point of purchase advertising can be used to increase sales of candy bars and smokeless tobacco, we reasoned, it can also be used to increase memory for pictures of missing children. In one of our studies, posters were placed near the cash registers of a local grocery store. In particular, the stores we worked with have metal housing running from the ceiling to the cash registers that contains the wiring for the registers. We placed a poster containing pictures of six missing children on these columns at each cash register location. In a second experiment, we placed posters at these locations and also created a contest to motivate customers to look at the posters. Customers were given small pictures of missing children as they checked out. They were told that if the picture matched one of the pictures on the poster they would win a $50 gift card.

As in the previous studies, customers were surveyed as they left the store and were asked, among other things, if they looked at the posters. Customers were also shown pictures of 12 children and were asked to pick the pictures that had been shown in the store. The point of purchase approach was a big improvement over presenting pictures at store exits. Consider the results shown in Figure 7.2. Once again, the data represented on the far left show how often customers looked at posters of missing children when they were placed at supermarket exits (i.e., the data from the original study). Note that the vast majority of participants (more than 70%) indicated that they did not look at the posters. The bars in the middle show the results when point of purchase advertising is used. Notice that the vast majority of customers in this study reported looking at the posters. Finally, the bars on the far right show the results when point of purchase advertising was combined with a contest designed to encourage looking at the posters. Notice that close to 80% of customers report looking at the posters when a point of purchase display is combined with a contest designed to encourage customers to look at the posters, which is a big improvement.

What about memory for the children? Figure 7.3 shows the percentage of true positives and false positives on the recognition memory test. Again the bars on the far left of the figure are from our initial study where posters were placed at grocery store exits. Memory for the children's pictures did not differ from chance in that situation (i.e., true positives equal false positives). The middle two bars show memory performance when point of purchase ads were used. In that situation, true positives were significantly more common than were false positives (by about 15%). The third pair of bars show the results when point of purchase advertising was combined with a contest designed to draw the customer's attention to the poster. In that case, the results were even better. There were significantly more true positives than false positives, a difference of about 30%. The results of these studies, combined with our prior research (Lampinen et al., 2009c), provide compelling evidence that current efforts to find missing children could be substantially improved. When posters were placed at the exits of a cooperating supermarket, as is done in most national missing children campaigns, a vast majority of customers reported not looking at the posters, and memory for the posters did not differ from chance. When posters of missing children were prominently displayed at the cash registers themselves (i.e., point of purchase display) a majority of customers reported looking at the posters, and memory was significantly better than chance. This effect was even greater when point of purchase displays were combined with a contest that encouraged customers to look at the posters.

Age Progression

Most children are recovered within hours or days of their disappearance, but sometimes children can remain missing for years. Our research team recently reviewed the missing children cases on the website for the National Center for Missing and Exploited

Children (NCMEC) and found that over half of the children listed have been missing for at least 3 years, and that one in four had been missing over a decade. When law enforcement is faced with these long-term cases a new set of problems arise because law enforcement officials no longer have a recent photo of the child to use in their search (Lampinen et al., 2009a).

The human face changes dramatically over the lifespan, and much of this transformation takes place during the rapid maturation that occurs during the course of childhood. In missing children cases where a recovery is not achieved quickly, there are no longer accurate photos of the missing child's current appearance (Feik & Glover, 1998). This is frustrating for the family members and law enforcement who are still searching for the child (McQueen, 1989). John Rabun, a spokesperson for the NCMEC, described the frustration in this way:

> When the case passes the one year anniversary, it's like everything dies on the vine. Like a magical switch in the sky turns off. No calls. No tips. No leads. And the case just withers away. Parents, and understandably so, get upset with the police because we have not kept their kid's case alive. They ask why aren't we trying harder. But in all honesty, the investigative team is not very active at this point. All the spade work has been done. The formal leads have been checked. The suspect's profile has been searched. They've had a whole year or more to work the evidence. Officers still are concerned about the unsolved cases, but there is no point redoing all that work when there is no new direction to go – until now. (cited in McQueen, 1989, p. 42)

In the 1980s a new technique was developed that gave law enforcement officials like Rabun hope in cases like this. In particular, advancements in computer technology enabled medical illustrators to digitally manipulate the photographs of missing children to produce estimates of the child's current appearance. As Rabun's statement suggests, the introduction of computer age progression was met with great enthusiasm from law enforcement and the families of missing children (Allen, 1990; McQueen, 1989; Sadler, 1986; Taylor, 2001).

Current computer age progression utilizes techniques initially developed by Barrows and Sadler. The technique alters the relative location of 40 anatomical landmarks based on average anthropometric growth patterns. Using the most recent image of the child, these techniques attempt to estimate the current appearance of the child. Forensic artists may also use images of the children's parents and siblings at the target age, as well as the medical history of the child, to manipulate the age-progressed images (Taylor, 2001). Forensic artists attempt to assimilate two categories of information when producing age-progressed images. The artist needs to capture what Sadler (1986) refers to as the "gnomic features," while also taking into consideration the changes that occur over the course of the lifetime. In her book on age progression, Taylor (2001) states that a main goal of the forensic artist is to locate and capture the "lifelong look" of the child. Sadler describes this lifelong look as follows:

> Although our face undergoes tremendous growth from youth to adulthood and into old age, it is also true that there is a constancy of appearance. The face of a man looks almost the same, regardless of age. Such growth is called "gnomic", a fact of importance in growth prediction. Gnomic growth is a process that leaves the resultant features similar to the original. This unity of the individual's looks cannot be destroyed by growth and decay. (Sadler, 1986, p. 11)

Forensic artists have to pinpoint and communicate the gnomic features of the child's face, but they also need to represent the changes that occur as the child ages. Sadler (1986) identified two types of facial changes, labeled "anabolic changes" and "catabolic changes." Anabolic changes are those that occur during the natural sexual and biological maturation process, while catabolic changes are those that occur during the decay cycle and aging process. Both changes occur during the lifespan, but anabolic changes have a greater impact during childhood. A forensic artist has to select the gnomic features of the child and then predict how anabolic and catabolic changes will impact those features. Within the field of forensic progression there is controversy over the importance of the inclusion of features of parents or siblings. Many artists are in favor of using photos of the parents or siblings at the target age to influence the age progression (Allen, 1990). Other forensic artists contend that gnomic features, combined with a prediction of anabolic and catabolic changes, are sufficient to produce an accurate age-progressed image. These artists hold that the parent and sibling photos do not increase the accuracy of the image (Sadler, 1986).

A second controversy within the field of forensic age progression focuses on how effective age progression is likely to be. For the age-progressed images to be effective they have to achieve two goals: first, the images have to be accurate, representing what the child currently looks like. Secondly, the images have to provide the public with more information than they could gain from the outdated photographs.

The first goal, to produce accurate images, means that forensic artists have to manage the wide variability in facial growth patterns across children. Forensic artists use the average growth patterns of the population when age progressing photos (Feik & Glover, 1998). Using the average growth patterns for a population provides an accurate depiction of the aging process in the average child, but may not provide an accurate depiction of the aging process in any specific individual child. As Feik and Glover (1998) put it, "[Information about average growth patterns] may be misleading in that specific events are said to occur at certain chronological ages. The values, however, are for the so called 'average' child, and individual children, who display different developmental rates, may not conform to this pattern, hence attaining certain landmarks at different ages from those specified" (p. 214). The variability in the growth rates of the children can be fairly large. A longitudinal study of mandibular sizes of children at ages 11, 12, 13, and 15 found that mandibles in boys grew an average of 0.206 cm/year, while mandibles in girls grew an average of 0.22 cm/year. The standard deviations for these average growth rates, however, are substantial. The standard deviation for the boys was 0.12 cm/year, while the standard deviation for girls was 0.13 cm/year. Beyond the standard deviations, it is likely that imprecise estimations of growth would become compounded in some children, so the end estimate could be dramatically off (Buschang, Tanguay, LaPalme, & Demirjian, 1990).

The other potential limitation of forensic age progression concerns the relevant comparison condition. For age progression to be warranted, not only must the technique be more effective than presenting no picture at all, but it should also be more effective than the alternative of simply presenting the most recent picture of the child. Indeed, it may be that people can accurately identify a child at one age based on an outdated photograph of that child at a younger age. A recent study by Keenan (2007) supports that view. Keenan's research suggests that people have an implicit understanding of the impact that anabolic and catabolic changes have on facial growth in children. If this is true, age-progressed photographs may not provide any advantages over and above providing an outdated photograph.

Indeed, the technique of age progression itself as described by Sadler suggests that possibility. According to Sadler (1986), one of the primary goals of age progression is to capture the gnomic features of the child's face. Yet those gnomic features, by definition, are invariant across development. If people have an implicit understanding of the impact of anabolic and catabolic changes, it is possible that the age-progressed photos add little that a layperson cannot glean from the outdated photo. Age progression may provide information that is superfluous at best and misleading at worst.

Research empirically testing the effectiveness of age-progressed missing children's photos has been sparse. What little research has been done does not offer conclusive support in favor of the technique. Sadler's age progression techniques were tested by Brown, a graduate student who worked with him at the University of Illinois at Chicago (Brown, 1987). Brown presented her participants with a target photo, and asked them to select the child's current photo from 75 photos of 13-year-old children. They were given 15 minutes to complete the task, and were allowed to keep the target photo as a reference during the task. Each participant was presented with five trials. There were two outdated trials where the photo of the child was shown at age 6, with one trial for each gender. The age-progressed trials showed a photo that had been age progressed from age 6 to age 13, with one trial for each gender. The fifth trial presented participants with both photos: the outdated photo and the age-progressed photo. The gender of the child in the fifth trial was randomly determined.

Consistent with Keenan's (2007) finding that people have an implicit understanding of aging, all five trials performed better than chance. However, if age progression increased the effectiveness of the participants in recognizing the children, we would expect the age-progressed trials to perform significantly better than the trials where participants were working from outdated photos. This was not what Brown found. Instead she found that participants were equally capable of selecting the correct child when using outdated photos. This fails to support the conclusion that age-progressed images aid in selecting the missing child. The results in the combined condition were more complicated. The combined condition did not produce significantly better performance than the outdated picture condition for the same gender, but did produce significantly better performance than the outdated picture condition when the genders did not match. When the combined condition for a subject involved a female child, then this condition did better than the outdated picture condition involving a male child but did not do significantly better than the outdated picture condition involving a female child. When the combined condition for a subject involved a male child, then this condition did better than the outdated picture condition involving a female child, but did not do significantly better than the outdated picture condition involving a male child. This is an odd result to say the least and warrants further examination. It is also important to note that Brown's participants were allowed to retain the target photo during the selections trials. Clearly in real-world contexts, memory is a key component of the effectiveness of missing children's posters.

We have recently begun to empirically investigate the effectiveness of missing children's posters using a memory-based paradigm (Lampinen et al., 2009b, 2009c; Lampinen, Arnal, Adams, Courtney, & Hicks, submitted). Specifically we have examined whether age-progressed photographs result in better recognition of children than outdated photographs. To test the effectiveness of age-progressed images, we used forensic artists recommended by law enforcement. The artists were provided with a photo of volunteers at age 7, as well as photos of their parents and siblings at age 12. The artists were compensated for their production of age-progressed images of the child at age 12. These professionally produced age-progressed photos were used to evaluate the effectiveness of these techniques. Participants were brought into the laboratory and asked to imagine that four children had gone missing. They were shown the "missing children" and then participated in both prospective and retrospective memory tasks simulating a search for the children. Participants were randomly assigned to three different conditions. In all the conditions the participants were shown each photo four times, with each presentation lasting 3 seconds. In the current condition, participants were shown four photographs of the targets at 12 years old. In the outdated photograph condition, participants were shown four photographs of the targets at 7 years old. In the age-progressed condition, participants were shown four age-progressed photographs. All conditions were tested on novel photos of the targets at 12 years old. The prospective memory task was designed to measure how well a person is able to "keep their eyes open" for a missing child. To simulate the distractions of daily life, participants were told that they would be playing the role of a camp counselor. They were told that they were going to have a series of children presented and they needed to place the children into two groups, with each group having an equal number of boys and girls. For each photo, the participant had to press the "P" key to place the child in one group or the "Q" key to place the child in the other group. However, if at any point they saw one of the missing children they were asked to press the "H" key. The participants were shown 44 photos of children. Along with the 4 target photos there were 40 distractor foils.

The retrospective memory task was designed to measure how well a person is able to select a child who is missing. Each participant was shown a series of four lineups. Each lineup showed the target photo as well as seven distractor photos. All of the distractor photos had been selected from the prospective memory task, eliminating familiarity as a selection device. Participants were asked to indicate if any of the children in the lineup were the missing children they had previously seen. To score the prospective memory task the proportion of false identification of the foils was subtracted from the proportion of correct identification of the targets (see Figure 7.4). In support of Keenan's (2007) finding that people have an implicit understanding of the anabolic and

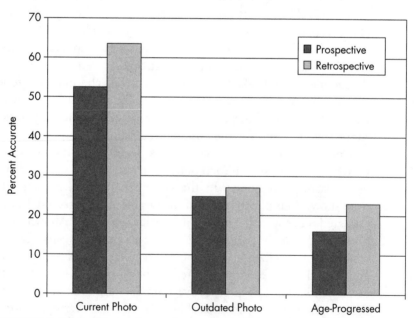

FIGURE 7.4 Prospective and retrospective memory for age-progressed pictures in the first age progression experiment.

catabolic changes a face undergoes, all three conditions scored significantly better than chance. Performance was best in the current photograph condition. However, the age-progressed condition did not significantly differ from the outdated photograph condition.

The participants performed similarly on the retrospective task. All conditions scored better than chance, but the group that was able to study the age-progressed images did not perform any better than the group that had the outdated photos. This suggests that the age-progressed photos did not aid our participants in searching for the missing children, although they did not hinder the search either.

To replicate these results, we ran a follow-up study where participants were again presented with mock missing children's photos. This time the photos were presented to look like the posters used in the popular supermarket campaigns. Participants were randomly assigned to the same three conditions as before, with one alteration. The age-progressed condition received a "combined" poster that showed both the age-progressed image and the outdated image. This change was made because age-progressed photographs are typically presented alongside outdated photos in actual missing child posters (Allen, 1990).

As in the prior experiment, participants did best in the current photograph condition, but the age-progressed and outdated photograph condition did not differ significantly (see Figure 7.5). Participants given the combined poster, including both the age-progressed and outdated photos, performed as well as those given only the outdated photo. These results failed to find evidence that age-progressed photographs lead to better recognition memory than outdated photographs. We are currently engaged in efforts to establish how generalizable these results are.

Public Perceptions

"Every 40 seconds a child goes missing in the United States" (AmberView, 2009). The claim is repeated in news reports, on the Internet, and on television ads. Is that really true? The evaluation of the claim depends on how you interpret the sentence, as much as it depends on the data itself. First, consider the connotation of the claim. Given what we know about public conceptions of missing children, the image conveyed by the "every 40 second" claim may well be that every 40 seconds a young child is snatched off the

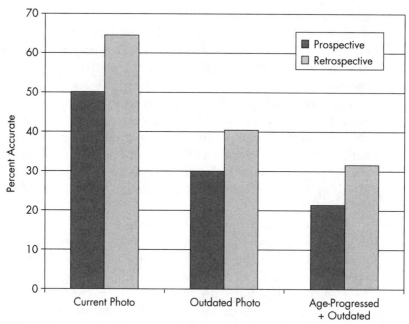

FIGURE 7.5 Prospective and retrospective memory for age-progressed pictures in the second age progression experiment.

street by a complete stranger. If that is what is meant, then no, of course, a child does not go missing *in that manner* every 40 seconds. Most children who go missing are not abducted at all. When a child is abducted, they are typically abducted by family members not strangers. Even when a child is abducted by a non-family member it is more often than not someone known to the child. And the majority of children who go missing are recovered relatively quickly. In the NISMART terminology a child does not go missing in a *policy-focal* manner every 40 seconds.

However, if one considers the denotation of the above claim, rather than its connotation, the claim is perfectly true. When one considers all types of reported missing child cases, the total incidence according to NISMART-2 is approximately 797,500. There are 31,449,600 seconds in a year. That results in a child being reported missing about every 39.44 seconds. These cases include children who have run away, children who have been lost, children abducted by family members, children abducted by non-family members, and children who are reported missing because of simple misunderstandings. Given the above considerations, should we be concerned about missing children? Of course. But it is important to ask what it is we should be concerned about. If we view the problem of missing children through the lens of the stereotypical kidnapping, then our public policy focus will also be focused through that very narrow lens. Stereotypical kidnappings are, of course, important. They are very dangerous events and require sustained public policy effort. However, it is also important for us to focus sustained attention on the other ways that children go missing. The most prevalent of these are cases where children run away. A substantial number of missing child cases also involve family abductions. And it is particularly important that long-term missing child cases be addressed. Although these cases are less common, they are also the cases where the most harm can befall the child and the most psychological harm can befall the family. Our own efforts in recent years have focused on how best to find children who are missing.

Public Policy

The purpose of the current chapter was threefold. First, we discussed the scope of the problem of missing children and presented statistics based on the NISMART studies and an archival examination of the NCMEC website (Lampinen et al., 2009a). Our goal was to give the reader a greater understanding of the variety of types of missing child cases and to provide base rates of these case types. Stereotypical kidnappings (i.e., those perpetrated by a complete stranger) represent only a small portion of the overall population of missing child cases (Sedlak et al., 2002). However, as made clear by the designated label for these cases, the general public believes this type of case to be typical of most missing child cases. Because of the degree of danger posed in these cases, it is important for resources to continue to be devoted to these cases. However, it would be a mistake to focus all research and public policy efforts on this particular type of missing child case. Instead, it is important to understand that children go missing for a variety of reasons and with a variety of outcomes.

Our second purpose was to further educate the reader about the harm caused by all types of missing child cases in order to emphasize the need for a broadening of research and public policy efforts. As previously stated, the problem of missing children can be harmful to the missing child, the family of the child, and the community as a whole. Runaways are often exposed to drugs and physical or sexual abuse (Flores, 2002), become involved in pornography and prostitution (Sadler, 1986), and engage in criminal activities such as theft or the dealing of drugs (Whitbeck & Hoyt, 1999). Child victims of family abductions exhibit symptoms of psychological trauma such as bedwetting and difficulty sleeping (Schetky & Haller, 1983) and depression (Senior et al., 1982). Non-family abductions include the risk of sexual and physical assault (Finkelhor et al., 2002), and labor and sex trafficking. Indeed, non-family abductions typically occur during the course of other crimes, most often sexual assaults. Stereotypical kidnappings often include physical and sexual assault (Finkelhor et al., 2002), and murder of the child (Brown, 2007). While this is not an exhaustive list of the harms that can befall missing children, their families, or the community, it is important to point out the variety of negative effects that all missing children might experience, not only those children missing in cases of stereotypical kidnappings.

The final purpose of the current chapter was to describe the research that our laboratory is conducting on the effectiveness of approaches and techniques used to find missing children. The approaches we have reviewed, while laudable, can certainly be improved. Initial examination of the effectiveness of missing children posters revealed disappointing results (Lampinen et al., 2009b). Many of the participants claimed that they were too busy completing their daily activities to take note of any information contained in those posters, including the photograph of the missing children.

One way to conceptualize "being busy" might be to consider the cost/benefit analysis a person in the above scenario might go through. Perhaps it seem so unlikely that an individual will come across a missing child that it does not seem worth the effort to interrupt their activities to study the posters. Two ways to improve this cost/benefit ratio would be to decrease the amount of effort needed to assimilate the information about the missing children and to increase the payoff for the potential witness. A recent study by Lampinen, Peters, Hicks, and Arnal (submitted) can be understood in terms of this dynamic. The researchers found that placing the missing children posters at the point of purchase and providing a potential $50 prize to customers led to a dramatic increase in the memory of those customers for the children in the posters. Providing posters at the point of purchase decreases the amount of effort required of the customer to look at the photographs and takes advantage of the captive audience effect (Bennett, 1998). Providing an incentive to look at the photographs provided further motivation. Although this is only the beginning of research into this area, the study suggests that small and simple changes in the presentation of the information about missing children can lead to more successful outcomes.

Our research on age-progressed photographs suggests that age progression may not always provide advantages over and above what one can find by simply providing outdated photographs of the child (Brown, 1987; Lampinen, Arnal, et al., submitted). The reasons for this appear to be twofold. On the one hand, people are much better than chance when it comes to recognizing a child based on an outdated photograph. In our studies, identification rates with outdated photographs hovered at around 20% after correcting for guessing. For age progression to be an effective technique, it would have to provide incremental improvements over and above what can be obtained with outdated photographs. The second factor to consider is that age progression techniques rely, to a considerable extent, on anthropometric growth trends. These are average rates of change of facial features in a sample of children. As Feik and Glover (1998) have pointed out, average growth trends do a good job of predicting the facial growth of the average child, but there is no average child. In fact, there is considerable interindividual variability in growth rates. This variability introduces potential error into age progression techniques.

With regard to public policy we believe that two points are important. First, controlled studies of the facial recognition using age-progressed photographs are few and far between. It is extremely important that the research we reported be replicated under a variety of circumstances, across a variety of age ranges, with a variety of ethnicities, subject populations, and forensic artists. It is quite possible that there is a range of situations under which age progression will be more effective than we have thus far found it to be. Particular artists may use techniques that maximize the effectiveness of their age progressions. If so, resources should be devoted to determine which techniques work best under which circumstances. We are currently engaging in a program of research aimed at addressing those questions.

It is also possible that the technique simply holds less promise than it was originally thought to hold. If this is the case, then the limited resources of law enforcement agencies and families should be utilized elsewhere. This does not mean that long-term missing child cases are hopeless. Far from it. If the identification rate for children based on outdated photographs is close to 20% then it may simply be that using multiple outdated photographs of the missing child and widely circulating them will be more effective and less costly than age progressing the pictures. As we discussed in the chapter, the probability of finding a child is a function of the number of people who see the photograph, the probability that those people encounter the child, and the conditional probability of identifying the child given that one has seen the photograph. Based on our current knowledge of the cognitive mechanisms involved, getting an outdated photograph to a large number of people who may have encountered the child may be the best way to maximize recoveries.

New technologies have led to novel approaches to finding missing children. For example, individuals can now enroll to receive AMBER (America's Missing: Broadcast Emergency Response) alert text messages via their cellular phones. New techniques such as this are certainly empirically testable, and might provide faster responses to situations in which time is a critical factor (i.e., missing child cases). Furthermore, these technologies can be examined in conjunction with basic cognitive processes, specifically retrospective and prospective memory, in a way that would inform both cognitive psychologists and policy-makers in their efforts to further the understanding on cognitive phenomena and increase the likelihood of finding missing children.

Concluding Comments

As previously reported (Lampinen et al., 2009b), individuals consider the problem of missing children to be important. We do too. A number of individuals and groups actively work in the area of finding missing children, including the Morgan Nick Foundation, the National Center for Missing and Exploited Children, the Walmart Missing Children's Network, and countless other groups. Other groups, such as Let's Bring Them Home, provide help to families of both missing children and missing adults. It is worth mentioning the contributions of these groups and to acknowledge their good works. Families are heart-broken and traumatized when their children go missing. These groups provide help and support, and their efforts have led to many recoveries. As cognitive psychologists who are interested in psychology and the legal system, the help we can provide is not help in organizing searches, putting out posters, or publicizing cases, but rather our efforts can best be utilized by trying to understand the nature of the problem and by testing the effectiveness of potential solutions. In the present chapter we have described some of that work, which is continuing on an ongoing basis.

Acknowledgments

The research we report in this chapter was partially funded by Let's Bring Them Home, a national non-profit organization dedicated to helping families of missing persons and to providing safety education. The views expressed in this chapter are those of the authors, and are not necessarily those of Let's Bring Them Home. Thank you to all the students from the law and psychology laboratory at the University of Arkansas who helped us conduct this research.

Note

1. The percentages represent percentages of children who are missing. Because some children were involved in more than one type of incident, the percentages sum to more than 100%. In Table 7.1 we provide other comparisons that are instead based on percentage of incidents (rather than percentage of children).

References

Acosta, R. A. (2003). Address of Assistant Attorney General R. Alexander Acosta, Shared Hope International Luncheon, December 8, 2003, Dominican Republic. *Anti-Trafficking News Bulletin, 1*(1), 3.

Allen, E. (1990). Computerized photo aging and the search for missing children. *International Criminal Police Review*, 4–10.

AmberView (2009). *Did you know.* Retrieved June 10, 2009, from http://AmberView.com

Asdigian, N. L., Finkelhor, D., & Hotaling, G. (1995). Varieties of non-family abductions of children and adolescents. *Criminal Justice and Behavior, 22*, 215–232.

Attorney General's Office NSW (2005). *Families and friends of missing persons counseling service.* Families and Friends of Missing Persons Unit, New South Wales.

Bales, K., & Robins, P. (2001). "No one shall be held in slavery or servitude": A critical analysis of international slavery agreements and concepts of slavery. *Human Rights Review, 2*, 18–45.

Bennett, R. (1998). Customer recall of promotional displays at supermarket checkouts: Arousal, memory and waiting in queues. *International Review of Retail, Distribution and Consumer Research, 8*, 383–398.

Booth, R. E., & Zhang, Y. (1997). Conduct disorder and HIV risk behaviors among runaway and homeless adolescents. *Drug and Alcohol Dependence, 48,* 69–76.

Briere, J. (1995). *Trauma Symptom Inventory professional manual.* Odessa, FL: Psychological Assessment Resources.

Brown, J. J. (1987). *Evaluation of a method of "aging" the human face for personal identification.* Masters Thesis, University of Illinois at Chicago.

Brown, K. M., & Keppel, R. D. (2007). *Child abduction murders: Incidence and impact on social and public policy.* Paper presented at the Annual Meeting of the American Society of Criminology, Atlanta, GA.

Buschang, P. H., Tanguay, R., LaPalme, L., & Demirjian, A. (1990). Mandibular growth prediction: Mean growth increments versus mathematical models. *European Journal of Orthodontics, 12,* 290–296.

Chaiyarachta, C. R. (1996). El Monte is the promised land: Why do Asian immigrants continue to risk their lives to work for substandard wages and conditions? *Loyola of Los Angeles International and Comparative Law Journal, 19,* 173–197.

Connor, K. M., & Davidson, J. R. T. (2003). Development of a new resilience scale: The Connor-Davidson resilience scale (CD-RISC). *Depression and Anxiety, 18,* 76–82.

De Baca, L., & Tisi, A. (2002). Working together to stop modern-day slavery. *The Police Chief,* August, 78–80.

DeYoung, R., & Buzzi, B. (2003). Ultimate coping strategies: The differences of parents of murdered or abducted, long-term missing children. *Omega: The Journal of Death and Dying, 47,* 343–360.

Farr, K. (2005). *Sex trafficking: The global market in women and children.* New York: Worth Publishers.

Farrell, A., McDevitt, J., & Fahy, S. (2008). *Understanding and improving law enforcement responses to human trafficking.* Final report prepared for the U.S. Department of Justice.

Feik, S., & Glover, J. (1998). Growth of children's faces. In J. G. Clement & D. L. Ranson (Eds.), *Craniofacial identification in forensic medicine* (pp. 203–224). New York: Oxford University Press.

Finkelhor, D., Hammer, H., & Sedlak, A. J. (2002). *Nonfamily abducted children: National estimates and characteristics* (National Incidence Studies of Missing, Abducted, Runaway and Throwaway Children). Washington, DC: U.S. Department of Justice.

Finkelhor, D., Hotaling, G., & Asdigian, N. L. (1995). Attempted nonfamily abductions. *Child Welfare, 74*(5), 941–955.

Finkelhor, D., Hotaling, G., & Sedlak, A. (1991). Children abducted by family members: A national household survey of incidence and episode characteristics. *Journal of Marriage and the Family, 53,* 805–817.

Finkelhor, D., Hotaling, G. T., & Sedlak, A. J. (1992). The abduction of children by strangers and nonfamily members: Estimating the incidence using multiple methods. *Journal of Interpersonal Violence*, 7(2), 226–243.

Finkelstein, M. (2005). With no direction home: Homeless youth on the road and in the streets. *Case Studies on Contemporary Social Issues*. Belmont, CA: Thomas/Wadsworth.

Flores, J. R. (2002). *Highlights from the NISMART Bulletins* (National Incidence Studies of Missing, Abducted, Runaway and Throwaway Children). Washington, DC: U.S. Department of Justice.

Furstenberg, F. F., Peterson, J. L., Nord, C. W., & Zill, N. (1983). The life course of children of divorce. Marital disruption and parental contact. *American Sociological Review, 48*, 656–668.

Gentry, C. (1988). The social construction of abducted children as a social problem. *Sociological Inquiry*, 58(4), 413–425.

Hammer, H., Finkelhor, D., Ormrod, R. K., Sedlak, A. J., & Bruce, C. (2008). *Caretaker satisfaction with law enforcement response to missing children* (National Incidence Studies of Missing, Abducted, Runaway and Throwaway Children). Washington, DC: U.S. Department of Justice.

Hammer, H., Finkelhor, D., & Sedlak, A. J. (2002a). *Runaway/throwaway children: National estimates and characteristics* (National Incidence Studies of Missing, Abducted, Runaway and Throwaway Children). Washington, DC: U.S. Department of Justice.

Hammer, H., Finkelhor, D., & Sedlak, A. J. (2002b). *Children abducted by family members: National estimates and characteristics* (National Incidence Studies of Missing, Abducted, Runaway and Throwaway Children). Washington, DC: U.S. Department of Justice.

Hammer, H., Finkelhor, D., Sedlak, A. J., & Porcellini, L. E. (2004). *National estimates of missing children: Selected trends, 1988–1999* (National Incidence Studies of Missing, Abducted, Runaway and Throwaway Children). Washington, DC: U.S. Department of Justice.

Johnston, J. R., Girdner, L. K., & Sagatun-Edwards, I. (1999). Developing profiles of risk for parental abduction of children from a comparison of families victimized by abduction with families litigating custody. *Behavioral Sciences and the Law, 17*, 305–322.

Keenan, C. A. (2007). *Implicit knowledge of facial growth patterns: Identification of normal vs. abnormal facial growth*. Unpublished doctoral dissertation, New School University.

Klain, E. J. (1999). *Prostitution of children and child-sex tourism: An analysis of domestic and international responses*. Washington, DC: National Center for Missing and Exploited Children.

Lampinen, J. M., Arnal, J. D., Adams, J., Courtney, K., & Hicks, J. L. (submitted). Forensic age progression and the search for missing children. Manuscript submitted.

Lampinen, J. M., Arnal, J. D., Courtney, K., & Adams, J. (2009a). *Archival study of cases listed on the website of the National Center for Missing and Exploited Children*. Annual Meeting of the Midwestern Psychological Association, Chicago, IL.

Lampinen, J. M., Arnal, J. D., & Hicks, J. L. (2009b). The effectiveness of supermarket posters in helping to find missing children. *Journal of Interpersonal Violence, 24*(3), 406–423.

Lampinen, J. M., Arnal, J. D., & Hicks, J. L. (2009c). Prospective person memory. In M. Kelley (Ed.), *Applied memory* (pp. 167–184). Hauppauge, NY: Nova Science Publishers.

Lampinen, J. M., Peters, C., Hicks, J. L., & Arnal, J. D. (submitted). Using point of purchase advertising to increase identifications of missing children. Manuscript submitted.

Lampinen, J. M., Peters, C., Petretic, P., Sweeney, L., & Culbertson-Faegre, A. (in prep). Trauma responses in family members of missing persons. Unpublished manuscript.

Liao, F. (1996). Illegal immigrants in garment sweatshops: The Universal Declaration of Human Rights and the International Covenant on Civil and Political Rights. *Southwestern Journal of Law and Trade in the Americas, 3*, 487–508.

Logan, T. K., Walker, R., & Hunt, G. (2009). Understanding human trafficking in the United States. *Trauma, Violence and Abuse, 10*, 3–30.

Markstrom, C. A., Marshall, S. K., & Tryon, R. J. (2000). Resiliency, social support, and coping in rural low-income Appalachian adolescents from two racial groups. *Journal of Adolescence, 23*, 693–703.

McQueen, I. (1989). Computer age: Computer enhanced aging. *Police,* June, 33–34, 42–43.

Missing Children's Assistance Act (1984). 42 USC 5771.

Morgan Nick Foundation (2009). *Morgan's story*. Retrieved August 14, 2009, from http://www.morgannick.com/morgans_story.html

Nelson, K. E. (2002). Sex trafficking and forced prostitution: Comprehensive new legal approaches. *Houston Journal of International Law, 24*, 551–578.

Picarelli, J., & Johnson, A. (2008). *Fostering imagination in fighting trafficking: Comparing strategies and policies to fight sex trafficking in the U.S. and Sweden*. Final report prepared for the U.S. Department of Justice.

Plass, P. S., Finkelhor, D., & Hotaling, G. T. (1995). Police response to family abduction episodes. *Crime and Delinquency, 41*, 205–218.

Plass, P. S., Finkelhor, D., & Hotaling, G. T. (1997). Risk factors for family abduction: Demographic and family interaction characteristics. *Journal of Family Violence, 12*, 333–348.

Raymond, J., & Hughes, D. (2001). *Sex trafficking of women in the United States: International and domestic trends. Coalition against trafficking in women*. Washington, DC: National Institute of Justice.

Roberts, M. C., & Ilardi, S. S. (2003). *The handbook of research methods in clinical psychology*. Oxford: Wiley-Blackwell.

Sadler, L. L. (1986). *Scientific art and the milk carton kids*. Paper presented at the 7th Annual Guild of Scientific Illustrators, Washington, DC.

Schetky, D. H., & Haller, L. H. (1983). Parental kidnapping. *Journal of the American Academy of Child Psychiatry, 22,* 279–285.

Sedlak, A. J., Finkelhor, D., & Hammer, H. (2005). *National estimates of children missing involuntarily or for benign reasons* (National Incidence Studies of Missing, Abducted, Runaway and Throwaway Children). Washington, DC: U.S. Department of Justice.

Sedlak, A. J., Finkelhor, D., Hammer, H., & Schultz, D. J. (2002). *National estimates of missing children: An overview* (National Incidence Studies of Missing, Abducted, Runaway and Throwaway Children). Washington, DC: U.S. Department of Justice.

Senior, N., Gladstone, T., & Nurcombe, B. (1982). Child snatching: A case report. *Journal of the American Academy of Child Psychiatry, 21,* 579–583.

Silbert, M. H., & Pines, A. M. (1982). Entrance into prostitution. *Youth and Society, 13,* 471–473.

Su, J. A. (1998). Making the invisible visible: The garment industry's dirty laundry. *Journal of Gender, Race, and Justice, 1,* 405–417.

Taran, P., & Geronimi, E. (2002, November). Globalization, labor, and migration: Protection is paramount. Paper presented at the Conferencia Hemisférica sobre Migración Internacional, Santiago, Chile.

Taylor, K. T. (2001). *Forensic art and illustration.* Boca Raton, FL: CRC Press.

Walmart Foundation (2001, June 21). *Wal-Mart's missing children's boards meet with more success. Walmart Foundation Press Release.* Retrieved July 22, 2005, from http://www.walmartstores.com/wmstore/wmstores/Mainnews.jsp?BV_SessionID=@@@@ 0634794216.1122048788@@@@&BV_EngineID= cccgaddfdldmdkdcfkfcfkjdgoodglh.0&pagetype=news &contentOID=9748&year=2001&prevPage=NewsShelf. jsp&template=NewsArticle.jsp&categoryOID=-8300&catID =-8248

Whitbeck, L., & Hoyt, D. (1999). *Nowhere to grow: Homeless and runaway adolescents and their families.* New York: Aldine de Gruyter.

Woodside, A. G., & Waddle, G. L. (1975). Sales effects of in-store advertising. *Journal of Advertising Research, 15,* 29–34.

CHAPTER 8

Looking Both Ways Before Crossing the Information Superhighway
Issues of Concern for Minors in Cyberspace

*Christopher S. Peters, Robin M. Kowalski, and
L. Alvin Malesky, Jr.*

Internet usage has increased dramatically since the 1980s
(Living Internet, 2008). In June 2008, approximately 1.4 billion
individuals worldwide had access to the Internet (Internet World
Stats, 2008). In the United States alone, it is estimated that 73.6%
of the population use the Internet (Internet World Stats, 2008).
Furthermore, the U.S. Department of Justice estimates that over
21 million teenagers are using the Internet in the United States
and 51% of these individuals use it daily (Lenhart, 2005). The
Internet permeates almost every aspect of our lives, ranging from
work and school to leisure and recreation activities. In fact, for
many of the nation's younger citizens, it is difficult to imagine life
without the Internet.

With that said, there are a number of negative aspects that have
arisen with widespread Internet usage. Two of the more prominent issues relevant to youth today are cyber bullying and online
sexual predators. Cyber bullying, as defined in this chapter, occurs
when an individual uses the Internet or cellular phones to torment
victims (Kowalski & Limber, 2007). Online sexual predators are
adults who use the Internet to locate, communicate, and, if
successful, sexually assault minors (Wolak, Finkelhor, Mitchell,
& Ybarra, 2008). Although these topics may seem divergent from

one another, they are included together in this chapter because they share a common theme: they both deal with how the Internet is used in the victimization of minors.

CYBER BULLYING

Case Illustration

My son was an early casualty and his death an early warning to our society that we'd better pay close attention to how our children use technology. We need to study this new societal problem with a sense of urgency and great diligence. We must also be swift and deliberate in our law-making and social policy development when it comes to protecting our youth from the misuse of technology against them and amongst them. (Kowalski, Limber, & Agatston, 2008, p. xi)

This statement was made by John Halligan in reference to his son, Ryan Patrick Halligan, who, at the age of 13, committed suicide, in part as a result of being cyber bullied. For several years preceding the suicide, Ryan had been bullied and picked on by a classmate. During the 7th grade, however, the bully "befriended" Ryan. Thinking that his new "friend" could be trusted, Ryan confided in him about a funny and embarrassing thing that had happened to him. His "friend" proceeded to share this incident with others, spreading the rumor that Ryan was gay. Perhaps to quell this rumor, Ryan established an online relationship with a girl from school, who appeared to reciprocate his feelings. She responded electronically to Ryan in a manner that led him to open up to her about his feelings, only to have these instant message exchanges shared with her friends. When the 8th grade school year began, Ryan approached the girl in person, unaware that she had been sharing his instant messages with others. The girl then told Ryan that he was a loser and that she wanted nothing to do with him. On the evening of October 7, 2003, after being told online to "go for it" by a "friend," Ryan hung himself, a victim of suicide by bullying, also known as "bullycide" (Marr & Field, 2001). With Ryan, the bullying occurred in both the real (i.e., traditional bullying) and the virtual (i.e., cyber bullying) worlds.

Overview of the Issues

When most people think of bullying, they think of the physical and verbal attacks, such as those initially experienced by Ryan. Bullying is most frequently defined as aggressive behavior intended to harm or injure another person that is generally repeated over time, and occurs when there is an imbalance of power between the individuals involved (Olweus, 1993). Commonly known as traditional bullying, the perpetrators are more likely to be male than female and the incidents are most likely to take place at school as opposed to outside school grounds (Nansel, Overpeck, Pilla, Ruan, Simmons-Morton, & Scheidt, 2001; Olweus, 1993; Rigby, 2003, 2007). In spite of common perception, most traditional bullying is not physical, but verbal (Nansel et al., 2001).

Recent years have seen a surge in a new wave of bullying known as cyber bullying (also known as electronic bullying, digital bullying, or online social cruelty). Cyber bullying refers to bullying through e-mail, instant messaging, video-gaming, chat rooms, websites, or through digital images or messages sent to a cellular phone (Kowalski & Limber, 2007; Kowalski, Limber, & Agatston, 2008; Li, 2007; Mason, 2008). Cyber bullying can take a number of different forms, including flaming (i.e., a heated exchange online), harassment (i.e., repeatedly sending emotionally distressing messages), denigration (i.e., posting defamatory or false information about another person online), impersonation (i.e., pretending to be someone else and electronically disseminating negative information as if you were that person), outing and trickery (i.e., electronically sharing another person's secret or embarrassing information), exclusion and ostracism (i.e., removing or blocking others from buddy lists), cyberstalking (i.e., electronically stalking or threatening another person), and happy slapping (i.e., assaulting someone while another individual videotapes the attack and distributes the video online) (Willard, 2006).

Although research on cyber bullying is still early in its development, a few consistent findings have emerged. First, although anyone can perpetrate cyber bullying, the greatest prevalence of cyber bullying is among middle school students. As children move through middle school, their involvement in cyber bullying increases, but it tends to drop off slightly during high school as they spend more time in face-to-face peer interactions and somewhat less time on the Internet. Second, few targets of cyber bullying report their victimization. Those who do tell someone generally tell a friend. Rarely do they report their victim status to a parent or other adult (Kowalski, Limber, & Agatston, 2008). Additionally, although cyber bullying can occur through any number of possible venues (e.g., instant messaging, chat rooms, social network sites), instant messaging currently is the most popular means reported by both targets and perpetrators (Kowalski & Limber, 2007; Kowalski, Limber, & Agatston, 2008). This is not all that surprising given that today's youth spend more of their time online instant messaging than engaging in any other type of online activity (Lenhart, Madden, & Hitlin, 2005). As online activities change, however, so too will the nature of cyber bullying.

Regardless of the venue by which the cyber bullying occurs, the most common forms that it takes are teasing and rumor-spreading. In their survey of over 3700 adolescents regarding their experiences with cyber bullying, Kowalski and Limber (2007) found that among those who had been cyber bullied, 68% had been teased online, 53% reported having lies and/or rumors about them circulated electronically, and 35% said that someone used their username to pick on others. Again, however, as the venue for cyber bullying changes, one would expect the form that the cyber bullying takes to change as well.

Prevalence of Cyber Bullying

Perhaps because of the recency of research on cyber bullying, researchers have not reached a consensus on defining cyber bullying or on the time parameters for assessing its prevalence. Whereas some studies ask participants the frequency with which they have experienced cyber bullying in their lifetime, others ask how often individuals have been cyber bullied within the past 2 months. Not surprisingly, then, prevalence rates of cyber bullying are variable across studies. Victimization rates range from a low of 4% (Ybarra & Mitchell, 2004) to a high of 72% (Juvonen & Gross, 2008). Rates of perpetrating electronic bullying range from a low of 3% (Kowalski & Witte, 2006) to a high of 23% (Aftab, 2006). One national study of over 3700 youths in grades 6–8 assessed participants' experiences with cyber bullying within the previous 2 months (Kowalski & Limber, 2007): 18% of the respondents indicated that they had been cyber bullied at least once within the previous 2 months and 11% said that they had cyber bullied others at least once within the previous 2 months (see also Kowalski, Limber, Zane, & Hassenfeldt, 2008).

Importantly, these statistics reflect overall prevalence rates of cyber bullying. The frequency with which individuals cyber bully or are cyber bullied through specific venues, such as e-mail, chat rooms, or instant messaging, varies from these overall rates (see Kowalski & Limber, 2007). In spite of the variability in prevalence rates of cyber bullying across studies and across venues, the point remains that cyber bullying is a problem and the situation will likely become worse before it becomes better. With rapid changes in technology, such as the most recent emergence of Twitter, new potential means of cyber bullying others exist. Sexting, or the sending of nude photos through electronic means (primarily cellular phones), similarly represents a new potential form of cyber bullying. Teens, who may think they are sending the photos to their girlfriend or boyfriend, arrive at school only to find that a large number of the students have also seen the photos. As teens and young adults become more and more tech savvy, rates of cyber bullying are likely to change.

Characteristics of Targets and Perpetrators of Cyber Bullying

To date, we know little about the characteristics of victims and perpetrators. One might assume that we could simply apply what we know about targets and perpetrators of traditional bullying to electronic bullying. Such does not appear to be the case, however. Unlike traditional bullying, which more frequently involves boys than girls (Olweus, 1993), cyber bullying seems to involve girls more than boys. Kowalski and Limber (2007) found that middle school girls (25%) were more than twice as likely to report being victims of cyber bullying than boys (11%). Similarly, girls (13%) were more likely than boys (9%) to report perpetrating cyber bullying.

In addition to gender differences in cyber bullying, personality variables also moderate involvement with electronic bullying. Heightened levels of social anxiety have been observed among perpetrators of cyber bullying (Kowalski, Limber, & Agatston, 2008). Additionally, among individuals who cyber bully, those who cyber bully with the greatest frequency show the highest levels of social anxiety. It is possible that some individuals who perpetrate cyber bullying may be seeking retaliation for traditional bullying. Perhaps the most socially anxious individuals are likely targets of traditional bullying and, therefore, members of a group that might retaliate online.

Victims of cyber bullying also report high levels of social anxiety (Kowalski, Limber, & Agatston, 2008). Of course, researchers have not determined whether heightened levels of social anxiety precede or follow cyber bullying. On the one hand, because of their inhibited nature, socially anxious individuals may be easy targets for cyber bullying (and traditional bullying as well). Alternatively, being a victim of cyber bullying may lead to feelings of tension and anxiety in both the real and virtual worlds.

Traditional Bullying versus Cyber Bullying

Researchers have debated whether cyber bullying is simply a new form of bullying or a qualitatively different phenomenon (Hinduja & Patchin, 2008; Juvonen & Gross, 2008; Kowalski, Limber, Zane, & Hassenfeldt, 2008; Raskauskas & Stoltz, 2007; Smith, Mahdavi, Carvalho, Fisher, Russell, & Tippett, 2008). The answer to this debate is informative because it addresses whether we can simply apply our existing knowledge of traditional bullying to cyber bullying, or whether we investigate cyber bullying as its own independent entity. An examination of the correspondence between involvement in traditional bullying and electronic bullying by Kowalski and colleagues suggested that traditional bullying and cyber bullying, although related, are not perfect predictors of one another (Kowalski, Limber, Zane, & Hassenfeldt, submitted). Using a criterion of having experienced traditional bullying two or three times a month or more, participants in their study were classified as victims only, bullies only, bully/victims, or not involved. Among victims of traditional bullying, 23% were also victims of cyber bullying and 9% perpetrated cyber bullying. Among perpetrators of traditional bullying, 19% were cyber victims and 20% cyber bullies. The largest overlap was observed with the traditional bully/victim group: 36% of these individuals were targets of cyber bullying and 23% had perpetrated cyber bullying. Only 9% of youth not involved with traditional bullying reported being targets of cyber bullying; 5% reported perpetrating electronic bullying.

Adapting the Olweus model of bullying, which views bullying as an aggressive behavior that is generally repeated over time between individuals who are on an unequal playing field, Kowalski, Limber, Zane, and Hassenfeldt (submitted) argued that cyber bullying shares three facets in common with traditional bullying: it is an act of aggression that is intended to harm another person; it is most often repeated (e.g., a single e-mail may be distributed to hundreds or thousands of individuals); and it occurs when there is a power imbalance between the perpetrator and the target. They suggest, however, that there are five key ways in which cyber bullying and traditional bullying are distinct from one another. First, unlike traditional bullying, where the perpetrator is a known entity to the victim, perpetrators of cyber bullying are often "anonymous." Just under 50% of the respondents in one study said that they did not know the identity of the individual who cyber bullied them (Kowalski & Limber, 2007). In another study, the percentage of perpetrators unknown to the victim was as high as 74% (Kowalski & Witte, 2006). This is very disconcerting to the victim, who is left wondering if the perpetrator is a friend, a fellow student, a sibling, or a stranger.

Second, because of their apparent anonymity, many perpetrators will say and do things online that they would be unwilling to say and do in person. Falling victim to this disinhibition effect, people's self-regulatory processes fall by the wayside as they communicate anonymously. Related to this, because targets and perpetrators are communicating with one another in a virtual world, they cannot see the emotional reactions of the person with whom they are communicating. Thus, targets do not have access to off-record markers that might indicate to them how to take the comments made by the perpetrator; nor can perpetrators see the emotional impact that their behavior is having on the target, often leading them to take their actions further than they might in a face-to-face encounter (Keltner, Capps, & Kring, 2001).

Third, because most traditional bullying occurs at school during the school day, the target can at least escape the bullying for certain periods of time. The same cannot be said for cyber bullying, where targets are accessible 24 hours a day, 7 days a week. Even if their cell phones are turned off or they are not currently logged on to the computer, messages and postings can still be left to be discovered by the target at a later date.

Fourth, the punitive fears of victims of traditional bullying and cyber bullying differ. Children and youth who are traditionally bullied often do not report the bullying because they are afraid that telling will lead to further victimization (Limber, 2002) or because they lack confidence in the ability of school personnel or other adults to effectively intervene (Hoover, Oliver, & Hazler, 1992). Targets of cyber bullying, however, may fear that reporting their victimization will result in their computer or cellular phone being taken away; in other words, they fear losing their social lifelines, even if those lifelines are the means by which they are being bullied.

Finally, as little as we know about bystanders of traditional bullying, we know even less about bystanders of cyber bullying. To date no research has examined the effects of cyber bullying on bystanders. However, because cyber-bullying bystanders are often inadvertently drawn into the aggression in a form of cyber bullying known as indirect cyber bullying or cyber bullying by proxy (Aftab, 2006), the effects of cyber bullying on them are estimated to be more problematic than those on bystanders to traditional bullying.

Public Perceptions

In June 2008, Lori Drew was indicted in Los Angeles County Court on three counts of illegally accessing private computers for the purpose of obtaining information to inflict emotional harm on another, and one count of criminal conspiracy. She allegedly had assumed a false identity on MySpace, communicating with a young girl, Megan Meier, as if she were a young boy named Josh Evans. Her plan was to find out what Megan was saying about her own daughter. According to the charges, in spite of knowing Megan's history of depression, Lori Drew, as Josh Evans, ultimately terminated "his" virtual "relationship" with Megan, telling her that the world would be better off without her. Devastated, Megan, at the age of 13, hung herself (Steinhauer, 2008).

Prior to this case, many people had never heard of cyber bullying. Even after this case made national headlines, many parents and educators still failed to recognize the seriousness of cyber bullying. Parents, in particular, claim that they are aware of and regulate their children's online activities. Children and youths, however, tell a different story. In a survey conducted by i-SAFE America (2005–2006), 92% of parents stated that they had established clear rules for their children's online activities whereas only 65% of the children said that their parents had established rules. Ninety-three percent of the parents felt they were aware of their children's online activities but only 41% of the children in grades 5–12 stated that they shared their online activities with their parents. Because many of the parents and educators did not grow up with the technology available to the youth of today, they often lack sufficient awareness of the misuses to which that technology can be put.

Even among parents and other adults who are aware of the online activities of today's youth, there is a lack of awareness of cyber bullying's devastating effects. Although only a small percentage of children and youths who have been the victims of cyber bullying have committed suicide, the effects can still be traumatic. A survey of 931 children and youths in grades 6–12 showed that victims of cyber bullying, particularly those who were also perpetrators (i.e., bully/victims), experienced lower self-esteem, higher anxiety, higher depression, a greater number of school absences, more physical symptomology, and lower grades relative to youths not involved with cyber bullying (Kowalski, Limber, Zane, & Hassenfeldt, submitted). Interestingly, the magnitude of these effects was greater following involvement in electronic bullying than traditional bullying.

Even with an awareness of the harmful effects of cyber bullying, some adults adopt the philosophy that kids will be kids and that this phase too will pass. Some even believe that cyber bullying is just part of the culture of some technological innovations, such as video-gaming. Even if that were true (which we are not suggesting it is), there is still a group of video-gamers, called griefers, who play multiplayer online games not for the love of the game but to destroy the gaming experience for others (Pham, 2002; Swartz, 2005).

Policy Recommendations

Legal and educational policies related to cyber bullying are early in their development but, importantly, they are developing. Prior to the shootings at Columbine High School in 1999, there were no state laws related to bullying in the United States. Since Columbine, however, 38 states have passed legislation related to bullying (Alley & Limber, 2009). Six of these include statutes specifically related to electronic bullying (Arkansas, Idaho, Iowa, South Carolina, Washington, Missouri). States that have legislation related to cyber bullying are mandating that programs related to cyber bullying prevention be incorporated within school curricula. Related to this, in October 2008 the Broadband Data Improvement Act (S.1492) was passed by both the Senate and the House of Representatives. This act legislated that schools receiving e-Rate discounts on telecommunication services and Internet access would now be required to educate students about cyber bullying and Internet safety (*Schools soon required to teach web safety*, 2008).

The state laws that have been passed related to bullying require schools in those states to create policies to address bullying within the school. Increasingly schools are broadening the scope of those policies to also include cyber bullying (Alley & Limber, 2009). Most schools (and certainly those receiving e-Rate discounts) have students sign Acceptable Use of Technology protocols. However, school administrators must be clear that cyber bullying is included as a touchpoint within these policies. The school's position on cyber bullying as well as the consequences for such behavior should be outlined in the policy (Kowalski, Limber, & Agatston, 2008). A model, Acceptable Use Policy for Information Technology Resources in the Schools, has been provided by the U.S. Department of Justice (http://www.usdoj.gov/criminal/cybercrime/rules/acceptableUsePolicy.htm).

Even with legislation and policies in place, however, lawmakers and educators face difficulties with defining the line between people's Constitutional rights (i.e., First Amendment Rights to freedom of speech and Fourth Amendment protection against illegal search and seizure) and protecting the reputations of those who are being defamed through cyber bullying (Hinduja & Patchin, 2008; Shariff, 2008). In addition, tracking published case law on cyber bullying is limited because of the recency of this phenomenon and the lack of legal clarity on issues related to cyber bullying, particularly when cyber bullying occurs outside school grounds (Kowalski, Limber, & Agatston, 2008; Willard, 2006). However, civil courts have taken action in some cases. For a more detailed examination of legal issues related to cyber bullying, the reader is referred to Hinduja and Patchin (2009). With time and additional research investigating cyber bullying, legal and policy recommendations should become more focused.

SEXUAL EXPLOITATION OF MINORS ON THE INTERNET

In addition to the Internet being used as tool in the victimization of minors via cyber bullying, this electronic medium has been used in the sexual exploitation of minors. Unlike cyber bullies, cyber sexual predators are often adults; however, as with cyber bullying, the victims are most often minors. In both cases this relatively new technology has changed the way offenders, be they cyber bullies or Internet sexual predators, approach their victims. We will now discuss how the Internet is being used in the sexual exploitation of minors as well as some of the misperceptions regarding this abuse. Finally, policy recommendations to minimize additional victims of this abuse will addressed.

The following hypothetical scenario depicts an adolescent being lured into sexual contact with an adult whom she initially met only online. While this situation is only hypothetical, it incorporates several aspects of the research literature that will be discussed in this section.

Case Illustration

Allie, a 15-year-old 10th grader, is isolated from her peers at school. She has a couple of friends whom she talks with during the day, but no one she is connected to or feels comfortable confiding in. She has been having difficulty focusing on her classes. Consequently, her mother and stepfather have pressured her about her seemingly lackluster academic performance. This has increased the rift that she feels between herself and her parents.

Allie set up accounts on several social networking websites (including Myspace and Facebook) in the past month and was initially surprised about the number of people who "randomly" contacted her. She was also surprised about how easy it seemed to be able to talk with people online.

Allie has started online "friendships" with several of the individuals who contacted her and now looks forward to checking her accounts to see if they have sent her a message. One of the individuals she has been talking with online is a 19-year-old named Calvin. She feels that Calvin understands her and looks forward to talking with him every day. However, last week Calvin admitted to Allie that he is not actually 19, but is in fact 29 years old.

At first Allie felt betrayed and upset with Calvin for lying to her. She cut off contact with him and even contemplated blocking him from sending her messages, but decided against that course of action. Truth be told, she missed communicating with Calvin. Two days ago, she finally responded to Calvin's messages, and they rapidly fell back into their intense online relationship. This morning Calvin suggested that they meet in person for the first time. Allie is not sure of what to do. . . .

Overview of the Issues

Beginning at a very young age, parents admonish their children with "do not talk to strangers" or "never get in the car of someone you do not know." Numerous books and articles have been published concerning child sexual abuse (for a review of the literature, see Ward, Laws, & Hudson, 2002). A consistent theme throughout the literature is that, in order for this type of sexual abuse to occur, the offender must have access to a minor. As a result, sexual predators will often place themselves in locations (such as near schools) or in situations (volunteering with the boy scouts or becoming close to a family) where they have easy access to children (Olson, Daggs, Ellevoid, & Rogers, 2007). With the proliferation of the Internet, however, a new medium to interact with minors has been created. As mentioned in the introduction to this chapter, an extremely large number of individuals now have access to the Internet in their homes and literally millions of minors are active Internet users (Internet World Stats, 2008). Thus, "sexual predators" do not need to maintain physical proximity to minors to have access to this population.

Broadly defined, an online sexual predator is an adult who locates minors and entices them into sexual activity via the Internet (Wolak, Finkelhor, Mitchell, & Ybarra, 2008). This type of behavior has been occurring for more than a decade; however, it was not until late 2004, with the first episode of Dateline's *To Catch a Predator*, that these offenders really gained the attention of the general public (*To catch a predator*, 2008). *To Catch a Predator*, hosted by Chris Hansen, was initially aired as a special on NBC's Dateline. These shows depict confrontations between Chris Hansen and "online predators" who were invited to a house via an online chat with an undercover agent to have sex with a minor. These Dateline segments have been extremely popular, averaging approximately 7 million viewers on each of the 11 episodes (Stelter, 2007). The show sparked a flurry of media attention, extolling the dangers of the Internet for children and sending parents into a panic. However, the question must be raised of whether this panic is actually warranted, and, if it is, what can parents do to protect their children?

Who is Most at Risk?

The first thing that needs to be done in order to protect minors is to identify who is most at risk. Approximately 4% of minors in one study received what was termed an "aggressive sexual solicitation" in which the solicitor attempted offline contact with the minor (Wolak, Finkelhor, & Mitchell, 2007). Although this may seem like a small percentage, it represents a large number of individuals being aggressively solicited when one considers the number of minors using the Internet. For example, if one considers that roughly 21 million adolescents use the Internet (Lenhart, 2005), then one can extrapolate that approximately 840,000 have received some sort of aggressive sexual solicitation online.

Certain trends can be identified among victims who were sexually solicited via the Internet. As represented in the case study at the beginning of this section, three-quarters of the victims were female and the overwhelming majority (99%) of the minors (defined as being under the age of 18) were teenagers, with 76% being between the ages of 13 and 15 (Wolak et al., 2007). Only a very small proportion (1%) were 12 years old, and none of the victims in this survey were under the age of 12. Thus, most victims are adolescents instead of young children (Wolak et al., 2007). This is somewhat different from the victims of non-online offenders, which run the full spectrum of ages (Wolak, Finkelhor, Mitchell, & Ybarra, 2008). The age of the victim is important to note when one examines the type of victimization that results from the initial online sexual solicitation. Most of the cases involving sexual assault (95%) were classified as statutory rape rather than violent rape (Wolak et al., 2007). Statutory rape is nonforcible sexual intercourse with a person who is younger than the statutory age of consent (Troup-Leasure & Snyder, 2005). Thus, the sexual activity would be considered legal if not for the age of one of the parties. Violent rape, on the other hand, is defined by Wolak, Finkelhor, Mitchell, and Ybarra (2008) as being committed by "offenders who abduct or assault victims because they have sadistic tendencies or lack the interpersonal skills to gain the confidence and acquiescence of victims" (p. 119). Violent rape is also relatively uncommon among non-Internet offenders, with younger children typically being coerced or manipulated into sexual activity (Wolak, Finkelhor, Mitchell, & Ybarra, 2008). The reason why most of the assaults with online predators are statutory in nature is likely related to the victim's age when these crimes occurred (Wolak, Finkelhor, Mitchell, & Ybarra, 2008). The teenage years are a time when adolescents are becoming curious about their sexuality and are seeking romantic relationships (Ponton & Judice, 2004). With this said, the typical adolescent often lacks the experience and good judgment necessary to make wise decisions about these relationships (Cauffman & Steinberg, 2000). It should also be noted that, regardless of what parents believe, most adolescents are unsupervised when they are online (i-SAFE America, 2005–2006). The combination of these factors (growing curiosity about sexuality, desire to be in a romantic relationship, and low parental supervision) makes them vulnerable to manipulation and exploitation by adults who simply desire to have sex with the adolescent.

Additional qualities appear to make specific populations of adolescents vulnerable to becoming victims of online sexual predators, many of whom are the same as their non-online counterparts. Minors who have been sexually or physically abused in the past may be especially vulnerable to becoming sexually exploited by an online predator (Finkelhor, Ormrod, & Turner, 2007). This is likely due to the fact that minors with a history of abuse may be more likely to seek the attention and affection that online predators offer (Lanning, 2002).

Other qualities that appear in online victims are higher incidences of delinquency, depression, and problems with social interaction (Wolak, Mitchell, & Finkelhor, 2008). Many of these adolescents have poor relationships with their parents or guardians, and a lower level of supervision. As a result, they may lack sufficient parental interaction to protect them against the overtures of online sexual predators (Wolak, Finkelhor, Mitchell, & Ybarra, 2008).

Although specific qualities appear to make certain minors more vulnerable, not all minors with those qualities will become victims. In addition to demographic and historical factors, a set of behaviors have been identified by Ybarra and her colleagues (Ybarra, Mitchell, Finkelhor, & Wolak, 2007) that elevate the potential for Internet-related sexual victimization. These researchers concluded that a combination of a number of the previously mentioned factors as well as specific behaviors (such as making rude comments to others or talking about sexual topics to strangers) interact to create this elevated risk (Ybarra et al., 2007). In order to better understand this interaction of factors, it is necessary to examine the characteristics of the online sexual predator as well.

Who are the Offenders and How do they Identify Potential Victims?

Sex offenders are a relatively heterogeneous group (Bourget & Bradford, 2008). Consequently, some researchers have questioned the accuracy of creating a subgroup of offenders and calling them "online predators" (Wolak, Finkelhor, Mitchell, & Ybarra, 2008). Although it is yet to be determined if Internet-related offenders comprise a unique subset of sex offenders or simply represent a diverse group of sex offenders using technology to access victims, a few generalizations about Internet offenders can be made at this time. The first of these is related to the age of the victims the offenders have chosen. As previously mentioned, online sexual predators predominantly target adolescents (Wolak, Finkelhor, Mitchell, & Ybarra, 2008). One thing to note, however, is that this does not automatically preclude the offender from desiring younger children. It is possible that online offenders as a group generally prefer adolescent victims. However, it is also possible that these victim characteristics reflect the victim pool available to the perpetrator and not the individual's sexual preferences. Furthermore, it is possible that Internet offenders have committed offenses against other younger children but these crimes were never reported (Hernandez, 2000). Nevertheless, available data suggest that Internet offenders most frequently target adolescent victims. A second apparent general characteristic of Internet offenders is that their contact offenses tend not to be violent, that is, they do not often use force in the commission of the sexual assault to gain compliance of their victim. Among the offenses committed by online sexual predators, only 5% actually involved violence (Wolak, Finkelhor, & Mitchell, 2004).

As far as demographic information is concerned, Wolak and her colleagues estimated that law enforcement officials made over 2500 arrests for Internet sex crimes against minors from July 2000 to July 2001 (Wolak, Mitchell, & Finkelhor, 2003). These offenses were categorized into three mutually exclusive categories: Internet-related sexual assaults such as the production of child pornography; Internet solicitation to undercover law enforcement posing as minors; and possession, distribution, or trading of Internet child pornography. The vast majority of these offenders acted on their own (97%), were Caucasian (92%), male (99%), and over the age of 25 (86%). Over two-thirds of the offenders who committed Internet sex crimes against minors were also found to possess child pornography (Wolak et al., 2003). It should also be noted that possession of child pornography has been shown to be a strong indicator of sexual interest in children (Seto, Cantor, & Blanchard, 2006). Yet, few (10%) had prior arrest for sexually offending against minors. Although these data provide a thumbnail demographic sketch of Internet offenders, one should keep in mind that as the demographics of Internet users change, so too may the demographic characteristics of those arrests for Internet-related sex crimes against minors.

Unfortunately, there are limited data available to provide insight into how offenders select their victims. A brief qualitative study questioned individuals convicted of Internet-related sex crimes about how they selected their online victims. Responses grouped according to theme of content suggest that offenders target victims when they have information as to the actual age and sex of the victim, if the victim is receptive to discussing sexual-related topics online, and if the offender could ascertain that the adolescent is under minimal parental supervision (Malesky, 2007). For example, some of the participants' comments in Malesky's (2007) study were:

> I said "Hi" to many girls. I would chat with those that responded. Those stating they were 10-yr-olds or so were attractive to me.

> I was talking to two female girls who were 13 and 14. They were in a bulletin board where sexual matter was being discussed. I was interested in them being sexual.

> Young-appearing nickname, sexually suggestive nicknames, my initial reactions to chatting.

> Need for friendship, appearing interested in sex.

> They usually had their age as part of their id, for example, LINDA 14.

The results of Malesky's (2007) study provide some evidence to suggest that the type of information posted could increase risk, especially if the material posted was sexual in nature. These finding were consistent with Wolak, Finkelhor, Mitchell, and Ybarra (2008) in that ". . . youths whose online interactions include sending personal information to and talking about sex with unknown people are more likely to encounter individuals who make online sexual advances and then try to move them offline" (p.116).

It is difficult for one theory to explain all facets of sexual offending; however, Social Learning Theory by Albert Bandura is a useful conceptualization in understanding some of the factors that enable one to engage in online sexually abusive behaviors. Bandura (1977) stated that learning occurs by observing and interacting with others. Further, he suggested that the individuals that one has the most contact with will have the greatest influence on a person's learning process. Therefore it is reasonable to suggest that if an individual spends a great deal of time corresponding online with others who support deviant sexual ideologies regarding minors, then the individual is less likely to find fault with these exploitive or illegal behaviors and perhaps is even more likely to engage in these acts.

Bandura (1977) also suggested that individuals use cognitive restructuring to engage in inappropriate behavior and avoid negative feelings associated with their actions. The view that cognitive restructuring plays a facilitatory role in enabling one to commit sexual abuse has substantial support in the sex offender literature (Abel, Gore, Holland, Camp, Becker, & Rathner, 1989; Bumby, 1996; Durkin & Bryant, 1999; Murphy, 1990). There are different types of cognitive restructuring that can be employed to minimize self-generated deterrents such as guilt or remorse (Bandura, 1977). For example, offenders may minimize, ignore, or misconstrue the consequences of their actions to excuse deplorable conduct. They may also contrast their illegal or abusive behavior with even more deplorable conduct to diminish the negative consequences of their actions (Bandura, 1977). For example, online offenders may admit to sending child pornography to a minor but then state that this action is not that bad (compared to raping a child). Online offenders may also use euphemistic language to mask the severity of their reprehensible thoughts or behaviors. For example, members of some cyber communities refer to themselves as "boy-lovers" or "girl-lovers" to conceal their exploitive thoughts or intentions. As previously mentioned, it is important to note that "distorted thinking" can be reinforced when interacting with other like-minded individuals and thus may increase an individual's propensity to engage in inappropriate or illegal conduct.

Public Perceptions

Online sexual "predators" have gained a great deal of media attention in recent years, largely due to Dateline's *To Catch a Predator* (Stelter, 2007) and high profile law enforcement sting operations. Some of the most sensational stories involve instances where a minor meets someone in real life whom they initially met online, only to be abducted, raped, and murdered (e.g., Foreman, 2007). Although tragic and extremely disconcerting, the existing literature suggests that this is an atypical scenario. Due in large part to these media stories, a number of articles have been written for parents on how to protect their children on the Internet (e.g., Mihelich, 2007). The problem is that many of the recommendations provided in these articles are inconsistent with what research in the area has actually found.

The first area of inconsistency involves how often minors are solicited online by an adult. The popular press often cites the figure that 1 in 7 youths are contacted by an Internet predator (e.g., Raskin, 2008). While this figure is actually taken from research, it is often used out of context. Thus, although a well-known study indicated that 1 in 7 youths surveyed acknowledged some sort of sexual solicitation, the majority of these were made by peers or were lewd inappropriate comments, instead of Internet predators (Wolak, Mitchell, & Finkelhor, 2006). A more accurate statistic is that 1 in 25 youths received an online sexual solicitation in which an adult attempted to make offline contact. This figure is obtained from the self-report of minors who use the Internet, and although it is still a high number it is not nearly as high as 1 in 7 (Wolak et al., 2006). Furthermore, even in this case, there is no guarantee that all of the aggressive solicitors were in fact adults. There is some evidence to suggest that a significant minority of adolescents report online to be older than they actually are (Hinduja & Patchin, 2008). Thus some of these adult "Internet Predators" could actually have been peers of the victims.

The second area of inconsistency involves the sex and age of the victims. The media often focuses on the victimization of females and, as a result, most protective suggestions in the articles are geared toward females (e.g., Schaumburg, 2005). However, according to victims and arresting officers, a quarter of all victims are males (Wolak et al., 2004). Similarly, the media tends to focus on young children as the primary victims; however, as mentioned previously, this has not usually been the case (Wolak et al., 2004).

The third area involves the type of victimization that occurs. The popular media tends to focus on the most violent stories involving the abduction, rape, and murder of minors after they meet someone in person that they initially met online. Research findings, however, suggest that these horrific stories are in fact relatively rare. In most cases, the victim "voluntarily" meets the offender offline with the expectations of sexual activity (Wolak et al., 2004). This is not to suggest, however, that coercion or manipulation is not being employed by the offender prior to engaging in sexual activity with the minor. In fact it should be noted, given the adolescents' age, naiveté, and inexperience in relations, that these individuals are exceptionally susceptible to this type of manipulation and exploitation. However, this type of abuse is very different to the abductions and rapes that are often reported in the media.

The fourth area involves tactics used by the offender when communicating online with minors. The popular press often report that online sexual predators lie about their age to potential victims in order to deceive them (Wolak, Finkelhor, Mitchell, & Ybarra, 2008). However, research suggests that age deception occurs less than what one might expect, ranging from 30% (Malesky, 2007) to as low as 5% of offenders (Wolak et al., 2004). Another example of misconceptions in the media involves specific "risky" behaviors that minors may be involved in. Most suggestions offered in the popular press to protect minors focus on common strategies employed with very young children, such as "never talk to strangers on the Internet" or "never give out personal information or have a personal webpage" (Wolak, Finkelhor, Mitchell, & Ybarra, 2008). These suggestions are based on the assumption that those at danger are young children. Although posting personal information may increase the likelihood of being contacted online by someone unknown to the adolescent (Lenhart & Madden, 2007; Smith, 2007), simply posting private information or having a social networking site profile does not appear to increase the risk of receiving a sexual solicitation (Wolak, Finkelhor, Mitchell, & Ybarra, 2008). Rather, what does appear to increase risk is the content of the posted information. Minors willing to talk about sex or those who seem more in need of attention and affection are at greater risk of falling prey to an online sexual predator (Wolak, Finkelhor, Mitchell, & Ybarra, 2008).

Overall, although the media has helped draw attention to the potential dangers of online sexual predators, it has focused too heavily on scare tactics and anecdotal advice without relying on research. It would be more effective if policy-makers utilize the existing literature to formulate strategies to protect minors when they venture online.

Policy Recommendations

A recent report by the Internet Safety Technical Task Force (2009) stated that parental involvement is the most important tool in protecting minors on the Internet; however, the advice that is often given to parents about Internet safety is more suited for young children and may not be appropriate for the age group actually at risk (Wolak, Finkelhor, Mitchell, & Ybarra, 2008). Telling an adolescent to avoid talking to strangers or not to have a social networking site profile loses its effectiveness, largely because they may simply not listen to such advice. A more effective option would be to tailor the advice to the at-risk age group, and focus the discussions toward the adolescents themselves. For example, it would likely be more effective to focus on risky behavior such as talking to strangers about sex, rather than just telling adolescents not to talk to strangers at all. Furthermore, considering that males make up 25% of victims, it is also necessary to include males in these discussions (Wolak, Finkelhor, Mitchell, & Ybarra, 2008). Currently, a number of recommendations are posted on the National Center for Missing and Exploited Children's website (National Center for Missing and Exploited Children, 2009) regarding Internet safety; however, at this time no known research has been conducted to determine the effectiveness of these strategies.

Another strategy that has been suggested is prohibiting convicted Internet sex offenders from having computers or Internet access once they are released from prison. Although some probation and parole officers receive specialized training in monitoring Internet-related sex offenders, it becomes increasingly difficult to supervise these individuals' online activity when they can go to public places like coffee shops or the library to use the Internet. This is particularly true when polygraphs are not used during supervision to verify the online activity of the offender. Furthermore, this recommendation will likely affect more than just the offender if, for instance, they have family members that need to use the Internet at home or if the offender has a job that requires using a computer (Malesky, 2007).

Online sting operations have also been utilized in an attempt to address concerns over Internet predators. As of this writing, Perverted Justice, a group dedicated to catching online predators, reported having contributed to the conviction of over 260 sexual predators, all caught through their online sting operations (Perverted Justice, 2008). Recently, some of these alleged predators and members of the general public have claimed that the actions of Perverted Justice and similar groups are actually a form of entrapment (Ross & Walter, 2007). A recent study found that, when the undercover law enforcement agent brought up the sexual solicitation, the participants were less likely to find the hypothetical defendant guilty and those who found him guilty were less confident in their verdict than when the defendant was the one who brought up sex (Peters & Malesky, 2008). Therefore, it is necessary that these online sting operations be performed carefully to avoid the perception of entrapping an innocent individual instead of actually catching a predator (Peters & Malesky, 2008). Considering the dearth of research concerning online sexual predators at this time, it is difficult to make more concrete policy recommendations. The ability to formulate further recommendations is likely to improve as additional research is conducted.

Conclusion

Despite all the benefits of the Internet, this technology is not without its downside. As previously mentioned, millions of adolescents go online each year. Fortunately, most of these individuals will transverse cyberspace with little or no complications; however, for some, their online venture will place them in harm's way. Ironically, as discussed in this chapter, the perpetrators of this abuse can be peers of the minor or adults, depending on the type of abuse. Given that the issues presented in this chapter are relatively new, there is limited empirical research to guide policies for protecting minors from cyber bullies and online sexual victimization. As a result, for both cyber bullying and online sexual victimization a number of misconceptions have been created and perpetuated by the popular media. For instance, online predators have received much greater attention than cyber bullies, as a result of shows like *To Catch a Predator*, when in fact a recent report indicated that cyber bullying is much more pervasive (Internet Safety Technical Task Force, 2008). Such misconceptions in both areas have resulted in ineffective prevention techniques that fail to adequately protect minors. However, it should be noted that the body of research addressing these topics is growing. New legislation is also being passed to protect minors from these and similar online abuses. In addition to new legislation, proper education needs to be conducted to inform the public as to what they can do to lower the number of minors victimized online.

References

Abel, G. G., Gore, K. K., Holland, C. L., Camp., N., Becker, J. V., & Rathner, J. (1989). The measurement of the cognitive distortions of child molesters. *Annals of Sex Research, 2,* 135–153.

Aftab, P. (2006). Retrieved November 15, 2006, from http://www.wiredsafety.org

Alley, R., & Limber, S. P. (2009). Bullying issues in the schools: Legal issues for school personnel. In S. M. Swearer & D. Espelage (Eds.), *Bullying prevention and intervention: Realistic strategies for schools* (pp. 53–73). New York: Sage.

Bandura, A. (1977). *Social learning theory.* Englewood Cliffs, NJ: Prentice-Hall.

Bourget, D., & Bradford, J. M. (2008) Evidential basis for the assessment and treatment of sex offenders. *Brief Treatment and Crisis Intervention, 8*(1), 130–146.

Bumby, K. M. (1996). Assessing the cognitive distortions of child molesters and rapists: Development and validation of the MOLEST and RAPE scales. *Sexual Abuse: A Journal of Research and Treatment, 8,* 37–54.

Cauffman, E., & Steinberg, L. (2000). (Im)maturity of judgment in adolescence: Why adolescents may be less culpable than adults. *Behavioral Sciences and the Law, 18,* 741–760.

Durkin, K. F., & Bryant, C. D. (1999). Propagandizing pederasty: A thematic analysis of the on-line exculpatory accounts of unrepentant pedophiles. *Deviant Behavior: An Interdisciplinary Journal, 20,* 103–127.

Finkelhor, D., Ormrod, R. K., & Turner, H. (2007). Revictimization patterns in a national longitudinal sample of children and youth. *Child Abuse and Neglect, 31,* 479–502.

Foreman, C. (2007). *Teen abducted by predator tells story to students.* Retrieved November 1, 2008, from http://www.pittsburghlive.com/x/pittsburghtrib/news/cityregion/s_533680.html

Hernandez, A. E. (2000, November). *Self-reported contact sexual offenses by participants in the Federal Bureau of Prisons' sex offender treatment program: Implications for Internet sex offenders.* Poster session presented at 19th Annual Research and Treatment Conference of the Association for the Treatment of Sexual Abusers, San Diego, CA.

Hinduja, S., & Patchin, J. W. (2008). Cyberbullying: An exploratory analysis of factors related to offending and victimization. *Deviant Behavior, 29,* 129–156.

Hinduja, S., & Patchin, J. W. (2009). *Bullying beyond the schoolyard: Preventing and responding to cyberbullying.* Thousand Oaks, CA: Corwin Press.

Hoover, J. H., Oliver, R., & Hazler, R. J. (1992). Bullies and victims. *Elementary and School Guidance Counseling, 25,* 212–219.

Internet Safety Technical Task Force (2008). *Enhancing child safety and online technologies: Final report of the Internet Safety Technical Task Force*: Cambridge, MA: The Berkman Center for Internet and Society.

Internet World Stats (2008). Retrieved November 15, 2008, from http://www.internetworldstats.com

i-SAFE America (2005–2006). *At risk online: National assessment of youth on the Internet and the effectiveness of i-SAFE Internet safety education*. Retrieved December 10, 2008, from www.http://www.isafe.org/

Juvonen, J., & Gross, E. F. (2008). Extending the school grounds? Bullying experiences in cyber space. *Journal of School Health*, *78*, 496–506.

Keltner, D., Capps, L., & Kring, A. M. (2001). Just teasing: A conceptual analysis and empirical review. *Psychological Bulletin*, *127*, 229–248.

Kowalski, R. M., & Limber, S. P. (2007). Electonic bullying among middle school students. *Journal of Adolescent Health*, *41*, S22–S30.

Kowalski, R. M., Limber, S. P., & Agatston, P. W. (2008). *Cyber bullying: Bullying in the digital age*. Malden, MA: Blackwell.

Kowalski, R. M., Limber, S. P., Zane, K., & Hassenfeldt, T. (submitted). *Psychological and physical consequences of traditional bullying and cyber bullying*. Manuscript submitted.

Kowalski, R. M., & Witte, J. (2006). *Youth internet survey*. Unpublished manuscript, Clemson University.

Lanning, K. V. (2002). Law enforcement perspective on the compliant child victim. *The APSAC Advisor*, *14*(2), 4–9.

Lenhart, A. (2005). *Protecting teens online*. Pew Internet and American Life Project. Retrieved July 1, 2008, from http://www.pewinternet.org/

Lenhart, A., Maddeen, M., & Hitlin, P. (2005) *Pew Internet & American Life Project: Teens and technology: Youth are leading the transition to a fully wired mobile nation*. Retrieved December 15, 2005, from http://www.pewinternet.org

Li, Q. (2007). New bottle but old wine: A research of cyberbullying in schools. *Computers in Human Behavior*, *23*, 1777–1791.

Limber, S. P. (2002). Addressing youth bullying behaviors. In M. Fleming & K. Towey (Eds.), *Proceedings of the educational forum on adolescent health: Youth bullying* (pp. 5–16). Chicago: American Medical Association.

Living Internet (2008). Retrieved November 15, 2008, from http://www.livinginternet.com

Malesky, L. A. (2007). Predatory online behavior: Modus operandi of convicted sex offenders in identifying potential victims and contacting minors over the Internet. *Child Sexual Abuse*, *16*, 23–32.

Marr, N., & Field, T. (2001). *Bullycide: Death at playtime – An exposé of child suicide caused by bullying*. London: Success Unlimited.

Mason, K. L. (2008). Cyberbullying: A preliminary assessment for school personnel. *Psychology in the Schools, 45,* 323–348.

Mihelich, P. (2007). *Protect your children from online predators.* Retrieved November 1, 2008, from http://www.cnn.com/2007/TECH/internet/03/23/safeonline.101/index.html

Murphy, W. D. (1990). Assessment and modification of cognitive distortions in sex offenders. In W. L. Marshall, D. R. Laws, & H. E. Barbaree (Eds.), *Handbook of sexual assault: Issues, theories, and treatment of the offender* (pp. 331–342). New York: Plenum Press.

Nansel, T. R., Overpeck, M., Pilla, R. S., Ruan, W. J., Simmons-Morton, B., & Scheidt, P. (2001). Bullying behavior among U.S. youth: Prevalence and association with psychosocial adjustment. *Journal of the American Medical Association, 285,* 2094–2100.

National Center for Missing and Exploited Children (2009). *Internet safety.* Retrieved May 24, 2009, from http://www.ncmec.org/missingkids/servlet/PageServlet?LanguageCountry=en_US&PageId=3026

Olson, L. N., Daggs, J. L., Ellevoid, B. L., & Rogers, T. K. (2007). Entrapping the innocent: Toward a theory of child sexual predators' luring communication. *Communication Theory, 17,* 231–251.

Olweus, D. (1993). *Bullying at school: What we know and what we can do.* Malden, MA: Blackwell.

Perverted Justice (2008). Retrieved July 3, 2008, from http://www.perverted-justice.com

Peters, C. S., & Malesky, L. A. (2008, March). *Online predator sting operations: Entrapment?* Poster session presented at 2008 American Psychology–Law Society Conference, Jacksonville, FL.

Pham, A. (2002, September 9). Enter the "griefers." *Chicago Tribune.* Retrieved September 1, 2006, from http://www.gamegirladvance.com/archives/2002/09/09/enter_the_griefers.html

Ponton, L. E., & Judice, S. (2004). Typical adolescent sexual development. *Child and Adolescent Psychiatric Clinics of North America, 13,* 497–511.

Raskauskas, J., & Stoltz, A. D. (2007). Involvement in traditional and electronic bullying among adolescents. *Developmental Psychology, 43,* 564–575.

Raskin, R. (2008). *Kids solicited less, but porn, bullying on the rise.* Retrieved November 1, 2008, from http://family.yahoo.com/?q=node/43&nodetype=article

Rigby, K. (2003). Consequences of bullying in schools. *Canadian Journal of Psychiatry, 48,* 583–590.

Rigby, K. (2007). *Children and bullying: How parents and educators can reduce bullying at school.* Malden, MA: Blackwell.

Ross, B., & Walter, V. (2007). *"To catch a predator": A sting gone bad.* Retrieved July 11, 2008, from http://blogs.abcnews.com/theblotter/2007/09/to-catch-a-pred.html

Schaumburg, D. (2005). *Girls learn about internet safety.* Retrieved November 28, 2008, from http://www.nexlan.com/press/corpart14.htm

Schools soon required to teach web safety (2008). Retrieved November 2, 2008, from http://www.eschoolnews.com/news/top-news/?i=55557

Seto, M., Cantor, J., & Blanchard, R. (2006). Child pornography offenses are a valid diagnostic indicator of pedophilia. *Journal of Abnormal Psychology, 115,* 610–615.

Shariff, S. (2008). *Cyber bullying: Issues and solutions for the school, for the classroom, and the home.* New York: Routledge.

Smith, A. (2007). *Teens who create social networking profiles or post photos online are more likely to be contacted online by people they do not know.* Pew Internet & American Life Project. Retrieved May 23, 2009, from http://www.pewinternet.org/Press-Releases/2007/Teenagers-who-create-social-networking-profiles-and-post-pictures-online-are-more-likely-t.aspx

Smith, P. K., Mahdavi, J., Carvalho, M., Fisher, S., Russell, S., & Tippett, N. (2008). Cyber bullying: Its nature and impact in secondary school pupils. *Journal of Child Psychology and Psychiatry, 49,* 376–385.

Steinhauer, J. (2008, November 26). Verdict in MySpace suicide case. *New York Times.* Retrieved June 15, 2009, from http://www.nytimes.com/2008/11/27/us/27myspace.html?_r=1&hp

Stelter, B. (2007). To catch a predator is falling prey to advertisers' sensibilities. *New York Times.* Retrieved October 15, 2008, from http://www.nytimes.com/2007/08/27/business/media/27predator.html?pagewanted=print

Swartz, J. (2005, March 7). Schoolyard bullies get nastier online. *USA Today,* p. 01a.

To catch a predator (2008). Dateline NBC. Retrieved February 6, 2008, from http://www.msnbc.msn.com/id/10912603/

Troup-Leasure, K., & Snyder, H. (2005). *Statutory rape known to law enforcement.* Office of Juvenile Justice and Delinquency Prevention. Retrieved November 16, 2008, from http://www.ncjrs.gov/pdf files1/ojjdp/208803.pdf

Ward, T., Laws, D. R., & Hudson, S. M. (2002). *Sexual deviance: Issues and controversies.* Newbury Park, CA: Sage Publications.

Willard, N. (2006). *Cyber bullying and cyber threats: Responding to the challenge of online social cruelty, threats, and distress.* Eugene, OR: Center for Safe and Responsible Internet Use.

Wolak, J., Finkelhor, D., & Mitchell, K. J. (2004). Internet-initiated sex crimes against minors: Implications for prevention based on findings from a national study. *Journal of Adolescent Health, 35,* 424.e11–424.e20.

Wolak, J., Finkelhor, D., & Mitchell, K. (2007). *1 in 7 youth: The statistics about online sexual solicitation.* Retrieved July 11, 2008, from http://www.unh.edu/ccrc/

Wolak, J., Finkelhor, D., Mitchell, K., & Ybarra, M. (2008). Online "predators" and their victims: Myths, realities, and implications for prevention and treatment. *American Psychologist, 63,* 111–128.

Wolak, J., Mitchell, K., & Finkelhor, D. (2003). *Internet sex crimes against minors: The response of law enforcement.* Alexandria, VA: National Center for Missing and Exploited Children.

Wolak, J., Mitchell, K., & Finklehor, D. (2006). *Online victimization: Five years later.* Retrieved March 1, 2008, from http://www.unh.edu/ccrc/pdf/kCV138.pdf

Wolak, J., Mitchell, K., & Finkelhor, D. (2008). Is talking online to unknown people always risky? Distinguishing online interaction styles in a national sample of youth internet users. *Cyberpsychology and Behavior, 11,* 340–343.

Ybarra, M. L., & Mitchell, K. J. (2004). Online aggressor/targets, aggressors, and targets: A comparison of associated youth characteristics. *Journal of Child Psychology and Psychiatry, 45,* 1308–1316.

Ybarra, M. L., Mitchell, K., Finkelhor, D., & Wolak, J. (2007). Internet prevention messages: Are we targeting the right online behaviors? *Archives of Pediatric and Adolescent Medicine, 161,* 138–145.

CHAPTER 9

Public Attitudes toward Applying Sex Offender Registration Laws to Juvenile Offenders

Jessica M. Salerno, Margaret C. Stevenson,
Tisha R. A. Wiley, Cynthia J. Najdowski, Bette L. Bottoms,
and Rachel A. Doran

There are many approaches to preventing child sexual abuse. One is to require convicted adult sex offenders to register with the police, often publicly on the Internet. The first federal registration law was the 1994 Jacob Wetterling Crimes Against Children and Sexually Violent Offender Registration Act (42 U.S.C. § 14071), which required all 50 United States to force sex offenders to register with local law enforcement agencies after serving their time in the prison system to ensure that their whereabouts were known. This legislation was intended to facilitate the prompt apprehension of repeat sexual offenders. In 1994, the Violent Crime Control and Law Enforcement Act (42 U.S.C. § 13701), commonly known as Megan's Law, added the requirement that states have community notification procedures in place to inform neighbors when sex offenders move into their community. The purpose of community notification is to enable community members to "take common sense measures for the protection of themselves and their families" (42 U.S.C. § 16911, p. 4).

In 2006, prior federal legislation was superseded and expanded with the Sex Offender Registration and Notification Act

(SORNA; 42 U.S.C. § 16911), also known as the Adam Walsh Act. The Adam Walsh Act requires all states to participate in an online registry that includes juvenile offenders (Caldwell, Ziemke, & Vitacco, 2008). Specifically, it requires registration for all juveniles who are convicted of a sex offense in adult criminal court and those adjudicated in juvenile court if they are at least 14 years old and attempted to commit or committed a sex offense involving aggravating circumstances (i.e., use of force or threat of serious violence, rendering the victim unconscious, or involuntarily drugging the victim). These guidelines are minimum standards, however, so states can register younger juveniles or juveniles who commit less severe crimes. (For a detailed history of the application of sex registration laws to juveniles, see Chaffin, 2008, and Trivits & Reppucci, 2002.)

It is important to determine the implications of these laws for protecting children from being victims of sex crimes. But it is also important to consider the potential for these laws to harm juveniles by placing them on a stigmatizing watchlist for years, even life. Although more work is needed, emerging research suggests that, overall, registry laws have not decreased the incidence of child molestation (nor general sex offending) for first-time or repeat offenders (Sandler, Freeman, & Socia, 2008). An important question, then, is whether the assumed protective effect of mandatory registry laws outweighs any harmful effects of these laws, particularly for juvenile offenders. In this chapter, we provide a summary of current registration laws for juvenile sex offenders across the United States and discuss the assumptions that drive these laws. We consider whether these assumptions have been supported or refuted by the research produced on the topic thus far. Then, turning to new data from our own laboratory, we discuss public perceptions of registration laws. This is an important issue because expansion of registry laws to juveniles might be driven by strong public support – or politicians' and policy makers' *perceptions* that there is public support – for expansion of the registry. As we discuss, research does indeed suggest that there is strong public support for registration laws for adult sex offenders, but is there such strong public support for registration laws for juvenile sex offenders? What factors influence support for these laws? To answer these questions, we present findings from new research investigating attorneys' and laypersons' perceptions of registration laws.

Case Illustration

The Jacob Wetterling Act, Megan's Law, and the Adam Walsh Act were each passed in reaction to heinous sexual crimes committed against children. For example, Megan's Law was passed in reaction to the sexual assault and murder of 7-year-old Megan Kanka in New Jersey. Jesse Timmendequas, a previously convicted sex offender who lived with two other convicted sex offenders, raped and murdered his 7-year-old neighbor after luring her into his apartment with a puppy. It is a compelling argument (emotionally surely, but also logically) that, had Megan's parents known about the potential danger next door, they might have been able to protect her. Thus, it is not hard to understand public support for these laws.

Although horrific violent sexual assault cases are often highly publicized, and although juveniles do sometimes commit serious sexual assaults, the majority of sex crimes committed by juveniles may not fit this prototype. For example, in 2007, forcible rapes accounted for only 15% of the sex crimes committed by persons under age 18 (U.S. Department of Justice, 2007). Some juveniles are even placed on the registry for behaviors that could be considered normative adolescent sexual experimentation, such as exposing themselves in classrooms (*No easy answers*, 2007), sending naked pictures of themselves to peers (*A. H. v. Florida*, 2007), or engaging in consensual sexual relationships with their peers (*No easy answers*, 2007; *Wilson v. State of Georgia*, 2006). For example, juveniles registered as sex offenders include a 12-year-old who mooned a class of 5- to 6-year-old classmates in Texas and a mildly mentally retarded 17-year-old who grabbed an 18-year-old's buttocks in Nebraska (Trivits & Reppucci, 2002). Thus, many juveniles on the registry do not fit the serious sex offender profile commonly portrayed in the media or commonly characterized by adult offenses.

Overview of the Issues

Current State Laws Governing Juvenile Sex Offender Registration

To determine the extent to which states have moved to include juveniles on sex offender registries, we reviewed registration laws from across the United States. Because juvenile sex offenders who are convicted in adult court are generally treated in accord with registration laws for adults, we were specifically interested in examining registration policies for juvenile sex offenders who are adjudicated in juvenile court. We visited each state's official website in the summer and fall of 2008 and reviewed statutes relevant to juvenile sex offender registration. We summarize what we found in Tables 9.1 and 9.2. Although the information in the tables is as accurate as possible, the reader should be aware that state laws are

TABLE 9.1   Summary of State Registration Laws for Juvenile Sex Offenders Adjudicated in Juvenile Court

Requirement and Discretion	N	States
Juveniles required to register as sex offenders		
Mandatory	26	AR, CA, CO, DE, IA, ID, IL, IN, KS, KY, MA, MI, MN, MO, NC, ND, NJ, NV, OH, OR, SC, SD, VA, VT, WA, WI
Sentencing court has discretion	3	AZ, FL, TX
Unknown discretion	4	LA, MS, OK, RI
Juveniles *not* required to register as sex offenders	13	AL, AK, GA, HI, ME, MT, NE, NH, NM, PA, TN, UT, CT
Unknown	4	MD, NY, WV, WY

TABLE 9.2   Summary of State Compliance of Adam Walsh Act Guidelines as of December 2008

Requirement and Discretion	N	States
State codes in compliance with Adam Walsh Act	5	DE, MS, MO, NH, OH
State codes *not* in compliance, but with progress being made toward compliance	24	AK, AR, AZ, CO, HI, ID, IA, LA, ME, MD, MA, MI, MN, MT, NE, NV, NJ, NM, NC, OK, PA, UT, VA, WA
State codes *not* in compliance, and with little or no progress being made toward compliance	9	CA, FL, GA, IL, KS, NY, OR, SC, TX
Unknown	12	AL, CT, IN, KY, ND, RI, SD, TN, VT, WV, WI, WY

currently in flux and state websites are not always updated. In an attempt to combat these problems ourselves, after we obtained information from all state websites we compared our findings with similar information that had been collected by Nicole Pittman, a juvenile justice policy analyst and attorney at the Defender Association of Philadelphia, who is also researching state laws about juvenile offenders. In some cases, we relied on her information rather than state web archives, because she had uncovered more recent information by directly contacting states. As shown in Table 9.1, only 13 states never require juvenile offenders who are adjudicated in juvenile court to register as sex offenders. Thirty-three states, however, currently require juveniles to register as sex offenders under some circumstances. In 26 of those states juvenile registration is mandatory, that is, if a juvenile is adjudicated guilty of certain offenses, the juvenile is legally required to register as a sex offender, and neither prosecutors nor judges can make case-by-case decisions about the appropriateness of registration.

In our opinion, registration laws in the 33 states in which juvenile sex offenders might be required to register reflect little acknowledgment of juveniles' developmental immaturity, which, from a psychological point of view, should make juveniles less culpable or at least less worthy of severe punishment than adults. Although Indiana, Ohio, Oklahoma, and South Dakota explicitly prohibit juveniles younger than 14 years old from being required to register, in other states there are no such prohibitions, and in some states juveniles as young as 7 years old may be placed on sex offender registries. Further, in the majority of states that require juvenile registration, registration extends long after adolescence, often with no opportunity for discretion, appeal, or petition. Specifically, 22 states require juveniles to register for at least 10 years, and in California and South Carolina, for example, juvenile (and adult) sex offenders remain on the registry their entire lives. In only nine of these states (including California) can the registration requirement be appealed or petitioned. Some states do appear to be sensitive to the role that age and immaturity might play in juvenile sex offending, however. Ohio stands out in particular: Individuals placed on sex offender registries as juveniles are allowed to petition to be removed from the registry after 3–5 years. And in at least eight other states (Arkansas, Arizona, Idaho, Kansas, Missouri, North Carolina, Nevada, and Oklahoma), registration length is determined by the juvenile's age, typically lasting until the juvenile is 18 or 21 years old.

Registration laws also vary across states with respect to the types of offenses for which a juvenile is required to register and the nature of registration itself. For example, in Kansas and Oregon, registration is required only in cases that involve threats, the use of force, or incapacitation, but in at least 19 other states juveniles adjudicated guilty of non-forceful offenses may be required to register. And, although registration typically requires only that offenders report their residential and work addresses to local law enforcement, juvenile sex offenders are also required to provide DNA samples in states such as Arkansas, Indiana, Kansas, and South Carolina. Further, information about juvenile sex offenders is publicly available via online databases in states such as Arkansas, Arizona, California, Delaware, Iowa, Kansas, Kentucky, New Jersey, and South Dakota.

Thus, although registration laws currently vary across states, the most common policy is to mandate registration for juvenile sex offenders adjudicated in juvenile court with no allowance for prosecutorial or judicial discretion. But the laws in these states and in states with more lenient juvenile registration policies will probably become more inclusive as they come into compliance with the most recent iteration of the SORNA guidelines governing the Adam Walsh Act. That is, states are federally mandated to either comply with the Adam Walsh Act or risk losing 10% of their federal funding for law enforcement activities (42 U.S.C. §16911; Caldwell et al., 2008). This threat has led some states to rapidly implement the new sex offender registration policy (Letourneau, 2008). Even so, many other states have been slow to come into compliance with the Adam Walsh Act, due in part to reservations and court challenges regarding its provisions for juvenile offenders (N. Pittman, personal communication, January 7, 2009). As of December 2008, only five states were in full compliance (see Table 9.2; for up-to-date information on Adam Walsh Act compliance, visit http://www.ojp.usdoj.gov/smart/). Therefore, many states' laws are in flux as legislators attempt to comply with the Act in ways that balance the goals of juvenile sex offender registration with concerns about their efficacy. We review these factors next.

Assumptions Underlying Registration Laws and Empirical Findings to Date

In general, registration laws are driven by the assumption that communities need protection from sex offenders who pose a uniquely dangerous threat to public safety. Implicit in this assumption is the belief that sex offenders represent a particularly bad breed of offenders who recidivate at high rates and cannot be rehabilitated. The recent expansion of such laws to juveniles is driven by the notion that juvenile sex offenders do not differ appreciably from adult sex offenders in terms of recidivism risk or rehabilitation potential; although more studies are needed, extant psychological research raises doubts about these suppositions, especially the appropriateness of sex offender registration for juveniles (for review, see Letourneau & Miner, 2005; Trivits & Reppucci, 2002). Next, we discuss the utility of expanding registration laws to a population that diverges in important ways from the prototypical adult sexual offenders for whom the laws were intended.

Recidivism

The extension of sex offender registration laws to juvenile sex offenders is based on the premise that juvenile sex offenders recidivate at a rate similar to adult sex offenders. Yet approximately 20–40% of adult sex offenders eventually re-offend (Trivits & Reppucci, 2002) in contrast to only 5–15% of juvenile sex offenders (Chaffin, 2008; Trivits & Reppucci, 2002). Pre-adolescents (5–12-year-olds) with sexual behavior problems have an even lower recidivism rate (2–7% over 10 years) (Carpentier, Silovsky, & Chaffin, 2006). Several studies even indicate that, compared to other juveniles who commit non-sexual offenses, juvenile sex offenders are no more likely to commit future sexual crimes and are even less likely to go on to commit non-sexual crimes (Caldwell, 2002, 2007; Caldwell et al., 2008; Carpentier, Silovsky, & Chaffin, 2006; Zimring, Piquero, & Jennings, 2007). Thus, the argument that registration is necessary to reduce juvenile sex offenders' high rate of recidivism is fundamentally flawed.

Do the laws fulfill the goal of reducing the amount of juvenile and/or adult sex offender recidivism? Sandler and colleagues (2008) collected arrest rates for child molestation, rape, general sexual offending, and non-sexual offenses in the state of New York from 1986 (10 years before the registration laws were enacted) to 2006 (11 years after the registration laws were enacted). They found no significant difference between arrest rates (in any category) before versus after the enactment of registration laws (for either first-time or repeat offenders). Further, they found that roughly 96% of sex offenses in New York between the years 1986 and 2006 were committed by new offenders (i.e., people who were not on the sex offender registry). Thus, only 4% of sexual offenses even had the *potential* to be influenced by sex offender registry laws.

Two studies comparing recidivism rates for registered versus non-registered juvenile and adult sex offenders have revealed no differences (Adkins, Huff, & Stageberg, 2000; Schram & Milloy, 1995), although registered offenders who did re-offend were apprehended more quickly than non-registered offenders who re-offended, which is arguably a positive outcome of the registry (Schram & Milloy, 1995). Adkins and colleagues did not, however, match their pre- and post-registry groups, which limits conclusions about the effectiveness of the registry.

In the only study we know of to focus on the effectiveness of registry laws exclusively for a sample of juvenile offenders, Letourneau and Armstrong (2008) matched 111 registered and non-registered juvenile sex offenders on a host of case and demographic characteristics (e.g., crime severity, age, race, prior offenses). Even after more than 4 years, there were no differences in recidivism rates between the registered and non-registered juveniles – but because only two subsequent sexual offenses were committed, statistical comparison was not possible, and it is clear that a study with a much larger sample is needed.

Thus, registration laws might not reduce recidivism, according to comparisons of recidivism rates of offenders who are registered versus not registered (Adkins et al., 2000; Letourneau & Armstrong, 2008; Schram & Milloy, 1995) and comparisons of general sexual offending incidence rates before and after registry law implementation (Sandler et al., 2008). According to a survey by Malesky and Keim (2001), mental health professionals are at least intuitively aware of this failure – many of them believe that registration laws do not decrease the number of children who are sexually abused each year through deterrence or better preparing parents to protect their children.

Rehabilitation and Amenability to Treatment

As noted previously, inherent in the inclusion of juveniles on the registry is the assumption that juvenile sex offenders represent a special class of juvenile offenders who are particularly dangerous and cannot be rehabilitated. This assumption runs counter to one of the central tenets of the juvenile justice system: that juveniles are amenable to rehabilitation and should be reformed. A recent meta-analysis revealed that the methods typically used to treat adult sex offenders (e.g., addressing specific sexual behaviors) did not affect recidivism rates in a sample of juvenile sex offenders. In contrast, treatments that have been shown effective with non-violent juvenile offenders (e.g., addressing family-level dynamics) effectively reduced the likelihood that juvenile sex offenders would re-offend (St. Amand, Bard, & Silovsky, 2008). Thus, in terms of rehabilitation potential, juvenile sex offenders appear to be more similar to juveniles who commit non-sexual crimes than they are to adult sex offenders. Of more importance, research suggests that juvenile sex offenders are amenable to treatment (for reviews, see Chaffin, 2008; Trivits & Reppucci, 2002), further calling into question one of the assumptions underlying the extension of registration laws to juveniles.

Juvenile Sex Offenders: The Rule or the Exception?

In 2007, forcible rapes accounted for only 15% of the sex crimes committed by persons under age 18 (U.S. Department of Justice, 2007). Therefore, many juveniles who are charged with sex crimes do not match the prototype of the perpetually dangerous sex offender for which the registry was created. Yet in some jurisdictions there is no distinction between juveniles who commit less serious offenses (e.g., exposing oneself to a classmate) and those who commit more serious offenses (e.g., forceful rape). In fact, in recognition that sex offenders represent different levels of threat based on the offenses they commit, the Adam Walsh Act established a tiered system of (among other things) the length of registration required, and whether details about the least serious offenses must be disclosed on online registries versus not (42 U.S.C. § 16911 p. 21). But jurisdictions are not required to use the tier system as long as they meet the minimum guidelines for each tier. That is, jurisdictions with registry laws that are more inclusive than the Adam Walsh minimum guidelines (i.e., laws that include younger juveniles, or juveniles that commit less severe offenses) are considered to be in compliance with the tier system.

This policy translates into a practice by which juvenile sex offenders are treated as a homogeneous group, even though juveniles vary in terms of causal patterns and typologies (for review, see Lambie & Seymour, 2006). Juvenile sex offenders vary not only in terms of the types of offenses they commit (e.g., whether they use force or weapons) but also in terms of factors related to the victim (e.g., prepubescent versus postpubescent) and their own characteristics (e.g., whether they have been abused, whether they engage in other non-sexual delinquent behavior) (Almond, Canter, & Salfati, 2006; Hunter, Figueredo, Malamuth, & Becker, 2003). It is important to recognize that there are different sub-groups of offenders because, even among those who commit similar crimes, their motivations may differ (e.g., sexual exploration; Becker, Kaplan, & Tenke, 1992; Moffitt, 1993). Further, although certainly some juveniles commit heinous sex offenses and persist in such behavior into adulthood, juvenile sex offenders also vary in recidivism rates and amenability to treatment (Trivits & Reppucci, 2002). Policies that do not recognize these differences are problematic.

Currently, the only factor used to differentiate juvenile sex offenders is age: The original Adam Walsh Act required registration for all juveniles aged 14 years or older who committed sex offenses against victims aged 12 years or younger. Of interest, research suggests that these criteria for juvenile sex offender registration are not predictive of sexual offense recidivism. Specifically, Caldwell and colleagues (2008) found that juvenile sex offenders who would be required to register according to the age guidelines set forth in the Adam Walsh Act were less likely to be charged with any subsequent violent offense (not sexual offenses specifically) compared to juvenile offenders who would *not* be required to register. Thus, registration laws based explicitly on the age of the offender and victim do not appear to be effective at protecting communities from those most likely to re-offend. Fortunately, the Adam Walsh Act guidelines were recently revised: Registration is still required for juveniles aged 14 years or older, but only for those who commit an offense that includes force or threat of force (42 U.S.C. § 16911). But, as mentioned earlier, the guidelines governing the Adam Walsh Act set a minimum standard and registration laws can be more inclusive.

The Iatrogenic Effects of Registration Laws: Unintended Consequences

Sex offender registration laws might even have a negative impact on adult and juvenile offenders' lives. Anecdotally, being listed on the registry might put offenders' lives in danger – four registered offenders were targeted through the registry and killed by strangers in 2005 and 2006 (*No easy answers*, 2007). Some sex offenders have committed suicide after being required to register, including a juvenile who was registered for exposing himself to a girl in gym class (*No easy answers*, 2007). Although these extreme outcomes are certainly noteworthy, they are of course not representative, so it is important to consider the more mundane, yet pervasive negative consequences that registration has on sex offenders' lives. Empirical research shows that sex offenders on the registry experience a wide variety of negative outcomes (Levenson, D'Amora, & Hern, 2007b; Levenson & Cotter, 2005; Tewksbury, 2005; Tewksbury & Lees, 2006). Researchers in these studies surveyed convicted sex offenders about their experiences related to being listed on the sex offender registry and found that the majority of registered sex offenders who were sampled reported feeling isolation, loss of close relationships, shame and embarrassment, hopelessness, and stress that interfered with recovery as a result of someone finding out that they were registered as a sex offender (Levenson & Cotter, 2005). Across a number of studies, registered sex offenders have also reported that as a consequence of their registry status being discovered by others they have experienced job loss (21–43%), being forced out of a place to live (10–45%), being harassed by neighbors (21–47%), being physically assaulted (5–16%), and having property damaged (18–21%) (Levenson, D'Amora, & Hern, 2007b; Levenson & Cotter, 2005; Tewksbury, 2005). Although these studies focused on adult sex offenders (even though there might have been some juveniles in these samples), these effects are likely to apply to juvenile sex offenders as well. As noted by Sampson and Laub (2005, p. 15), juvenile delinquency is more likely to occur when "individuals' bonds to society are attenuated." Registration laws appear to do just this. Thus, Letourneau and Miner (2005) have argued that iatrogenic effects of sex offender registration might inadvertently lead to re-offending.

Summary

Although research does not provide empirical support for legal assumptions about juvenile sex offenders' recidivism rates, amenability to treatment, and homogeneity, registration laws for juveniles have become more inclusive. The gap between data and public policy appears to be widening (Chaffin, 2008). Not only is there growing evidence that registration laws might be ineffective and less necessary for preventing juvenile sex offenders from recidivating, they might also unintentionally increase recidivism among juvenile sex offenders. Clearly there are dangerous juvenile sex offenders for whom registration might be appropriate. But for juveniles who commit less serious offenses, the potential protection offered to the community may be outweighed by the negative impact of being stigmatized as a sex offender during an important developmental phase (Chaffin, 2008; Letourneau & Miner, 2005; Trivits & Reppucci, 2002). Why, then, do registration policies continue to move in the direction of greater inclusion of juvenile sex offenders?

Public Perceptions

The expansion of sex offender registration laws to include more and more juveniles might be due to strong public support – or perceptions that there is public support – for the registry. That is, politicians and policy-makers might be hesitant to reconsider juvenile registration laws, even in the face of mounting empirical evidence calling them into question, because they believe that the public wants juvenile registration laws. Is this assumption correct? First, we review the growing literature regarding public perceptions of adult sex offender registration laws. Second, we describe our recent research examining public perceptions of the application of registration laws to juveniles. To our knowledge, our work is the first to investigate this controversial issue.

Perceptions of Registration Laws for *Adult* Sex Offenders

Malesky and Keim (2001) found that 80% of mental health professionals believed registries to be ineffective in reducing the incidence of child sexual abuse. Seventy percent believed that registries give parents a false sense of security. Yet there is very strong public support for registration laws for adult sex offenders (Levenson, Brannon, Fortney, & Baker, 2007a; Phillips, 1998). Levenson et al. (2007a) surveyed community members and found that 76% believed that *all* adult sex offenders should register. Only 6% believed low risk offenders with no history of violence should *not* have to register. Such support might be based on inaccurate beliefs about the effectiveness of registration and offender characteristics. For example, 83% of Levenson et al.'s (2007a) respondents agreed that registration is effective in reducing sex offenses and 74% agreed that the majority of adult sex offenders recidivate – a gross overestimation of the actual 20–40% recidivism rate for adults (Trivits & Reppucci, 2002). Other surveys found that the public believes sex offender registries to be very important (Caputo & Brodsky, 2004; Phillips, 1998). Further, the more one believes the registry to be important, the more fearful one is about crime in general (Caputo & Brodsky, 2004).

This strong public support for adult sex offender registration might deter politicians and policy-makers from reconsidering these laws in light of the social science evidence we have reviewed. The research on perceptions of adult sex offender registration laws suggests that a "tough on sex crimes" platform would be much more popular with the public than a platform based on making sex offender registration laws more lenient. Chaffin (2008) remarked that "the sound bite that we should put our kids' safety before the rights of sexual offenders, adult or juvenile, sounds so intuitively correct that it is a guaranteed political winner, even if the policy it promotes is ultimately destructive and fails to deliver the child protection goods" (p. 120). Many politicians use a "tough on sex crimes" platform when running for office for this very reason. For example, in May 2008, Tim Fox, a Republican candidate for Montana Attorney General, announced during his campaign that enforcing sex offender registration laws was his top priority. Politicians who question the laws might face trouble: The only Iowa House member to vote against a 2002 bill to implement housing restrictions for sex offenders was targeted with negative campaign flyers with a photograph depicting a prisoner in an orange jumpsuit looking through a fence at a schoolyard full of children, with a tagline asking, "Why does Ed Fallon think it's ok for sex offenders to live near schools?" (Brenton, 2008).

Perceptions of Registration Laws for Juvenile Sex Offenders: New Empirical Evidence

Would politicians and policy-makers be correct in assuming that the public supports the extension of registration laws to juvenile sex offenders? Is public support for juvenile registration laws sensitive to developmental or case factors? Surprisingly, research has not yet explored public perceptions of registration laws for juveniles. Next, we describe some findings from our program of research on public perceptions of juvenile sex offender registration. To our knowledge, ours is the first research to address this issue directly. In our first study, we examined general attitudes toward registration laws for juveniles versus adults, and whether these attitudes differ between laypeople and legal professionals. In our second study, we examined whether support for registration laws and estimates of recidivism are influenced by juvenile and case characteristics.

Study 1: General Support for Adult versus Juvenile Sex Offender Registration

Our first research question was whether public support for registration laws would differ as a function of whether the offender was an adult or juvenile. We predicted that participants would support registration laws more for adult sex offenders than for juvenile sex offenders. We were also interested in examining potential differences between laypeople and legal professionals, so we compared samples of undergraduate students, family law attorneys, and prosecuting attorneys. We expected that prosecutors would support harsher registration laws than would family law attorneys, who are more likely to have had experience working with juvenile sex offenders in an advocacy role. Because we expected undergraduates to have less crystallized opinions about these laws and the punishment of offenders generally, we predicted that they would fall in the middle of the two polarized attorney groups in terms of registration support.

Our participants were undergraduates at the University of Illinois at Chicago (UIC), a large, ethnically diverse urban university ($N = 150$, 66% women), family law attorneys ($N = 57$, 39% women), and prosecuting attorneys ($N = 82$, 45% women). Participants received one of two versions of a survey assessing attitudes about registration laws: Half of the surveys asked about the laws with regard to adult sex offenders and the other half asked about the law with regard to juvenile sex offenders (i.e., aged 16 years or younger). Participants indicated their support for sex offender registration on a 3-point measure: 1 (*[Adult/juvenile] sex offenders should never be required to register at all with law enforcement in their communities*), 2 (*[Adult/juvenile] sex offenders should be required to register, but their information should never be posted on the Internet*), or 3 (*[Adult/juvenile] sex offenders should be required to register and their information should be publicly posted on the Internet beginning at the time they are convicted*). We treated this variable as a continuous scale of registry support with higher numbers denoting support for harsher registration laws. Participants also answered the question, "In your opinion, what percentage of all [juvenile/adult] sex offenders eventually commit another sex offense?" Participants responded on an 11-point scale ranging from 0% to 100%, in intervals of 10%.

A 2 (offender age: juvenile, adult) × 3 (sample: undergraduates, family law attorneys, prosecutors) between-subject analysis of variance (ANOVA) on our measure of registry support showed that, as predicted, participants supported harsher registration laws for adult sex offenders than for juvenile sex offenders, $F(1, 238) =$ 10.59, $p < .05$. In addition, support for registration laws differed as a function of sample, $F(2, 238) = 20.22$, $p < .05$. As predicted, family law attorneys supported significantly less harsh registration laws than did undergraduates or prosecutors, all simple effects: $F \geq 26.68$, $p < .05$. Undergraduates' and prosecutors' support for registration laws did not significantly differ, $F(1, 238) = 2.85$, *ns*. A significant interaction between offender age and sample, with $F(2, 238) = 6.68$, $p < .05$, however, revealed that offender age affected only family law attorneys. That is, only family law attorneys supported more lenient laws for juveniles than for adults, with $F(1, 238) = 17.44$, $p < .05$, but this effect was not significant for undergraduates or prosecutors, with $F(1, 238) \leq 1.10$, *ns*, as shown in Figure 9.1.

A similar ANOVA revealed that estimations of recidivism rates

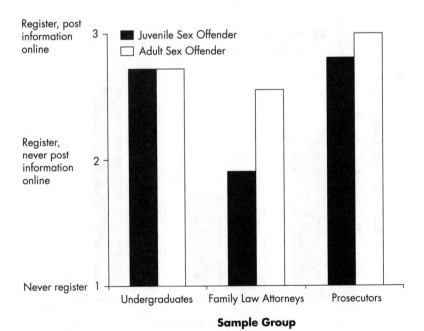

FIGURE 9.1 Mean support for registration laws as a function of offender age and sample group for Study 1.

were, overall, lower for juvenile sex offenders than for adult sex offenders, $F(1, 233) = 6.75$, $p < .05$. Of course, estimations for both groups are overestimations compared to actual recidivism rates. Also, estimates of recidivism differed as a function of sample, $F(2, 233) = 21.02$, $p < .05$. Prosecutors estimated that sex offenders recidivate at higher rates than did undergraduates, who in turn estimated that sex offenders recidivate at higher rates than did family law attorneys, all Fs $(1, 238) \geq 14.46$, $p < .05$. As with support for registration laws, a marginally significant interaction between offender age and sample, $F(2, 233) = 2.88$, $p = .06$, indicated that only family law attorneys estimated that adult sex offenders recidivate at higher rates than juvenile sex offenders, $F(1, 233) = 11.13$, $p < .05$, as shown in Figure 9.2.

Thus, we found that only family law attorneys (who might be more likely to act as advocates for juvenile sex offenders) make age-related adjustments in their beliefs about sex offenders and their attitudes towards registration laws, supporting significantly more lenient sex offender registration laws for juveniles compared to adults, and correctly judging that juvenile sex offenders recidivate at significantly lower rates than do adults. Finally, it is worth noting that our finding that undergraduates, family law attorneys,

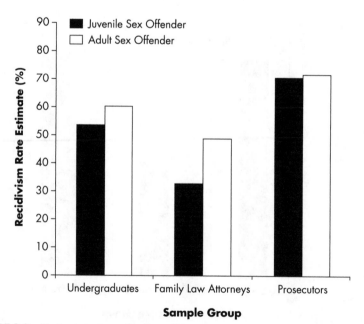

FIGURE 9.2 Estimates of sex offender recidivism rates as a function of offender age and sample group for Study 1.

and prosecutors all overestimated actual recidivism rates for adult offenders is consistent with prior research (Levenson et al., 2007a), and the finding that they also overestimate recidivism rates for juvenile sex offenders is novel.

Study 2: Case-Specific Support for Juvenile Sex Offender Registration

In a second study, we explored our suspicion that undergraduates' and prosecutors' judgments were not influenced by offender age because our survey asked them about their attitudes toward sex offenders *in the abstract*. Family law attorneys, who presumably have more experience advocating for juvenile offenders, might have been thinking of more typical juvenile sex offenders who commit less serious offenses, recidivate at low rates, and are amenable to treatment. In contrast, prosecutors and undergraduates might have been thinking of the prototypical sex offender (e.g., repeat rapist) when making their judgments. This is an interesting possibility, in light of the fact that many states' mandatory registration laws require juveniles to register, regardless of the severity of the offense, and their online registries do not differentiate between offenders who committed less versus more severe offenses. Is public support for registration laws moderated by offense severity? In our second study, we presented participants with different types of cases and examined their support for registration as a function of offense severity and, again, the age of the juvenile.

Participants were 384 UIC undergraduates (55% women) who each read one brief vignette describing a juvenile as either 12 years old or 16 years old and as having committed either rape (raped a girl in a park) or one of the following less severe offenses, descriptions of which were based on real cases: (1) child pornography (was caught looking at naked pictures of his underage girlfriend; Stockinger, 2009); (2) harassment (ran through school hallways slapping girls' buttocks; Goldsmith, 2007); or (3) statutory rape (participated in mutually desired sexual activity with an underage girl; *Wilson* v. *State of Georgia*, 2006). Participants then indicated their level of registry support for the juvenile and estimated the likelihood that the juvenile would recidivate. These measures were similar to those used in Study 1, but asked about the specific juvenile in the case (i.e., David), not sex offenders in general. Also, because we were not asking about support for adult offenders in this study, our item assessing registry support was altered to include an additional option that is sometimes available for juvenile offenders. Thus, participants in Study 2 indicated their support for registration on a 4-point scale: 1 (*David should not be required to register at all with law enforcement in his community*), 2 (*David should be required to register, but his information should never be posted on the Internet*), 3 (*David should be required to register, but his information should not be posted on the Internet until he turns 18, at which time his information should be publicly posted on the Internet*), or 4 (*David should be required to register and his information should be publicly posted on the Internet immediately*).

A 2 (juvenile offender age: 12 years old, 16 years old) × 4 (offense severity: child pornography, harassment, statutory rape, rape) between-subjects ANOVA on registry support revealed that participants supported significantly more lenient registry laws for a 12-year-old than a 16-year-old juvenile sex offender: $F(1, 376) = 14.05, p < .05$ (see Figure 9.3). In addition, registry support differed as a function of case severity, $F(3, 376) = 47.16, p < .05$. Specifically, planned comparisons revealed that participants who read about the rape case supported significantly harsher laws than did those who read about either the statutory rape case or the harassment case, who did not differ from each other but who both supported harsher laws than did participants who read the pornography case, all $Fs ≥ 9.85, p < .05$. The case severity by offender age interaction was not significant, $F(3, 366) = 1.64, ns$.

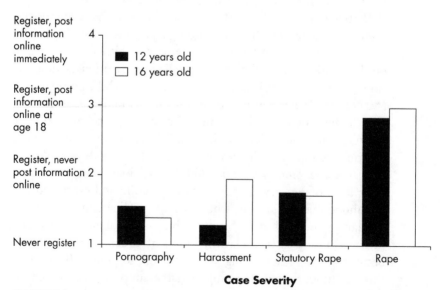

FIGURE 9.3 Mean support for registry as a function of offender age and case severity for Study 2.

A similar ANOVA on participants' estimates of recidivism likelihood (see Figure 9.4) revealed no significant differences in estimates for a younger juvenile and an older juvenile, $F(1, 366) = 2.81, p = .09$. Recidivism estimates differed significantly as a function of offense severity, $F(3, 366) = 23.10, p < .05$. The pattern of this effect is the same as the pattern described above. Specifically, planned comparisons revealed that participants who read about the rape case estimated greater recidivism than did participants who read about the statutory rape case or the harassment case, who both estimated greater recidivism rates than did participants who read about the pornography case, all $Fs \geq 8.45$, $p < .05$. The case severity by offender age interaction was not significant: $F(3, 366) = 0.98, ns$.

The results of our second study provided some indirect support for our speculation that the public would be less likely to support registration laws for juvenile sex offenders when given specific cases to consider as compared to when thinking of juveniles in the abstract. We found that participants were significantly less likely to recommend registration for a juvenile who committed child pornography rather than the other three more serious offenses. The harassment and mutually desired sexual activity cases did not differ from each other, and both elicited support for more lenient

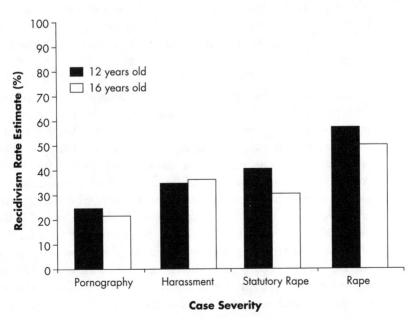

FIGURE 9.4 Estimates of sex offender recidivism rates as a function of offender age and case severity for Study 2.

registration laws compared to the rape case. The rape case was the only offense for which the majority of participants supported registration (in fact 100% supported the registry in this condition), whereas the participants who supported registration in the less severe case conditions were in the minority (pornography = 22%, harassment = 42%, statutory rape = 44%). Even for a rape case, the majority (65%) did not support posting the juvenile's information online immediately (25% thought the juvenile's information should never be posted online, 20% thought it should not be posted online until the juvenile turned 18).

It is interesting to compare the percentage of people who were opposed to registration laws when asked about them abstractly in Study 1 (3% thought juvenile sex offenders in general should "never register") to the percentage of participants who were opposed to registration laws when asked about a rape case in Study 2 (0% thought such an offender should "never register") and to the percentage of participants who were opposed to registration laws for the less severe cases in Study 2 (67% thought perpetrators of those crimes should "never register"). Thus, when asked *in the abstract* about their support for juvenile sex offender registration, it seems that members of the public are probably envisioning the most extreme cases of sex offenders on the registry (i.e., rapists) and not the many other lesser offenses for which juveniles are sometimes registered. These findings suggest that application of registration laws to juveniles without consideration of age or offense severity does not align with public sentiment.

It was also interesting that participants did not view the case of mutually desired sexual activity between teenagers as an offense for which a juvenile should be registered. In fact, they were no more likely to support registration for that than for a juvenile who ran down the hall slapping girls' buttocks. Yet, many juveniles are currently on the registry for having engaged in what some consider to be "consensual" sex. Our depiction of this offense was based on the actual case of Genarlow Wilson, who engaged in non-forced oral sex with a 15-year-old girl when he was 17 years old (*Wilson* v. *State of Georgia*, 2006). In an attempt to avoid sex offender registration, he refused a plea bargain for only 1 year in jail and chose to contest the offense in adult court, where he was subsequently convicted of aggravated sexual molestation and sentenced to 10 years in prison. He was recently released after serving 2 years. Thus, registering juveniles for some instances of mutually desired sexual acts with a similarly aged peer is not only contrary to public sentiment, but fear of registration might influence juveniles' legal decisions (e.g., decisions about plea bargains) in adverse ways. Of course, it is a difficult and controversial task to define consensual sex among youths, one that involves consideration of social mores as well as psychological evidence (Ondersma, Chaffin, Berliner, Cordon, Goodman, & Barnett, 2001), and we are not suggesting that young adolescents can make such decisions, especially with older-aged partners.

Conclusions and Policy Recommendations

The sex offender registry was created in the United States with the best of intentions – to protect children from dangerous sexual predators. This, of course, is a commendable goal, one to which this entire book is dedicated. Unfortunately, there is little scientific evidence that sex offender registration actually protects children by decreasing sex offenders' recidivism rates (Adkins et al., 2000; Letourneau & Armstrong, 2008; Sandler et al., 2008; Schram & Milloy, 1995). Even so, recent policy changes have extended registration requirements to juvenile sex offenders. The application of the registry to juveniles is particularly questionable given that: (1) juvenile sex offenders can be rehabilitated; (2) juvenile sex offenders recidivate at low base rates, especially as compared to adult sex offenders; and (3) registration has negative consequences that might inadvertently increase recidivism rates. The movement to include juveniles on the registry might be due in part to politicians' and policy-makers' perceptions of public support for such policies. Our research, however, demonstrates that perceived public support for these laws might only be an artifact of the way questions have been framed. Our research suggests that the public supports juvenile sex offender registration *in the abstract*, but support wanes when considering registration for a specific juvenile accused of a specific, less severe offense (i.e., not rape).

Whether sex offender registration laws should be challenged is not a popular question to ask. It is, however, an important one. To advocate a re-examination of policies that require juveniles to register as sex offenders might at first seem contrary to the goal of protecting children. But we recommend that more research be conducted on the issue and that current policies be revisited, for several reasons. First, these laws might have iatrogenic effects that may unintentionally increase recidivism, ultimately resulting in *more* rather than less child sexual abuse. Second, these laws could instill a sense of false security in parents. The vast majority of child sexual abuse perpetrators are not strangers, but instead are known to their victims (Lieb, Quinsey, & Berliner, 1998). Thus, parents may falsely believe that the registry protects their children from sex crimes, when in reality the registry does not protect children from those most likely to abuse them. Finally, one could question whether requiring juveniles to register for offenses that are arguably acts of immature, but not dangerous, adolescent sexual experimentation constitutes child abuse in and of itself. This concern is highlighted in tragic cases in which juveniles have committed suicide after being put on the registry for arguably harmless crimes (e.g., a boy exposing himself to a group of girls on their way to gym class, *No easy answers*, 2007). Few would suggest that juveniles who commit sexual crimes should not be identified and treated, in line with the goal of rehabilitation. But labeling juveniles as sex offenders stigmatizes them in ways that might lead to feelings of deviance and alienation. Ultimately, sex offender registration could be a self-fulfilling prophecy.

Protecting children means protecting them from sexual abuse, but we believe it also means protecting juveniles from unnecessarily being placed on a public registry for behavior that the public perceives as not necessitating registration. Mandatory across-the-board application of sex offender laws to low risk juvenile sex offenders might do more harm than good. We hope to inform politicians and policy-makers of the research we have presented in this chapter, so they can understand that their constituents might not be as supportive of mandatory or universal application of registration laws to juveniles as they might assume.

Acknowledgments

We thank Pamela S. Pimentel and Roberto A. Vaca, Jr. for their invaluable research assistance and Nicole Pittman and Peter Parry for their consultation regarding legal issues.

References

Adkins, G., Huff, D., & Stageberg, P. (2000). *The Iowa sex offender registry and recidivism*. Des Moines: Iowa Department of Human Rights.

A. H. v. *Florida* (2007). 949 So. 2d 234 (Fla. 1st Dist. 2007).

Almond, L., Canter, D., & Salfati, C. (2006). Youths who sexually harm: A multivariate model of characteristics. *Journal of Sexual Aggression, 12*, 97–114.

Becker, J. V., Kaplan, M. S., & Tenke, C. E. (1992). The relationship of abuse history, denial and erectile response profiles of adolescent sexual perpetrators. *Behavior Therapy, 23*, 87–97.

Brenton, S. (2008, May 28). *Fallon Campaign: Sex offender law makes children less safe – Fallon was right!* [Press release]. Retrieved March 9, 2009 from www.iowapolitics.com.

Caldwell, M. F. (2002). What we do not know about juvenile sexual reoffense risk. *Child Maltreatment, 7*, 291–302.

Caldwell, M. F. (2007). Sexual offense adjudication and sexual recidivism among juvenile offenders. *Sex Abuse, 19*, 107–113.

Caldwell, M. F., Ziemke, M. H., & Vitacco, M. J. (2008). An examination of the sex offender registration and notification act as applied to juveniles: Evaluating the ability to predict sexual recidivism. *Psychology, Public Policy, and Law, 89*, 89–114.

Caputo, A. A., & Brodsky, S. L. (2004). Citizen coping with community notification of released sex offenders. *Behavioral Sciences and the Law, 22*, 239–252.

Carpentier, M., Silovsky, J. F., & Chaffin, M. (2006). Randomized trial of treatment for children with sexual behavior problems: Ten-year follow-up. *Journal of Consulting and Clinical Psychology, 74*, 482–488.

Chaffin, M. (2008). Our minds are made up – Don't confuse us with the facts: Commentary on policies concerning children with sexual behavior problems and juvenile sex offenders. *Child Maltreatment, 13*, 110–121.

Goldsmith, S. (2007, July 22). Unruly schoolboys or sex offenders. *The Oregonian*, p. A01.

Hunter, J. A., Figueredo, A. J., Malamuth, N. M., & Becker, J. V. (2003). Juvenile sex offenders: Toward the development of a typology. *Sexual Abuse: A Journal of Research and Treatment, 15*, 27–48.

Jacob Wetterling Crimes Against Children and Sexually Violent Offender Registration Program, 42 U.S.C. § 14071 (1994).

Lambie, I., & Seymour, F. (2006). One size does not fit all: Future directions for the treatment of sexually abusive youth in New Zealand. *Journal of Sexual Aggression, 12*, 175–187.

Letourneau, E. J. (2008). Legal consequences of juvenile sex offending in the United States. In H. E. Barbaree & W. L. Marshall (Eds.), *The juvenile sex offender* (pp. 275–290). New York: Guilford Press.

Letourneau, E. J., & Armstrong, K. S. (2008). Recidivism rates for registered and nonregistered juvenile sexual offenders. *Sexual Abuse: Journal of Research and Treatment, 20*, 393–408.

Letourneau, E. J., & Miner, M. (2005). Juvenile sex offenders: A case against the legal and clinical status quo. *Sexual Abuse: Journal of Research and Treatment, 17*, 293–312.

Levenson, J., Brannon, Y., Fortney, T., & Baker, J. (2007a). Public perceptions about sex offenders and community protection policies. *Analyses of Social Issues and Public Policy, 7,* 1–25.

Levenson, J., & Cotter, L. (2005). The effect of Megan's law on sex offender reintegration. *Journal of Contemporary Criminal Justice, 21,* 49–66.

Levenson, J., D'Amora, D., & Hern, A. (2007b). Megan's Law and its impact on community re-entry for sex offenders. *Behavioral Sciences and the Law, 25,* 587–602.

Lieb, R., Quinsey, V., & Berliner, L. (1998). Sexual predators and social policy. *Crime and Justice, 23,* 43–114.

Malesky, A., & Keim, J. (2001). Mental health professionals' perspectives on sex offender registry web sites. *Sexual Abuse: Journal of Research and Treatment, 13,* 53–63.

Moffitt, T. E. (1993). Adolescence-limited and life-course-persistent antisocial behavior: A developmental taxonomy. *Psychological Review, 100,* 674–701.

No easy answers (2007). Sex offender laws in the US. *Human Rights Watch, 19.* Retrieved January 7, 2008, from http://www.hrw.org/en/reports/2007/09/11/no-easy-answers.

Ondersma, S. J., Chaffin, M., Berliner, L., Cordon, I., Goodman, G. S., & Barnett, D. (2001). Sex with children is abuse: Comment on Rind, Tromovitch, & Bauserman (1998). *Psychological Bulletin, 127,* 707–714.

Phillips, D. (1998). *Community notification as viewed by Washington's citizens.* Olympia, WA: Washington State Institute for Public Policy.

Sampson, R. J., & Laub, J. H. (2005). A life-course view of the development of crime. *Annals of the American Academy of Political and Social Science, 602,* 12–45.

Sandler, J. C., Freeman, N. J., & Socia, K. M. (2008). Does a watched pot boil? A time-series analysis of New York State's sex offender registration and notification law. *Psychology, Public Policy, and Law, 14,* 284–302.

Schram, D. D., & Milloy, C. D. (1995). *Community notification: A study of offender characteristics and recidivism.* Olympia, WA: Washington State Institute for Public Policy.

Sex Offender Registration and Notification Act (SORNA), 42 U.S.C. § 16911 (2006).

St. Amand, A., Bard, D. B., & Silovsky, J. F. (2008). Meta-analysis of treatment for child sexual behavior problems: Practice elements and outcomes. *Child Maltreatment, 13,* 145–166.

Stockinger, J. (2009, March 26). Nude photos at St. Charles East lead to arrest. *Daily Herald.* Retrieved March 31, 2009, from http://www.dailyherald.com/story/?id=281904&src=5

Tewksbury, R. (2005). Collateral consequences of sex offender registration. *Journal of Contemporary Criminal Justice, 21,* 67–81.

Tewksbury, R., & Lees, M. (2006). Perceptions of sex offender registration: Collateral consequences and community experiences. *Sociological Spectrum, 26,* 309–334.

Trivits, L., & Reppucci, N. (2002). Application of Megan's Law to juveniles. *American Psychologist, 57,* 690–704.

U.S. Department of Justice (2007). *Crime in the United States, 2007* (Federal Bureau of Investigation, Criminal Justice Information Services Division). Retrieved March 9, 2009, from http://www.fbi.gov/ucr/cius2007/index.html

Violent Crime Control and Law Enforcement Act, 42 U.S.C. § 13701 (1994).

Wilson v. State of Georgia (2006). 279 Ga. App. 459.

Zimring, F. E., Piquero, A. R., & Jennings, W. G. (2007). Sexual delinquency in Racine: Does early sex offending predict later sex offending in youth and young adulthood? *Criminology and Public Policy, 6,* 507–534.

CHAPTER 10

Mediating Factors in the Long-Term Outcome Following Childhood Abuse

Cognitive and Other Factors Predicting Personal Distress, Intimacy Functioning, and Resilience

Patricia A. Petretic and Elizabeth White Chaisson

Case Illustrations

As a child Anna lived with her divorced mother and two younger sisters in a small apartment. There was no contact with her father. One sister was severely developmentally disabled, and her mother was unemployed since she cared for the younger sister, who required full-time home care. Anna was regularly beaten by her mother, but confided in no one. The beatings increased in severity over time, but her mother hit her on her torso so that no bruising was apparent to others. By the time she was an adolescent, Anna's father, whom she described as "the only good adult person I knew while I was growing up" came back into her life and she moved out of her mother's house to live with him during her junior high and high school years. Her father, much to Anna's amazement, remarried her mother when Anna was 17. Subsequently, both Anna and her father were beaten severely by her mother. When Anna was 19 and going to nursing school, her father gave her money that allowed her to move away. Anna stated that she believed that her mother would surely kill her if she remained in her parents' home. Using "escape" money given to her by her father, Anna bought an airline ticket to Germany. She reported not being sure why she chose to go there except that it was as far away from her mother she could get geographically with the money her father had given her. Struggling with self-esteem issues, she married soon after and had a daughter. While the marriage was not problematic by her report, she subsequently divorced her husband. She stated that she was not sure why she married him in the first place since they did not have much in common, but attributed it to "feeling lost at the time." After raising her daughter as a single mother for several years she met the man who was to become her second husband. She credits him for a major shift in her life. She stated that he had "faith in her as person" and strongly encouraged her to start her own business after working for others for several years. He was also a good father to her daughter. Happily married for 25 years, at age 59 she now owns her own highly successful business. She speaks with and visits with her daughter and her family on a regular basis, and she and her husband travel frequently with their two grandsons. She stated that she believes that her greatest accomplishment in life has been that she has broken the cycle of abuse in her family.

Bill, a highly successful and charismatic businessman, was the older of two children in a middle class family and was raised in the suburbs of a large Eastern metropolitan area. He entered therapy with the first author when he was in his late 40s, reporting a history of chronic depression and relationship difficulties, including two divorces and a string of troubled intimate relationships. He was seeking treatment following his frustration with his lack of "a satisfying life." He reported prior treatment with three therapists over a period of nearly 10 years, primarily to address his chronic depression. Bill's father was a successful salesman and his mother was a homemaker. While on the surface the family appeared functional, Bill's father was emotionally abusive and his mother experienced both severe anxiety and depression, which she self-medicated with alcohol. She admitted to him in his adulthood that following his birth she was too afraid to pick him up and it was necessary to have a relative care for him. She also responded to his crying by slamming his baby carriage against a wall to make him stop. When Bill was 5 years old, several older boys coerced him into sexual activity on several occasions, and several years later a teenage female babysitter routinely engaged him in sexual activities with her during the times she babysat for him and his younger sister. Despite his success in both school and the business world, Bill reported that he was unhappy in both his professional and personal life. He stated that he felt a need to be liked by everyone, and this explained why he could not refuse any woman's request to sleep with her despite the fact that sex had always been unsatisfying for him. Former friends and partners often expressed surprise that, with no warning, he seemed to become detached and disinterested, after appearing to have close relationships with them. He also admitted to a number of other problems, including periods of severely disordered eating, impaired sleep, reckless behaviors (e.g., excessive spending, polysubstance abuse, unprotected sex), hoarding behavior, debilitating anxiety, and chronic suicidal ideation. He said he was constantly "searching for something or someone who could make him happy," but with every new acquisition and/or relationship his initial pleasure was soon followed by disappointment and a renewed quest for whatever would make him happy. He stated that if he were asked to describe himself, he imagined himself as "nothing more than red, angry, beady eyes staring out of blackness under a log."

Overview of the Issues

As clinical psychologists and researchers, the authors have worked with many individuals over the years who have experienced abuse or maltreatment as children. However, Anna has not been one of our clients or research participants. Rather, she was the very first "best friend" of the first author during her childhood and recently "reconnected" with me following the untimely death of a classmate. We had not spoken or been in contact for more than 40 years. As a child I was at Anna's house often before she moved but I had no knowledge of her abuse. Her mother never hit her when I was in their home. No one at school addressed her home situation, but this was long before mandatory reporting statutes for child abuse were instituted. As we began to renew our friendship via e-mail and I told her of my professional interest and work in family violence, she disclosed her story to me. The positive long-term outcome for Anna illustrates the resilience that is demonstrated by many individuals who experience child abuse. By contrast, Bill's life trajectory following his childhood abuses had a different path. Even with professional intervention, a variety of personal and interpersonal problems were difficult to overcome.

Many individuals who interacted with Bill in his professional and personal life would say that "he had everything," and would, no doubt, have been surprised had they known of the scope and severity of his distress.

The lesson to be learned? We all likely know one or several individuals who have a history of child abuse, but we may not "know about" the abuse or its long-term consequences. Family violence often remains a "secret" to those outside the family, despite the fact that statistics indicate that child abuse is an all too common problem (U.S. Department of Health and Human Services, 2008). The reason we chose these two personal histories to introduce this chapter was to illustrate that our ideas about child abuse, most often formed by media reports, may or may not reflect the reality of abuse outcome for an individual child. Long-term outcome is affected by many variables, leading to vastly different outcomes. But first, what do we know about child abuse and, more specifically, its outcome?

A Brief History of Child Abuse Outcome Research

Historically, child abuse research began with the work of Kempe and his colleagues (Kempe, Silverman, Steele, Droegemueller, & Silver, 1962), who published a seminal article on child physical abuse (e.g., the battered child) almost 50 years ago. Subsequent to this initial focus on child physical abuse, increased attention to the issue of child abuse by researchers and the general public was evident in the 1970s. Similar attention to other forms of family and interpersonal violence, such as domestic violence, rape, and sexual assault, was occurring during this period.

In the 1970s the focus of the child abuse literature shifted to the problem of child sexual abuse (Finkelhor & Hotaling, 1984), which has been the most extensively investigated of all forms of child maltreatment. Early outcome studies examined characteristics of the abuse experience to determine the cause of differential outcome. Researchers concluded that child sexual abuse resulted in harm, and that this harm was pervasive and long-lasting. While these conclusions were not initially questioned, these findings came under increased scrutiny in the 1980s and 1990s, with the findings of negative outcome being called into question. Some researchers challenged the causal link between child abuse and negative outcome, and posited that the negative outcomes obtained in the early outcome studies were an effect of other co-occurring variables, such as a negative home environment (Bauserman & Rind, 1997; Beitchman, Zucher, Hood, DaCosta, Akman, & Cassavia, 1992; Rind & Tromovitch, 1997; Rind, Tromovitch & Bauserman, 1998). At the same time others (Briere & Runtz, 1990; Glod, 1993) concluded that a causal relationship could be inferred between child sexual abuse and negative outcome. This debate in the literature has become quite contentious and continues to this day, with disagreement now focusing on the interpretation of the statistical analyses used in meta-analytic reviews of outcome studies (Hyde, 2007; Tromovitch & Rind, 2007; Ulrich, Randolph, & Acheson, 2005–2006).

The most recent type of abuse to be studied is emotional maltreatment, which includes both emotional abuse and emotional neglect (Egeland, 2009). However, a number of issues have made the study of this type of child abuse problematic, with the result that it is the type least investigated (O'Dougherty-Wright, Crawford, & Del Castillo, 2009). This is true despite it being posited to be the most pervasive form of child abuse, as well as a "core issue" that is inherent in all forms of abuse (Hart & Brassard, 1987).

Another recent focus has been the investigation of the impact of multiple abuse experiences, termed "poly-victimization" (Finkelhor, Ormrod, & Turner, 2007). Individuals reporting poly-victimization appear to have greater severity of distress than those reporting one form of childhood abuse (Mullen, Martin, Anderson, Romans, & Herbison, 1996). Childhood abuse also appears to put at least some childhood victims at risk for subsequent victimization in adulthood. Women sexually abused in childhood are two to four times more likely to be revictimized as adults when compared to women who were not abused (Fergusson, Horwood, & Lynskey, 1997; Marx, Heidr, & Gold, 2005) and six times more likely to have probable posttraumatic stress disorder (PTSD; Schumm, Briggs-Phillips, & Hobfoll, 2006).

Because the literature on long-term outcome of child abuse is so vast and, as such, a comprehensive review is beyond the scope of this chapter, only a brief summary of symptomatic outcome for each type of child abuse will be provided here. The reader is referred to the following articles, which provide comprehensive literature reviews of the long-term consequences for each of the major types of child abuse: Springer, Sheridan, Kuo, and Carnes (2007) for physical abuse; O'Dougherty-Wright et al. (2009) and Egeland (2009) for psychological maltreatment;

and Jumper (1995), Neumann, Houskamp, Pollock, and Briere (1996), Paolucci, Genuis, and Violato (2001), and Ulrich et al. (2005–2006) for sexual abuse.

Within the victimology literature, symptoms that may occur following interpersonal trauma are often grouped into several categories or domains: emotional, behavioral, cognitive, and interpersonal. Symptomatic distress may be severe enough to meet the criteria for diagnosable psychiatric disorders, most commonly depression or PTSD, but not all victims of child abuse report symptoms of such severity. Briere (1995), in reviewing the trauma literature, notes that symptoms associated with childhood interpersonal victimization include a wide range of potential adverse sequelae. In addition to symptoms commonly associated with PTSD (the cluster of intrusive and avoidant symptoms, such as flashbacks, nightmares, psychic numbing, and autonomic hyperarousal), Briere identified anger, depression, dissociation, sexual problems, interpersonal difficulties, disturbance in self-functions, and "acting out" behavior, such as self-mutilation and compulsive or dysfunctional sexual activity. Briere and Runtz (1990) suggest that there are abuse-specific outcomes, with physical abuse resulting more often in aggression toward others, emotional abuse resulting in low self-esteem, and sexual abuse resulting in maladaptive sexual behavior. Other research suggests a common cluster of overlapping patterns of symptomatic distress across different types of abuse (Mullen et al., 1996).

In reviewing the literature the following outcomes appear to be commonly associated with each of the three major types of abuse. Negative outcome reported to be associated with child sexual abuse include the psychiatric disorders of PTSD, major depression, generalized anxiety disorder (GAD), alcohol dependence, drug dependence, panic disorder, and bulimia nervosa (Kendler, Bulik, Silberg, Hettema, Mylers, & Prescott, 2000), along with symptoms of borderline personality disorder, inappropriate sexual behavior, sexual dysfunction, intimacy and relationship dysfunction, occupational dysfunction, and increased risk of a variety of health problems as well as subsequent sexual revictimization. Negative outcomes associated with physical abuse include depression, anxiety, increased risk of medical diagnoses, increased risk of physical revictimization, and anger (Springer et al., 2007). Negative outcomes associated with emotional abuse include high rates of dissociative, anxious, and depressive symptomatology (O'Doughtery-Wright et al., 2009), elevated PTSD symptomatology, and dating violence (Wekerle, Wolfe, Hawkins, Glickman, & Lovald, 2001).

Egeland made the following statement in reference to emotional abuse, but it clearly has applicability to investigating the impact of any form of child abuse:

> determining the impact of . . . abuse and differentiating the effects of . . . maltreatment from the many other factors that influence a child's development – including other forms of maltreatment, which are likely to co-occur with . . . maltreatment – is challenging. . . . Each ecological level of the caregiving environment in a maltreating context contains many risk factors . . . such risk factors are not useless statistical "noise," but rather important features of the family's ecology that must be considered in developing prevention and intervention programs for maltreating families. (Egeland, 2009, p. 25)

Scope of the Problem: Rates of Abuse

Child abuse is not uncommon, as was once thought. During 2006, an estimated 905,000 children were determined to be victims of abuse or neglect (U.S. Department of Health and Human Services, 2008) based on confirmed cases of victimization by CPS agencies. The DHHS statistics suggest that children aged up to 1 year had the highest rate of victimization at 24.4 per 1000 children of the same age group in the national population. The DHHS report, *Child Abuse: 2006*, further states that boys and girls are abused at similar rates, with 51.5% girls and 48.2% boys. Approximately half of all reported cases involved Caucasians (48.8%) while 22.8% were African-American and 18.4% were Hispanic. Neglect cases (61.4%) were most often reported and substantiated, followed by physical abuse (16%), sexual abuse (8.8%), and emotional abuse/maltreatment (6.6%). However, experts generally agree, based on retrospective studies, that the actual number of abuse cases is much higher than estimated by cases reported to DHHS agencies, suggesting that the number of reported cases vastly underestimates the true incidence of child abuse. Adult retrospective reports of childhood abuse vary as a function of the type of sample studied, with higher rates reported in clinical as compared to college or community samples for all forms of abuse, and criteria for inclusion in abuse groups across studies. The reader is referred to a well written and highly readable review of the issues relevant to abuse statistics (Hopper, 2009).

Variability in the long-term outcome of adults reporting histories of child maltreatment/abuse has been well-documented in the research literature. This variability has led researchers to investigate a variety of variables believed to mediate or moderate the relation between maltreatment and subsequent adult psychiatric symptomatic distress that may or may not meet the criteria for psychiatric diagnosis (e.g., PTSD, depression, anxiety). As mentioned above, more recently, researchers have begun to document that early interpersonal trauma may play a role in a variety of problems in addition to psychiatric symptoms and disorders, including revictimization, interpersonal dysfunction, and adult physical health concerns (Springer, Sheridan, Kuo, & Carnes, 2003). While many pre-abuse and abuse event experiences (e.g., family functioning, other environmental stressors or adversity, type of abuse) may affect subsequent long-term functioning, in our research group we have focused our efforts on identifying post-abuse variables that would influence subsequent psychological functioning in adulthood. Such variables could have applicability for incorporation within translational research that focuses on developing effective treatment programs. Post-abuse variables that have been hypothesized to affect symptomatic outcome include factors such as cognitive distortions, locus of control, coping strategies, perceptions of family of origin, emotional dysregulation, adult attachment styles, revictimization, intimacy functioning, and social support.

Outcome variability has been documented not only among individuals experiencing a particular type of abuse but also across abuse types (Briere & Runtz, 1990). Although researchers sometimes choose to focus on the impact of one form of abuse, others have focused on the impact of multiple forms of abuse along with other contextual variables. In our research group we have further expanded the variable of outcome to include several dimensions beyond individual symptomatic distress, investigating both adaptive functioning (e.g., resilience) and interpersonal functioning (e.g., intimate partner violence and intimacy functioning). In a series of studies over the last decade we have sampled young adults (both men and women) reporting a broad range of childhood abuse experiences (e.g., physical, sexual, and/or psychological maltreatment, and multiple/concurrent forms of abuse) as well as other traumatic or adverse experiences of childhood and adolescence.

Data collected during this period have allowed for empirical evaluation of the role of several mediating variables on posttraumatic outcome and have generated hypotheses concerning the relation of trauma and subsequent adaptive functioning (resilience, positive affect, optimism), symptomatic expression (negative affect, depression, PTSD), and interpersonal/relational functioning (intimacy, relationship satisfaction) as mediated by cognitive variables (distortions, locus of control, family of origin/social support in childhood) related to perceptions of traumatic events, self, and others. In this chapter we are summarizing several studies that attempt to evaluate the predictive ability of specific risk (e.g., perceptions of family of origin health/functioning, cognitive distortions, locus of control) and protective (e.g., resilience) factors associated with psychological functioning (e.g., distress) in samples of young adults who retrospectively report experiences with different forms of child abuse. A second purpose has been to evaluate the relation between symptomatic distress and adaptive (resilient) functioning and the relation of cognitive and contextual (environmental) factors to resilience.

Risk Factors: The Role of Cognitive Distortions in Predicting Symptomatic Distress

The first study we review from our research lab group examined the relation between cognitive distortions and symptoms of psychological distress (Petretic, White, & Jacobs, 2008). Participants were 762 undergraduate male and female respondents at a southeastern university who were a subset of a larger sample of young adults in which the impact of child abuse on intimacy functioning was being investigated. Group assignment was to single and multiple abuse groups and no abuse control. Due to group sizes, groups of interest in this study were the Emotional Abuse Alone group (CEA; $n = 33$) and the Emotional + Physical Abuse group (CEA + CPA; $n = 159$). Respondents completed one of two specific child abuse incident scales: the Parent-Child Conflict Tactics Scales (CTSPC; Straus, Hamby, Boney-McCoy, & Sugarman, 1996) or the Critical Incident Checklist (CIC; Petretic et al., 2004). Other variables and measures included negative cognitions about self and the world (Cognitive Distortion Scales, CDS; Briere, 2000), adult attachment/relational style (Experiences in Close Relationships, ECR; Brennan, Clark, & Shaver, 1996), perceptions of family health (Family of Origin Scale, FOS; Hovestadt,

Anderson, Piercy, Cochran, & Fine, 1985), and symptomatic distress (Trauma Symptom Inventory, TSI; Briere, 1995).

Symptomatic distress subscale mean scores for both abuse groups were within the average range ($t = 50s$; below clinical cutoff of $t = 65s$), with greater variability in the CEA + CPA group. However, compared with non-abused participants, those reporting physical or emotional abuse had significantly higher symptoms of anxious arousal, depression, dissociation, and tension-reducing behavior. Cognitive distortions (CDS) were considerably more elevated, with subscale means in the clinical range, and with self-criticism and blame scores showing the highest elevations. Compared to non-abused participants, those reporting abuse reported significantly greater levels of helplessness, self-blame, and preoccupation with danger.

For those in the CEA group, while cognitive distortions account for a substantial amount of variance in symptoms, few specific distortions predicted distress uniquely. However, three forms of cognitive distortions predicted negative outcome: (1) *self-blame*, which explained impaired sense of self, concerns about sex/intimate relationships, and use of maladaptive behaviors to cope; (2) *self-critical cognitions*, which predicted PTSD-like symptoms; and (3) *helplessness*, which predicted anger.

With a history of both physical and emotional abuse (CEA + CPA group), negative cognitions about self and the world were substantially greater than with physical abuse alone. Further, it was found that (1) cognitions that view the world as a dangerous place predicted a number of PTSD symptoms; (2) cognitions of hopelessness predicted both interpersonal dysfunction and poor self-esteem and coping; and (3) symptomatic distress involving impaired self-reference (e.g., low self-esteem), anxious arousal, and sexual concerns were predicted by several types of distorted cognitions.

Similarities found when comparing participants endorsing child physical and emotional abuse experiences included the following relations between cognitive distortions and personal distress/psychological symptom clusters: (1) cognitive distortions of *hopelessness* predicted depressive symptoms; (2) distortions of *preoccupation with danger* predicted defensive avoidance; and (3) *self-blame* predicted sexual concerns and impaired self-reference.

Compared to young adults reporting no experiences of child emotional or physical abuse, those in the abuse groups also reported significantly more interpersonal impairment based on scores on adult attachment dimensions, with significantly higher levels of separation anxiety, anger, discomfort with dependence, tough independence, and repellant desire to merge. This suggests that childhood abuse history in this sample was associated with considerable risk for adult intimate relationship dysfunction, which appears to be characterized by ambivalence.

Protective Factors: Resilience

While some victims report considerable psychological distress following trauma in both the short and long term, others report relatively unimpaired functioning. Identification of specific variables that predict adaptive and positive interpersonal functioning (e.g., well-being, resilience) would have significant implications both for theoretical formulations of trauma response and recovery, and for clinical practice. Such knowledge could result in the identification of adaptive strategies that are associated with positive outcome (resilience or positive affect). These adaptive strategies could then be incorporated into treatment plans for symptomatic victims through translational research. For example, cognitive attributions/styles (e.g., low self-blame, high optimism, internal locus of control), which might be associated with minimal symptomatic expression, positive affect, good interpersonal functioning, and general positive self-perceptions, could be integrated into existing treatment research protocols.

Recently there has been growing interest in the variable of post-traumatic resilience among trauma researchers, yet little empirical investigation of resilience and abuse outcome. Additionally, it has been suggested that a primary factor in resilience is "having caring and supportive relationships within and outside the family" (American Psychological Association, 2008) while the relation between perceived family support, resilience, and symptoms of distress in young adults reporting childhood abuse is not well-studied. Our research group has, to date, conducted two studies in which these variables have been examined in samples of young adults.

Definition and History of the Study of the Construct of Resilience

Until recently, the investigation into how individuals maintain positive functioning and show resilience has been a topic on which relatively little research has been done (Foley & McNeil, 2007; Kelley et al., 2007; Palyo & Beck, 2007). Most information on resilience comes from studies on the process or framework of resilience. There has been much work done on the identification of risk and protective factors, and their interaction with environmental and other factors to produce a particular positive or negative outcome. In these studies resilience is defined both in terms of successful adaptation, as well as the process of interpersonal and environmental transaction that produces a successful outcome. Other longitudinal studies of resilience have operationalized the construct as a resulting positive outcome in high risk populations such as a low-income environment, or one that is rife with conflict and external stressors (Kumpfer, 1999). These positive outcomes include adaptive success in future expectation, self-reliance, capacity for healthy interpersonal relations, absence of substance use, lack of delinquent behavior, and absence of psychopathology such as anxiety, depression, and somatization (Rutter, 1987). Resilience has also been conceptualized as the dynamic processes that lead to adaptive outcomes in the face of adversity (Lepore & Revenson, 2006). In general, these definitions all point to the idea of resilience as overall positive functioning in the face of adversity, whether from developmental and environmental stressors or negative life events such as trauma.

The study of resilience and resilience theory has been presented in three waves of inquiry focus, according to Richardson (2002). He identifies the focus of the first wave as "characterized through phenomenological identification of developmental assets and protective factors" (Richardson, 2002). Here, within this first wave, qualities that help people grow through adversity, including self-esteem, internal locus of control (LOC), humor, and outside support systems, were specified as resilience factors. The focus of the second stage was an examination of the process of acquiring identified resilience factors. It was during this phase that resilience was defined as "the process of coping with adversity, change, or opportunity in a manner that results in the identification, fortification, and enrichment of resilient qualities or protective factors" (Richardson, 2002). Researchers viewed resilience as overcoming the homeostatic disruption of a traumatic life event by positively reintegrating, via introspection and recognition of qualities of strength and substance. It was during this phase of study that the idea of "posttraumatic growth" emerged, as many theorists suggested that resilience could result in personal growth, self-understanding, and an increase in the already present resilient qualities. This conceptualization also suggested that resilience could be considered a positive outcome following trauma or other disruptive and distressing life events, and pointed to the presence of psychopathology as a lack of resilience (Richardson, 2002). The third wave of resiliency research, according to Richardson (2002), is focused on the concept of resilience in terms of the inner motivation that drives people to seek wisdom, self-actualization, and harmony with spiritual strength. The main question in this line of inquiry is "where does the energy or motivation to reintegrate resiliently come from?" Findings and conceptualizations from this line of research are being applied in current resilience education and interventions, which work on identifying inner strengths and building an innate moral framework around one's spiritual strength in order to gain introspection and reintegrate resiliently following traumatic life experiences.

Measurement of Resilience

Much of the resilience literature has looked at variables that are associated with effective coping, successful achievement, and lack of psychopathology (Garmezy, 1993; Kumpfer, 1999; Rutter, 1987). There has been a two-pronged approach to the assessment of resilience, with some attempts at developing measures of a specific model of resilience, and many studies that have combined multiple existing measures, each examining a single characteristic thought to contribute to resilience (Wicks, 2006). While several measures have been developed to measure the phenomenon of resilience, none of these have become the standard tool with which to measure resilience. Some of the individual measures of resilience that have been used in the place of multiple single index measures are the Connor-Davidson Resilience Scale (CD-RISC; Connor & Davidson, 2003), the Resilience Scale for Adults (RSA; Ahern, Kiehl, Sole, & Byers, 2006), and the Resilience Scale (RS; Ahern et al., 2006). These measures examine the sums of risk by simultaneously considering multiple individual and environmental factors, an acknowledgment that such risk and protective factors co-occur in the real world. This consideration of multiple-influencing variables contributes to these measures having better validity than a combination of single index measures (Connor & Davidson, 2003).

Recent Findings on the Nature of Resilience

A recent study (White, 2009) examined the relation between individual and environmental factors as they contributed to resilience following a traumatic or adverse life event. Specifically, the study investigated the relationship between locus of control, family of origin functioning, resilience, and trauma symptoms in various trauma group victims to identify "personal qualities that enable one to thrive in the face of adversity" (Connor & Davidson, 2003). Participants were college students from a southeastern university. They completed standardized measures of resilience (CD-RISC), perceptions of family health (FOS), locus of control (LOC) (Rotter, 1966), and symptomatic distress (TSI), as well as a check-list of traumatic and stressful life events (modified from Davidson, 1998).

It was noted that although 97% of the participants reported at least one traumatic event in their lifetime, the sample as a whole was quite resilient as measured by CD-RISC scores. Regression analyses revealed that resilience was a significant predictor of the level of posttraumatic distress reported, but also showed that high levels of resilience did not necessarily predict the absence of symptomatic distress. These results suggest that it may be possible to view oneself as resilient and/or "better," yet continue to experience significant psychological symptoms. However, despite the presence of distress, these individuals appear to consider themselves resilient overall.

Locus of control was a significant predictor of resilience, while family of origin influences were not. Additionally, LOC was a significant predictor for traumatic distress, along with resilience and perceived impact of the traumatic event. Family of origin influences did not predict the level of psychological distress. These findings are significant in that they contradict the widely accepted view that the family of origin strongly influences the psychological health of its offspring, particularly in terms of how a person reacts to and copes with adversity and stress (Hovestadt et al., 1985).

Further analysis of this dataset (Petretic, White, & Jacobs, 2008) identified participants who endorsed experiences of child physical abuse and child sexual abuse (using responses to global questions versus specific incidents of abuse) and compared them to participants who reported general trauma and other normative life stressors or adverse experiences. Those who endorsed childhood abuse experiences indicated that these experiences affected them only slightly more negatively than those in the general sample, both at the time the abuse occurred and at the time of their participation in the study (current impact). However, it was noted that the respondents endorsing childhood abuse were less resilient based on CD-RISC scores. They also reported a higher level of distress compared to those who did not endorse any childhood abuse experiences. Additionally, these participants had a more external LOC and reported more dysfunction in their family of origin. These findings were not unexpected, as child abuse tends to occur within the context of the family.

This analysis also revealed that various dimensions of resilience significantly predicted trauma symptoms. Specifically, a low sense of personal competence and lack of tenacity, two dimensions of resilience, were found to predict higher levels of traumatic symptoms. Also, a lack of high standards, personal and otherwise, was associated with higher levels of distress. Less acceptance of change and fewer secure relationships predicted higher levels of posttraumatic distress. It is important to note that, overall, the participants in this abused sample reported a high level of resilience. However, the results indicate that their exposure to violence in childhood had a negative impact on their level of functioning, as evidenced by their increased report of internalizing and externalizing posttraumatic symptoms.

Using a global measure of resilience, our research group (Petretic, White, Limberg, Jacobs, Addison-Brown, & Makin-Byrd, 2008) evaluated the relation between symptomatic distress and adaptive resilient functioning, and how family functioning might predict both negative (trauma symptoms) and positive (resilient) functioning in a second sample of young adults reporting childhood physical and emotional abuse. Family functioning, resilience, and distress were measured respectively by the FOS (Hovestadt et al., 1985), RS (Wagnild & Young, 1993), and TSI (Briere, 1995). Abuse was measured using CIC, in which abusive events were endorsed compared to global endorsement of child abuse. In this sample 57.1% ($n = 172$) endorsed critical incidents of child physical abuse, while 45.2% ($n = 136$) endorsed critical incidents of child emotional abuse.

Respondents in both abuse groups had significantly lower levels of family of origin (FOS) functioning and elevated levels of trauma (TSI) symptoms, yet no difference in resilience (RS) scores compared to non-abused respondents. In regression analyses, perceptions of family health did not predict resilience for either form of abuse. By contrast, perceptions of family health predicted seven dimensions of symptomatic distress for those reporting physical abuse and three dimensions for those reporting emotional abuse. The relation of resilience and symptomatic distress is complex. For both abuse groups the personal competence dimension of resilience predicted only depression, while the acceptance of self and life dimensions predicted level of anxious arousal, depression, anger–irritability, and impaired self-reference.

Implications: Resilience as the Absence of PTSD?

Resilience makes a significant contribution to how one functions in terms of symptomatic distress following trauma, such that low levels of resilience are likely to contribute to more distress and high levels to less distress. Recent empirical evidence suggests that resilience is not simply the opposite or absence of distress and psychological symptomology, as it has been previously conceptualized (White, 2009). Instead, resilience may have more to do with one's subjective cognitive perception of how they are functioning rather than an objective listing of the presence or absence of psychological symptoms. These findings provide further evidence that resilience is a very complex construct that cannot be explained simply in terms of absence of symptoms or other negative outcomes. It is also possible that these findings may reflect the presence of a recovery curve following negative life events. Perhaps one can be cognitively resilient and still exhibit emotional and behavioral symptomatic distress. It is possible that the presence of distress reflects different stages of recovery, such that individuals perceive themselves as resilient but have not yet achieved a level of reintegrated homeostasis. It is also possible that people are able to acknowledge their experience of symptomatic distress and perceive themselves as resilient despite their level of distress, perhaps because they feel that it could be or had been much worse than it is currently.

Implications: The Cognitive Nature of Resilience

Recent findings suggest that resilience is more related to an individual's cognitive style or interpretation of the events in their lives rather than the negative or positive nature of the events themselves (White, 2009). However, one must question when and how a particular person develops his or her cognitive interpretive style. There is evidence to support multiple sources of cognitive style development, from genetics (Schulman, Keith, & Seligman, 1993) to learning history, both from individual experiences (Gibb, Alloy, Walshaw, Comer, Shen, & Villari, 2006) and social influences from the family (Bruce, Cole, Dallaire, Jacquez, Pineda, & LaGrange, 2006), to the media (Krahe & Moller, 2004). Perhaps it is in the development of a resilient cognitive style that individual and environmental interaction is most important, rather than in the development of resilience itself. Regardless of how and when cognitive styles more amenable to a resilient reaction to life events develop, it is clear from the results of this study that individual cognitive characteristics are crucial to the capacity for resilience following traumatic events. One must interpret the negative events that occur in their environment in a manner that both protects and strengthens the individual to overcome the negative impact on multiple areas of their lives.

It may be more accurate to conceptualize resilience as the ability to minimize or counter the impact of other psychological risk factors (e.g., maladaptive coping style, cognitive distortions, external LOC) rather than the presence of something acting as a buffer from the consequences of a traumatic event. It may be that resilient individuals experience traumatic events differently, such that the events are not as emotionally intense as they are for those who go on to develop posttraumatic psychopathology. On the other hand, it may be that all individuals experience a negative event the same way, but resilient people are able to move past because they are not impaired by other psychological risk factors making inroads for the disorder to develop.

Other evidence pointing to the importance of cognitive interpretation is the strong predictive nature of participants' current subjective impact ratings and their relation to symptomatic distress (White, 2009). It was apparent that those who perceived themselves as doing well (i.e., low impact), in fact displayed significantly less psychological distress than did those who perceived themselves as suffering more from the events of their traumatic experience. This finding may suggest the presence of a negative or positive cognitive bias in participants' self-evaluation of their level of functioning.

Research and Public Perception: Goodness of Fit?

Perceptions among the public often represent stereotypic views of victims of child abuse. They include the following: child abuse itself does not have a negative impact or, alternatively, child abuse leads to significant impairment in all victims; there is a clearly identifiable pattern of responses characteristic of all victims; all victims are female; and all perpetrators are male.

Public perceptions may be shaped by information gleaned from the media, which may present a skewed view. A study by Bornstein,

Kaplan, and Perry (2007), for example, indicated that people have stereotypes about circumstances and consequences of child abuse. Stereotypes are sometimes, though not always, consistent with existing empirical findings.

In contrast to the public perception of stereotypic victim responses, our research supports the finding of considerable variability both within a specific type of abuse as well as across abuse types in terms of symptomatic distress, which is consistent with the findings of other researchers. However, there is some indication of a common pattern of distress across abuse groups. Multiple childhood abuse experiences result in greater levels of distress with a high functioning college sample, and self-blame and self-criticism are more likely cognitive distortions at this age than a sense of hopelessness. Yet, based on an examination of the range of variable scores, not all victims with the same type of abuse experiences have the same symptomatic pattern. Mediating and moderating variables, both individual and contextual, exist. It also appears that some victims may be symptomatic yet perceive themselves as quite resilient, which would be borne out by their ability to function well enough to attend college as opposed to dropping out of school or having psychiatric treatment. At the same time, our research also supports a negative symptomatic impact (e.g., internalizing, externalizing) and elevated negative cognitions in a substantial subset of "high functioning" young adults reporting a past history of exposure to various forms of violence in childhood, despite reports of a reduced impact of this violence over time.

Policy Recommendations

Based on the findings from our laboratory's research program we have a number of suggestions that, if implemented, could mediate, in both the short and long term, the negative impact of violence, minimizing personal and interpersonal distress and promoting resiliency. We believe that although our culture is not focused on primary prevention, the costs, both financial and emotional, of such programs are inherently far less than interventions targeted at victims after abuse has occurred. Thus we would recommend a three-pronged approach for children: primary preventive strategies targeted at all children that teach resilience and self-esteem; secondary prevention efforts aimed at those identified to be at risk based on their childhood circumstances/context, to which we would add coping and interpersonal skills training; and programs designed for those in treatment for abuse.

For victims in treatment it is desirable for mental health professionals to evaluate possible cognitive distortions, particularly those of self-blame and self-criticism. Clinicians should also evaluate the levels of personal distress and the perceptions of attachment styles, which have the possibility of negatively affecting the quality and satisfaction of interpersonal relationships (e.g., repellant desire to merge; tough independence; anger toward partner). Therapists should inform themselves about and incorporate contemporary resiliency interventions. Clients should be encouraged to identify personal and interpersonal sources that foster positive functioning (e.g., personal competence; social support network/ secure relationships). It is also important to assess, and if necessary teach, adaptive self-care skills that provide structure (e.g., conflict resolution, problem solving, positive communication) and nurture (e.g., empathy). Certainly self-care skills can be incorporated within an academic curriculum in schools for all students (primary prevention), as well as with identified high risk (secondary prevention) children and within the therapeutic context.

Perpetration or revictimization may occur following one's victimization if no alternatives to abusive parenting strategies or self-protective strategies are available. Children who have been victimized need to be exposed to healthy role models who foster and exemplify positive skills regarding developmental expectations for children and also positive parenting strategies, such as how to provide both structure and nurturance and how to adaptively deal with negative emotions. For example, a previously badly physically abused and aggressive 4-year-old child in a preschool program, with which the first author was working a number of years ago, attacked and ripped out "a hunk of hair" from a younger child. I put him in "time out" and took a "time out" myself, since I said I also needed a "time out" to calm down. I felt helpless and, yes, angry at myself and the child. Although his 5 minute "time out" was completed, the child refused to go back to class until I told him directly that his "time out" was over. When I felt calm enough to go to him we had a brief talk. His most notable response was the comment that, "You were angry at me, weren't you? But you did not hit me. Does that mean that when I am angry I can do something else rather than hurt someone, like maybe ride my tricycle until I feel OK? Just because I feel bad or angry I do not have to hurt someone else." His aggressive behavior stopped that day. Yes, even very young children have the capacity to learn from their experiences, model adult coping behavior, incorporate positive coping strategies, and regulate their emotional states.

Although our treatment and research focus has been on victims, they are only one part of the equation. To protect children from victimization we need to have a more comprehensive plan that will address the behaviors of perpetrators, a plan that is compassionate and yet will keep children from harm. In addition to treatment for abusive adults, it is advisable to incorporate prevention efforts as well, targeting parents to promote positive parenting and reduce parental stress. Perhaps it would even be most desirable, in order to reduce adult perpetration of abuse of children, to offer services to adolescents and adults prior to the onset of caretaking responsibilities. Child abuse is a community problem that needs a community plan and response.

References

Ahern, N. R., Kiehl, E. M., Sole, M. L., & Byers, J. (2006). A review of instruments measuring resilience. *Issues in Comprehensive Pediatric Nursing, 29*, 103–125.

American Psychological Association (2008). *The road to resilience* [Brochure]. Washington, DC: APA.

Bauserman, R., & Rind, B. (1997). Psychological correlates of male child and adolescent sexual experiences with adults: A review of the nonclinical literature. *Archives of Sexual Behavior, 26*, 105–141.

Beitchman, J. H., Zucher, K. J., Hood, J. E., DaCosta, G. A., Akman, D., & Cassavia, E. (1992). A review of the long-term effects of child sexual abuse. *Child Abuse and Neglect, 16*, 101–118.

Bornstein, B. H., Kaplan, D. L., & Perry, A. R. (2007). Child abuse in the eye of the beholder: Lay perceptions of child sexual and physical abuse. *Child Abuse and Neglect, 31*, 375–391.

Brennan, K. A., Clark, C. L., & Shaver, P. R. (1996). *Development of a new multi-item measure of adult romantic attachment: A preliminary report*. Paper presented at the meeting of the International Society for the Study of Personal Relationships. Banff, Alberta, CA.

Briere, J. (1995). *Trauma Symptom Inventory, professional manual*. Palo Alto, CA: Psychological Assessment Resources.

Briere, J. (2000). *Cognitive Distortion Scales, professional manual*. Palo Alto, CA; Psychological Assessment Resources.

Briere, J., & Runtz, M. (1990). Differential adult symptomology associated with three types of child abuse histories. *Child Abuse and Neglect, 14*, 357–364.

Bruce, A. E., Cole, D. A., Dallaire, D. H., Jacquez, F. M., Pineda, A. Q., & LaGrange, B. (2006). Relations of parenting and negative life events to cognitive diatheses for depression in children. *Journal of Abnormal Child Psychology, 34,* 321–333.

Connor, K. M., & Davidson, J. R. T. (2003). Development of a new resilience scale: The Connor-Davidson resilience scale (CD-RISC). *Depression and Anxiety, 18,* 76–82.

Davidson, J. R. T. (1998). *Trauma Questionnaire.* Retrieved January 3, 2009, from http://psychiatry.mc.duke.edu/Research/Programs/TQ%20Scale.pdf

Egeland, B. (2009). Taking stock: Child emotional maltreatment and developmental psychopathology. *Child Abuse and Neglect, 33,* 22–26.

Finkelhor, D., & Hotaling, G. T. (1984). Sexual abuse in the National Incidence Survey of Child Abuse and Neglect: An appraisal. *Child Abuse and Neglect, 8,* 23–32.

Finkelhor, D., Ormrod, R. K., Turner, H. (2007). Poly-victimization: A neglected component in child victimization. *Child Abuse and Neglect, 31,* 7–26.

Fergusson, D., Horwood, L., & Lynskey, M. (1997). Childhood sexual abuse, adolescent sexual behaviors and revictimization. *Child Abuse and Neglect, 14,* 19–28.

Foley, K. P., & McNeil, C. B. (2007, November). *Children exposed to intimate partner violence: Exploring factors that promote resiliency.* Paper presented at the meeting of the Association for Behavioral and Cognitive Therapies, Philadelphia, PA.

Garmezy, N. (1993). Children in poverty: Resilience despite risk. *Psychiatry, 56,* 127–136.

Gibb, B. E., Alloy, L. B., Walshaw, P. D., Comer, J. S., Shen, G. H., & Villari, A. G. (2006). Predictors of attributional style change in children. *Journal of Abnormal Child Psychology, 34,* 425–439.

Glod, C. A. (1993). Long-term consequences of childhood physical and sexual abuse. *Archives of Psychiatric Nursing, 7,* 163–173.

Hart, S. N., & Brassard, M. R. (1987). A major threat to children's mental health: Psychological maltreatment. *American Psychologist, 42,* 160–165.

Hopper, J. (2009). *Child abuse: Statistics, research, and resources.* Retrieved June 4, 2009, from http://www.jimhopper.com/abstats/

Hovestadt, A. J., Anderson, W. T., Piercy, F. P., Cochran, S. W., & Fine, M. (1985). A family of origin scale. *Journal of Marital and Family Therapy, 11,* 287–297.

Hyde, J. S. (2007). Methodological issues in inferences from meta-analysis about the effects of child sexual abuse. *International Journal of Sexual Health, 19,* 15–19.

Jumper, S. A. (1995). A meta-analysis of the relationship of child sexual abuse to adult psychological adjustment. *Child Abuse and Neglect, 19,* 715–728.

Kelley, M. L., Davidson, K., Palcic, J., Spell, A. E., Self-Brown, S., Gresham, F., et al. (2007, November). *Children's adjustment in the aftermath of Hurricane Katrina: A prospective study of risk and resiliency factors*. Paper presented at the meeting of the Association for Behavioral and Cognitive Therapies, Philadelphia, PA.

Kempe, H. C., Silverman, F. N., Steele, B. F., Droegemueller, W., & Silver, H. K. (1962). The battered child syndrome. *Journal of the American Medical Association, 181*, 17–24.

Kendler, K. S., Bulik, C., Silberg, J., Hettema, J. M., Mylers, J., & Prescott, C. A. (2000). Childhood sexual abuse and adult psychiatric and substance use disorders in women: An epidemiological and co-twin control analysis. *Archives of General Psychiatry, 57*, 953–959.

Krahe, B., & Moller, I. (2004). Playing violent electronic games, hostile attributional style, and aggression-related norms in German adolescents. *Journal of Adolescence, 27*, 53–69.

Kumpfer, K. (1999). Factors and processes contributing to resilience: The resilience framework. *Resilience and Development: Positive Life Adaptations, 14*, 179–224.

Lepore, S. J., & Revenson, T. A. (2006). Resilience and posttraumatic growth: Recovery, resistance, and reconfiguration. *Handbook of posttraumatic growth: Research and practice* (pp. 24–46). Mahwah, NJ: Lawrence Erlbaum Associates, Inc.

Marx, B., Heidr, J., & Gold, S. (2005). Perceived uncontrollability and unpredictability, self-regulation, and sexual revictimization. *Review of General Psychology, 9*, 67–90.

Mullen, P. E., Martin, J. L., Anderson, J. C., Romans, S. E., & Herbison, G. P. (1996). The long-term impact of the physical, emotional and sexual abuse of children: A community study. *Child Abuse and Neglect, 20*, 7–21.

Neuman, D. A., Houskamp, B. M., Pollock, V. E., & Briere, J. (1996). The long-term sequelae of childhood sexual abuse in women: A meta-analytic review. *Child Maltreatment, 1*, 6–16.

O'Dougherty-Wright, M. O., Crawford, E., & Del Castillo, D. (2009). Childhood emotional maltreatment and later psychological distress among college students: The mediating role of maladaptive schemas. *Child Abuse and Neglect, 33*, 59–68.

Palyo, S. A., & Beck, J. G. (2007, November). *Capturing resilient outcomes using an analogue stressor paradigm: Hardiness as a buffer against "posttrauma" symptoms*. Paper presented at the meeting of the Association for Behavioral and Cognitive Therapies, Philadelphia, PA.

Paolucci, E. O., Genuis, M. L., & Violato C. (2001). A meta-analysis of the published research on the effects of child sexual abuse. *Journal of Psychology, 135* (1), 17–36.

Petretic, P., Addison, K., Limberg, N., Griffin, G., Shewmaker, S., & Perdew, I. (2004, July). *Childhood abuse experiences, dimensions of attachment and subsequent victimization and perpetration in dating relationships*. Paper presented at the 9th International Family Violence Research Conference/UNH, Portsmouth, NH.

Petretic, P., White, E., & Jacobs, I. (2008, May). *Mediating factors in the long-term outcome following childhood abuse: Cognitive and other factors predicting personal distress, intimacy functioning and resilience.* Paper presented at the Protecting Children From Violence: Emerging Trends and Research Mini-Conference, Chicago, IL.

Petretic, P., White, E., Limberg, N., Jacobs, I., Addison-Brown, K., & Makin-Byrd, L. (2008, July). *The relation among traumatic symptoms, family functioning, and resilience in a college sample reporting child physical and/or emotional abuse.* Paper presented at the International Family Violence and Child Victimization Research Conference, Portsmouth, NH.

Richardson, G. (2002). The metatheory of resilience and resiliency. *Journal of Clinical Psychology, 58,* 307–321.

Rind, B., & Tromovitch, P. (1997). A meta-analytic review of findings from national samples on psychological correlates of child sexual abuse. *Journal of Sex Research, 34,* 237–255.

Rind, B., Tromovitch, P., & Bauserman, R. (1998). A meta-analytic examination of assumed properties of child sexual abuse using college samples. *Psychological Bulletin, 124,* 22–53.

Rotter, J. (1966). Generalized expectancies for internal versus external control of reinforcements. *Psychological Monographs, 80,* Whole No. 609.

Rutter, M. (1987). Psychosocial resilience and proactive mechanisms. *American Journal of Orthopsychiatry, 57,* 316–331.

Schulman, P., Keith, D., & Seligman, M. E. (1993). Is optimism heritable? A study of twins. *Behavior Research and Therapy, 31,* 569–574.

Schumm, J., Briggs-Phillips, M., & Hobfoll, S. (2006). Cumulative interpersonal traumas and social support as risk and resiliency factors in predicting PTSD and depression among inner-city women. *Journal of Traumatic Stress, 19,* 825–836.

Springer, K. W., Sheridan, J., Kuo, D., & Carnes, M. (2003). The long-term health outcomes of childhood abuse: An overview and a call to action. *Journal of General Internal Medicine, 18,* 862–870.

Springer, K. W., Sheridan, J., Kuo, D., & Carnes, M. (2007). Long-term physical and mental health consequences of childhood physical abuse: Results from a large population-based sample of men and women, *Child Abuse and Neglect, 31,* 517–530.

Straus, M. A., Hamby, S. L., Boney-McCoy, S., & Sugarman, D. B. (1996). The Revised Conflict Tactics Scales (CTS2): Development and psychometric data. *Journal of Family Issues, 17,* 283–316.

Straus, M. A., Hamby, S. L., Finkelhor, D., Moore, D. W., & Rungan, D. K. (1998). Identification of child maltreatment with the parent-child conflict tactics scales (CTSPC): Development and psychometric data for a national sample of American parents. *Child Abuse & Neglect, 22,* 249–270.

Tromovitch, P., & Rind, B. (2007). Child sexual abuse definitions, meta-analytic findings, and a response to the methodological concerns raised by Hyde (2007). *International Journal of Sexual Health, 19,* 1–13.

Ulrich, H., Randolph, M., & Acheson, S. (2005–2006). Child sexual abuse: A replication of the metal-analytic examination of child sexual abuse by Rind, Tromovitch, and Bauserman (1998). *Scientific Review of Mental Health Practice, 4,* 37–51.

U.S. Department of Health and Human Services, Administration on Children, Youth and Families (2008). *Child Maltreatment: 2006.* Washington, DC: U.S. Government Printing Office.

Wagnild, G. M., & Young, H. M. (1993). Development and psychometric evaluation of the Resilience Scale. *Journal of Nursing Measurement, 1,* 165–178.

Wekerle, C., Wolfe, D. A., Hawkins, D. L., Glickman, A., & Lovald, B. E. (2001). Childhood maltreatment, post-traumatic stress symptomatology, and adolescent dating violence: Considering the value of adolescent perceptions of abuse in a trauma meditational model. *Development and Psychopathology, 33,* 847–871.

White, E. (2009). *An examination of locus of control, family dynamics, and resilience: How do they impact traumatic outcome?* Unpublished master's thesis, University of Arkansas, Fayetteville, AR.

Wicks, C. R. (2006). Resilience: An integrative framework for measurement. *Dissertation Abstracts International, 66,* 10-B. (UMI No. 3191869)

CHAPTER 11

Cognitive Development and Exposure to Violence in Children

Robert Schleser and Mary E. Bodzy

Overview of the Issues

The effects of violence on a child can only be understood in the context of the changing child and his or her changing environment, including familial and societal expectations for the child (Pynoos, 1993). Violence is interpreted based on the child's own capacities to appraise and understand violence, to respond to and cope with danger, and to utilize environmental resources that offer protection and support (Finkelhor & Kendall-Tackett 1997).

School-aged children face the developmental challenges of adapting to the school environment and establishing relations with peers and teachers. These tasks require the ability to regulate emotions, show empathy, and attend to increasingly complex cognitive material. In school-aged children, according to Aber and Allen (1987), children who have safe, secure relationships demonstrate a greater readiness to learn and show overall higher levels of cognitive competence. Alternatively, a child overly concerned with security issues (Cicchetti & Toth 1995) and possibly hypervigilance to aggressive responses may process social information with a bias toward interpreting hostile intent (Dodge, Bates, & Pettit 1990). These processes may result in children with limited social competence and negative responses to social situations.

Children who are physically abused demonstrate aggressive

behavior during play with peers (Alessandri 1991, Hoffman-Plotkin & Twentyman, 1984; Kaufman & Cicchetti, 1989). Peers rate these children as more likely to fight, be aggressive and mean, and engage in antisocial behaviors (Manly, Cicchetti, & Barnett, 1994; Salzinger, Feldman, Hammer, & Rosario, 1993). Parents and teachers rate these children as being more aggressive and exhibiting greater behavioral problems (Haskett & Kistener, 1991; Hoffman-Plotkin & Twentyman, 1984; Trickett, 1993).

School-age children are less dependent on parent or caretaker responses than younger children for specific cues regarding how to respond to threatening situations, but monitoring of their children's behavior is still important to children's development. A parent or caretaker's emotional responsiveness to the child can impact their perspectives of a violent event. Parents or caretakers may be negatively affected by their own feelings of helplessness, fear, and grief. Efforts to protect the child may be exhibited in authoritarian and restrictive parenting practices, as well as in certain precautions that may heighten the child's anxiety (Garbarino, 1993).

Children exposed to violence, although in greater need of nurturance and protection than children without such stressors, may have less access to social support from their caretakers if the parent is protecting the child by keeping them in the home away from other people. A parent or caretaker who listens to the child, validates his or her feelings about the event, and normalizes the experience will have a child who is more adapted and less distressed. A child who does not have caretaker support may learn to rely on him or herself and approach caretakers only after having assessed the caretaker's mood, or to attempt to develop other sources of interpersonal support. A child at this stage of development may not understand that the violent event does not occur everywhere or with all people. A child may be protected if the mother-figure models assertive, non-violent approaches to violence and is emotionally available to the child (Egeland, Carlson, & Sroufe, 1993; Mullender, Kelly, Hague, Malos, & Imam, 2000) because it is found that having one reliable source of support provides comfort to the child.

Typical developmental tasks may be altered when a child is exposed to violence (Boney-McCoy & Finkelhor, 1995). Initially, the child exposed to violence may develop an increase in bed-wetting, decreased verbalization, or separation anxiety (Osofsky, 1995). In turn, this may lead to the development of anxiety, depression, or posttraumatic stress disorder symptoms, which then disrupts the child's progress through age-appropriate developmental tasks. As a result, social skills or the ability to concentrate at home or in school may be affected. Exposure to violence may lead the child to cope with adult issues, further disrupting normal development. When the home and the neighborhood are not considered a safe place, the child may lose his or her protective and comforting qualities (Margolin, 1998).

Parental or caregiver protection and support is essential to guide the child through each developmental stage. When children are exposed to physical, emotional, or sexual abuse by the parent or caregiver, this support is diminished. As a result, children may learn to be self-reliant, only approach caretakers after having assessed the caretaker's mood, or attempt to develop other sources of interpersonal support that may or may not be appropriate. Without caretaker support to guide the child, the child is left to make these decisions alone. In addition, caretakers may be less available to the child if they are involved in domestic abuse, with unpredictable moods by the perpetrator and the victim distracted by basic issues of safety and survival for the family (Margolin, 1998). Observing and experiencing this punitive style of communication between caretakers may lead to the child developing similar methods (Margolin, Christensen, & John, 1996).

Childhood exposure to violence can be evaluated in the context of normal developmental processes and identifying the links between disrupted and normal development (Cicchetti, 1993; Pynoos, 1993). Piaget named four continual stages of development with approximate age ranges: sensory motor (age 0–2 years), preoperational (age 2–7 years), concrete operational (age 7–12 years), and formal operational (age 13 to adult) (Wadsworth, 1996). Abuse and violence experienced by a child can disrupt different developmental challenges at each stage. Understanding the effects of exposure to violence must be informed by an understanding of normal adaptation across developmental stages. Violence affects how children view the world and themselves. In turn, this disrupts typical cognitive development.

For example, violence during the sensory motor stage can alter the developmental task of learning to trust others and to form secure attachment relationships (Janoff-Bulman, 1992). These disrupted attachments can then lead to difficulties in subsequent relationships throughout life. However, although infants and young children are at risk of physical injury and death when abused or neglected, very young children are partially protected from psychological distress because they do not fully comprehend violence and the risk involved. Osofsky (1995) challenges the belief that very young children are too young to be affected by violence. Osofsky and Scheeringa (1997) and Zeanah and Scheeringa (1997) suggested that infants display distress based on observed changes in behavior, including irritability, sleep disturbances, emotional distress, somatic complaints, fears of being alone, and regression in toileting behavior and language. However, these changes were inferred and did not take into account the parental or caretaker responses to the violent event.

Infants and young children rely on parent figures not only to protect them from danger and to make the world predictable and safe, but also to guide their understanding of violence. An infant or young child does not understand or comprehend that an event is dangerous or unsafe unless the parent responds in a way that evokes a negative reaction. For example, if a family hears a gunshot nearby, a young child may not know that the sound is dangerous unless the parent or caretaker reacts by running the child quickly into the house and telling the child to hide. The child may then become fearful because of the parent or caretaker response. If the parent instead walked the child calmly but briskly into the house and had the child read a book or play a game with the parent, then the child may not perceive or understand that the sound was dangerous.

Preoperational Stage of Development

As children progress into the preoperational stage of development, children begin to use language, memory, and imagination. Children in this stage can classify objects and events based on attribute recognition to develop trial-and-error strategies and transductive reasoning (the idea that a special explanation belongs to each object and consequently special relations that can only result in special reasoning). A cause–effect relation may become unclear if a logical sequence is broken. When young children experience a "break" in patterns (e.g., daily routines), they dissociate from their usual thinking pattern. According to Wadsworth (1996), discrepancies in young children's environments encourage them to look for answers. This allows children to construct their knowledge. Parents or caretakers who have specific routines in the home allow the child to develop the understanding that the home and environment are safe and predictable. In terms of violence, if the parent or caretaker always reacts calmly to a violent event and protects the child, then the child will develop secure relationships and understand the violent event to be less distressing. The violent event may then be perceived as producing protection and support.

Children in the preoperational stage of development tend to see the world from their own perspective. They have difficulty distinguishing between their own perspective and that of others. These children often describe people, objects, and events in terms of physical characteristics rather than internal states. Children may explain the world in magical or vague terms, creating confusion about causal relationships. As a result, reasoning about violence is likely to be different and obscure compared with adult perspectives. Children at this stage tend to describe a particular detail of the violent event rather than how the violence occurred. The child observes the behavior or event from his or her view instead of how something actually happened.

These children may have difficulty focusing on more than one portion of the violent event and focus more on the object involved, such as a fist or gun. Children at this age have difficulty understanding the psychological perspective of others and may view violence as a tactic to get what one wants. These observable physical appearances or actions are typically the focus, rather than unobservable attributes such as intentions and underlying psychological states. The child may be protected or deescalated if the caregiver is able to redirect the child towards a more positive normalizing physical event such as going to McDonalds.

Young children reason differently than adults, and the child's unique interpretations should be considered. Children may wish to share their explanations and perceptions with a non-judgmental, supportive adult who understands the unique logic of children, but the child may also feel that the event is insignificant according to how the caretaker responds. For example, a child may discuss the physical, observable fact that a child's clothing was torn after witnessing an episode of violence (Pynoos, 1993). Recognizing that this is a reflection of the child's cognitive-developmental level helps the adult better understand the perceptual experience for the child. A child may feel that he lacks control over his life and needs to be provided with a sense of security and protection. A simple explanation explaining that most children are not victims of a shooting or witness such events (if relevant) will help the child feel safe. Children at this age do not understand cause–effect relationships and will not understand a lengthy explanation. Preoperational children do not have the capacity to understand empathic perspective taking (Brondolo, Baruch, Conway, & Marsh, 1994).

These children may act aggressively to obtain a goal without thinking about the long-term consequence of their actions. For example, a child may hit a peer to obtain a toy, but not consider the pain caused towards the peer or that in the future this child may not want to play with him. A child's immediate concern about obtaining the desired object or being hit by a peer during an argument over a toy may be a more relevant focus than a recent neighborhood shooting. The child may not understand or feel the effects of such an event in the same way as an adult. It is important to explore the child's understanding and reactions from his or her perspective rather than attempting to explain the event in complex adult terms. The specific characteristic of the event that the child focuses on may become the topic of discussion rather than the cause. Adults can articulate the connection between events and emotions but children at this age cannot. It is necessary to offer children at this age the opportunity to work through concerns without the constraints of reality or pressures from the adult. This allows for enhanced development (Rogoff, 1998).

Concrete Stage of Development

As a child progresses into the concrete operational stage, the child's thought processes are directed to real events observed by the child. The child is able to reason systematically about the world and a scene can be viewed from a different perspective and still contain the same elements (Wadsworth, 1996). The child develops reversibility for any action that exists other than those actions that can cancel them out. Development of class inclusion ideas is evident during the concrete operational stage. The child is able to think about parts and the whole independently in whole–part relationships. Children at this stage (who are not able to master reversibility) are unable to reverse the thought of a "part" to the whole again. For example, in relation to exposure to violence, a child who has witnessed an event such as domestic violence in one home can comprehend that this type of violence may not occur in every home. The child can understand that this one experience is not the same for all couples (the whole picture).

Children in the concrete stage of development are able to understand logic and cause–effect relationships. These logical abilities allow the child to analyze concretely and take on the perspective of others. Children at this stage emphasize rules, and organize and classify the environment. However, these children have difficulty understanding that people can experience more than one feeling at a time.

In relation to violence, children at this stage consider both internal and external factors. For example, the effects of violence can be understood as, "someone took my bike because they are mean and this makes me feel mad." The child is able to explain logically that the child stole because he or she wanted the desired object. The link is in concrete terms. The child can also reason alternatives that maybe the child did not steal the bike but instead borrowed the bike and will bring it back later. In terms of physical violence, a child who hits another child because they stole from him or her may feel that hitting allows that child to experience the same feeling he or she felt when the item was stolen. At this stage, intentions are considered and psychological explanations are offered.

Understanding the cause–effect relationship exhibits an appreciation for rules, viewed as concrete and fixed. Rules are followed to meet personal interest. The child may view a violent event in concrete terms such as, "he hit me so I will hit him." At this point, the child is able to self-reflect and recognizes that others may have similar views. The child is able to allow for internal conceptualization of the violent event (e.g., "they hit me, now I'll hit them back so they can see how it feels"). This process allows the child to compare his or her own level of competency to others. Actions begin to be influenced by peers and modeling. Group rules are understood as beneficial for the group and not just the individual. The child can pair violence with going to jail because this may be the societal expectation. Children who think in concrete terms can categorize violent events.

Children may struggle to reconcile differences in perspectives on their own. Kruger (1992) and Kruger and Tomasello (1986) found that children understand more about problems when discussed with a child at the same stage of development. Rogoff (1998) found that collaborating with a child slightly above their own developmental level enhances understanding of conflicts. Either way, these children may benefit from continual guidance to remember internal emotions related to concrete external factors.

Caregiver and adult support is necessary in violent situations to facilitate growth.

A child develops cognitive schemas based on patterns of social cognition. The more the child experiences the world as a hostile place, the more acceptable violence becomes encoded into memory. The child may develop social scripts based on these previous experiences and become aggressive in response to a perceived threatening situation. This further emphasizes the importance of understanding cognition from a child's perspective, particularly the link between a child's cognition of observed aggression and reacting aggressively (Bandura, 1986; Dodge et al., 1990). Huesmann (1998) suggested that children who are repeatedly exposed to violence feel less aversive to the behavior, making it easier to think and act aggressively. Some children may also have difficulty regulating their emotions after such experiences (Eisenberg, Fabes, Nyman, Bernzweig, & Pinuelas, 1994). Most of this literature focuses on either specific age groups or a broad range of ages without considering differences in a child's developmental level. Huesman and Guerra (1997) found that early aggression predicted aggressive beliefs during the elementary years, and aggressive beliefs predicted aggression during later elementary years. This indicates that aggressive behaviors influence aggressive beliefs as a child develops more stable cognitions. Guerra, Huesmann, and Spindler (2002) found that exposure to violence predicted aggressive behavior in grades 1–3 (ages 5–8 years), but social cognitions surrounding violence was only evident in grades 4–6 (ages 9–12 years). This may be because children in earlier grades may not have the cognitive capacity to understand violence in the same way as children in older grades. Children in the concrete stage of development are able to understand why or how the violence is occurring, whereas a younger child may only be reacting to a feared stimulus with no or limited understanding.

If a family experiences economic stressors, this may or may not impact on the children based on the parents' reactions. Jorge's family (see Chapter 13) were struggling economically. The children experienced abuse from the father as a result of the stress; the mother also became concerned. These smaller children may not know or understand logically why different events may be occurring in the home until the adults change their own behaviors. The children would likely be playing and experiencing life at home as normal with no indication of distress. If the mother began to play less with the children, began to yell or cry, or appeared upset, then the children may become scared because they do not understand what is happening. Younger children look to adults for understanding of the world because they themselves have no or limited ability to process adult information. If this same mother were to continue doing what she usually does on a regular basis, then the children would continue to feel safe and secure. Once a parent physically abuses a child, the child becomes fearful and looks to find a safe place, but also may depend on the other adult to help make sense of what is happening. Younger children rely on this dependence to feel safe and secure in the home and environment. If neither parent is available to the child, attachment may be compromised and the child may begin to rely on him or herself.

A child's perspective may also be related to the environmental conditioning and survival instincts. As discussed in Chapter 14, a child may be afraid of the dark or of the light, depending on the particular circumstance. As mentioned, children in Kosovo became afraid of the light because during the day you were in danger of sniper fire. Again, despite the situation, the preoperational child is dependent on the reaction by the adult. A child at the concrete level can comprehend the adult understanding that people may shoot you in the daytime and remaining inside is important. A preoperational child would follow an adult's lead and be fearful because the adult is afraid but without this understanding.

Violence in the world can trickle down to the welfare of the child and affect his or her perspective because this situation influences the parent. The parent takes the information obtained and reacts, which then trickles down to the child. The preoperational child is not going to understand that war in their country is dangerous and scary unless the parent begins to hide the family in the basement or appears frightened. If the parent is able to keep a stable, steady home environment despite stressors, the child will continue to feel safe. The concrete child can process the information more logically and may become distressed, regardless of the parental reaction; however, the parent can ease the child by remaining calm and keeping a predictable structure at home.

Children can become resilient despite exposure to violence or a difficult situation if the adults can provide a place for the child to feel safe, secure, and help the child find ways to be a child. For example, as mentioned in Chapter 14, the teachers in Bolivia's prison school used boxes as toys for the children. The teachers found a way to meet the needs of the children and, as a result, the children demonstrated resiliency despite living in closed quarters with limited space. In addition, these teachers have found ways to teach the children about music and art, providing a sense of mastery and the stimulating environment that children need to feel secure. These supports are necessary for the child to process the environment, particularly when the child does not have the ability to comprehend adult problems, such as prison or war. This sense of normality promotes balance and positive mental health for children.

In the Tanzanian example, the caretakers were able to change the child's view based on their own. Once given the tools, the caretakers felt confident in their ability to provide support and, in turn, the children felt the support of the caretakers. The children were able to process their feelings of sadness based upon the availability of the adult to provide emotional support for the child. Preoperational children depend on this type of exchange, while concrete-stage children benefit from the guidance to promote positive well-being and protection against exposure to all forms of violence.

The Laurie Dann Shootings

On May 20, 1988, at approximately 10:30 a.m., Laurie Dann entered the Hubbard Woods Grammar School in Winnetka, Illinois. She was armed with three handguns that she had purchased legally, despite her extensive history of mental illness. Initially, she went to a 2nd grade classroom where Amy Moses was teaching bicycle safety. After briefly observing the class, she left. In the hallway, she saw a 6-year-old boy at a water fountain. She dragged him into a boys' room and shot him in the upper right chest. He recovered. Laurie Dann returned to the 2nd grade classroom and ordered Amy Moses to gather the children in a corner of the room, who refused and struggled with Dann. Dann broke free and shot five more children, killing 8-year-old Nicholas Corwin. The other four children survived. Later in the day, Dann broke into the home of Phillip Andrew, a 20-year-old University of Illinois student. Andrew negotiated the release of his parents. He attempted to disarm Dann, who shot him in the chest. In the immediate aftermath of the shooting, the children, their parents, school teachers, and staff received massive support from psychologists, social workers, and other mental health professionals to cope with the psychological impact of the shootings. Later in the week, 1500 people attended the memorial service for 8-year-old Nicholas Corwin, led by Rabbi Robert Schriebman at the Temple Jeremiah in Northbrook, Illinois.

Chicago Tribune reporters Lisa Black and Bonnie Miller Rubin wrote an article for the 20th anniversary of the Laurie Dann shootings. They interviewed Amy Moses, Phillip Andrew, and Rabbi Schriebman. Amy Moses was refused tenure at Hubbard Woods and subsequently left teaching. She became an artist. She reports lingering guilt and anxiety and wonders what more she could have done that day. Phillip Andrew survived, became a lawyer, and later an FBI agent. He also served as the executive director of the Illinois Council Against Handgun Violence. Rabbi Schriebman, who had to inform Nicholas Corwin's parents of his death, reported that his faith was sorely tested. He is retired, and stated that he remains "decidedly skeptical" about the existence of God. The surviving children are in their late twenties. Although they talk about it privately, they all refused to be publicly interviewed.

The impact of an event like the Laurie Dann shootings is diverse and enduring. The responses of the individuals who were adults at the time seem to be, at least superficially, understandable. The teacher who wonders what more she should have done feels guilt and turns to art to express her feelings. The college student who bravely protected his family becomes an advocate against gun violence and a federal law enforcement agent. And, sadly, the clergyman who loses his faith is left wondering why God would allow this to happen. We can empathize with these responses. The responses of the children, who were willing to talk privately among themselves but not publicly, are more perplexing.

One explanation for the differential responses of the adults and children is that they experienced profoundly different events that day. We noted previously that broad differences occur in the cognitive processes of younger children and adults. Preoperational children are egocentric, unable to de-center and understand an event objectively. Their attention is centered on small idiosyncratic details and they often miss the larger picture. Their reasoning is infralogical and their concept of causality, time, and life and death is undeveloped. They also focus on end-states and not transformations. Finally, through assimilation, they tend to use existing categories to understand novel events and objects.

As adults, we would agree that a deeply troubled woman with a history of severe mental illness walked into Hubbard Woods School, killed one child, and seriously injured five others. As adults, we would understand the horror of this tragedy. This is not the case for preoperational children.

Second grade is a time of great diversity in the cognitive abilities of students. Some have almost adult-like processing styles while others are magical in their thinking. Two concepts that are immediately relevant to understanding the possible perceptions of the Laurie Dann shootings are the concepts of violence and death. As adults we would generally agree that violence involves the intentional infliction of harm on another. We would also generally agree that death is associated with the cessation of biological functions. These are not innate concepts. They develop over time.

Buckley and Walsh (1998) conducted a developmental analysis of children's understanding of violence. They hypothesized that children's understanding of the definition, cause, and prevention of violence follows an ordered sequence of categories that corresponds to the development of causal reasoning. To test this, they grouped 72 children into three age categories (5–7, 8–10, and 11–13 years old) that approximated Piaget's preoperational, concrete, and formal operational stages of development. Children were administered the Developmental Concepts of Violence Protocol (DCVP). The DCVP developed for this study was composed of vignettes describing hitting and shooting events. A social role-taking task to differentiate preoperational children from the other two groups was also administered. The DCVP assessed children's causal reasoning about hitting and shooting violence. Scores on the DCVP produced three distinct developmental levels of reasoning about violence: associative, sequential, and interactional.

Results indicated that the youngest group provided significantly more associative answers. These answers essentially described specific actions without any indication of the inferred characteristics or psychological state of the actors. In general, they demonstrated little capacity to comprehend violence at anything remotely close to an adult. A majority of children in both older groups provided significantly more sequential explanations. These explanations included a sequence or causal chain, multiple perspectives, and a tendency to see violence as an effective, albeit less desirable, means to accomplish specific goals. Psychological states, motivation, and intent are considered. Older children from both groups provided interactional explanations that included multiple cause–effect scenarios. Physical, psychological, and societal factors were considered. Reasoning was multidimensional and often hypothetical in nature.

Performance on the social role-taking task indicated that the older group displayed significantly more mature social skills. The younger two groups did not differ from one another and relied on strategies based on idiosyncratic and egocentric reasoning. Although preliminary in nature, the results of Buckley and Walsh (1998) have serious implications in dealing with children's fears of and ability to predict violence. They also suggest the need to develop age-appropriate interventions following violent incidents, and programs to prevent violence.

Just as children's concept of violence follows a developmental sequence, so does their concept of life and death. Numerous studies have demonstrated that a child's concept of death is not complete until around the age of 9 or 10 (Candy-Gibbs, Sharp, & Petrun, 1984–1985; Childers & Wimmer, 1971; Hyslop-Christ, 2000; Speece & Brent, 1992). Traditionally researchers have focused on four subconcepts of death: irreversibility, nonfunctionality, universality, and inevitability.

Lazar and Torney-Purta (1991) investigated the relationship between Piagetian conservation status and the subconcepts of death. Their results indicated that children acquired the subconcepts in a particular developmental sequence. The order was universality, inevitability, and irreversibility. Hunter and Smith (2008) investigated a number of predictors of children's understanding of death. Participants were 37 mother–child dyads. Child measures include three Piagetian conservation tasks and a seriation task: age, cognitive ability, death experience, and maternal communication competence. The maternal measure was the Children's Questions About Death Scale. Results indicated that age predicted irreversibility, non-functionality, and universality but not inevitability. Conservation ability and seriation predicted universality and inevitability but not non-functionality. Death experience of a family member or pet predicted the subconcept of universality. Parental communication was not related to any of the four subconcepts of death. The latter finding is of special significance because it indicates that parental communication about death does not facilitate the acquisition of the subconcepts. This has implications for postdeath interventions with younger children.

Implications of a Developmental Model of Childhood Violence

Formal Operations

It was noted above that in the immediate aftermath of the Laurie Dann shootings, the children, their parents, school teachers, and staff received massive support from psychologists, social workers, and other mental health professionals to cope with the psychological impact of the shootings. This is a good plan to help the adults. They clearly understand the magnitude of the tragedy. They are overwhelmed by grief and the need to process their feelings with others. Therapy and support will help them to do this.

Adults, with their formal operational capacity for abstract thought and hypothetical reasoning, have an endless number of questions. Unfortunately there are no satisfactory answers. The objective facts are clear. A woman with severe mental illness shot six people and killed an 8-year-old boy. The most meaningful questions the adults have, however, are not about facts but about why this happened. They will never really know why because Laurie Dann killed herself before they could ask her. In the end, they will probably agree that it was just fate or bad luck that led Laurie Dann to the Hubbard Woods School with three handguns in the waistband of her pants. Professional interventions can help to facilitate this emotional closure.

The next most likely question would center on what could have been done to prevent this from occurring or reoccurring. The answer is probably very little, but that is unsatisfactory. Later that year the Illinois State Legislature provided a satisfactory answer. They enacted a law that requires the doors of every school in Illinois to remain locked during school. Visitors were required to be "buzzed" in. Despite the fact that almost anyone will be buzzed in without visual inspection, this too brought emotional closure.

A final issue for the adults is the fact that a young boy lost his life. Adults, with their capacity for hypothetical thought, can ponder what he might have become, and grieve the loss of that potential. Again, mutual support and professional facilitation help them to find closure. In the end they can conclude that he was a happy child who led a rich life.

Concrete Operations

As noted, support was also provided to the children. Despite the massive developmental literature documenting the tremendous difference in the cognitive abilities of same-age children, most professionals tend to view development in terms of age or grade. In all likelihood, all 2nd graders receive similar interventions. Concrete operational children would probably benefit, while preoperational children would not.

Concrete operational children have adult-like reasoning about causality and time. Through the process of accommodation, they have many more categories to help understand objects and events. Unlike adults, they do not have the capacity for abstract or hypothetical reasoning. Their concept of death is not fully developed. As the results of Hunter and Smith's (2008) study indicate, they have likely mastered the subconcepts of inevitability and universality but not irreversibility and non-functionality. Thus, they understand that death will happen to everybody at some point, but they do not grasp the complete finality of death.

Concrete operational children will understand that something "bad" has occurred and will have questions about their personal safety. They will not wonder why the shootings occurred. They will accept the fact that a woman with mental problems did a horrible thing. They will understand that their friend has died. They may miss their friend, but they will not mourn him. Since they do not have abstract and hypothetical reasoning, they will not have the adult sense of lost potential.

Concrete operational children will benefit from a straightforward presentation describing what happened. As noted, they base their emotional reaction on cues from adults. Dwelling on issues of loss and grief are likely to elicit, but not resolve, negative responses. An attempt should be made to normalize the situation as quickly as possible. The children should be encouraged to return to normal activities, including play, as soon as they are ready.

Preoperations

As described earlier, preoperational children live in a magical world. Their concept of time is based on events, not the abstract adult sense of minutes and hours. Their concept of causality is idiosyncratic. They are egocentric and cannot understand the perspective of others. Their focus is primarily on themselves. In this situation, they cannot understand that something terrible has happened to a classmate. They may, however, become quite upset because their routine has been disrupted.

Preoperational children have very little understanding of the concept of death. They also have limited categories in which to assimilate this new information. The closest category they have to understand death is sleep. This is readily apparent to a mother or father who, while trying to rein in their 6-year-old at a funeral, is horrified to see the child chatting with the deceased in an attempt to wake him/her up. As Hunter and Smith's (2008) results indicate, they cannot accommodate or develop a new category to understand death through verbal discussion. Since they are even more sensitive to adult cues for their emotional response, extended discussion with a distraught adult is likely to severely upset them.

Preoperational children live in a here-and-now world. Their attention is captured by salient features of the environment. Specifically, they are highly distractible. For a preoperational child it is truly out of sight, out of mind. Interventions that dwell on the violence and ask children to express emotions that they cannot feel are likely to do more harm than good. Verbal interventions are unlikely to help. Positive distraction is the treatment of choice. Although counterintuitive to some, the best intervention with preoperational children may be a trip to a fast-food restaurant or some other venue unrelated to the site of the violence.

Summary

There is a vast body of literature based on the developmental theory of Jean Piaget. Literally thousands of studies have revealed profound qualitative differences in the cognitive abilities of same-age children. These differences should help us to develop clinical interventions, educational programs, and other child-focused activities. Unfortunately, this body of research is largely ignored by applied child psychology researchers, therapists, and teachers. In many respects we have not moved beyond the "short adult" concept of childhood. We infer adult emotions, motivations, and understanding that are simply not possible based on children's cognitive capabilities.

It is not in the scope of this chapter to present other than a few samples of the fascinating differences in which children construct and understand their world. The purpose is to encourage readers to explore the developmental literature and determine how it might inform their work with children. One final incentive, the developmental literature has helped us to reconcile the memory of the day when we realized irrevocably that Santa Claus does not exist.

References

Aber, J. L., & Allen, J. P. (1987). Effects of maltreatment on young children. *Developmental Psychology, 23*, 406–414.

Alessandri, S. M. (1991). Play and social behavior in maltreated preschoolers. *Developmental Psychopathology, 3*, 191–205.

Bandura, A. (1986). *Aggression: A social learning analysis.* New York: Holt.

Boney-McCoy, S., & Finkelhor, D. (1995). Psychosocial sequelae of violent victimization in a national youth sample. *Journal of Consulting and Clinical Psychology, 63*, 726–736.

Brondolo, E., Baruch, C., Conway, E., & Marsh, E. (1994). Aggression among innercity minority youth: A biopsychosocial model for school-based evaluation and treatment. *Journal of Social Distress and the Homeless, 3*, 53–80.

Buckley, M. A., & Walsh, M. E. (1998). Children's understanding of violence: A developmental analysis. *Applied Developmental Science, 2*, 182–193.

Candy-Gibbs, S. E., Sharp, K. C., & Petrun, C. J. (1984–1985). The effects of age, object, and cultural/religious background on children's concepts of death. *Omega, 15*, 329–346.

Childers, P., & Wimmer, M. (1971). The concept of death in early childhood. *Child Development, 42*, 1299–1301.

Cicchetti, D. (1993). Developmental psychopathology: Reactions, reflections and projections. *Developmental Review, 13*, 471–502.

Cicchetti, D., & Toth, S. L. (1995). A developmental perspective on child abuse and neglect. *Journal of the American Academy of Child and Adolescence Psychiatry, 34*, 541–565.

Dodge, K. A., Bates, J. E., & Pettit, G. A. (1990). Mechanisms in the cycle of violence. *Science, 250*, 1678–1683.

Egeland, B. R., Carlson, E., & Sroufe, L. A. (1993). Resilience as a process. *Development and Psychopathology, 5*, 517–528.

Eisenberg, N., Fabes, R. A., Nyman, M., Bernzweig, J., & Pinuelas, A. (1994). The relations of emotionality and regulation to children's anger-related reactions. *Child Development, 65*, 109–128.

Finkelhor, D., & Kendall-Tackett, K. (1997). A developmental perspective on the childhood impact of crime, abuse, and violent victimization. In D. Cicchetti & S. Toth (Eds.), *Developmental perspectives on trauma: Theory, research, and intervention* (pp. 1–32). New York: University of Rochester Press.

Garbarino, J. (1993). Children's response to community violence: What do we know? *Infant Mental Health Journal, 14*, 103–115.

Guerra, N. G., Huesmann, L. R., & Spindler, A. (2002) Community violence exposure, social cognition, and aggression among urban elementary school children, *Child Development, 74,* 1561–1576.

Haskett, M. E., & Kistener, J. A. (1991). Social interaction and peer perceptions of young physically abused children. *Child Development, 62,* 979–990.

Hoffman-Plotkin, D., & Twentyman, C. T. (1984). A multimodal assessment of behavioral and cognitive deficits in abused and neglected preschoolers. *Child Development, 55,* 794–802.

Huesmann, L. R. (1998). The role of social information processing and cognitive schemas in the acquisitions and maintenance of habitual aggressive behavior. In R. E. Green & E. Donnerstein (Eds.), *Human aggression: Theories, research and implications for policy* (pp. 73–109). New York: Academic Press.

Huesmann, L. R., & Guerra, N. G. (1987). Children's normative beliefs about aggression and aggressive behavior. *Journal of Personality and Social Psychology, 72,* 408–419.

Hunter, S. B., & Smith, D. E. (2008). Predictors of children's understandings of death: Age, cognitive ability, death experience and maternal communicative competence. *Omega. 5,* 143–152.

Hyslop-Christ, G. (2000). *Healing children's grief: Surviving a parent's death from cancer.* New York: Oxford University Press.

Janoff-Bulman, R. (1992). *Shattered assumptions: Toward a new psychology of trauma.* New York: Free Press.

Kaufman, J., & Cicchetti, D. (1989). Effects of maltreatment on school-age children's socio-emotional development: Assessments in a day-camp setting. *Developmental Psychology, 25,* 516–524.

Kruger, A. C. (1992). The effects of peer and adult–child transactive discussion on moral reasoning. *Merrill-Palmer Quarterly, 38,* 191–211.

Kruger, A. C., & Tomasello, M. (1986). Transactive discussions with peers and adults. *Developmental Psychology, 22,* 681–685.

Lazar, A., & Torney-Purta, J. (1991). The development of the subconcepts of death in young children: A short-term longitudinal study. *Child Development, 62,* 1321–1333.

Manly, J. T., Cicchetti, D., & Barnett, D. (1994). The impact of subtype, frequency, chronicity, and severity of child maltreatment on social competence and behavior problems. *Developmental Psychopathology, 6,* 121–143.

Margolin, G. (1998). Effects of domestic violence on children. In P. K. Trickett & C. J. Schellenbach (Eds.), *Violence against children in the family and the community* (pp. 57–102). Washington, DC: American Psychological Association.

Margolin, G., Christensen, A., & John, R. (1996). The continuance and spillover of everyday tensions in distressed and nondistressed families. *Journal of Family Psychology, 10,* 304–321.

Mullender, A., Kelly, L., Hague, G., Malos, E., & Imam, U. (2000).

Children's needs, coping, strategies, and understanding of women abuse. Coventry, UK: Economic and Social Research Council.

Osofsky, J. D. (1995). The effects of exposure to violence on young children. *American Psychologist, 50,* 782–788.

Osofsky, J. D., & Scheeringa, M. S. (1997). Community and domestic violence exposure: effects of development and psychopathology. In D. Cicchetti & S. Toth (Eds.), *Developmental perspectives on trauma: Theory, research, and intervention* (pp. 155–80). New York: University of Rochester Press.

Pynoos, R. S. (1993). Traumatic stress and developmental psychopathology in children and adolescents. In J. Oldham, A. Tasman, & M. Riba (Eds.), *Tasman American Psychiatric review of psychiatry* (Vol. 12, pp. 205–238). Washington, DC: American Psychiatric Press.

Rogoff, B. (1998). Cognition as a collaborative process. In W. Damon (Series Ed.), D. Kuhn, & R. S. Siegler (Vol. Eds.), *Handbook of child psychiatry: Vol. 2. Cognition, perception and language* (5th ed., pp. 679–744). New York: John Wiley.

Salzinger, S., Feldman, R. S., Hammer, M., & Rosario, M. (1993). The effects of physical abuse on children's social relationships. *Child Development, 64,* 169–187.

Speece, M. W., & Brent, S. B. (1992). The acquisition of a mature understanding of the concept of death. *Death Studies, 16,* 211–229.

Trickett. P. K. (1993). Maladaptive development of school-aged, physically abused children: Relationship with the child rearing context. *Journal of Family Psychology, 7,* 134–147.

Wadsworth, B. (1996). *Piaget's theory of cognitive and affective development.* White Plains, NY: Longman.

Zeanah, C. H., & Scheeringa, M. S. (1997). The experience and effects of violence in infancy. In J. D. Osofsky (Ed.), *Children in a violent society* (pp. 97–123). New York: Guilford Press.

CHAPTER 12

Snakes, Spiders, Strangers

How the Evolved Fear of Strangers may Misdirect Efforts to Protect Children from Harm

Jennifer Hahn-Holbrook, Colin Holbrook, and Jesse Bering

Case Illustrations

> The men began to kill the children; little ones, bigger ones, they killed many of them. They tried to run away but [the Karawetari raiders] caught them, and struck them with bows.
>
> (Valero & Biocca, 1970, p. 34)

Eleven-year-old Helen Valero was abducted by Yanomamo warriors while working as a Christian missionary near the Amazon in 1937. During her years of captivity, she witnessed male raiders of rival tribal groups targeting infants and children, especially boys. On one such occasion, Valero recalls a woman's pleas to save a male infant, "Don't kill him, he's your son. The mother was with you and she ran away when she was already pregnant with this child. He's one of your sons!" The raider paused to weigh this possibility, then replied, "No, he's [another group's] child. It's too long since she ran away from us" (Valero & Biocca, 1970, pp. 34–35). The man then seized the baby by his feet and bashed him against the rocks. Following her initial kidnapping, Valero was abducted once again by raiders from yet another village, where she was forced to marry and provide children for her new captors. Before she ultimately escaped, Valero witnessed frequent, violent intertribal raids in which men and children were regularly murdered and women were kidnapped as a sexual commodity. For the traditional Yanomamo, whose hunter–gatherer lifestyle likely resembles that of ancestral humans, the appearance of a strange male signaled imminent and dire peril.

Thousands of miles to the north in a contemporary urban metropolis, a 9-year-old boy named Izzy Skenazy asked his mother whether he could ride the subway home from Manhattan by himself (Skenazy, 2008). Lenore Skenazy, who would subsequently be dubbed "the worst mother in the world," readily agreed, and later wrote about Izzy's adventure in her weekly newspaper column. Within hours, Skenazy began receiving a torrent of outraged responses from all over the world. Many parents even accused her of criminal child neglect (Celizic, 2008). The public uproar over her decision to permit her young son to ride the subway alone was so intense that soon Skenazy was giving internationally broadcast television interviews. Her defense was straightforward: in contemporary New York City, parents' fear of murderous strangers waiting to pounce on their children is based on hysteria. In reality, her young son, traveling alone among strangers, was safe.

Overview of the Issues

"Stranger danger" is a widely used term to describe the perceived threats that strangers pose towards children. Critics of contemporary stranger danger preoccupations typically blame the mass media for opportunistically sensationalizing incidents of child assault by strangers (e.g., Skenazy, 2008). Although we agree that the media influences public perceptions of stranger danger, the question remains: why do stranger abuse scenarios, rather than far more likely and equally severe threats to children, garner so much attention and concern from contemporary audiences? In this chapter, we will argue that stranger fear is an evolved predisposition that increased fitness over the course of human history. In modern, developed societies, however, the same native bias against strangers may obscure perception of the greater threat of child harm posed by familiar peers, acquaintances, friends, and kin.

Literature Review

Stranger abductions and homicides account for less than 1% of the actual harm that befalls children in the United States (Center for Disease Control and Prevention, 1982). By contrast, automobile accidents account for 41% of all non-natural child deaths each year (UNICEF, 2001). Yet despite the drastic differences in the actual frequency of these potential sources of harm to children, parents worry over them equivalently (Stickler, Salter, Broughton, & Alario, 1991). In fact, several surveys report that stranger violence and abduction are the primary concern for parents (Kantrowitz, 1997; Kidscape, 1993). This emotional disconnect between the actual versus perceived risk posed by strangers toward children may stem from an innate human aversion that evolved in response to stranger violence in the ancestral past.

In the present chapter, we review evidence that strangers, particularly adult males aligned with outgroups, posed sufficient risk over evolutionary time to warrant the evolution of a "prepared" fear. Unlike prepared fears of snakes or spiders, which typically appear later in life after initial learning (Seligman, 1971), *stranger anxiety* emerges spontaneously. Stranger anxiety, also known as *"stranger wariness"*, *"fear of strangers"*, or *"8-month anxiety"*, is a developmental universal characterized by a marked increase in fearful reactions toward strangers, such as withdrawal, crying on sight, and gaze aversion, during the second half of the first year of life (Campos, Emde, Gaensbauer, & Henderson, 1975; Emde, Gaensbauer, & Harmon, 1976; Ricciuti, 1974; Schaffer, 1966; Schaffer & Emerson, 1964; Skarin, 1977; Sroufe, 1977; Tennes & Lampl, 1964; Waters, Matas, & Sroufe, 1975).[1] Infants who display stranger anxiety often cry out and crawl toward their caregivers, behaviors that presumably defended them in the ancestral past against infanticidal attacks (Feinman, 1980). Such attacks have been documented in modern hunter–gatherer societies such as the Ache Indians (Hill & Hurtado, 1996) and the Yanomamo (Chagnon, 1983; Valero & Biocca, 1970). These infanticidal behaviors are phenotypically ancient. Adult males from many non-human primate species, for example, target outgroup infants (Goodall, 1977; Hrdy, 1977, 1984; van Schaik & Kappeler, 1997; Watts, Muller, Amsler, Mbabazi, & Mitani, 2006).

Whereas infants demonstrate their fear of strangers overtly, adults often exhibit their aversion implicitly (Amodio, Harmon-Jones, Devine, Curtin, Hartley, & Covert, 2004; Devine, 1989; Navarrete, Olsson, Ho, Mendes, Thomsen, & Sidanius, 2009). Stranger anxiety may therefore be viewed as the onset of a psychological tendency that persists over the entire lifespan. Far from disappearing after the first year of life, stranger aversion seems to manifest in different ways throughout ontogeny, increasingly tempered by habituation and executive inhibition. One contemporary expression of this enduring bias may be the exaggerated concern commonly referenced as "stranger danger."

We begin with an overview of infant stranger anxiety research, followed by a brief review of research on stranger aversion over childhood and into adulthood. We also review the evidence that strangers were sufficiently deleterious to our ancestors' genetic fitness to have posed an adaptive problem fostering an evolved solution. We next discuss the realities of stranger threat in the modern era, and examine the possibility that our innate biases against strangers may ironically undermine child protection today. We end by reviewing programs that may assist parents and policymakers to perceive the actual hazards facing children in the present environment, rather than those we have evolved naturally to fear.

Infant Stranger Anxiety

Humans everywhere are born with a firm dislike of stimuli such as hunger, cold, pain, and loud noises, whereas other aversions manifest later. Fearful reactions, for instance, often develop just when the relevant danger would first be encountered (Marks, 1987). A good example of this phenomenon is the fear of heights, the appearance of which roughly coincides with the newfound capacity to crawl. Bertenthal, Campos, and Caplovitz (1983) found that within 41 days of initial crawling, 80% of infants refuse to cross an apparent visual cliff despite encouragement to do so by their mothers. Before this time, infants exhibit no distress when perched over the illusion of a cliff and willingly crawl over the apparent edge. Similarly, stranger anxiety may emerge with the fear of heights at around the 8th month because the capacity to crawl allows infants to move away from caregivers and toward strangers or steep drops, both of which posed significant survival threats in the ancestral environment (Heerwagen & Orians, 2002; Marks & Nesse, 1994). In both cases, fear motivates infants to alert caregivers and to withdraw from threat, thereby increasing the child's odds of survival and subsequent reproductive success. In this manner, natural selection may have favored the proliferation of psychological traits that prepared our ancestors to begin to fear strangers at an early age.

Novelty and size of the stranger alone do not predict infants' fearful reactions. The age, gender, and distance of the stranger all mediate the infant's responses. Stranger anxiety increases as the stranger approaches, as their speed of approach increases, and when the stranger is male (Feinman, 1980). Infants also exhibit exaggeratedly fearful reactions towards strangers when their caregivers are farther away, even by a few feet (Morgan & Ricciuti, 1969). Although strange adults elicit fear, infants respond positively to unfamiliar children (Lewis & Brooks, 1974). Likewise, adult faces elicit more gaze aversion than child faces presented at an equivalent, typically adult height (Bigelow, MacLean, Wood, & Smith, 1990). Theories of stranger anxiety based solely on stimulus familiarity would predict that child faces presented at adult height would elicit more anxiety, not less, due to their inherent bizarreness.

Infants are more fearful of male strangers than female strangers (Benjamin, 1961; Morgan & Ricciuti, 1969; Shaffran & Decarie, 1973; Skarin, 1977). Males are typically taller, but incidental height discrepancies fail to account for infants' disproportionately fearful reactions towards male strangers, as taller males do not evoke more fear than shorter ones (Weinraub & Putney, 1978). Infants' greater fear of adult males cannot be explained by their simple lack of experience with male adults, because infants raised by male caregivers still react with greater anxiety toward male strangers than they do female strangers (Lamb, Hwang, Frodi, & Frodi, 1982).

Noticing that adult male strangers evoked the greatest fear, Feinman (1980) first argued that infants respond to strangers as if stranger anxiety were a psychological adaptation designed to protect them from outgroup strangers. Infants' fear increases with the danger that a stranger would actually pose. Moreover, behaviors typical of stranger anxiety would help to provide infants with protection from strangers. As strangers near, infants typically seek closer proximity to the caregiver or cry for their attention (Bretherton & Ainsworth, 1974; Skarin, 1977). Given their physical helplessness, soliciting aid from caregivers constitutes the infants' only defense (Bowlby, 1969).

Other evolutionary-minded researchers have also cited these factors to argue that stranger anxiety represents a true *ontogenetic adaptation*, one calibrated to protect infants from homicidal attacks by male strangers (Heerwagen & Orians, 2002; Hrdy, 1999; Marks, 1987; Marks & Nesse, 1994). The principal evidence posed by most previous evolutionary theorists that violent male strangers presented an adaptive problem (e.g., Heerwagen &

Orians, 2002; Marks & Nesse, 1994) has been Daly and Wilson's (1988) finding that infants living with stepfathers are far more likely to be murdered than infants living with their biological fathers. However, step-parent perpetrators are, by definition, not strangers. Stranger anxiety disappears after mere minutes of exposure (Rheingold & Eckerman, 1973), yet the stepfathers in the Daly and Wilson data were co-habiting with the infants they killed. Stranger anxiety reactions are not elicited by familiar men, and therefore cannot protect infants from stepfathers. Consequently, Daly and Wilson's stepfather data do not pertain to hypotheses concerning the adaptive utility of stranger anxiety. Archeological, historical, and anthropological approaches to stranger violence among humans, as well as comparative findings from non-human primate species, provide better evidence that strangers posed an adaptive threat.

Infanticide by strange males is commonplace throughout the animal world (van Schaik & Janson, 1997). Hrdy (1999) compares the prevalence of strange males committing infanticide across primate species with evidence gathered from the Ache Indians. Among this Paraguayan hunter–gatherer society, outgroup male tribe members constituted the single greatest cause of mortality for children aged 4–14, accounting for 56% of deaths, and 16% of the deaths of children 0–3 years of age (Hill & Hurtado, 1989). History presents a gruesome litany of similar cases; prehistory appears to have been even more fraught with intergroup bloodshed (see Keeley, 1997, and Komar, 2008, for reviews). During the 19th century, American soldiers were known to deliberately murder infants and children as part of the genocidal campaigns against native peoples (Kane, 1999). Likewise, archeologists uncovered a mass grave containing nearly 500 bodies of children, men, and women who had been murdered, scalped, and mutilated during a rival tribe's attack on their village in 1325 CE (Willey, 1990).

If outgroup violence precipitated the evolution of stranger aversion, then outgroup membership cues such as foreign accents, skin pigmentation, or features might be expected to heighten fearful reactions.[2] In fact, infants do respond more fearfully towards strangers of differing race (Feinman, 1980). Kinzler, Dupoux, and Spelke (2007) also found that younger infants would rather look at people who previously spoke their native language, older infants are more likely to accept toys from native speakers, and toddlers preferentially select native speakers as friends.[3] Future research is needed to determine whether this preference for native speakers interacts with stranger anxiety to elicit more fearful reactions towards strangers with accents.

In the context of intergroup conflict over disputed resources, killing outgroup infants of either gender benefits the attacker by reducing the ability of the rival group to reconstitute or retaliate (Manson & Wrangham, 1991). Simultaneously, killing outgroup infants increases the fertility of potential outgroup females by ending the postpartum infertility brought on by lactation amenorrhea (Hrdy, 1984). Although killing outgroup male infants decreases the numbers of future adult outgroup male competitors, who typically play a larger role in retaliation and defense of resources, killing female infants suffers the drawback of squandering a future reproductive resource for outgroup males and their kin. There is some evidence to support the notion that outgroup males target young boys (including infants) to a greater degree than girls. For example, the Yanomamo of Brazil, renowned for frequent intertribal warfare and female abduction (Chagnon, 1983), have been observed to target boys to reduce the warrior population of opposing tribes (Valero & Biocca, 1970). In other primate species, chimpanzees and langurs have also been observed to target outgroup male infants (Hamai, Nishida, Takasaki, & Turner, 1992; Sommer, 1994; Watts et al., 2006).

Thus, the male predisposition for greater anxiety toward strange males may be a "logical" selective response to a genuinely greater threat. Indeed, male infants do show more anxiety than female infants when confronted by a male stranger (Greenberg, Hillman, & Grice, 1973; Morgan & Ricciuti, 1969; Shaffran & Decarie, 1973; Skarin, 1977). To be sure, females have also had much to fear from strange males, and infant girls display clear stranger anxiety toward strange males. However, if females tended to be abducted and impregnated by strange males rather than killed outright in the evolutionary past, then stranger attack would pose less of a drain on female reproductive fitness. For instance, in the mass grave site from 1325 CE mentioned previously, young women were underrepresented among the remains, suggesting they were taken captive (Willey, 1990). The selective incentive to eliminate outgroup male competitors and exploit outgroup female fertility continues to hold for outgroup children and adults. Indeed, even in adulthood, men display a heightened perception of male outgroup members as threats (Neuberg, Kenrick, Maner, & Schaller, 2004; Williams & Mattingley, 2006).

Stranger Anxiety Beyond Infancy

The threats of violence posed by outgroup members remained constant over our ancestors' lifecycles. If stranger anxiety reflects an adaptive reply to outgroup violence, why should it disappear as infants enter their second year, or ever? Although any full treatment of these questions must consider a confluence of environmental and cognitive factors interacting in a formidably complex dynamic interplay, the basic explanation may be condensed to two fundamental processes: *habituation* and *executive inhibition*. Rather than end with the first year, stranger anxiety may instead express itself in increasingly subtle behaviors over development, as individuals grow increasingly habituated to encounters with strangers and as executive systems develop greater control over overtly negative displays.

In the context of stranger anxiety, *habituation* refers to the ameliorating influence of routinely innocuous encounters with strangers. In most modern, large-scale cultures, children observe strangers in great numbers, and parents typically socialize their children to be friendly with others and reassure them when they seem distressed. These experiences should help to ameliorate infants' natural inclination to withdraw from strangers. By the same logic, individuals exposed to fewer strangers over their lifespan should preserve their native aversion and display it more intensely. Indeed, the children of an isolated, small-scale traditional society were found to exhibit a relatively extreme fear of strangers until the end of the second year (Konner, 1972), a full year longer than observed in highly populous cultures. Similarly, 3-year-olds who had attended preschool, and thus gained more exposure to strangers, showed lower physiological stress responses (as measured by cortisol levels) at the approach of a stranger than children who had not attended preschool (Zimmermann & Stansbury, 2004). Infants' habituation to strangers may couple with their growing executive capacity to inhibit the expression of negative reactions as outwardly visible behaviors.

Executive inhibition refers to cognitive supervisory regulation of otherwise reflexive responses. The earliest forms of executive inhibition normally develop between 10 and 12 months (Diamond, 2006), at the same time that overt infant stranger anxiety reactions tend to dissipate. Executive processes inhibit reactions to difficult or novel situations when prepotent response tendencies are at odds with intended outcomes (Amodio et al., 2004; Botvinick,

Cohen, & Carter, 2004; Geary, 2005; Greene, Nystrom, Engell, Darley, & Cohen, 2004; Miller & Cohen, 2001; Norman & Shallice, 1986). Executive inhibition operates across domains of human cognition involving goals (Bargh, 1997; Bjorklund & Harnishferger, 1995; Geary, 2005; Monsell, 2003), including social contexts related to reputation management and intergroup bias (Adolphs, 1999; Amodio et al., 2004; Devine, 1989; Lieberman, 2007; Wheeler & Fiske, 2005). Directly relating executive control with masking stranger anxiety, Hill-Soderlund and Braungrat-Rieker (2007) found that infants who display stranger anxiety of greater severity and duration later show impoverished executive inhibition as 5-year-olds. Executive inhibition may explain the transition from the blatantly observable fear of strangers in infancy to an increasingly clandestine fear of strangers, particularly out-group male strangers, detected in later stages of development (e.g., "shyness").

If executive inhibition curtails the outwardly fearful behaviors characteristic of stranger anxiety by the end of the child's first year, children should show implicit signs of persisting stranger fear belying their outward calm. Although few studies have investigated covert stranger anxiety reactions beyond infancy, implicit indicators of stranger anxiety have been reported to endure well beyond the first year. In a longitudinal study of children at 10 and 25 months, the amount of fearful behaviors and increased heart rate displayed in 10-month-old infants during a stranger's approach were found to predict the degree of stranger shyness subsequently exhibited as toddlers at 25 months (Andersson, Bohlin, & Hagekull, 1999). This finding suggests that stranger shyness at age 2 reflects a muted version of the child's previous infant stranger anxiety.

In addition, 3-year-olds habituated to strangers through preschool attendance continue to display a significant increase in cortisol (a hormonal measure of stress and negative affect) during a stranger's approach (Zimmermann & Stansbury, 2004). In a comparison of implicit and explicit negative attitudes toward outgroup members among 6-year-olds, 10-year-olds, and adults, implicit aversion was constant for all three groups but self-reported aversion decreased with age (Baron & Banaji, 2005). In this fashion, the executive capacity for self-regulation steadily improves as children transition to adulthood (Davidson, Amso, Anderson, & Diamond, 2006).

Aversion to outgroup males, first displayed in infant stranger anxiety reactions, persists into adulthood. Adopting a classic prepared fear paradigm previously used to study automatic reactions to stimuli such as snakes and spiders (see Seligman, 1971, for review), Navarrete and colleagues (2009; also see Olsson, Ebert, Banaji, & Phelps, 2005) paired faces of racial ingroup versus outgroup male and female strangers with mild but unpleasant electric shocks. Participants' subsequent implicit fear reactions (measured through skin conductance) endured longer when the paired face belonged to male outgroup members. In a related study of fear-primed participants' tendencies to attribute anger to emotionally neutral outgroup faces of both genders, participants attributed more anger to outgroup males rather than outgroup females, with male participants attributing more anger than female participants (Neuberg et al., 2004). Similarly, Williams and Mattingley (2006) found that although both genders are better at detecting an angry male face than an angry female face in an array of distracting neutral faces, male participants were significantly faster at doing so, suggesting a greater covert vigilance toward male threats. These adult data complement the previous finding that male infants find male strangers more intensely threatening than female infants, presumably for the same reason: Males are more likely than females to fall victim to violence inflicted by strange males, a contemporary trend that probably persisted over the course of our ancestral history (Daly & Wilson, 1988).

In addition to being unfamiliar, strangers from racial outgroups further cue lack of kinship by their novel appearance. Recalling that infants exhibit more acute fear of strangers of differing accent or appearance, adults should be expected to share, but inhibit, this negative reflex. Wheeler and Fiske (2005) manipulated participants' task goals during exposure to outgroup images and stereotypically associated words, monitoring amygdala responses with fMRI to gauge the arousal of automatic threat reactions (also see Macrae, Bodenhausen, Milne, Thorn, & Castelli, 1997). They found that "controlled efforts to inhibit expression of automatically activated stereotyped [negative] thoughts differentiate observers who display prejudice and discrimination from those who do not" (Wheeler & Fiske, 2005, p. 57; also see Devine, 1989). In another study, Amodio and colleagues (2004) presented White participants with an artifact identification task in which a Black or White male face was followed by an image of a handgun or a hand tool. Preceding tool images with Black faces increased the chance of incorrectly identifying the tools as weapons. The authors correlated participants' artifact choices with electroencephalogram recordings that monitored activation of executive areas, finding that participants who compensated for their automatic race bias in order to choose correctly displayed an enhanced signal for executive control. Although these findings relate more directly to the inhibition of prejudice rather than fear reactions per se, they demonstrate that executive control inhibits prepotent negative responses to strange members of racial outgroups.

To summarize, humans are born inclined to fear strangers, particularly strange males aligned with outgroups, because this predisposition would have encouraged adaptive responses to the rampant stranger violence of the ancestral past. The evidence linking stranger aversion throughout the lifespan is also compelling, suggesting that children's stranger anxiety and adults' aversion to strangers arise via a shared mechanism. This largely unconscious, reflexive tendency toward fear and suspicion may distort parents' perceptions of the danger posed to their children by strangers today.

Public Perceptions

Humans of all ages appear to possess an inborn aversion to strangers, which may have contributed to our ancestors' survival and reproduction. But is it still useful to fear strangers in developed societies, or has this native predisposition fallen out of date? Evolutionary psychologists refer to mismatches between inborn predilections and modern conditions as cases of *disequilibrium*. Consider our innate, universal preference for rich foods. For most of human history, and in many parts of the world today, calories were scarce and feasting was a wholesome activity when possible. In modern developed societies, the exorbitant cravings for fat and sugar that formerly prompted adaptive eating behaviors contribute to serious health problems. Stranger aversion may similarly represent a case of at least partial disequilibrium.[4] In what follows, we review current statistics on child abduction, violence, and sexual abuse to assess the risks posed by strangers.

In many surveys, parents report kidnapping as the most worrisome stranger threat scenario (Kidscape, 1993; Stickler et al., 1991). Children also cite strange intruders (e.g., kidnappers) as their most common nighttime fear (Muris, Merckelbach, Ollendick, King, & Bogie, 2001). Concerns regarding stranger abduction are disproportional to the frequency of this type of crime. According to the U.S. Department of Justice (Finkelhor,

Hammer, & Sedlak, 2002), there were 115 child abductions in 1999 in the United States that met the definition of a "stereotypical kidnapping" in which a stranger (or slight acquaintance) killed, detained overnight, held for ransom, or intended to keep a child permanently. Only 20 of these child abductees were under the age of 5 years. This means that the odds of a child under 5 being kidnapped by a stranger in 1999 were 1 in 1,157,848. For children between the ages of 6 and 11 years, the odds of being kidnapped were 1 in 954,348. The odds of stranger kidnapping were slightly less astronomical for older children: 1 in 265,096 for children between the ages of 12 and 14, and 1 in 596,467 for teenagers between 15 and 17.[5] During the same period, an estimated 58,200 children were abducted by family or adult acquaintances, although these kidnappings were usually less severe, lasting less than a day and not involving homicide or ransom.[6] Ironically, then, the most prototypical fear held by parents and children today is also among the least likely to occur.

Stranger violence ranks as a major concern for 54% of parents of children in the United States under the age of 4 years (Kantrowitz, 1997). Again, the concern greatly outweighs the risk. According to the U.S. Department of Justice (Durose, Harlow, Langan, Motivans, Rantala, & Smith, 2005), only 19% of the victims of stranger violence were under the age of 18, with the large majority of these child victims over the age of 13. Conversely, 76% of stranger violence victims were adults between the ages of 18 and 54. Of the 2362 victims murdered by strangers in 2002, only 2% were under the age of 13 and only 6% were between the ages of 13 and 17. Although the most frequent type of criminal violence is stranger violence, which accounted for nearly half (46.1%) of all fatal and non-fatal violence between 1998 and 2002, practically all of the victims of these crimes were adults. Strangers today may be dangerously violent, but rarely towards children.

Child sexual abuse presents a somewhat more realistic stranger-related hazard than violence or kidnapping. Meta-analyses reveal that roughly 20% of female and 7% of male children in the United States are sexually abused (Bolen & Scannapieco, 1999). Despite these figures, however, strangers are much less likely to sexually abuse children than familiar adults (Finkelhor, 1994). According to a survey of state correctional facilities, one-third of the inmates charged with child sexual abuse had molested their own children, while half had a prior relationship with their victim as a friend, acquaintance, or relative; only 1 in 7 inmates had been a stranger to their victim (Greenfeld, 1996). Other studies affirm the general conclusion that perpetrators of child sexual abuse are overwhelmingly known by their victims, with 70–90% of abuse perpetrated by familiar persons (see Finkelhor, 1994, for a review).

Although strangers are less likely to sexually assault children than familiar adults or peers, sexual abuse is the most prevalent threat that strangers pose to children today. In a survey of 2420 children conducted in the United Kingdom, 41% of reported sexual abuses were attributed to strangers (Gallagher, Bradford, & Pease, 2002). This amounts to 9% of the total number of children surveyed reporting one or more incidents of sexual abuse by a stranger. This figure may have been inflated in this study because sexual abuse was broadly defined to include indecent exposure, which comprised 44% of the reports. The remaining children recollected more serious acts, such as strangers attempting to lure the child to accompany them elsewhere (28%), touching the child (18%), attempting to touch the child (14%), attempting to make the child touch them (5%), convincing the child to accompany them elsewhere (3%), and making the child touch them (1%). Of the total children interviewed, only 1.7% reported stranger abuse involving physical contact. In another UK study that employed a narrower definition of sexual abuse, 4% of British children reported being abused in some fashion by a stranger (Cawson, Wattam, Brooker, & Kelly, 2000).

To combat these disturbing crimes against children, we must acknowledge that children are at far greater risk of sexual assault than of violence or abduction, and direct our energies accordingly. We must also recognize that sexual abuse is more likely to be committed by family members, adult acquaintances, and peers, without disregarding the fact that stranger sexual abuse, though less common, also occurs.

Strangers no longer warrant the menace with which they are perceived in contemporary industrialized cultures. The remarkable absence of stranger attacks on children may result from a number of factors, such as severe legal penalties, societal vigilance, and contemporary norms. For whatever reasons, modern strangers are culpable for a negligible number of child kidnappings, a tiny fraction of violent assaults on children, and a relatively minor percentage of child sexual abuse. In comparison, everyday accidents pose far greater peril to children. For example, 80% of students reported being bitten by dogs, being struck by cars, or falling off bicycles, with 36% sustaining injuries severe enough to require medical treatment (Gallagher et al., 2002). When these statistics are compared with the chances of children being hurt by a stranger, then road safety, bicycle, and dog wariness classes appear to take precedence over courses in stranger danger. Confining our concerns to dangers posed by fellow humans, the data clearly suggest that harm reduction programs should focus their energies on the risk posed by the people children already know. Policies designed to reduce childhood stranger danger should certainly not be abandoned, but appropriately scaled to reflect the actual risks.

Policy Recommendations

Strangers no longer present the threat they once did, yet our innate biases to avoid them persist unabated. To the extent that they focus attention and energy away from the actual loci of risk to children, stranger danger initiatives can inadvertently misdirect resources better invested in preventing abuse perpetrated by family, friends, and acquaintances. In addition, exaggerated stranger danger hysteria can potentially be harmful to children when stranger fear adversely affects child mobility, freedom, and independence. For example, in 1970, 80% of British children were allowed to go to school without supervision, but by 1990 this figure had fallen to 9% due primarily to parents' concerns over stranger attacks (Hillman, Adams, & Whitelegg, 1990). A similar decline in children walking to school, partially owing to stranger fear, has been observed in the United States, falling from more than 50% in 1969 to only 13% in 2004 (Kweon, Naderi, Maghelal, & Shin, 2005). Studies have identified fears of molestation and other stranger crime as chief motivators for parents driving their children to school (Hillman, 1993). Similarly, media attention and traditional stranger danger education programs may be fueling children's experiences of anxiety more than parents appreciate. The majority of parents appear to be unaware of or drastically underestimate their children's level of terror about strangers (Muris et al., 2001).

Lying awake at night fixating on unwarranted concerns over strangers is distressing to children, but abandoning stranger education programs is certainly not the answer, as strangers do pose a relatively small but real threat. Education initiatives designed to minimize child abuse should therefore incorporate stranger danger techniques into more comprehensive programs that focus on training children to cope with the far more likely, though perhaps more innately counterintuitive, threats of abuse from familiar adults or peers. Fortunately, many contemporary abuse prevention programs endeavor to do just that. Estimates indicate that nearly three-quarters of all students participate in some form of abuse prevention program at school (Daro, 1994). In what follows, we will review the efficacy and policy goals of school-based abuse prevention programs.

Stranger danger education remained at the heart of protection programs through the 1980s. Traditional stranger danger abduction prevention programs take many forms, but they typically consist of verbal presentations on three main themes: (1) realizing that strangers are dangerous even if they seem nice; (2) learning about common lures used by strangers; and (3) escaping from abductors. Of the few studies evaluating the effectiveness of programs of this type, children were not found to have retained the skills and knowledge necessary to avoid abduction (see Blumberg & Johnson, 1997, for a review). According to the National Center for Missing and Exploited Children (2005), the stranger danger message by itself is not effective, as children consider strangers to be "ugly" and "mean," and often do not consider that a person they have seen before or talked to once is a stranger. These experts also argue that "don't talk to strangers" campaigns may actually be deleterious to children's safety, because the great majority of strangers would provide aid if children were to find themselves in danger. Since the 1980s, however, many programs have broadened from verbally presented stranger danger instruction to include more interactive ways of teaching children how to handle issues such as peer bullying and sexual abuse by familiar adults (Child Assault Prevention Project, 2004).

Behavioral approaches to prevention training, which have been shown to be more effective (Blumberg & Johnson, 1997), combine verbal instruction with modeling, behavioral rehearsal, corrective feedback, and practice until a criterion level of performance is achieved. The nationally implemented Child Assault Prevention Project (CAP), for example, emphasizes a three-pronged focus on training students, parents, and teachers to anticipate and resolve interactive abuse scenarios involving other children, familiar adults, and strangers (Child Assault Prevention Project, 2004). These topics are tailored to suit the different learning styles of kindergarteners, elementary school students, teenagers, and disabled children. CAP's most widespread workshop involves elementary school children role-playing a bully confrontation, a stranger attempting to kidnap a child through trickery, and a familiar adult inappropriately kissing a child and then directing the child to keep it secret. Each situation is dramatized in two variations; the child is initially portrayed as a victim, but after a brainstorming session on preventive techniques the scenario is re-enacted as a "success story." In a third and final role-play, the classroom teacher is invited to portray a supportive adult who responds to a child's request for help.

Meta-analyses reveal that abuse prevention programs presented over four or more physically interactive sessions yielded the greatest retention of program materials (Davis & Gidycz, 2000). Ray and Dietzal (1984) evaluated a program that consisted of three 1-hour presentations to 5th grade students and found that although children performed better immediately afterwards on a questionnaire, crucial concepts were lost during a subsequent 8-month period. For example, the students often failed to recall whether molesters were frequently people whom they knew, who was to blame when an adult touches a child in a sexual way, or whether it was acceptable to break promises made to molesters. In another study, after participating in only one instruction session, over half of the children stated that they would comply with an unfamiliar adult's direction to accompany him (Moran, Warden, Macleod, Mayes, & Gillies, 1997). Including a review component to prevention programs significantly improves knowledge retention (Plummer, 1984). In addition, one-on-one follow-up sessions held on the same day can reinforce knowledge and simultaneously provide children with an opportunity to report abuse. For example, the New Jersey CAP program uncovered 705 cases of abuse requiring outside intervention over a 5-year period by providing children with additional one-on-one review and discussion time in a safe setting (Riesser & Borys, 2005).

Some evidence indicates that the implementation of abuse prevention programs has decreased the incidence of childhood abuse. One correlational study found that college-aged women who reported participating in a "good-touch, bad-touch" prevention program as children were half as likely to report having been sexually abused than women who did not recall participating in a prevention program (Gibson & Leitenberg, 2000). Research with convicted sex offenders suggests that children who participate in prevention programs may be less likely to be targeted by offenders, who prefer passivity, lack of confidence, and low self-esteem when identifying victims who will accede to their wishes (Budin &

Johnson, 1989). To the extent that prevention programs endeavor to reduce shame and increase children's ability to react effectively to abuse, they may help children to project more assertiveness and understanding than child predators are comfortable with. Encouragingly, there has been a massive decline in sexual abuse cases over the last decade, which may in part be due to prevention programs (Finkelhor & Jones, 2004). However, it is impossible to derive causal conclusions from these correlations, and other researchers have failed to uncover evidence that children exposed to prevention programs suffered lower incidences of sexual abuse or physical injury (Bolen, 2003).

Findings that prevention programs do not clearly reduce the incidence of abuse have often been advanced to negate these programs' usefulness (e.g., Catholic Medical Association Task Force, 2006). For example, studies suggest that the strategies taught in abuse prevention programs do not help children to escape acts of sexual assault once they are underway. Although children exposed to prevention programs evince more prior awareness of sexual abuse and are more likely to attempt prevention strategies such as yelling, threatening to tell, insisting on being left alone, and actually telling, they appear equally likely to be victimized as children without prevention training after an attack is initiated (Finkelhor, Asdigian, & Dziuba-Leatherman, 1995). However, the prevention of abuse should not be the sole barometer of the success of policies intended to reduce child harm.

Prevention programs have been correlated with better outcomes in the aftermath of abuse. Finkelhor, Asdigian, and Dziuba-Leatherman (1995) found that prevention program participation increased the likelihood that children reported abuse, did not blame themselves, and felt satisfied that they had successfully tried to protect themselves. By promoting abuse disclosure, prevention programs may help to shorten the durations of abuse and mobilize assistance for victims (Finkelhor, 2007). Though laudable, the goal of outright prevention may unduly overshadow equally valuable achievements in minimizing abuse or marshalling emotional and material support for children who have already been subjected to abuse. These contributions justify the utility of abuse prevention programs even if the actual "prevention of abuse" outcomes turn out to be disappointingly modest.

As the focus shifts from stranger harm to the harm inflicted by familiar persons, effective interventions appear more complicated: It is much easier to run away from a stranger than from your home or church. For example, abused children often rely on their attackers as caregivers; resisting assaults can therefore be severely costly if the child must forsake vital resources as the price of refusal (Taal & Edalaar, 1997). The trauma some children may experience attendant to being separated from their attackers should be taken into account as well. To be truly effective, abuse reduction programs must therefore direct the children of abusive caregivers toward agencies equipped to provide practical options rooted in their specific needs and circumstances.

Some critics have argued that prevention programs unduly burden children with troubling information about potential sexual abuse, violence, and abduction (e.g., Catholic Medical Association Task Force, 2006). Although very little research has been done on the potential negative impact of prevention programs, there is some evidence of temporarily adverse effects. Taal and Edelaar (1997) surveyed students between 8 and 12 years of age who had recently completed a sexual abuse prevention program. Immediately after participating, the youngest and oldest children reported feeling less capable of managing a potentially abusive interaction, and the youngest children considered refusing to cooperate with abusers less plausible. Six weeks later, however, the same groups of children reported increased confidence in prevention strategies, and younger children reported decreased social anxiety. Another study found that some children and parents report increased worry after the training but that these same people also report the most positive feelings about the program and effective use of program skills (Finkelhor & Dziuba-Leatherman, 1995). In addition, studies have shown no correlation between participation in abuse prevention programs and the quality of later sexual satisfaction or intimate relationships (Gibson & Leitenberg, 2000). Therefore, the negative effects of abuse prevention programs appear to be minimal, short-lived, and well worth the benefits.

Although the emphasis must be on recognizing and combating harms perpetrated by friends, family, and acquaintances, the stranger danger component of prevention training should of course not be discarded. Based on a national telephone survey, Finkelhor, Hotaling, and Asdigian (1995) estimated that over 100,000 failed stranger abduction attempts occur each year. Victims of attempted abduction in this study were most likely to be solicited by a stranger in a passing car and to be between the ages of 4 and 11 years of age. Although it is important to keep in mind that even at this estimated frequency attempted abductions would still be quite rare relative to population size, the enormous difference between actual and attempted abductions lends credence to arguments that children are capable of resisting stranger abductions. When utilizing interactive instruction, stranger abduction prevention training has also been experimentally confirmed to help children to respond appropriately to confederates who mimic dangerous strangers in naturalistic environments (Flanagan, 1986). Being struck by lightning may not be likely, but the consequences are dire enough to warrant taking the time to equip children with the basic principles of lightning safety. When children are taught about lightning safety, the dangers are stressed, but so are the chances of avoiding being struck if you employ simple precautions. Stranger danger training programs should similarly inform parents and children about the real risks, and thereby alleviate their fears while imparting stranger abuse prevention skills.

In sum, there is reason to believe that prevention programs that acknowledge the threat posed by familiar adults as well as strangers reduce children's likelihood of being targeted by abusers (Gibson & Leitenberg, 2000), increase disclosures of abuse (Riesser & Borys, 2005), and help children who are abused to achieve better outcomes (Finkelhor, 2007). Pedagogically, abandoning purely verbal instruction in favor of interactive, behavioral approaches to skills training appears to be vital (Blumberg & Johnson, 1997). Follow-up review also appears to be crucial to reinforce children's retention of key concepts (Ray & Dietzal, 1984), and one-to-one review sessions gain the added benefit of simultaneously providing a safe space in which abused children may disclose abuse (Riesser & Borys, 2005). Child abductions by strangers may be infrequent, but their potential seriousness justifies continued efforts to warn and empower children against stranger abuse. We simply advocate seeking ways of doing so that simultaneously minimize fueling children's (and adults') natural fear and paranoia about strangers.

Conclusion

In this chapter, we have presented evidence that humans innately fear strangers, especially males, because male strangers posed a significant threat to both children and adults in the evolutionary past. Stranger aversion is first observed as blatant behavioral displays (e.g., crying, recoiling, etc.) in the second half of the first year, after which mechanisms of habituation and executive inhibition enable emotion regulation. As the capacity for executive inhibition matures, stranger aversion becomes increasingly covert but the bias remains. Regardless of the massive evidence that strangers no longer pose a serious threat to children, modern adults continue to exhibit an inordinate, perhaps evolutionarily prepared, fear that strangers will harm their children. However, humans have also inherited the executive capacity to override gut reactions when they conflict with our goals. To prevent harm to children, we must endeavor to meet the dangers where they are, rather than where our ancestrally derived minds lead us to expect them.

Notes

1. At one time, most psychologists considered stranger anxiety a developmental milestone reflecting the child's achievement of normal cognitive, social, and emotional development (Spritz, 1965). Nevertheless, some researchers challenged the very existence of stranger anxiety because in certain contexts infants usually react positively towards strangers (Rheingold & Eckerman, 1973). However, when variables such as the amount of time spent interacting with the stranger before their approach, the proximity of the caregiver, and the gender of the stranger are considered, the behavioral aversion toward strangers is apparent (Sroufe, 1977).

2. Differences in skin pigmentation would have been exceedingly rare in the ancestral past, if they occurred at all. Encounters with other races today are an artifact of relatively recent technology. The accent data may therefore be more relevant to the conditions in which stranger anxiety evolved, as dialect shifts rapidly over time with group isolation and would have been a more plausibly encountered indicator of outgroup status. However, distinctive modes of dress and appearance signaling group orientation may have also been common; racial skin and feature characteristics may be seen as a similar visual cue in this respect.

3. These findings do not necessarily indicate that babies are born afraid of all adults whose skin pigment or accent differs from their own, but only that when paired with a previously aversive factor, such as being a strange adult, novelty produces a more intensely negative reaction. For example, babies raised in families with diverse skin colors and accents would not be predicted to show increased fear of strangers with these characteristics.

4. These data and interpretations apply only to Western societies such as the United States and the United Kingdom. Stranger aversion may still be warranted for much of the remainder of the world's population.

5. These probabilities were extrapolated from the U.S. Department of Justice (Finkelhor et al., 2002) figures by multiplying the total

population of children in 1999 by the percentage of children in each age group and then dividing the number of children in each age group by the number of abductees in each age group.
6. In 21% of these cases, police recovered the children in less than an hour (Finkelhor et al., 2002).

References

Adolphs, R. (1999). Social cognition and the human brain. *Trends in Cognitive Science, 3*, 469–479.

Amodio, D. M., Harmon-Jones, E., Devine, P. G., Curtin, J. J., Hartley, S. L., & Covert, A. E. (2004). Neural signals for the detection of unintentional race bias. *Psychological Science, 15*, 88–93.

Andersson, K., Bohlin, G., & Hagekull, B. (1999). Early temperament and stranger wariness as predictors of social inhibition in 2-year-olds. *British Journal of Developmental Psychology, 17*, 421–434.

Bargh, J. A. (1997). The automaticity of everyday life. In R. S. Wyer, Jr. (Ed.), *The automaticity of everyday life: Advances in social cognition* (Vol. 10, pp. 1–61). Mahwah, NJ: Lawrence Erlbaum Associates, Inc.

Baron, A., S., & Banaji, M. R. (2005). The development of implicit attitudes. *Psychological Science, 17*, 53–58.

Benjamin, J. D. (1961). Some developmental observations relating to the theory of anxiety. *Journal of the American Psychoanalytic Association, 9*, 652–668.

Bertenthal, B. I., Campos, J. J., & Caplovitz, K. S. (1983). Self produced locomotion: An organizer of emotional, cognitive and social development in infancy. In R. N. Emde & R. Harmon (Eds.), *Continuities and discontinuities in development* (pp. 175–209). New York: Plenum Press.

Bigelow, A., MacLean, J., Wood, C., & Smith, J. (1990). Infants' responses to child and adult strangers: An investigation of height and facial configuration. *Infant Behavior and Development, 13*, 21–32.

Bjorklund, D. F., & Harnishfeger, K. K. (1995). The evolution of inhibition mechanisms and their role in human cognition and behavior. In F. Dempster & C. Brainerd (Eds.), *New perspectives on interference and inhibition in cognition* (pp. 175–204). New York: Academic Press.

Blumberg, D. S., & Johnson, B. (1997). Behavioral versus traditional approaches to prevention of child abduction. *School Psychology Review, 26*, 662–633.

Bolen, R. M. (2003). Child sexual abuse: Prevention or promotion? *Social Work, 48*, 174–185.

Bolen, R. M., & Scannapieco, M. (1999). Prevalence of child sexual abuse: A corrective meta-analysis. *Social Service Review, 73*, 281–312.

Botvinick, M., Cohen, J. D., & Carter, C. S. (2004). Conflict monitoring and anterior cingulate cortex: An update. *Trends in Cognitive Sciences, 12*, 201–208.

Bowlby, J. (1969). *Attachment and loss (Vol. 1)*. London: Random House.

Bretherton, I., & Ainsworth, M. S. (1974). Responses of one year olds to strangers in a strange situation. In M. Lewis & L. Rosenblum (Eds.), *The origins of fear* (pp. 131–164). New York: Wiley.

Budin, L., & Johnson, C. F. (1989). Sex abuse prevention programs: Offenders' attitudes about their efficacy. *Child Abuse and Neglect, 13*, 77–87.

Campos, J., Emde, R., Gaensbauer, T., & Henderson, C. (1975). Cardiac and behavioural interrelationships in the reactions of infants to strangers. *Developmental Psychology, 11*, 589–601.

Catholic Medical Association Task Force (2006). *To prevent and to protect: Report of the task force of the Catholic Medical Association on the sexual abuse of children and its prevention*. Wynnewood, PA: Catholic Medical Association.

Cawson, P., Wattam, C., Brooker, S., & Kelly, G. (2000). *Child maltreatment in the United Kingdom: A study of the prevalence of child abuse and neglect*. London: NSPCC.

Celizic, M. (2008). *Mom lets 9-year-old take subway home alone: Columnist stirs controversy with experiment in childhood independence*. Retrieved November 15, 2008, from http://www.msnbc.com/id/23935847/

Center for Disease Control and Prevention (1982). Perspectives on disease prevention and health promotion: Child homicide – United States. *Morbidity and Mortality Weekly, 31*, 292–294.

Chagnon, N. (1983). *Yanomamo: The fierce people*. New York: Holt, Rinehart, & Winston.

Child Assault Prevention Project (2004). *Child Assault Prevention Project*. Retrieved October 17, 2008, from http://www.teamwv.org/Pages/cap_new.html

Daly, M., & Wilson, M. I. (1988). *Homicide*. Hawthorne, NY: Aldine de Gruyter.

Daro, D. (1994). Prevention of child sexual abuse. *The Future of Children, 4*, 198–223.

Davidson, M. S., Amso, D., Anderson, D., & Diamond, A. (2006). Development of cognitive control and executive functions from 4 to 13 years: Evidence from manipulations of memory, inhibition, and task switching. *Neuropsychologia, 44*, 2037–2078.

Davis, M. K., & Gidycz, C. A. (2000). Child sexual abuse prevention programs: A meta-analysis. *Journal of Clinical Child Psychology, 29*, 257–265.

Devine, P. G. (1989). Stereotypes and prejudice: Their automatic and controlled components. *Journal of Personality and Social Psychology, 56*, 5–18.

Diamond, A. (2006). The early development of executive functions. In E. Bialystok & F. Craik (Eds.), *Lifespan cognition: Mechanisms of change* (pp. 70–95). New York: Oxford University Press.

Durose, M. R., Harlow, C. W., Langan, P. A., Motivans, M., Rantala, R. R., & Smith, E. L. (2005). *Family violence statistics: Including statistics on strangers and acquaintances*. Washington, DC: U.S. Government Printing Office.

Emde, R., Gaensbauer, T., & Harmon, R. (1976). Emotional expression in infancy: A biobehavioural study. *Psychological Issues, 10*, 1–37.

Feinman, S. (1980). Infant response to race, size, proximity, and movement of strangers. *Infant Behaviour and Development, 3*, 187–204.

Finkelhor, D. (1994). Current information on the scope and nature of child sexual abuse. *The Future of Children, 4*, 31–53.

Finkelhor, D. (2007). Prevention of sexual abuse through educational programs directed toward children. *Pediatrics, 120*, 640–645.

Finkelhor, D., Asdigian, N., & Dziuba-Leatherman, J. (1995). The effectiveness of victimization prevention instruction: An evaluation of children's responses to actual threats and assaults. *Child Abuse and Neglect, 19*, 141–153.

Finkelhor, D., & Dziuba-Leatherman, J. (1995). Victimization prevention programs: A national survey of children's exposure and reactions. *Child Abuse and Neglect, 19*, 129–139.

Finkelhor, D., Hammer, H., & Sedlak, A. J. (2002). *Nonfamily abducted children: National estimates and characteristics*. Washington, DC: U.S. Government Printing Office.

Finkelhor, D., Hotaling, G., & Asdigian, N. (1995). Attempted non-family abductions. *Child Welfare, 74*, 941–955.

Finkelhor, D., & Jones, L. M. (2004). *Explanations for the decline in child sexual abuse cases*. Washington, DC: U.S. Government Printing Office.

Flanagan, R. (1986). Teaching young children responses to inappropriate approaches by strangers in public places. *Child and Family Behaviour Therapy, 8*, 27–44.

Gallagher, B., Bradford, M., & Pease, K. (2002). The sexual abuse of children by strangers: Its extent, nature and victims' characteristics. *Children and Society, 16*, 346–359.

Geary, D. C. (2005). *The origin of mind: Evolution of brain, cognition, and general intelligence*. Washington, DC: American Psychological Association.

Gibson, L. E., & Leitenberg, H. (2000). Child sexual abuse prevention programs: Do they decrease the occurrence of child sexual abuse? *Child Abuse and Neglect, 24*, 1115–1125.

Goodall, J. (1977). Infant killings and cannibalism in free-living chimpanzees. *Folia Primatologica, 28*, 259–282.

Greenberg, D. J., Hillman, D., & Grice, D. (1973). Infant and stranger variables related to stranger anxiety in the first year of life. *Developmental Psychology, 9*, 207–212.

Greene, J. D., Nystrom, L. E., Engell, A. D., Darley, J. M., & Cohen, J. D. (2004). The neural bases of cognitive conflict and control in moral judgment. *Neuron, 44*, 389–400.

Greenfeld, L. A. (1996). *Child victimizers: Violent offenders and their victims* (Publication number: NCJ-153258). Washington, DC: Office of Justice Statistics.

Hamai, M., Nishida, T., Takasaki, H., & Turner, L. A. (1992). New records of within-group infanticide and cannibalism in wild chimpanzees. *Primate, 33,* 151–162.

Heerwagen, J. H., & Orians, G. H. (2002). The ecological world of children. In P. H. Kahn, & S. R. Kellert (Eds.), *Children and nature: Psychological, sociocultural and evolutionary investigations* (pp. 29–64). London: MIT Press.

Hill, K., & Hurtado, M. A. (1996). *Ache life history: The ecology and life history of a foraging people.* Hawthorn, NY: Aldine de Gruyter.

Hillman, M. (1993). *Children, transport and the quality of life.* London: Policy Studies Institute.

Hillman, M., Adams, J., & Whitelegg, J. (1990). *One false move . . . a study of independent mobility.* London: PSI Publishers.

Hill-Soderlund, A. L., & Braungrat-Rieker, J. M. (2007). Early individual differences in temperamental reactivity and regulation: Implications for effortful control in early childhood. *Infant Behavior and Development, 31,* 386–397.

Hrdy, S. B. (1977). *The langurs of abu: Female and male strategies of reproduction.* Cambridge, MA: Harvard University Press.

Hrdy, S. B. (1984). Assumptions and evidence regarding the sexual selection hypothesis: A reply to Boggess. In G. Hausfater & S. B. Hrdy (Eds.), *Infanticide: Comparative and evolutionary perspectives* (pp. 315–321). New York: Aldine Publishing Company.

Hrdy, S. B. (1999). *Mother nature: Maternal instincts and how they shape the human species.* New York: Ballantine.

Kane, K. (1999). Nits make lice: Drogheda, Sand Creek, and the poetics of colonial extermination. *Cultural Critique, 42,* 81–103.

Kantrowitz, B. (1997, March). Off to a good start: Why the first few years are so crucial to a child's development. *Newsweek Special Issue, 7,* 6–9.

Keeley, L. H. (1997). *War before civilization: The myth of the peaceful savage.* London: Oxford University Press.

Kidscape (1993). *How safe are our children? A Kidscape special report.* London: Kidscape.

Kinzler, K. D., Dupoux, E., & Spelke, E. S. (2007). The native language of social cognition. *Science, 321,* 1844–1849.

Komar, D. (2008). Patterns of mortuary practice associated with genocide: Implications for archaeological research. *Current Anthropology, 49,* 123–133.

Konner, M. J. (1972). Aspects of the developmental ethology of a foraging people. In B. N. Jones (Ed.), *Ethological studies of child behavior* (pp. 285–304). London: Cambridge University Press.

Kweon, B., K., Naderi, J., Maghelal, P., & Shin, W. (2005, October). *Pedestrian environments and children's commute to school: Parent's decision making path to let children walk and bike to school.* Paper presented at the Association of Collegiate School of Planning (ACSP) annual conference, Kansas City, MO.

Lamb, M. E., Hwang, C. P., Frodi, A. M., & Frodi, M. (1982). Security of mother– and father–infant attachment and its relation to sociability with strangers in traditional and non-traditional Swedish families. *Infant Behaviour and Development, 5*, 355–367.

Lewis, M., & Brooks, J. (1974). Self, others, and fear: Infants' reactions to people. In M. Lewis & M. Rosenblum (Eds.), *The origins of fear* (pp. 195–228). New York: Wiley.

Lieberman, M. (2007). The X- and C-systems: The neural basis of automatic and controlled social cognition. In E. Harmon-Jones & P. Winkielman (Eds.), *Fundamentals of social neuroscience* (pp. 290–315). New York: Guilford Press.

Macrae, C., Bodenhausen, G., Milne, A., Thorn, T., & Castelli, L. (1997). On the activation of social stereotypes: The moderating role of processing objectives. *Journal of Experimental Social Psychology, 33*, 471–489.

Manson, J. H., & Wrangham, R. W. (1991). Intergroup aggression in chimpanzees and humans. *Current Anthropology, 32*, 369–390.

Marks, I. M. (1987). *Fears, phobias, and rituals.* New York: Oxford University Press.

Marks, I. M., & Nesse, R. M. (1994). Fear and fitness: An evolutionary analysis of anxiety disorders. *Ethology and Sociobiology, 15*, 247–261.

Miller, E., & Cohen, J. (2001). An integrative theory of prefrontal cortex function. *Annual Review of Neuroscience, 24*, 167–202.

Monsell, S. (2003). Task switching. *Trends in Cognitive Science, 7*, 134–140.

Moran, E., Warden, D., Macleod, L., Mayes, G., & Gillies, J. (1997). Stranger-danger: What do children know? *Child Abuse Review, 6*, 11–23.

Morgan, G., & Ricciuti, H. (1969). Infants' responses to strangers during the first year. In B. M. Foss (Ed.), *Determinants of infant behavior* (Vol. 4, pp. 253–272). London: Methuen.

Muris, P., Merckelbach, H., Ollendick, T. H., King, N. J., & Bogie, N. (2001). Children's nighttime fears: Parent–child ratings of frequency, content, origins, coping behaviours and severity. *Behaviour Research and Therapy, 39*, 13–28.

National Center for Missing and Exploited Children (2005). *Child safety is more than a slogan: "Stranger-danger" warnings not effective at keeping kids safer.* Retrieved November 15, 2008, from http://www.missingkids.com/missingkids/servlet/NewsEventServlet?LanguageCountry=en_US&Pageid=2034

Navarrete, C. D., Olsson, A., Ho, A., Mendes, W., Thomsen, L., & Sidanius, J. (2009). Fear extinction to an outgroup face: The role of target gender. *Psychological Science, 20*, 155–158.

Neuberg, S. L., Kenrick, D. T., Maner, J. K., & Schaller, M. (2004). From evolved motives to everyday mentation: Evolution, goals and cognition. In J. Forgas & K. Williams (Eds.), *Social motivations: Conscious and unconscious processes* (pp. 133–152). New York: Cambridge University Press.

Norman, D. A., & Shallice, T. (1986). Attention to action: Willed and automatic control of behavior. In R. J. Davidson, G. E. Schwartz, & D. Shapiro (Eds.), *Consciousness and self-regulation* (pp. 1–18). New York: Plenum Press.

Olsson, A., Ebert, J. P., Banaji, M. R., & Phelps, E. A. (2005). The role of social groups in persistence of learned fear. *Science, 29,* 785–787.

Plummer, C. (1984). *Preventing sexual abuse: What in-school programs teach children.* Unpublished manuscript.

Ray, J., & Dietzel, M. (1984). *Teaching child abuse prevention.* Unpublished manuscript.

Rheingold, H., & Eckerman, C. (1973). Fear of the stranger: A critical examination. In H. Reese (Ed.), *Advances in child development and behavior* (Vol. 8, pp. 185–222). New York: Academic Press.

Ricciuti, H. (1974). Fear and the development of social attachments in the first year of life. In M. Lewis & L. Rosenblum (Eds.), *The origins of fear* (pp. 73–106). New York: Wiley.

Riesser, G., & Borys, S. (2005). *An evaluation of the New Jersey Child Assault Prevention (CAP) Program.* Retrieved October 25, 2008, from http://www.njcap.org/evaluation_research.wbp

Schaffer, H. (1966). The onset of fear of strangers and the incongruity hypothesis. *Journal of Child Psychology and Psychiatry, 7,* 95–106.

Schaffer, H., & Emerson, P. (1964). The development of social attachments in infancy. *Monographs of the Society for Research in Child Development, 29* (3, Serial No. 94).

Seligman, M. E. P. (1971). Phobias and preparedness. *Behavior Therapy, 2,* 307–320.

Shaffran, R., & Decarie, T. G. (1973, March–April). *Short-term stability of infants' responses to strangers.* Paper presented at the Society for Research in Child Development, Philadelphia.

Skarin, K. (1977). Cognitive and contextual determinants of stranger fear in six- and eleven-month old infants. *Child Development, 48,* 537–544.

Skenazy, L. (2008). *"America's worst mom?"* Retrieved November 15, 2008, from http://www.creators.com/opinion/lenore-skenazy/-america-s-worst-mom.html

Sommer, V. (1994). Infanticide among the langurs of Jodhpur: Testing the sexual selection hypothesis with a long-term record. In S. Parmigiani & F. S. vom Saal (Eds.), *Infanticide and parental care* (pp. 155–198). London: Harwood Academic.

Spritz, R. A. (1965). *The first year of life.* New York: International Universities Press.

Sroufe, L. A. (1977). Wariness of strangers and the study of infant development. *Child Development, 48,* 731–746.

Stickler, M., Salter, M., Broughton, D. D., & Alario, A. (1991). Parents' worries about children compared to actual risks. *Clinical Pediatrics, 30,* 522–528.

Taal, M., & Edelaar, M. (1997). Positive and negative effects of a child sexual abuse prevention program. *Child Abuse and Neglect, 21,* 399–410.

Tennes, K. H., & Lampl, E. L. (1964). Stranger and separation anxiety in infancy. *Journal of Nervous and Mental Health Disease, 139,* 247–254.

UNICEF (2001). *A league table of child deaths by injury in rich nations.* Florence: Innocenti Research Centre.

Valero, H., & Biocca, E. (1970). *Yanoama: The narrative of a white girl kidnapped by Amazonian Indians.* New York: E. P. Dutton.

Van Schaik, C. P., & Janson, C. H. (1997). *Infanticide by males and its implications.* London: Cambridge University Press.

Van Schaik, C. P., & Kappeler, P. M. (1997). Infanticide risk and the evolution of male–female association in primates. *Proceedings of the Royal Society London, 26,* 1687–1694.

Waters, E., Matas, L., & Sroufe, L. A. (1975). Infants' reactions to an approaching stranger: Description, validation and functional significance of wariness. *Child Development, 46,* 348–356.

Watts, D. P., Muller, M., Amsler, S. J., Mbabazi, G., & Mitani, J. C. (2006). Lethal intergroup aggression by chimpanzees in Kibale National Park, Uganda. *American Journal of Primatology, 68,* 161–180.

Weinraub, M., & Putney, E. (1978). The effects of height on infants' social responses to unfamiliar persons. *Child Development, 49,* 598–603.

Wheeler, M., & Fiske, S. (2005). Controlling racial prejudice: Social-cognitive goals affect amygdala and stereotype activation. *Psychological Science, 16,* 56–63.

Willey, P. (1990). *Prehistoric warfare on the Great Plains: Skeletal analysis of the Crow Creek massacre.* New York: Garland.

Williams, M. A., & Mattingley, J. B. (2006). Do angry men get noticed? *Current Biology, 16,* 402–404.

Zimmermann, L. K., & Stansbury, S. (2004). The influence of emotion regulation, level of shyness, and habituation on the neuroendocrine response of three-year-old children. *Psychoneuroendocrinology, 29,* 973–982.

CHAPTER 13

International Perspectives on Domestic Violence

Paula T. McWhirter and Elizabeth Altshuler Bard

Case Illustration

The Chilean economic miracle lifted over a million people out of poverty by 1995, a booming economic growth for 20% of those living in poverty prior to the mid-1990s. The Supara family living in a poor barrio of Peñalolen, Chile, were among the remaining 4 million whose economic struggles actually worsened during this period, sinking the family into an even deeper level of poverty. The four-member family live in a small home built of plywood and tarpaper, with a main gathering area about 12 feet by 12 feet across and an extension for sleeping, created out of more plywood pieces on a dirt floor covered with plastic. There is electricity and running water to the sink, but no plumbing in the home itself. An outhouse at the back of the small property serves as a toilet. Jorge, the father and implied head of the Supara household, formerly owned his own truck, but the maintenance costs and repair expenses became overwhelming. He was forced to sell his truck for parts and he has been at the mercy of small business owners who employ him as a part-time driver as needed. Jorge's wife, Mirabel, stayed at home caring for their two young children, Pablo and Laura. She became increasingly very concerned, both for their economic situation and for Jorge's response to their circumstances. Lack of work and limited resources frustrated Jorge; over time, his frustration turned to rage. "That is when the beating began," recalls Mirabel. "Before he lost the truck, he would only hit me out of anger and his anger was much less often. Now he knows that he can't provide for the family. He has nothing to do and then he starts drinking. I know that when he drinks, he will become angry. I then must try to convince my neighbor, Ana, to watch the children. I do this because he not only hits me; he also sometimes beats the children. But, Jorge wanted us (and our neighbors) to know that he is the one in charge of the family, and that he is the one they needed to obey, and so trying to send them to Ana's made him even more angry."

In talking with Mirabel about her experiences, she would often explain, "It isn't Jorge's fault. When he was drunk, his father used to hit Jorge and I remember my father was the same way when I was a child. My father used to hit my mother and he would also hurt me and especially my brothers. My mother tried to help me understand that men with nothing to take pride in become angry and full of rage."

Overview of the Issues

Children's vulnerability to violence varies internationally as a function of each nation's political structure, shared religious beliefs, and culturally subjective attitudes regarding violence in general, including state-sponsored violence such as civil conflict and war. In this chapter, we review issues of domestic violence from an international perspective, with particular attention to children's exposure to violence. Similarities across countries are explored in terms of violence prevalence, expression, and consequences to vulnerable populations: women and children. We hope to explicate varying historical and sociocultural influences, including implications manifest in economic, political, and legal beliefs and practices across countries. Risk factors at societal, community, relational, and individual levels are then delineated, and we conclude with a discussion regarding culturally specific public perception of the issues and related policy recommendations.

Prevalence

A comparison of rates of domestic violence across countries reveals wide-ranging family conflict and suggests variable violence etiology from country to country. Unfortunately, reporting accurate data about child abuse as a type of domestic violence is very difficult because of the various individual country standards. As a result, intimate partner abuse typically is more accurate and serves as our best indicator of the prevalence of child abuse from three perspectives. First, men who victimize their intimate partners are also more likely to abuse their children. Second, mothers who are abused often take out their own abuse on their children. Finally, child observation of maternal victimization is a form of vicarious abuse with very serious negative consequences. Providing some insight as to the extent of domestic violence globally, women from 32 countries who were physically victimized by an intimate partner were presented by the World Health Organization (Krug, Dahlberg, Mercy, Zwi, & Lozano, 2002). The highest figures for lifetime prevalence were from Nicaragua (69%) and Papua New Guinea (67%). The lowest incident came from Paraguay (10%) and the Philippines (10%). Rates in other studies (Waters, Hyder, Rajkotia, Basu, & Butchart, 2005) vary from the lowest rates among married women found in Australia (3%) to the highest rates in the West Bank and Gaza (53%), South Korea (38%), Egypt (34%), and Nicaragua (27%).

A recent comparative review of 33 international studies revealed that lifetime prevalence of women's experience of physical violence by an intimate partner ranged from 52% (Nicaragua) and 45% (Ethiopia) to 3% (Germany) and 12% (Mexico) (Krahé, Bieneck, & Moller, 2005). High occurrences were reported from Palestine (54%) and South Africa (41.7%). Lifetime prevalence rates of women's sexual victimization ranged from 7% (Germany) and 10% (Mexico) to 76.9% (New Zealand). Interestingly, 12 of the studies presented data on the rate of both women's and men's victimization. Two Australian and one Dutch study showed considerably higher rates for women victimization as compared to men. Five studies (within New Zealand, Germany, Hong Kong, South Africa, and the United Kingdom) showed similar levels of victimization for both women and men. The remaining three studies (also within Germany, the United Kingdom, and New Zealand) showed higher victimization rates for men than women (Krahé et al., 2005).

Reports generated within countries further reflect the overall high incidence and suggest vulnerability among children from a global perspective. For example, "one in four women with children in the United Kingdom report having experienced domestic violence from a male partner at some time in their adult lives" (Mirlees-Black, 1999, p. 18). In 1992, the first Japanese national survey on spousal abuse or abuse by male intimates was conducted with nearly 800 women, the majority with children living in the home. Most women (77%) reported "at least one type of physical, emotional, or sexual abuse, with more than half reporting all three" (Kozu, 1999, p. 51). The majority (59%) experienced physical abuse, most frequently being slapped or punched. A large incidence of sexual abuse (60%) was reported, with most reporting being forced (80%). Emotional abuse was reported in many instances (66%), with verbal abuse as the most frequently reported (Kozu, 1999). There is a common belief in Japanese society that the prevalence of family violence has decreased. However, this is somewhat contradicted by data indicating that violence in the home remains the primary reason Japanese women with children seek divorce (Hada, 1995). In a related study, as many as "1 in 10 Japanese women had experienced intimate partner abuse in the previous 12 months" (Stanko, Marion, Crisp, Manning, Smith, & Crouch, 1998, p. 20). A more recent government survey found "one in three Japanese women had sustained some physical injuries from male partners and 1 in 20 women had experienced violence they described as being life threatening" (Cabinet Office, 2002, p. 24). Japanese women are increasingly seeking advice about domestic violence at Asian Women's and Family Centers. A steady increase was reported from 49 women in 1988 to 748 in 2002. In one 4-month period (between October 2001 and February 2002), 233 protection orders were granted to Japanese women, many with children (Radford & Tsutsumi, 2004).

Similar concerns are revealed in local Russian-generated research. An estimated 14,000 Russian women were killed by their male partner in 1996 (Human Rights Watch Report, 1997). Some report that Russia leads the world in murders per female capita, with rates that grossly exceed those observed in the United States (Semenoff, 1997). Results from a pilot program in Russia showed that, in a sample of 545 women, 26% reported that they had been physically assaulted by their partner. Of these women, nearly half (12%) reported that they deserved to be hit. Russian women in their 20s and 30s reported the highest rates of abuse. The results also documented that men were more likely to define violence as serving a specific purpose, typically explaining it, for example, as a way for them to relax. Conversely, Russian women explain domestic violence as a "consequence of misunderstanding or a result of conflict or as a way of striving to control and dominate" (Horne, 1999, p. 59). These high rates of abuse reported by women correlate with victimization of children who suffer increased vulnerability to experiencing abuse both as a witness or a direct target.

A culturally representative study of Egypt involved 1000 married women between the ages of 16 and 49 presenting at general hospitals, maternal and child health care centers, and family planning centers (Elnashar, Ibrahim, Eldesoky, Aly, & Hassan, 2007). Results showed that 108 (11.5%) women reported having some previous sexual abuse experience in addition to other sexual problems. Many experiences of the sexual abuse recounted occurred during childhood, adolescence, and early adulthood. Sexual abuse correlated negatively with having received secondary education and positively with poor literacy, a history of surgical gynecologic interventions, and five or more deliveries. Furthermore, husband's education level, age, illiteracy, tobacco, and drug use correlated with the wife's report of sexual abuse. Less educated women with multiple marriages were more likely to be involved in spousal violence.

In Latin American countries, violence against women is similarly demonstrated through emotional and physical abuse, marital rape, isolation, and murder (Meyer, 1998). Almost two-thirds (60%) of women sampled in both Chile and Ecuador report having been beaten by their partner, and the statistic approaches three-quarters (74%) of the population studied in Guatemala (Heise, Pitanguy, & Germain, 1994). Roughly half (54%) of the women sampled at a child welfare clinic in Costa Rica reported experiencing physical abuse at the hand of an intimate partner. This is similar to findings in Mexico City where 55% of married women report similar experiences (Torres, Jimenez, 1993). Heise et al. (1994) found that spousal rape was frequent in Guatemala, Bolivia, Puerto Rico, and Colombia and cited specific evidence in Colombia of husbands imprisoning wives to ensure fidelity. Violence experienced by women in these situations increases the vulnerability to children, who are more likely to experience abuse by their fathers (whose violence is socially condoned) and their mothers, in response to various forms of victimization or by witnessing violence.

Two recent studies from Spain and Sweden reveal the domestic violence incidence within Europe. In the Swedish survey prevalence rates for partner violence varied between 8% and 20%, in relation to the respondent's age. Medina-Ariza and Barberet (2003) found in Spain that 16.2% of the surveyed women reported sexual abuse or severe sexual abuse and 12.9 % reported physical or severe physical abuse from an intimate partner. Interestingly, these studies associate increases in poverty with parallel increases in family violence, an obvious factor in our case illustration.

Consequences to Women, Children, and Society

Vulnerability among Children as Direct Targets

International studies reveal that domestic violence carries undercurrents of serious consequences to children. A study in Italy revealed that 750,000 boys and 700,000 girls aged 11–15 witness family violence (Baldry & Winkel, 2004). Intimate partner violence in the home places children at greater risk of becoming direct targets of abuse. For example Kozu (1999) observed that half of spousal abusers in Japan openly acknowledged the use of violence with their children. According to research in several countries, children become victims of abuse even prior to birth. A study in the obstetric wards of four tertiary hospitals in Pakistan revealed that 44% of pregnant women had experienced abuse by their husbands. Reports of abuse included either "verbal humiliation, isolation from family and friends, or threats made toward their loved ones (43%), or being slapped, pushed, kicked, beaten, choked, burned, or threatened with a weapon (12.6 %)" (Farid, Saleem, Karim, & Hatcher, 2008, p. 143). Many reported an increase of frequency and type of abuse as the pregnancy progressed (17%).

Vulnerability among Children as Witnesses

Children who witness marital violence face increased risk of emotional and behavioral problems such as anxiety, depression, poor school performance, low self-esteem, disobedience, nightmares, and physical health complaints (McCloskey, Figueredo, & Koss, 1995; McWhirter, 2008). Italian and Finnish girls are found to internalize symptoms of depression and anxiety whereas boys are shown to externalize symptoms through aggression, delinquency, or bullying (Baldry & Winkel, 2004; Kaltiala-Heino, Rimpela, Marttunen, Rimpela, & Rantanen, 1999). Similar to findings in North America, research from Australia and Singapore reveals that the long-term effects of children exposed to domestic violence include, "school failure, the inability to trust others and maintain relationships, physical and mental ill health, drug and alcohol abuse, antisocial/criminal as well as self destructive behavior and suicide and family breakdown" (Briggs & Potter, 2004, p. 339).

Vulnerability in a Relational Context

Researchers in several countries investigate parent–child relationships in conjunction with domestic violence and have found that a child's attachment may be compromised when children experience violence in the home. Exposure to domestic violence has been found to affect caregiver well-being and quality of caregiver interaction with their children, consequently resulting in poor health of the child (English, Marshall, & Stewart, 2003). A study in Jerusalem investigated children's perceptions of non-abusive and abusive parents in domestic violence situations (Sternberg, Lamb, Greenbaum, Dawud, Cortes, & Lorey, 1994). The Department of Family Services classified 110 children aged 8–12 into three quasi-experimental groups: (1) those who were physically abused by at least one parent (*abuse*), (2) those who witnessed physical violence between parents (*spousal witness*); and (3) those who both experienced and witnessed physical abuse (*abuse with witness*). Pablo and Laura, the children in our case illustration, would obviously be included in the *abuse with witness* grouping. The control (*comparison*) group was comprised of children who had not experienced or observed any form of domestic abuse. Results revealed that children in all exposure groups accurately identified their fathers as primary perpetrators of abuse. Not surprisingly, children in the *abuse* and *abuse with witness* groups had more negative perceptions of the abusive parent than children in the *spousal witness* group or the *comparison* group. Children in the abuse conditions did not appear to generalize feelings about the abusive parent to the non-abusive parent, which is perhaps a function of resilience. This is consistent with studies conducted in North America, suggesting that although relationships with the abusive parent are compromised, children are still able to form secure attachments to the non-abusive parent (Lamb, Thompson, Gardner, & Charnov, 1985). Furthermore, the similarity among the *spousal witness* and *comparison* group children suggests that children's appraisals were based on parental behavior as opposed to spousal roles. In terms of child witnesses to violence in the home, children in the *spousal witness* group, as compared to the *comparison*, rated their mothers more negatively, suggesting a relationship between witnessing spousal abuse and consequential negative maternal attachment. If a study conducted in Israel generalizes to children in Chile, Pablo and Laura are at risk of alienation from their mother, Mirabel, as well as their father.

Vulnerability of Women: Children's Primary Caregivers

Internationally, the consequences of intimate partner violence to the women victims are beginning to be documented and findings reveal similarities across the psychological consequences of intimate partner violence. An Israeli study showed that, relative to controls, lower self-esteem and higher stress, depression, and anxiety were found in women who have been victims of both physical and sexual violence (Romkens, 1997). The same findings were seen among Dutch women, with victims indicating significantly more psychosomatic and depressive complaints than non-victims. An international classification of adverse health outcomes resulting from violence against women included categories of physical health (e.g., injuries), negative health behaviors (e.g., excessive alcohol consumption), chronic conditions (e.g., somatic complaints), reproductive health (e.g., STD/HIV, low birth rate, miscarriages), and mental health (e.g., PTSD, depression, anxiety, phobias) (Center for Health and Gender Equity, 1999, p. 18).

A Legacy of Financial Burden: Children Paying the Price

Another consequence of violence in the home is the economic cost to society, with enduring effects on societies' children. The estimated cost of violence is considerably higher within low- and middle-income countries, as compared to high-income countries, when considered as a percentage of each country's GDP (Gross Domestic Product). In Canada, the cost is estimated to be 1.2 billion when considering healthcare, policing, legal fees, incarceration, lost earnings, and psychological care. Based solely on lost productivity of victimized women in Chile and Nicaragua, total costs reach $1.73 billion (Chile) and 32.7 million (Nicaragua), equivalent to approximately 2% of these countries' GDP (Morrison & Orlando, 1999). Extrapolated costs for one region of London reached 13.3 million, averaging $159 per household, and included costs of public services, policing, court costs, medical care, and refuge (Stanko, Crisp, Hale, & Lucraft, 1998). In 2001 the total annual cost for treating victims of intimate partner violence in Jamaica was nearly 0.5 million dollars and in New Zealand the total annual cost was nearly 0.75 million dollars (Waters et al., 2005).

Public Perception

Public perception of abuse within families is strongly influenced by differing cultural norms and attitudes. Differences emerge even in the way in which cultures define the word *abuse*, and the word itself is difficult to translate across languages. In Somalia and Turkey, for example, there exists no exact word or synonym for *abuse*. Physical abuse is the term that comes closest to the English meaning for the term *abuse* in Russia and China; sexual abuse is the more appropriate translation in Germany and Iceland.

These varying definitions reflect the culturally accepted understanding of what constitutes maltreatment. Increases in public awareness involve a gradual change in cultural norms and attitudes. In the 1960s the term "battered child syndrome" became recognizable in the United States, which led to an increase in public awareness resulting in mandatory reporting laws (Rapoza & Malley-Morrison, 2004). Even though child abuse is rarely recognized or litigated, awareness in Japan is increasing (Kozu, 1999). The establishment of international treaties (e.g., the United Nations' Convention of the Rights of the Child) has increased understanding of what constitutes child abuse, ultimately improving public awareness (Shetty & Edleson, 2005).

Gender differences persist in terms of perceived level and judgment of severity regarding familial abuse. In Canada and England, women perpetrators of abuse toward their husbands are typically judged less harshly compared to husbands inflicting the same level of abuse toward their wives. In Italy, Israel, and Turkey, physical abuse toward a son is considered less abusive than the same abuse directed toward a daughter. Similarly, cultural norms have evolved at disparate rates based on perpetrator gender. From 1968 to 1994, physical abuse acceptance against male partners has remained stable, while physical abuse acceptance against females has gradually decreased (Patterson, 2004).

Various forms of abuse are justified differentially across cultures. Greece and the Philippines justify abuse directed toward unfaithful wives, and Turkish wives viewed as disobedient are often subsequently abused, which is justified as a form of punishment. Misbehavior by children (in England and Greece) and disobedience by children (in Turkey, Iceland, and the Philippines) are considered justification for physical or psychological abuse. In several countries, public aggression against family members is considered to be a more severe crime than private acts of aggression (e.g., Israel, Turkey, Saudi Arabia, Canada, and Korea).

The majority of Singaporeans (72%) approve of "putting children down" as a form of motivation (Tong, Elliott, & Tan, 1996). Chinese respondents were more accepting of emotional and physical abuse than other ethnic groups in Singapore. In a survey of 368 Singapore professionals, medical practitioners (62%), hospital doctors (59%), and lawyers (32%) believe that children are their parents' "property," required to obey parents at all times. Similarly, medical practitioners (86.1%), hospital doctors (83%), and lawyers (77.5%) view physical punishment to be a form of parental love (Fung & Chow, 1998).

Chinese culture appears to perpetuate a tradition of physical punishment as a form of discipline. The majority of Chinese educators (84.1%) view the caning of children (beating with a cane administered in school settings) as a suitable form of punishment (Chan, Elliott, & Chow, 2000). As compared to the general public, Chinese teachers show more tolerance for caning. In Singapore, a public survey found that 94% believe that severe physical abuse should always be reported; however, 73% found caning acceptable and therefore not reportable (Tong et al., 1996). Other studies associated caning with "parental love" (Briggs & Potter, 2004).

In Singapore, Briggs and Potter (2004) found that the majority of special education (60%) and kindergarten teachers (86%) were unaware of the procedures for reporting child abuse or neglect. The authors concluded that this unawareness could result in false reporting or not reporting severe cases. Kindergarten teachers (18%) and special education teachers (24%) report that parents are not concerned with educating children about safety. In addition, teachers report that there is no cause to educate children on safety when there is not a threat of child abuse. Both kindergarten (50%) and special education (46%) teachers report educating children to maintain secrets, most importantly family secrets. Some kindergarten teachers advocated the use of criticism for motivation, believing that "praising children is bad because it results in a reduction in effort and conceit (20%), and that telling children that they are 'unlovable' or 'a nuisance' will improve their behavior (16%)" (Briggs & Potter, 2004, p. 351).

In Japan, violence is justified as a means of discipline. The majority of girls (60%) reported parental violence as discipline (Idemitsu, 1994), and parents and teachers consider strangling and kicking to be valid and even frequently used forms of corporal punishment (Kozu, 1999).

Across cultures, violence in the home can be explained according to risk factors at four levels: societal, community, relational, and individual. *Societal*-level risk factors are those in which men are allowed dominance over women, violence is a method of conflict resolution, and only traditional gender roles are tolerated (Heise, 1998). Societies oriented toward collectivism, including Arab and Latin countries, tend to pressure battered wives to assume responsibility for their husband's violent behavior and to resist engaging in self-protective strategies (e.g., seeking help from formal agencies) that might risk breaking up the traditional family unit (Bezerra-Flanders, 2004; Haj-Yahia, 2002; Patterson, 2004). In Nicaragua, roughly half of co-habitating women reported experiencing physical abuse at least once. This finding has been attributed to societal norms related to gender roles, such as female subservience (Ellsberg, Peña, Herrera, Liljestrand, & Winkvist, 2000). Studies conducted in Korea and Hong Kong found a relationship between degree of male dominance and rate of physical violence (Kim & Emery, 2003; Tang, 1999). Italian women report "that they expect to be physically mistreated by their partner, and more respondents reported physical aggression of husband against wife than vice versa" (Patterson, 2004, p. 484). As compared to liberal Jews, in Israel, traditional Jews and Muslims reported higher rates of intimate partner violence, perhaps suggesting some degree of religious zeal underlying acceptance of perpetual home violence that affects women and children (Eisikovitz, Winstok, & Fishman, 2004).

Societal-level risk is further evident in studies that reveal gender-based discrepancies concerning what is considered abuse. One British respondent stated that it would be considered severely abusive for "a woman to withhold sex from her spouse," an act considered equivalent to a "drunken husband physically beating his wife" (Donovan, 2004, p. 42). Respondents in Brazil did not mention any form of husband abuse and those in South Africa said it was "impossible" for a husband to be abused. These societal factors place children at greater risk of abuse, if not directly from the male then indirectly from their mothers. In Japan, the overwhelming majority (90%) of Japanese perpetrators of child abuse are mothers, purportedly a result of culturally sanctioned obligation of the mother to cope single-handedly with the stressors and consequences of child rearing.

At the societal level, children are at risk when women are at risk. A society that tolerates unfettered, excessive, and socially sanctioned male privilege sets the stage for domestic violence that is harmful to children. In Italy, a fairly common occurrence along the crowded bus system involves men approaching and physically isolating a young woman in order to rub up against her for his sexual gratification. From a psychological perspective, this behavior is termed "fotteurism," and is considered a sexual perversion because of the lack of consent of the female recipient. A group of activist Italian women developed a grassroots strategy to counteract this manifestation of "male privilege." Use of the strategy has become widespread within the bus system in the city and surrounding areas. Whenever a man initiates this behavior, the targeted woman yells out in a loud voice: "Stop that, pervert." All women on the bus begin supportive calls: "Pervert!", "Jerk!", "What's the matter with you!", and similar statements. The strategy effectively results in the hasty exit of the perpetrator at the next stop.

Risk factors at the *community* level include poverty, low socioeconomic status, unemployment, and seclusion of females and children (Heise, 1998). A review of 35 international studies found that the risk markers most commonly addressed by researchers were these *community*-level demographic variables, such as education and economic status (Krahé et al., 2005). In the case study described earlier, the Supara family reside in Peñalolen, a very poor barrio outside of Santiago. The family income is marginal and the educational level of Jorge and Mirabel is low. Clearly, child abuse occurs at every level of socioeconomic status. Nevertheless, the rate of abuse is greater when poverty is chronic and pervasive.

As well as the specific local community, the prevalence of physical abuse within families is found to be higher in low income countries and in rural areas. In India prevalence ranges from 13% to 28%, while in Pakistan it was found to be 23% (Farid et al., 2008, p. 141). Two recent studies from Spain and Sweden associated increases in poverty with parallel increases in family violence (Medina-Ariza & Barberet, 2003). Reports from Japan indicate that women are left more vulnerable to abuse due to increased rate of poverty and limited access to support following decreased welfare services (Kozu, 1999). In Japan, most women are shown to be financially dependent on their spouses and therefore stay in abusive relationships (Kozu, 1999).

Communities across the globe are susceptible to the reality of *peripheral regions*. A *peripheral region* is one in which women and children in situations of poverty, rural isolation, social exclusion, and domestic violence are vulnerable to being distanced economically, physically, or mentally from their basic human and civil rights. As such, women and children in these *peripheral regions* are excluded from the rights and protections afforded other citizens, including members of their own society. *Peripheral regions* occur within poor and rural communities, but can be found in pockets of poverty throughout affluent communities or via social isolation within prosperous societies. Studies conducted in Japan and the UK find that women and children in geographically *peripheral regions* are held accountable for their own victimization, burdened with both blame and consequence of the domestic violence perpetrated against them. Particularly in rural and poverty-stricken *peripheral regions*, men are found to target women and children known to have limited awareness and/or access to their rights, and who consequently lack the protection from violence afforded to those less vulnerable (Radford & Tsutsumi, 2004).

A clear example of a *peripheral region* is found in Latino communities within the United States. Undocumented workers simply do not report domestic violence, including child abuse, for fear of deportation not only of the abuser – who may be the major source of financial support – but also of the abused. This situation is not uncommon among those undocumented in many countries internationally.

The third level of risk, *relational*, includes partner conflict and male authority over family finances and decisions (Heise, 1998). In Pakistan, for example, "a certain level of abuse is seen as a husband's right and considered socially acceptable. Decisions about family size rest with the paternal mother-in-law. The close involvement of the family leads to higher rates of conflict and is likely to increase a woman's vulnerability to spousal abuse" (Farid et al., 2008, p. 143). Certain cultural norms legitimize forced intercourse by husbands for sexual gratification. Hadi (2000) finds that a quarter of married Bangladeshi women report forced sex by their spouse.

Similarly, Japan maintains a patriarchy in which traditional gender roles dictate familial interactional patterns. With a paternal hierarchy women and children have lower status, which creates a family structure susceptible to conflict. Children are more likely to disrespect their parents' authority as a backlash to extreme parental pressure to conform to expectations and demands. Due to the Japanese tendency to avoid conflict and to discourage verbal communication within the family, children's resentments build, resulting in increasingly common acts of violence against parents (filial violence). Furthermore, the Japanese tradition of maintaining secrets to avoid bringing shame to the family results in a systematic underreporting of domestic violence, and prolonged secrecy causes women to avoid divorce, even in the most dangerous of situations. Considered a socially inappropriate topic of conversation, sexuality is not openly discussed in Japan. Women who have experienced sexual abuse feel shame and embarrassment and seldom speak out about the abuse (Kozu, 1999).

In our case illustration, Jorge's blustering insistence that he was in charge and must be obeyed was accepted by Mirabel, Ana, their extended family, the neighbors, and others in the family's relational network. Mirabel also reflects the relational level of risk. Her explanations – excuses really – for Jorge's actions reflect an internalization of relationship patterns that makes abuse of her and of her children, Pablo and Laura, more likely.

The last level of risk factors, *individual perpetrator*, includes childhood history of violence exposure and victimization, lack of father figure, and substance abuse (Heise, 1998). Jorge is a good example of the *individual perpetrator* level of risk. His own abuse as a child, his distant relationship with his father, and his substance abuse increase his abuse potential and, reciprocally, exposure to societal, community, and relational risk may increase the presence of these *individual* risk factors. Again, Jorge illustrates this cumulative effect of risk factors. Support from family and friends has been linked to decreased violence, suggesting that such support acts as a protective factor in countering risk. Studies conducted in Israel, Turkey, and Saudi Arabia, for example, associate the presence of supportive family members with a decrease in wife beating (Counts, Brown, & Campbell, 1992; Patterson, 2004).

Policy Recommendations

Previously outlined risk factors suggest corresponding interventions at societal, community, relational, and individual levels. Below, we consider international and domestic initiatives, both governmental and grassroots responses, and macro to micro systemic approaches to protect children from domestic violence. To contextualize these interventions, we begin with a discussion of political and legal sanctions of violence across nations, perpetuating children's vulnerability to domestic violence and signaling a need for increased initiatives targeting each level of risk.

Political and Legal Sanctions

State-sanctioned violence, embedded in legal mandates and political structure, increases the vulnerability of women and children and serves to perpetuate violence in the home. The first author examined family violence and found aspects of Chilean culture insidiously permissive of beliefs that perpetuate violence within the home (McWhirter, 1999). The Pinochet dictatorship (1973–1988) provided a brutally violent example of authority, culturally accommodated and reflected in Chilean family structure. During and following this period, men maintained the role of authority within the home and demonstrated love through violent acts; women accepted and associated violence as congruent with their family role, placing women and children at greater risk of exposure to violence (Larrain, 1994).

Legal mandates in several countries perpetuate leniency regarding violence in the home. In Japan, for example, sexual abuse and incest are not considered crimes (Ikeda, 1992). Moreover, the rights of children in Japan take a backseat to those of their parents (Kinoshita, 1993), as was evident when only one in almost 2000 child abuse cases resulted in custody rights loss (Koseisho Daijin Kanbo Tokei Johobukyoku, 1995).

Hundreds of women in Pakistan are killed by their families each year in the name of "honor." Laws typically do not protect victims of violence, as is evident when rape victims in Pakistan and Afghanistan are sent to prison for participating in illegal sex (Ahmad, 2004). These acts legitimize continued familial violence, placing children – the society's most vulnerable – at greater risk for victimization.

For decades, the Civil Code of Chile affirmed that wives obey their husbands and that husbands protect their wives (McWhirter, 1999). The code further stipulated that husbands have complete control over their wife and her possessions. Finally, as late as 1989, this law was revised, which currently mandates that a husband and wife mutually respect and protect one another.

The Japanese government's gender equality strategy only recently began to include violence against women in 2000, and a new law on domestic violence was introduced the following year.

"Recorded crimes of domestic violence against women, many who are mothers, have since sky-rocketed, with 233 protection orders granted within the first four months from October 2001 to February 2002" (Cabinet Office, 2002, p. 27). Family violence continues to be undercounted. "It is estimated that less than 1% of Japanese women who experience domestic violence contact the police" (Cabinet Office, 2002, p. 25). Although domestic violence continues to be a problem, women are increasingly standing up against domestic violence, as is evident by an increase in reporting (Radford & Tsutsumi, 2004). Undercounting and otherwise overlooking instances of women and family violence increase children's vulnerability to family violence and victimization.

Children's vulnerability to violence is further compromised due to law enforcement reluctance to intervene in instances of familial violence. In Chile, although women report that they are treated well by the police, evidence suggests that police officers still oppose recent laws designed to protect women. A police officer was quoted saying that "he feels the law is bad since it tends to separate the couple, disempowering the man" (McWhirter, 1999, p. 38). In Japan, police intervention in situations of familial violence is rare, and domestic violence is not seen as a serious criminal act (Kozu, 1999). Russian laws established to protect women from domestic violence frequently go unenforced. Most law officials perceive domestic violence as a matter best resolved privately, in the home (Horne, 1999). There is a lack of sensitivity training and Russian police are known to try to persuade women to go back to their abusers. Visibly abused females are often denied aid in the absence of physician documentation (Horne, 1999).

Personally and culturally based biases of judges and other legal personnel perpetuate familial violence in several countries. In the final 6 months of 2000, 78% of Hague Convention appeal cases involving women who abducted their children cited claims of domestic violence (Weiner, 2003). Article 13(b) of the Convention "provides an exception to the return of the child to his or her habitual residence if there exists grave risk that his or her return would expose the child to physical or psychological harm" (Hague Convention, 1980, Article 13(b)). However, despite the evidence and the prevalence of domestic violence in abduction cases, many judges do not consider exposure to domestic violence as increasing a child's vulnerability to physical or psychological harm. Many believe that unless the child is abused directly, stipulated legal protections of children are unwarranted (Shetty & Edleson, 2005).

International Initiatives

Internationally, there is widespread agreement that greater protections are needed to decrease family violence and its risk to those abused. Although domestic violence is commonly viewed as an intimate family problem in many countries, macro-system social structures and social attitudes regarding treatment of vulnerable populations are beginning to receive increasing attention from researchers and family advocates internationally. Many countries have joined international treaties, and as such have begun to address family violence in the context of human rights. These treaties provide no enforcement of law internationally, but instead define social and political policy, with clarifications as to what constitutes abuse and how it should be justly addressed. As such, these international organizational treaties effectively socialize cultures, providing consciousness-raising for the breadth of abuse that occurs within families in terms of prevalence, frequency, forms, and consequences. In time, consciousness-raising gradually reveals specific forms of family abuse that a given culture may be predisposed to overlook. This inevitably results in wider protection of vulnerable populations (Patterson, 2004).

Many countries face challenges in preventing family violence and protecting its vulnerable citizens. Limited access to necessary funding limits the breadth and availability of resources needed to confront societal, community, relational, and individual risk factors previously outlined (Heise, 1998; Kozu, 1999; Patterson, 2004).

In addition to funding limitations, many countries lack trained mental health, medical, and legal personnel. Social services are essential to tackle family violence, and yet available resources and services vary considerably. Although some countries have developed shelters, safe houses, and centers, not all within those countries have access to these services, which is the case for the rural poor (Patterson, 2004). In fact, even considering the many barriers to reporting domestic violence, shortages in resources continue to be the chief explanation as to why people fail to report (Bezerra-Flanders, 2004).

Domestic Social, Organizational, and Indigenous Initiatives

Various countries have embarked on initiatives to reduce vulnerability to family violence, including the establishment of statewide agencies and community-based services. For example, several governmental agencies in Chile have been established to deal with issues of domestic violence, and in 1990 shelters were opened to protect children from abuse. Also in the 1990s, the Chilean's National Service for Women created several domestic violence shelters in five different towns, providing counseling for victims and perpetrators in rural and urban communities (McWhirter, 1999). Also in the 1990s, Japan began initiatives to increase the public's awareness of child and spousal abuse, although the majority of the services continue to target child victims of physical and sexual abuse, with only limited services for individuals seeking support for spousal abuse. The Ministry of Health and Welfare began implementing a nationwide program that aimed to protect children's rights and directly addresses child abuse. Bar Associations initiated hotlines for consultation. "The first crisis centers in Russia designed to aid women victims of abuse were developed in Moscow in 1992, providing hotlines, legal consultation, and counseling" (Horne, 1999, p. 59). During this same period, the Russian Lawyers Advocacy Project was formed to improve legal responses to domestic violence and to develop legal advocacy skills of lawyers associated with the centers; and the Research, Education, and Advocacy Project was started to educate the public, to strengthen laws and conduct research, and to share outreach plans with other women's organizations. Police and probation agencies in Japan and the United Kingdom initiated use of the Spousal Assault Risk Assessment (SARA) to guide interviews with victims of domestic violence, which assesses victim risk based on indicators drawn from research (Radford & Tsutsumi, 2004, p. 8).

A host of governmental agencies (Brazil, Chile, Mexico) have devoted themselves to addressing domestic violence through "specialized police forces, public information, and education programs to prevent family violence, and the compilation of some official statistics on the problem" (Meyer, 1998, p. 140). Progress has been demonstrated in Costa Rica as family and divorce laws are updated and as public programs, local non-government agencies, legal services, and psychological counseling emphasize the treatment of domestic violence. In attempts to raise public awareness, many countries (Bosnia, Rwanda, El Salvador, Peru, and Haiti) have increased media coverage of domestic violence (Meyer, 1998).

Although governmentally sponsored groups help to promote awareness and recognition of issues of violence within the family, many are accused of perpetuating belief systems that maintain societal and relational risks associated with family violence, thus creating barriers to tangible social change. For example, the

Organization of American States' specialized commission, the Inter-American Commission of Women (or Comision Inter-americana de Mujeres, CIM), drafted a treaty "holding nation states in the Americas accountable for preventing, punishing, and eradicating violence against women. Since its creation, CIM has worked with women's groups and feminist organizations to implement its programs in promoting women's education, development, and political equality" (Meyer, 1998, pp. 136–137). However, contrary to its initial purpose, CIM has been called an example of gender politics in international organization and global governance, functioning as "a regional intergovernmental organization, made up of states with long standing authoritarian political traditions, of societies with deeply imbedded cultural values of machismo, and of families in which women's subordination to men is considered natural and right" (Meyer, 1998, p. 136). As a result, many governmentally sponsored organizations, designed to protect families from violence, struggle to make long-lasting cultural change from within. As a result, in many countries, local grassroots organizations provide leadership for family violence change efforts.

In addition to the governmentally sanctioned agencies mentioned above, non-government grassroots organizations play a critical role in promoting human rights for populations most vulnerable to family violence. Social networking groups and indigenous protest movements in Brazil, Turkey, the United Kingdom, Philippines, Israel, Nicaragua, and India, for example, provide culturally grounded mechanisms for changing social norms and behaviors related to family violence (Patterson, 2004). These charitable, locally based groups, empowered by international organizations and treaties, initially served as service-based relief organizations; however, in response to macro-level social and political forces perpetuating family violence, these organizations have evolved to protect families from violence at the local level by promoting public recognition of global human rights in the context of the family (Patterson, 2004).

International, state, and local movements to decrease child vulnerability are on the rise, but more is needed. Practical, micro-level interventions implemented by grassroots organizations should be systematically and methodically increased globally. Much in the same way that city planning involves consideration of water, sewer, roadway, and other services, programs and resources should be implemented in a planful way to protect children from the varied risk factors of violence. This includes use of media (i.e., TV, radio, internet) to increase awareness and encourage family support to children in need. Telephone hotlines should be available, increasing access to information and service availability. As in many countries but especially in the Middle and Far East, disclosure of family violence is only entrusted with friends and family (Haj-Yahia & Shor, 1995). Community-based support groups should be encouraged to increase awareness about issues of family violence, and to treat and prevent violence against children.

In this chapter, we addressed domestic violence from an international perspective, considering the types and prevalence of domestic violence, particularly in terms of its effect on children. In addition to discussions regarding specific consequences to children and families, violence was explored in the context of sociocultural issues highlighting historical, economic, and political influences. We reviewed ways to keep children safe and decrease their vulnerability. We suggested systematic interventions and methodical prevention to address societal, community, relational, and individual levels of risk. We hope that you come away from this chapter with a deeper understanding as to the complexity of contextual issues surrounding family violence internationally and its impact on children, the most vulnerable population across all cultures.

References

Ahmad, K. (2004, January 17). Violence prevention receives international attention. *Medicine and Health Policy, 363.* Retrieved October 20, 2008, from www.thelancet.com

Baldry, A. C., & Winkel, F. W. (2004). Mental and physical health of Italian youngsters directly and indirectly victimized at school and at home. *International Journal of Forensic Mental Health, 3*(1), 77–91.

Bezerra-Flanders, W. (2004). Brazil. In K. Malley-Morrison (Ed.), *International perspectives on family violence and abuse: A cognitive ecological approach* (pp. 397–414). Mahwah, NJ: Lawrence Erlbaum Associates, Inc.

Briggs, F., & Potter, G. (2004). Singaporean early childhood teachers' responses to myths about child abuse. *Early Child Development and Care, 174*(4), 339–355.

Cabinet Office (2002). *FY 2001 annual report on the state formation of a gender equal society.* Tokyo, Japan: Cabinet Office.

Center for Health and Gender Equity (CHANGE) (1999). Population reports. Ending violence against women. *Issues in World Health, 17*(4).

Chan, J. S., Elliott, J. M., & Chow, Y. (2000). Professional and public perceptions of physical child abuse and neglect in Singapore. *Research Monograph No. 3.* Singapore: Singapore Children's Society.

Counts, D. A., Brown, J. K., & Campbell, J. C. (1992). *Sanctions and sanctuary: Cultural perspectives on the beating of wives.* Boulder, CO: Westview Press.

Donovan, E. (2004). England. In K. Malley-Morrison (Ed.), *International perspectives on family violence and abuse: A cognitive ecological approach* (pp. 33–50). Mahwah, NJ: Lawrence Erlbaum Associates, Inc.

Eisikovitz, Z., Winstok, Z., & Fishman, G. (2004). The first Israeli national survey on domestic violence. *Violence Against Women, 10*(7), 729–748.

Ellsberg, M., Peña, R., Herrera, A., Liljestrand, J., & Winkvist, A. (2000). Candies in hell: Women's experiences of violence in Nicaragua. *Social Science and Medicine, 51*(11), 1595–1610.

Elnashar, A. M., Ibrahim, M. E.-D., Eldesoky, M. M., Aly, O. M., & Hassan, M. E.-S. M. (2007). Sexual abuse experienced by married Egyptian women. *International Journal of Gynecology and Obstetrics, 99*, 216–220.

English, D. J., Marshall, D. B., & Stewart, A. J. (2003). Effects of family violence on child behavior and health during early childhood. *Journal of Family Violence, 18*(1), 43–57.

Farid, M., Saleem, S., Karim, M., & Hatcher, J. (2008). Spousal abuse during pregnancy in Karachi, Pakistan. *International Journal of Gynecology and Obstetrics, 101*, 141–145.

Fung, D. D. S., & Chow, M. H. (1998). Doctors' and lawyers' perspectives of child abuse and neglect in Singapore. *Singapore Medical Journal, 39*(4), 160–165.

Hada, A. (1995). Domestic violence. In K. Fujimura-Fanselow & Kameda, A. (Eds.), *Japanese women.* New York: Feminist Press.

Hadi, A. (2000). Prevalence and correlates of the risk of marital sexual violence in Bangladesh. *Journal of Interpersonal Violence, 15*(8), 787–805.

Hague Convention (1980). *Convention on the civil aspects of international child abduction.* The Hague, The Netherlands: World Organisation for Cross-border Cooperation in Civil and Commerical Matters.

Haj-Yahia, M. M. (2002). Attitudes of Arab women toward different patterns of coping with wife abuse. *Journal of Interpersonal Violence, 17*(7), 721–745.

Haj-Yahia, M. M., & Shor, R. (1995). Child maltreatment as perceived by Arab students of social science in the West Bank. *Child Abuse and Neglect, 19*(10), 1209–1219.

Heise, L. L. (1998). Violence against women: An integrated, ecological framework. *Violence Against Women, 4*(3), 262–290.

Heise, L. L., Pitanguy, J., & Germain, A. (1994). *Violence against women: The hidden health burden.* World Bank Discussion Papers. Washington, DC: The World Bank.

Horne, S. (1999). Domestic violence in Russia. *American Psychologist,* *54*(1), 55–61.

Human Rights Watch Report (1997). *Russia: Too little too late. State response to violence against women, 9,* 13(d).

Idemitsu, M. (1994). Hikoshojo niokeru oyakarano boryoku keiken [Parental violence in delinquent girls]. *Gendaino Esupuri [L'espirit d'aujourd'hui], 320,* 154–164.

Ikeda, Y. (1992). Letters to the editor. *Child Abuse and Neglect, 16,* 313–314.

Kaltiala-Heino, R., Rimpela, M., Marttunen, M., Rimpela, A., & Rantanen, P. (1999). Bullying, depression, and suicidal ideation in Finnish adolescents: School survey. *British Medical Journal, 319*(7206), 348–351.

Kim, J. Y., & Emery, C. (2003). Marital power, conflict, norm consensus, and marital violence in a nationally representative sample of Korean couples. *Journal of Interpersonal Violence, 18*(2), 197–219.

Kinoshita, A. (1993). Shinkento kodomo no jinken [Parental rights and children's rights]. *Imago, 4–6,* 80–85.

Koseisho Daijin Kanbo Tokei Johobukyoku [Office of Ministry of Health and Welfare, Statistics and Information Bureau] (1995). *Shakaifukushi gyosei gyomu hokoku: Heisei nendo ban [Report on social welfare administration 1994].* Koseisho Tokeikyokai: Tokyo.

Kozu, J. (1999). Domestic violence in Japan. *American Psychologist,* *54*(1), 50–54.

Krahé, B., Bieneck, S., & Möller, I. (2005). Understanding gender and intimate partner violence from an international perspective. *Sex Roles, 52*(11), 807–827.

Krug, E. G., Dahlberg, L. L., Mercy, J. A., Zwi, A. B., & Lozano, R. (2002). *World report on violence and health.* Geneva: World Health Organization.

Lamb, M. E., Thompson, R. A., Gardner, W., & Charnov, E. L. (1985). *Infant–mother attachment: The origins and developmental significance of individual differences in strange situation behavior.* Hillsdale, NJ: Lawrence Erlbaum Associates, Inc.

Larrain, S. H. (1994). *Violencia puertas adentro: La mujer golpeada [Violence behind doors: Battered women].* Santiago, Chile: Editorial Universitaria.

McCloskey, L. A., Figueredo, A. J., & Koss, M. P. (1995). The effects of systemic family violence on children's mental health. *Child Development, 66,* 1239–1261.

McWhirter, P. T. (1999). La violencia privada domestic violence in Chile. *The American Psychologist, 54*(1), 37–40.

McWhirter, P. T. (2008). An empirical evaluation of a collaborative child and family violence prevention and intervention program. In G. R. Walz, J. C. Bleuer, & R. K. Yep (Eds.), *Compelling counseling interventions* (pp. 221–228). Alexandria, VA: Counseling Outfitters, American Counseling Association.

Medina-Ariza, J., & Barberet, R. (2003). Intimate partner violence in Spain: Findings from a national survey. *Violence Against Women*, *9*(3), 302–322.

Meyer, M. K. (1998). Negotiating international norms: The inter-American commission of women and the convention on violence against women. *Aggressive Behavior, 24*, 135–146.

Mirlees-Black, C. (1999). *Domestic violence: Findings from the British Crime Survey Self Completion Questionnaire Research Study*, Vol. 191. London: Home Office.

Morrison, A. R., & Orlando, M. B. (1999). Social and economic costs of domestic violence: Chile and Nicaragua. In A. R. Morrison & M. B. Orlando (Eds.), *Too close to home: Domestic violence in the Americas* (pp. 51–80). New York: Inter-American Development Bank.

Patterson, M. D. (2004). Contextualizing human rights: A response to international family violence. In K. Malley-Morrison (Ed.), *International perspectives on family violence and abuse: A cognitive ecological approach* (pp. 473–500). Mahwah, NJ: Lawrence Erlbaum Associates, Inc.

Radford, L., & Tsutsumi, K. (2004). Globalization and violence against women – inequalities in risks, responsibilities and blame in the UK and Japan. *Women's Studies International Forum, 27*, 1–12.

Rapoza, K. A., & Malley-Morrison, K. (2004). United States. In K. Malley-Morrison (Ed.), *International perspectives on family violence and abuse: A cognitive ecological approach.* (pp. 451–470). Mahwah, NJ: Lawrence Erlbaum Associates, Inc.

Romkens, R. (1997). Prevalence of wife abuse in the Netherlands: Combining quantitative and qualitative methods in survey research. *Journal of Interpersonal Violence, 12*(1), 99–125.

Semenoff, L. (1997). *The women's movement and the responses to violence against women in the USSR and post-Soviet Russia.* Ottawa, Ontario: Institute of Central/East European and Russian Area Studies, Carleton University.

Shetty, S., & Edleson, J. L. (2005). Adult domestic violence in cases of international parental child abduction. *Violence Against Women, 11*(1), 115–138.

Stanko, E., Crisp, D. H., Hale, C., & Lucraft, H. (1998). *Counting the costs: Estimating the impact of domestic violence in the London borough of Hackney.* Crime concern report funded by Hackney Safer Cities and the Children's Home Society with the cooperation of the London Borough of Hackney.

Stanko, E., Marion, L., Crisp, D., Manning, R., Smith, J., & Crouch, S. (1998). *Taking stock: What we know about violence.* Royal Holloway College, University of London: ESRC Violence Research Programme.

Sternberg, K. J., Lamb, M. E., Greenbaum, C., Dawud, S., Cortes, R. M., & Lorey, F. (1994). The effects of domestic violence on children's perceptions of their perpetrating and nonperpetrating parents. *International Journal of Behavioral Development, 17*(4), 779–795.

Tang, C. (1999). Marital power and aggression in a community sample of Hong Kong Chinese families. *Journal of Interpersonal Violence, 14*(6), 586–602.

Tong, C. K., Elliott, J. M., & Tan, P. (1996). Public perceptions of child abuse and neglect in Singapore. *Research Monograph No. 1.* Singapore: Singapore Children's Society.

Torres Jimenez, R. (1993, October 24). *Women, victims of violence at home. InterPress Service, Mexico Newspack,* p. 10.

Waters, H. R., Hyder, A. A., Rajkotia, Y., Basu, S., & Butchart, A. (2005). The costs of interpersonal violence – an international review. *Health Policy, 73*(3), 303–315.

Weiner, M. H. (2003). Potential and challenges of transnational litigation for feminists concerned about domestic violence here and abroad. *American University Journal of Gender, Social Policy and the Law, 11,* 749–800.

CHAPTER 14

Protecting Children from the Violence of Global Health Inequities
Working Beyond Academic Halls and Clinic Walls[1]

Chris E. Stout

> Of all the forms of inequality, injustice in health care is the
> most shocking and inhumane.
>
> (King, 1966)

Public Perception

This chapter is likely different from many of the others herein,
as it relates to a personal journey of sorts. As such, I have
asked the editors to allow a little license in using first-person and a
shift in format of this chapter.

I began my clinical career working with children and families.
As a significant portion of that work was done in an inpatient
setting, it seemed that many of the children I worked with had
been abused, and some even tortured, mostly by a parent or both
parents. This caused me to learn a great deal about the consequences of trauma and the methods of treatment. I then began
to get involved in some international clinical work and in the area
of resilience, and I quickly saw the value that I believed could be
provided, but I was not too sure about the cultural translation.

There is alchemy to psychology that can produce an incredible set of opportunities and experiences. The alchemy of psychology that I have focused on is in the area of global health disparities. But there is a great divide between behavioral health, public health, and primary healthcare that has long mystified me.

I have served on a Board of Health for almost a decade, along with completing a Fellowship in Public Health, and believe me the *psychological* aspects of violence, health compliance/non-compliance issues, smoking cessation, mental illness, domestic violence, drug and alcohol use, etc., all overlap with public health successes and failures. The State of Illinois' Division of Mental Heath got it right when they coined the phase: "Without mental health, there is no health."

I worked with Dr. Stevan Weine, who is well known for his clinical and research work in Kosovo and with refugees from the Balkans. Therein I learned that aspects of what I believed to be universal developmental phenomena were alterable under conditions of war, conflict, or trauma. For example, fear of the dark became fear of the light in Kosovo due to sniper fire. In the daytime it was not safe because you could be targeted by a sniper and killed or maimed. But at night you were safe from such threats. The proverbial bogie-man hid in the daylight, not at night.

I also came to learn about child soldiers, the methods of conscription, and the horrors they experienced and caused, but thankfully now there are projects and programs to help them adapt in non-conflict situations and begin the healing process. My transition from working solely as a traditional clinical psychologist (i.e., private practice, consulting, teaching, research, and writing) to something a bit less parochial started in Cairo. A speech that I gave was well received by a multidisciplinary audience. It focused on how psychological principles could be used as a vehicle to impact global concerns such as poverty, healthcare and illness prevention, peace/conflict/warfare, demilitarization and economic viability, and policy development. The conceptualizations used psychology as the "most common denominator" for creating change and as an integrating point of citizen/community with government/ruling order along with private business/industry.

This concept evolved into a book, *The Integration of Psychological Principles in Policy Development* (Stout, 1994), along with an opportunity to become involved in domestic policy advocacy with a focus on healthcare via the American Psychological Association in the role of Federal Advocacy Coordinator for the state of Illinois. Doing so provided an excellent education and understanding of the power of networking, as well as how policy can be developed, influenced, and advocated. This methodology then was applied beyond psychology to other disciplines. The conceptualization that I developed is that psychology can and should be used as a vehicle of additional, key tools that can have their application and their value realized in a variety of ways and venues.

Case Illustrations

The following are two detailed examples of the impact that psychology can have on helping to mitigate the violence that innocent children experience due to their circumstances. They highlight the amplified impact that a person or group of individuals can achieve to the betterment of these children and hundreds of others.

Bolivia

I was invited to go to Bolivia and work with Flying Doctors of America to provide medical and dental care to prisoners and their families in La Paz. One of the prisons visited was a maximum security facility for women, called Miraflores. The other prisons, not maximum security, were San Pedro (men) and Obrajes (women). While the manifest mission of this trip focused on physical and dental healthcare, it also illuminated the emotional needs of the youngest inhabitants of the prisons, the children of the inmates, because in Bolivia if you are an incarcerated parent with no one else to care for your child then your child comes to prison with you.

In non-maximum security prisons, the families of the inmates are allowed to come and go. The children can attend school, and the spouses may leave during the day. However in Miraflores no one leaves the prison; even the guards have places to sleep there. With so many of the women needing to provide not only for themselves but also for their children, the prison warden allows them to take in laundry and make and sell crafts to generate money. As for the children, they not only live in the prison but they also have to go to school there. Those children do not get to leave, not for school, not for visits, not at all. So, the things that you and I would take for granted while going to school, such as simply seeing the world, going to market, or buying clothes, do not occur with these children. They are basically on house-arrest and sequestered in this prison.

The teachers in the prison's school approached the pharmacy volunteers to ask for the boxes that the medications had come in. The reason? So that they could use them as toys for the children. They are basically saying: "Can we use your trash, because we have nothing to even play with these kids with. Your trash will serve as our toys." As for the children themselves, even in such circumstances they displayed a beautiful resiliency that made the unfairness of the situation stand out even more. We saw the obvious dedication that these teachers had for the children, as well as the dearth of resources available for them to use with the children. So we began to think of ways to help.

You can fly in to fill a tooth but you cannot fly in and fix a trauma. We look at these children in a very holistic way – we want them to have good teeth, we want them to have good hygiene, we want them to have proper nutrition, and we want them to have, as best they can in a psychologically unhealthy environment, as many psychological positives as possible. These children are victims of circumstance and although we may not be able to change political structures and systems, we can provide medical services periodically but we also wanted to do something more sustainable.

The answer was to start small, but what may seem little to one person can be huge to someone with nothing. So, the Center for Global Initiatives (CGI) is developing a "virtual" library of tools and resources for the teachers to be able to use with the children in the prison. They do not have Internet access, but they do have a computer with a functioning CD-ROM drive. We are compiling materials in Spanish that include coloring-book images, picture cards for vocabulary building, and instructions for activities and non-competitive games, along with Spanish-language journal articles on education and classroom management, and non-violent parenting methods and behavior management tools that could be used by the mothers and guards. This type of teaching tool can be used for years and can be viewed on older computers. Along with the CD-ROMs, the CGI will also be sending art supplies such as crayons, colored pencils, and paper, as well as printer paper and ink. We can also create updated versions in years to come.

The materials will also include activities that can introduce and teach resilience and adaptive coping mechanisms to the children. The activities, designed to teach communication skills, empathy, and active listening, can be implemented by the teachers and do not require any extra supplies or additional therapeutic training on the teachers part.

The CGI's use of expressive arts to address the children's needs is the most unique aspect of this project. We thought that creative arts, expressive arts, and music could all be things to bring more life to these children. We want to help to rejuvenate aspects of what "school" could bring to these children. We have an orchestra instructor who volunteered to get music to us and once the music is translated the children can begin basic music education, with or without instruments because you can teach singing without instruments. We are exploring basic kinds of instruments such as triangles, as well as wanting to learn more about the indigenous musical instruments they have there. The CGI continues to explore options for funding for the necessary materials and their transport to Bolivia.

The overall perspective throughout these efforts is to aid the children and enhance what is already there, not disparage it. Every child has strengths, and it is our job to help find those strengths and then build from them. To this end, the CGI plans to coordinate with the teachers in the prison school to find a local music teacher who could come to the school and teach the children music. We are already working with a Bolivian foundation to secure the funding that would be required.

We are also working with a volunteer who is an art therapist, to develop art therapy exercises that the teachers can use with the kids to help them express and process their feelings. The art the children create could do more than provide them with a way to emotionally work through their experiences in the prison. We hope that it can aid in the sustainability of the project.

Our thinking is that art would be therapeutic and beneficial for them, and it would provide more activities for the teachers to be able to engage with the children. We then wish to have the artwork of the children (with appropriate permissions) compiled into an art-book. Once the permissions were obtained, the CGI would look for a publishing house that could donate the production and sales proceeds to the prison school in order to pay for a music/art teacher's salary and materials. We hope that this would also result in more exposure for the plight of these children, and hopefully lead to more help and other opportunities for these children. An added benefit is the pride the children would have in having their art published for others to see and their stories told for others to feel.

Tanzania

As was noted earlier in this chapter, we have a strong relationship working with Tanzanian children in both a kindergarten that we co-founded as well as working with the Huruma Designated Hospital in the Rombo district. This quite simply stemmed from a personal relationship I had with a guide I met while on a climbing trip there and predated the CGI's start but certainly was catalytic to its coming into being. What is amazing to me is the amplification effect of what are very easy and simple "interventions" on our part. These are things that *any* psychologist/ individual could do and likewise have a wonderful impact.

I work with my dear friend Fr. Aloyce Urio, who is in charge of a group of orphaned children as well as being a chaplain at a local hospital. He and I are pen-pals in the most classic sense – ink on paper and a stamp. Over the years he would query me about a child having a certain physical or emotional problem and I would respond back with suggestions, materials, and whatever I could get my hands on. If it was outside my skills, I would consult with an ad hoc team of friends in medicine, physical therapy, occupational therapy, or what-have-you specialty for help, and they always come through.

Aloyce once mailed me a note about many of the children being manifestly sad and tearful. The caretakers did not know how to respond, so they felt that not discussing the children's emotionality was best for the children. I sent Aloyce a set of basic counseling materials on grief and loss, some group exercises, active listening, empathic responding, Rogerian methods, and other "counseling 101" materials that were for children, with the caveat that they were developed and used in the West and that he needed to use his best judgment in adapting them for his use. I also explained ways in which he could consider their use, as well as contraindications.

This seemed to be very useful for him and the caretakers felt supported and empowered to have tools, supervision, and the approval to indeed talk about the children's emotional lives with them. Over time I learned that the children also had experienced therapeutic benefit. But what happened next is a great example of a quite incredible but unintended consequence.

One day a bishop who was responsible for the region was visiting and happened to see the materials I had sent Aloyce sitting on his desk. After being asked what they were and learning more about them, he asked if he could borrow them to make copies and distribute to the other clinics, hospitals, and orphanages he would be visiting, and if Aloyce would be able to "consult" with his counterparts at those sites as a follow-up.

So, what took me perhaps 3 hours to compile and write, and cost less than 9 dollars to send, was now being used not only in Aloyce's area but with many, many other children who otherwise would not have had such therapeutic and emotional support. This is what I mean by amplification. Aloyce's time and postage cost in writing to me, and mine in return, yielded an immense impact on the staff and the children in a number of villages, both now and in the future. I could never have planned nor imagined that would happen. This is the kind of thing that I encourage readers to think about if they are so inclined to be involved in this kind of work, as the bang-for-the-buck can be exponential. Imagine the impact we could make in the lives of others if each one of us did something like this just once in our lifetimes.

The CGI has also consulted on managing the emotional health problems of some of the nursing students who came to the Huruma Hospital for practical training, again with my tutorial coaching notes and sending copies of materials suitable for group and individual use. Similarly, I had never really thought about how (or even if) the orphaned children went to school, and I learned that they did not. Aloyce believed their chances for a better life were improved if they could read and had knowledge-based skills as well as labor-based training. I agreed and we set forth on creating a modest school. In 2005 we received word that the Ministry of Education had approved a kindergarten for the children, which Aloyce now "manages." We continue to be on-call for any help we can give, and always for free. In fact we conduct fundraisers for them and are active in fiscally supporting the children in any way we can under Aloyce's watchful and measured stewardship.

The CGI's philosophy for the projects it works on is to continuously be a free consultant; we really do not want to have "ownership" of any projects. We want to help incubate them, greenhouse them, and then launch them. We will always be available, if needed, ever-after.

Overview of the Issues

While I believe psychology is playing catch-up with public health and global health disparities, there are good models and methods already available and being imported. Paul Farmer (2007), through Partners in Health (PIH), found that one of the keys in his work has been to intervene at the community level via training community health workers rather than doctors and nurses. Their results indicate that AIDS treatment outcome in rural areas of poor countries is significantly better than in inner-city America! So, Farmer is now taking a model that PIH pioneered in Haiti and seeing if it can be made to fit the needs of Boston.

Easterly (2006) describes successful examples and promising programs. He ratchets it up a notch and keeps things current with his discussion of the website and organization GlobalGiving.org, which makes it easy for the rest of us to focus our giving to organizations vetted by a funding algorithm that Easterly developed. In a similar vein, *Millions Saved* (Levine & Kinder, 2004) is a cleverly titled double entendre and a quick-read resource that provides chapter-by-chapter examples of various successful programs worldwide that required only modest investments of capital.

De Waal (2007), in response to a Foreign Affairs piece on global health issues, sums things up:

> The complicated interrelationship between poverty and ill health is unsuited to simple numerical indicators of progress, which is why the Millennium Development Goals (MDGs) attempt the difficult balancing act of crystallizing simple measures that span different sectors. Like any policy designed by an international committee, the MDGs are full of the compromises and ambiguities necessary to obtain consensus, leaving them with inevitable shortcomings. We all have our criticisms of the indicators chosen and doubtless a better job could be done today if health and development experts were to reconvene for a year's deliberations. But that isn't feasible. So the challenge is to identify subordinate targets that can become the focus for mobilization by activist constituencies and that can be used to hold governments and aid donors accountable.

While not as strident as *Neoliberalism, Globalization and Inequalities: Consequences for Health and Quality of Life* (Navarro, 2007) is at times, de Waal certainly understands the key problems confronting global health initiatives.

As psychologists, many of us too often sit on the global health sidelines, feeling as if we are in the wrong arena. There is a great divide between behavioral health, public health, and primary healthcare, and this has long mystified me. For a long time, "health" held little interest for psychology. Noreen Johnson changed that during the year she served as President of the American Psychological Association (APA), when she had the Council of Representatives add the word "health" to the APA's mission statement (Garcia-Shelton, 2006).

Another APA Past-President, Pat DeLeon, rightfully chides us, noting that psychology ". . . as both a science and as a profession . . . has yet to develop a highly visible and proactive international agenda" (DeLeon, 2003). Shame on us, as I believe that psychologists are better prepared by our training than most other disciplines to provide the culturally competent services, along with a myriad of psychological tools, necessary to effect change in individuals, families, systems of care, and policy. I think that reading the works of Navarro and others can help to expand our vision, and hopefully our participation.

Illnesses' Impacts

I have learned that the link from violence to health is clear: Wars and violence kill and injure combatants and civilians, but they also destroy infrastructure and social structures, in both cases with adverse effects on the population's general health. Even less obvious to most of us is the reciprocal nature of this (Kassalow, 2001). There is also evidence of the reverse effect, that of health on war. Combatants in new wars are often the socially excluded. Poor health shortens people's time horizons, making them more likely to engage in risky behavior; conversely, strong democracies and strong communities with broad support from healthy populations are less likely to engage in conflict.

When I worked in South Africa, they noted their top three public health problems as HIV/AIDS, tuberculosis, and violence. They included violence because it is a matter of public well-being and health. I also find it curious to note that the three factors that lead to state failures, such as wars, genocides, or disruptive regimen changes, are: (1) lack of democracy; (2) lack of economic openness; and (3) a rising infant mortality rate. In other words, societies that do not listen to their people, that close themselves off from the world, and that do not care for their most vulnerable tend to fail, producing war and chaos.

Failed states inevitably become seedbeds of violence, terrorism, international criminality, mass migration and refugee movements, drug trafficking, and disease. To prevent war we might better look more closely at the means to bring health and social stability to poor countries, which is something psychology could be quite good at.

Actions Speak Louder

I was fortunate to have been selected to serve as a non-governmental organization (NGO) special representative to the United Nations (UN) via Division 9 of the APA, blending my background in clinical psychology with my UN experiences in sustainable development. I presented a paper that was the result of a year-long project on behavioral health's role in health and sustainable development vis-à-vis a UN document known as the Copenhagen Declaration.

Yet papers and talks, while necessary, did not seem sufficient, so I applied to the Flying Doctors of America to go on a medical mission in Vietnam. This impactful experience demonstrated that active participation in international work is critical for a real understanding of others, of cultures, and of events. And now, from many medical missions, I found myself primarily working with children, where I saw the violence of poverty on health and well-being as well as the violence of illness and trauma.

Paralleling these activities, I took up mountaineering, as very much the amateur. During my first major climb, Mt. Kilimanjaro, I met a Tanzanian guide who was studying in the seminary. We kept in touch over the ensuing years and he became involved in running an orphanage for children who had lost both parents to AIDS or tribal warring. Mixing in what I learned in Vietnam and from the Flying Doctors' organization, along with a passion for public health in a context of battling the inequities experienced by those less fortunate, marginalized, or disenfranchised, the idea for the CGI was born, with more on that below.

The Power of the Small Project

One of my favorite and most influential books is *The White Man's Burden* (Easterly, 2006). Easterly's thesis is pretty simple: Big organizations create big plans that draw big donors or big attention to do big things. The problem is that they tend to be equally big flops. Additionally, such large organizations have such concomitantly large internal operational cost-needs that it often seems that very few dollars or Euros ever make it to the end-recipient.

Making matters even worse is that there is little accountability in such bureaucratic mega-organizations as the World Health Organization, the World Bank, the International Monetary Fund, or even the United Nations. Nevertheless, there is something compelling in the vision or fantasy of really making a dent. And when one hears of large funding, it spurs hope that *this time* it can be different. Donors also like such heroics. Their perspective is that fast, clean solutions trump longer term messier ones every time, but that is true only if they work. All the same, such schemes are sexy and compelling. And it would seem that many bureaucrats have pitifully short-term memories when it comes to assessing outcomes at all, or less-than-expected results are often explained away by so-called intervening and uncontrolled contaminating variables (such as conflict and warring situations or catastrophic climatic events) that mitigated the hoped-for effect. Such variables unfortunately do not likewise mitigate the monies spent.

The wunderkind of making health projects work, Farmer (2007) notes that "A first principle for the emerging global health movement, in fact, might well be: 'Don't emulate the mainstream aid industry.' That said, aid is not bad in itself, and if managed appropriately it can achieve impressive results." He would know, as his work is a showcase for silk purse healthcare results from sow's ears materials.

I am all for more funding but, as Easterly (2006) points out, there is not always a direct or positive correlation between bang and buck. His calculus pegs Western foreign aid thus far to be around $2.3 trillion, with pitifully little to show for it. The point is that small projects do make a difference – perhaps not always at a "statistically significant level" suitable for peer-reviewed journal publication, but quite significantly to that person, or that family, or that clinic, or that community. This is something I can bear witness to having seen with my own eyes, and also added to the formation of the CGI.

This issue of outcomes is a tricky one. While I and many others wholeheartedly support empirical, outcome-based approaches, there is also a caution that should go along with such accountability concepts. And while it is reasonable for funding sources to establish efficacy expectations for projects they support, the metrics should be gauged to most accurately measure what is supposed to be measured, contaminating/contributing variables must be identified and considered, and the timeline should be adequate to allow for accurate measurement of effect (Garrett, 2007). Outcomes should always be additionally judged by those worked with, and communicated to all involved – patients, donors, and board members. This means that it can take a while to see what impact a project has on life expectancy or live births or disability-adjusted life years (DALYs) or whatever. Such metrics simply cannot always be accurately measured in 18 months time postintervention.

Responses to Global Demand

When I use the word "global," it is not simply as a synonym for overseas or international, but I consider both the local and transnational disparities of health risk and illness outcomes. At Harvard Medical School half of all medical students spend time on service projects in the urban United States or abroad. The Adler School, in Chicago, has a required practicum for non-profit experiences and the Chicago School has community partnerships. Alliant University, in California, has campuses not only through-out California but also in Mexico and Nairobi (Kenya), along with programs in Japan, Thailand, and numerous other countries on the drawing board. *Bravo!*

Brigham and Women's Hospital in Boston had so much demand for more serious attention to be paid to health inequal-ities that a special residency program was started to address health disparities in the United States and in the poorest parts of the world. Along similar lines, the APA's upcoming Education Leadership Conference will address "The emerging single global market places for health care," along with other global issues (Belar, 2008, p. 86).

Charity or Social Justice?

We can best create change by sharing our knowledge, our wealth, and a valuable resource – each of you. I'm not just talking about charity work. There is nothing wrong with charity, per se, but most charitable work is focused on the giver. A typical medical mission describes how a group of healthcare workers provided care in a poor setting, left, and then expressed thanks for the opportunity to call a place like the United States home.

Those they cared for remain poor unfortunate people, unable to help themselves. It is therefore important for us to reflect on our motivations for undertaking such work. We must look behind the veil of humanitarianism to understand how our own motivations may clash with the needs and desires of those whom we hope to serve.

The question for me, then, is how may we augment this desire? Perhaps it lies in the concept of social justice? Charity focuses our attention on the comfortable, familiar domain of the giver, while social justice demands that we focus our attention on the often unseemly and disturbing world of those on the receiving end.

In charity we can send surplus supplies abroad, but to arrive at justice we must also look at activism within governmental systems, policy, and political forces – all things that psychology can do and that the CGI does do.

The Center for Global Initiatives

After having worked with many top-tier NGOs, the UN, and many international for- and not-for-profit organizations, many of my friends and colleagues urged me to form a freestanding center devoted to training multidisciplinary healthcare professionals and students to bring integrated services that are sustainable and have publicly accountable outcomes to areas of need. Thus, the CGI was born.

Conceptually, we see the problem we address as healthcare services, sciences, systems, education, and research all suffer from disconnections – globally and locally, biologically and behaviorally, training and practice. Health inequities are global in scale; however it is the philosophy of the CGI that the optimal way of successfully addressing these injustices is by multiple, smaller scale projects, with a coordinated focus and outcome accountability (as with Easterly's perspective). Until now, there has not been a truly integrated center that is at once mindful of all the complex aspects of global health inequities while also focused on small, outcome-oriented projects or cases that will be agile, responsive, and empowering in clinical, training, and research domains. The mission of the CGI is to create self-sustaining programs that improve access to healthcare in underserved communities throughout the world.

The Most Unique Aspects of the CGI

Perhaps the most important aspects of the CGI are the simplest:

1. We serve as an incubator and hothouse for new projects. We help to nurture, grow, and launch them to be self-sustaining.
2. After a project has taken hold, we will continue to serve as pro bono consultants as long as we are needed, with whatever is needed – materials, medicines, case consultation, introductions, etc.
3. The majority (95%) of all of our projects are the result of being invited to do the work. When we are not a good fit, we recommend and link them to a more suitable organization.
4. As best we can, depending on the project, we seek to blend primary care, behavioral health, and public health into an ultimately self-sustaining, outcome-accountable, culturally consonant result.

The goals of the CGI are to:

1. Advance the education and performance of local and international health professionals and students in health-related fields to meet the challenges of health inequalities.
2. Maintain a philosophy and approach as that of a collaborator and colleague.
3. Foster a sense of control over the lives of those we work with.
4. Augment inherent strengths and resilience.
5. Improve people's lives by decreasing premature death and disability, with a special focus on the underserved, refugee, and immigrant populations' needs.
6. Provide clinical services, directly or via channeled funding.
7. Augment existing medical, psychological, and science education, research, and service capacity (including health education).
8. Build the capacity of local communities to improve health and healthcare access.
9. Motivate the public and private sectors to drive consensus and action for the improvement of health globally.

We do this by:

1. Serving as an incubator for new initiatives that creatively solve healthcare inequities throughout the world.
2. Acting as a collaborator with individuals and organizations in developing and launching projects that address the needs of medically impoverished populations.
3. Functioning as a facilitator in directing public and private resources towards programs aimed at improving health.
4. Working as an educator to provide new information and tools for empowering others.

The CGI is currently involved in many no-cost service projects worldwide, as detailed below.

XDR-TB Collaborative

The CGI has responded to the request to sign-on to help battle extreme drug-resistant tuberculosis or XDR-TB. This concern has now been added to our projects in Bolivia and Cambodia.

Bolivia: Project Niños

The CGI collaborated with the Flying Doctors of America in a pioneering and critical project called Project Niños (Alexander, 2008). We were the first non-Bolivian group to be granted access to three Bolivian prisons. Hundreds of children live with their parent(s) in these prisons. We provided care with a focus on general medicine, pediatrics, and gynecology. The CGI will be embarking on helping these non-criminal yet imprisoned children through a unique and pioneering effort. Basically, we plan (pending funding) to develop and deploy educational and social skills training for educators (there are schools in the prisons!) and guards, as well as parenting skills training and resilience development instruction. A detailed case study was provided earlier in this chapter.

Ecuador/Amazon: CONTACT (Coordination and Online Tracking of Activities and Clinical Teams)

This work involves the development of a freely accessible, web-based database that functions as a coordinating center for medical missions, medication distribution, medical equipment donations, and evidence-based practice (EBP) guidelines and protocols for triage, diagnostics, and therapeutics for groups working in the Equatorial Amazon Basin (with goals of expansion worldwide).

It will also serve as a nascent epidemiological database and potentially the first electronic health record for indigenous tribespeople for medical aid and population health workers.

Tanzania: THRIVE (Tanzanian Health and Resilience Initiative Valuing Education)

The kindergarten I helped to found in 2005 is expanding its scope via THRIVE. We are using education as a basis for developing the resilience of the orphans as well as those providing healthcare in the neighboring clinic/hospital. We will be developing programs for local nursing students and orphan children in collaboration with local doctors, nurses, and staff. We will have a particular focus on counseling people with HIV infection and AIDS. We will be in Moshi. The ages of children are between 3 and 12 years. The name of the hospital is Huruma Designated Hospital and it is in the Kilimanjaro region in the Rombo district. The primary illnesses of patients in our hospital are malaria, TB, pneumonia, immunosuppression, diabetes, and hypertension.

Cambodia: SMART (Sustainable Medical Arts, Research, and Technology)

We are developing a project that will bring training and potentially telehealth services to rural areas, delivered by indigenous village women. Public heath, primary care, first aid, and emergency services are all but absent in rural areas of Cambodia. "Itinerant" medical ex-pats may be the currently best available healthcare resource in such areas. This project seeks to empower indigenous women by providing training in basic public health practices and emergency medical care/first aid so they may be of aid to those in their villages. They would be supported by a training program that will enable them to provide sufficient help until the patient can be taken to the nearest medical facility or a traveling physician can come to the village. It will be unique because it will not require literacy to operate.

Benin: Medical InterAction (Linking Sustainable Ecology and Medical Innovation)

Contacts and relationships have been developed with colleagues in Benin that crosscut various areas: health and illness, poverty and sustainability, environmental concerns, traditional and medical sciences/health treatment, and education. We plan to develop a scientific and economic mechanism of researching the medicinal properties of specific plant materials used by our Benin partners (university scientists and traditional healers) to further develop medicines and use the resultant knowledge to refine the compounds to have fewer side-effects and improved dosing characteristics, and to develop that intellectual property into concomitant economic value that will provide economic sustainability, self-sufficiency, and independence for ongoing research.

Ukraine: Nutritional and Health Assessment of the Physically and Mentally Challenged Children in Level 3 and 4 Internauts (Orphanages) in Ukraine for the Purpose of Treatment of Malnourished Children and the Education of Their Caretakers

This collaboration with the Ukrainian Congress Committee of America and the National Assembly of Disabled in Ukraine for a USAID grant is another life-saving project.

India: WorldWise

Through a collaborative with partners in rural India who have developed a comprehensive, community-based primary healthcare approach, we are helping to recruit students for summer experiences that will provide a life-changing perspective on healthcare. The project is called WorldWise and it is being made available only to graduate students (in any health discipline), medical students, and Fellows.

Training and Doing

The CGI also offers various training opportunities. The newest is MENTOR (Methods, Experiences, Networking and Training, Organizing and Research). This is a very special and unique new program that provides individualized mentorship for people wanting to learn how to conduct their own project(s). Upon acceptance into the MENTOR Program, we help awardees to obtain project funding and we provide skills training along with the contacts and tools to actualize their plans. In some instances, undergraduate and graduate credits or Continuing Education Units for some licensed healthcare professionals are also able to be provided. Our motto for this is *"Where do you want to go? What do you want to do? We can make it happen."*

University Model and Fear and Loathing with the Internal Revenue Service (IRS)

If you have ever worked at a university and won a grant, you quickly learn that the university receives 25–55% of the funds. The reason is that there is a mutual need between faculty and research universities. Professors need a not-for-profit setting to receive funding. Grantors do *not* fund individuals; they fund institutions that have been properly vetted and deemed legitimate entities capable of managing funds for the work to be done by the professor. So faculty not only need this safety mechanism provided by an institution but also the support services provided by the university, which help the faculty in their work. The CGI has adopted a similar model.

I now understand why there are not more not-for-profit organizations – I never knew what a time-consuming and expensive process it is. In Illinois, we first had to become incorporated, which took about 3 months, cost $750 in fees to the State of Illinois, plus legal fees. Then we had to complete a daunting IRS application form, called Form 1023 (look it up online, it's a doozie). In it we had to forecast budgets 3 years ahead, provide a myriad of spreadsheets, and other various puzzling whatnots that you hope to goodness you have correctly completed. All of this took a massive amount of my time and that of our attorneys. Then we had to apply for tax-exempt status in the State. Fortunately we were successful, but in all it took about 14 months, almost $1000 in application fees, and almost $6000 in attorneys' fees. Then we had to file our state and federal tax returns on Form 990 (and all of its supporting forms and documents) and Form AG 990-IL (note "AG" stands for Attorney General, so it maximizes one's anxieties in completing it as well). The federal form notes that it takes about 24 person-hours to complete, and I can attest that it did. And that was for our *first* year with *non-complex* financial activities, and not a great deal of money. I do not look forward to next year's tax time . . .

But the point is, after going through all this, I fully understand why more people interested in doing their own projects do not follow through. These hurdles do not do anyone any good. While I do fully understand why they exist to serve as very rigorous protections and assurances, they nevertheless are difficult, costly, and time consuming, and that is if you complete everything properly.

So, as it has always been CGI's philosophy to not "own" projects but to support, augment, and incubate them, it made perfect sense to meld with the university model. For example, a colleague has the desire to take early retirement and, in some of his free time, to create music education projects for needy children in developing countries. The problem is, he does not have the time or money to build his own not-for-profit organization, he just wants to do the work. An additional problem is that while he already has donors who want to contribute both funds and instruments to support his work, they also want to be able to gain a tax deduction for doing so. This is totally understandable, but they cannot donate *and* gain the tax deduction because my colleague is "just" an individual. So, no donations, no project, no children being given instruments and educated on how to use them, and thus no music and no benefit to these children.

But, the CGI (university) model allows my colleague to develop his project within the structure of CGI, a not-for-profit organization, as one of its projects. We provide him with the tools and infrastructure he needs for organizing his project. We connect him with contacts we have in the geographic regions he plans on working in. We conduct research for him that is needed in order to operationalize the project. We help structure a budget, we purchase air-fare and hotel stay for his site-scouting in South America, and we help design his fund-raising and awareness-raising efforts. We also provide him with a website for his project, along with the ability to process credit card donations or mailed-in checks. The purchases he needs to make will be tax free, and all donations would be tax-deductable for the contributors. We even do the year-end tax reporting, filing, and auditing. Our business model is thus like that of a university – 25% of the donations go to support these project efforts and the CGI. It costs him nothing – financially, time-wise, or hassle-wise. The CGI gets to be involved and support more projects, and talented individuals get to accomplish their dream project(s) much sooner than if they built their own not-for-profit organization.

Global Health Fellowship

We have also developed what we call the Global Health Fellowship, following the MENTOR model. The Fellowship addresses four key areas:

1. We have an unmet demand for training opportunities for psychologists and graduate students, which can be done both locally and in-country.
2. As DeLeon (2003) notes, we also have a responsibility to be internationally aware, and Buckminster Fuller called for us to be globally active as "Citizens-of-the-World."
3. We need to provide the tools and support needed to do the work.
4. We need to be advocates, activists, and actors, in the full and complete integration and synthesis of behavioral healthcare, primary healthcare, and public health as *health*. The time is over for disconnected distinctions in one's health to be parsed out by organ system or by social system.

But why should psychologists or graduate students who have spent years learning the science of human behavior invest precious time learning the complex fields of global health? Quite simply, because ours is a profession dedicated to healing – from the individual to the family to the community – and perhaps for the first time in history we can truly create multiple, local impacts as individuals.

A Calling

We are fortunate that ours is a profession that allows for doing well while doing good. We each have a responsibility to live up to the promise of our profession. It is a tall order for psychology, but I know of no other profession better suited. I challenge you to make it part of your work as a psychologist. You can become a psychologist and be in the world, but if you become a part of CGI, you can help to change it.

Note

1. Parts of this chapter are based on excerpts from:

Stout, C. E. (2004). Global initiatives. *American Psychologist, 59*(8), 844–853.

Stout, C. E. (2008). What psychologists could learn about global health inequities, a review of neoliberalism, globalization and inequalities: Consequences for health and quality of life. *PsycCRITIQUES, 53* (Release 26, Article 1554–0138), 1–6.

Stout, C. E. (2008). Psychology, social justice, and global works. Invited feature article. *The California Psychologist, Nov/Dec,* 6, 8–9.
Stout, C. E. (2009). Center for Global Initiatives. In C. E. Stout (Ed.), *The new humanitarians: Inspirations, innovations, and blueprints for visionaries.* Westport, CT: Praeger.

References

Alexander, R. (October, 2008). Project Niños. *Angels in Medicine.* http://www.medangel.org/ninos/ninos020.shtml

Belar, C. (2008). Internationalizing psychology education. *Monitor on Psychology, July,* 86.

DeLeon, P. (2003, July 25). A time for psychology's proactive involvement. *Division 52 International Psychology Newsletter.* Washington, DC: American Psychological Association.

De Waal, A. (2007, January 24). *Pick the right targets.* Retrieved September 21, 2007, from http://www.foreignaffairs.org/special/global_health/dewaal2

Easterly, W. (2006). *The white man's burden: Why the West's efforts to aid the rest have done so much ill and so little good.* New York: Penguin Press.

Farmer, P. (2007, January 23). *From "marvelous momentum" to health care for all.* Retrieved September 21, 2007, from http://www.foreignaffairs.org/special/global_health/farmer

Garcia-Shelton, L. (2006). Meeting US health care needs: A challenge to psychology. *American Psychologist, 37*(6), 676–682.

Garrett, L. (2007, January/February). The challenge of global health. *Foreign Affairs, 86*(1).

Kassalow, J. (2001). *Why health is important to US foreign policy.* Washington, DC: Council on Foreign Relations.

King, M. L. (1966). Presentation at the *Second National Convention of the Medical Committee for Human Rights,* Chicago, IL.

Levine, R., & Kinder, M. (2004). *Millions saved: Proven successes in global health.* Washington, DC: Center for Global Development.

Navarro, V. (2007). *Neoliberalism, globalization and inequalities: Consequences for health and quality of life.* Amityville, NY: Baywood Publishing.

Stout, C. E. (1994). *The integration of psychological principles in policy development.* Westport, CT: Praeger.

CHAPTER 15

Protecting Children from Violence

Historical Roots and Emerging Trends: Conclusions

Kathy Sexton-Radek and James Michael Lampinen

The maltreatment of children in any context is unacceptable. Yet recent statistics indicate that violence against children is all too frequent and is a worldwide problem. These findings necessitate that steps be taken to help protect children from violence. This book has presented several conceptual, clinical, and applied ways of providing safe environments for children. Taken in its entirety, the book provides various platforms and viewpoints that we believe can aid the reader in planning and sustaining this essential mission. In this final chapter we review key themes that have emerged throughout this book: the importance of clearly defined terms, the needs children have after they have suffered from an act of violence, and plausible mechanisms for action. Finally, we will indicate some recommendations for future planning and design in this area and some outstanding resources.

Definition: What is It that we Have in Our World that Compromises the Safety of Our Children?

Before any problem can be solved, the nature of the problem first needs to be documented and understood. This includes developing clear conceptual models of the nature of the underlying problem, the types of abuse and violence that occur, and the incidence and prevalence of the problem. Understanding the scope of the problem in terms of the statistics, demographics, and long-term effects provides a starting ground to determining how change can occur to remedy the problem. Clearly defining the nature of the myriad of problems that children face, and in turn that our world as a whole faces, often indicates clear action pathways. Several chapter authors' approaches provided breadth and scope to this definition of protecting our children from violence. The scope of their treatment of the issues was broad and spanned from the individual child perspective to the family/community/world focus.

At an individual level, we learned from Galezewski (Chapter 2) that three common factors are viable contributors to a child mimicking, exploring, and demonstrating violent behavior. The three factors – family violence, directly or indirectly being a victim of domestic violence, and media (television, film, video games) – are sufficient to influence all ages of children to explore their behavior with an aggressive element. Galezewski wrote that the need to identify with factors they perceive as rewarding and the aftermath of difficulty understanding what they see due to their "pattern of processing" is compelling. Included in this consideration is the often excluded troubled child – the bully. Strikingly, this situation is amplified, Galezewski writes, by the prolonged exposure to violence that is increasing in our society. Newgent wrote at the individual level, we believe, to underscore the need to tailor a program to meet the selective needs of the individual child. In their clear definitions, Newgent and colleagues (Chapter 5) described the concepts of low self-esteem, loneliness, and depression and anxiety in children as being sad, realistic outcomes from exposure to violence. They poignantly termed this "selective identification." Newgent and colleagues furthered their perspective with results from their empirical investigations using the statistics of ROC on objective (selectively identified) assessment measures with logistic regression tools to predict optimal scores for intervention. This empirical substantiation of Newgent and colleagues, approach will determine how best to meet the individual needs of the child. In Chapter 6 by Odegard and colleagues we learn many individualized key ideas to the interviewing of children who have had the misfortune of being victimized. The meta-messages of the accuracy of the child's account are to be accepted and no longer challenge/discounted. Essential elements of using open-ended questions, the use of anatomical dolls, and intermittent interviewing of the child identified by Odegard and colleagues imply that intense focus on the child and their experiences is valid. We read the startling and all too familiar outcomes for the individual child who has succumbed to a violent situation in Chapter 10 by Petretic and White-Chaisson. These authors itemized the pathological results in children's mental health secondary to victimization and witness to intimacy partner violence, emotional abuse, physical abuse, and neglect. Our international historical perspective from Hahn-Holbrook and colleagues (Chapter 12) provides the reader with intriguing considerations of the role of ontological sources in relation to the fear of strangers. Hahn-Holbrook provided the reader with the message, we believe, that the adaptive changes in the fear response are such that emotional regulation, particularly in parents, is eroded. This explanation provides hypothetical reasoning as to why the individual child is left alone to manage violent situations. The work of Schleser and Bodzy (Chapter 11) strongly points out this individual focus in relation to the basics of applying developmental theory when appraising the child's capacity to understand violence. We learn from Schleser and Bodzy that the context of the child's conceptual ability is changing and that factors of the environment and familial and society expectations for the child impinge upon these developing schemas.

A broad perspective that includes the role of the family, community, and the world is provided by many of our chapter authors in relation to the problem of violence and children. Here, we learn of the missteps and provisions of organized approaches. To the child's world this larger sphere provides direct and indirect influences on their behaviors. The value and regard of the family, the school, the afterschool and park district programs, the religious institutions, law enforcement, and governmental and world organizations, by their very existence, provide a haven of protection and care to children. Thus, when they fail, the outcome is as magnified as it is ironic.

Abrams and Portwood (Chapter 3) indicated that tertiary prevention programs are the narrowest in scope in that they target families with a history of maltreatment and seek to prevent reoccurrence of abuse. Further messages from Abrams and Portwood indicate that while the rate of abuse of children is declining, familial factors propagating violence toward children prevail. They wrote that the familiar triad of lack of knowledge of child development (as Schleser and Bodzy also pointed out in Chapter 11), single parenting, and a history of abuse sustains the problem of violence and children; a programmatic focus on parent education and organized, scripted materials released at a national level are needed. They creatively indicated the use of media to provide instruction to parents as well. Empirical investigations conducted by Lampinen and colleagues (Chapter 7) highlighted the problem of identifying missing children. The designs included a community element with practical yet experimentally rigorous elements to prompt remembrances of photos with negative, disturbing findings. But Lampinen and colleagues cited the outdated legislature of the Missing Children's Assistance Act of 1984 and a lack of funding as problems with its implementation. Lampinen and colleagues remind us of the broad need for up-to-date legislation and additional research in this area. Salerno and colleagues (Chapter 9) provided additional evidence of the mismatch of legislation to the scope of the violence and children problem with mandated registry laws. McWhirter and Altshuler Bard (Chapter 13), in their international perspective on domestic violence, highlight the similarity of concerns worldwide for children. McWhirter and Altshuler Bard write of the undercurrents of serious consequences for children witnessing domestic violence. The emotional costs are joined by financial loss, social loss, changes in healthcare, and policing violations/inadequacies. Based on world travels, Stout (Chapter 14) writes of the child health inequalities resulting from poverty, incarceration, abuse, and general societal disregard. A proactive agenda for change of such conditions includes blending the individual needs of the child and family with behavioral health and public health initiatives.

In summary, the individual and group perspectives of the authors span those perspectives pertinent to the issues of violence and children. In their research approaches, clinical experiences, and service, the authors write as experts on these issues to compassionately identify what can be done to move to better resolutions for our children.

What is Needed to Protect Our Children?

Perceptive actions have been identified by our authors but other factors that could not be addressed in a full chapter need to be considered. For example, the Red Cross has long considered the problems of humanity with an action focus. Their "Respect Ed" program is designed to build strengths and provides healthy role models through the enactment of comprehensive intervention.

The Red Cross uses the development of a plan to control risk, to develop policies and procedures, and to handle occurrences. Completed risk assessments along with developed plans and procedures in the program not only address the education of adults, youth, and children but provide for follow through to maintain a safe environment for children.

Another example program that addresses the needs underscored by the authors is the Mendez Foundation program endorsed by SAMHSA's National Registry of Evidence Based Programs. The Mendez Foundation program not only includes program materials and evaluation instruments but also cultural components that need to be addressed. Additionally, it incorporates "review sessions" for students to reinforce their learning about antiviolence programs. Also, the Mendez Foundation program incorporates the engagement of the community in interfaces with the children.

The American Psychological Association has a program, Adults and Children Together (ACT) Against Violence, that was initiated in 2001 and includes scripted materials and planning for partnerships with local agencies. It uses child development-based strategies for strengthening families and educating parents on positive parenting. The focus includes regard for local cultural, social, spiritual, and emotional needs of the very young child, with the philosophy: "caring adults is what a child needs." Data from preliminary studies and a full description are contained on their website: www.actagainstviolence.org. This program is congruent to the nationwide effort to provide for a healthier nation, a safer nation, and a better educated nation in the Decade of Behavior (2000–2010).

These model programs incorporate the themes identified in this book and important additional components: a comprehensive program, incorporation of the community, and regard for cultural issues. In each of the examples, an extension of what has been discussed is provided. However, much more can be done in this area, we believe.

What Can be Done to Further Provide for the Safety of Children?

We believe the experimental methods presented in these chapters provide a solid foundation to investigative approaches. The lack of randomized treatment control designs to provide increased confidence in the findings of programs has to be addressed. Funding for treatment outcome studies to definitively identify the pre-intervention and post-intervention changes for child, youth, and parent participants has to increase. The use of creative, applied approaches such as action research designs, where design participants are involved in the intervention, would release reality-tested generalizable findings, we believe. While the ROC technique to assessment provides strong statistical findings, it may not be available in all settings, thus approaches such as the Mendez Foundation program and APA's ACT with standard measures at the ready are useful.

Programmatic efforts need to be comprehensive to incorporate all elements of the child's environment. The strengths and resources of the agency provide for the sustainment of the program benefits to the child/youth/parent participants. The inclusion of "women and elders and domestic violence" has to be considered in programming. With the comprehensive approach, a social activism component for policy development and eventual legislation becomes essential. An inspection of the social policies mentioned in this book reveals that they are dated. Now, at the close of 2009, new policies and resulting legislature to protect children are needed.

Alongside program development we also need to consider skill building. As indicated in the Red Cross "Respect Ed" program, the building of strengths of the participants is paramount. It is possible that continued training to professionals that encounter the results of violence and children, such as law enforcement officers, would be helpful to promote competence in these areas. Also, the continued design of training opportunities for health-care professionals, with internships, practicums, and externship training opportunities, is necessary. Further, funding resources at the national and international level is essential to the development of programming and the corresponding training opportunities.

To reiterate, we conclude that the individual and community-wide approaches to addressing the issue of violence and children by the authors underscored many considerations. From the consideration of the child's actions, to their reactions to violence, to the broader view of measurement and conceptualization at a community/world focus, viable solutions have been suggested.

For further information there are some excellent websites in this area:

- Adults and Children Together (ACT) Against Violence
  www.actagainstviolence.org

- National Clearinghouse on Child Abuse and Neglect
  www.calib.com/nccanch
- ChildHelp USA
  www.childhelpusa.org
- National Organization for Victim Assistance
  www.try-nova.org
- Rape, Abuse and Incest National Network
  www.rainn.org
- Trauma Focused Cognitive Behavioral Therapy
  http://tfcbt.music.edu

Bibliography

Aigler, E., Taussig, C., & Black, K. (1992). Early childhood intervention: A promising preventative for juvenile delinquency. *American Psychologist, 47,* 997–1006.

Barrington, B., & Hendricks, B. (1989). Differentiating characteristics of high school graduates, dropouts, and nongraduates. *Journal of Educational Research, 82,* 309–319.

Birch, S., & Ladd, G. (1997). The teacher–child relationship and children's early school adjustment. *Journal of School Psychology, 35,* 61–79.

Bohart, A. C., & Stipek, D. J. (2001). *Constructive and Destructive Behavior.* Washington, DC: American Psychological Association Press.

Bradley, R., Caldwell, B., & Rock, S. (1988). Home environment and school performance: A ten year follow-up and examination of three models of environmental action. *Child Development, 59,* 852–867.

Carlson, B. E. (2008). The most important things learned about violence and trauma in the past 20 years. *Journal of Interpersonal Violence, 20*(1), 119–126.

Carlson, C. R., Collins, F. L., Stewart, J. F., Porzelius, J., Nitz, J. A., & Lind, C. O. (1989). The assessment of emotional reactivity: A scale development and validation study. *Journal of Psychopathology and Behavioral Assessment, 11,* 313–325.

Cooper, W. O., Lutenbach, M., Faccia, K., & Hepworth, J. T. (2003). Planning a youth violence prevention program: Development of a guiding measure. *Public Health Nursing, 20*(6), 432–439.

Entwisle, D. R. (1995). The role of schools in sustaining early childhood program benefits. *Future of Children, 5*(3), 133–144.

Erickson, C. L., Mattaini, M. A., & McGuire, M. S. (2004). Constructing nonviolent cultures in schools: The state of the science. *Children and Schools, 25*(2), 102–116.

Furlong, M., Paige, L. Z., & Osher, D. (2003). The Safe Schools/ Healthy Students (SS/HS) Initiative: Lessons learned from implementing comprehensive youth development programs. *Psychology in the School, 40*(5), 447–456.

Hinshaw, S. (1992). Externalizing behavior problems and academic underachievement in childhood and adolescence: Causal relationships and underlying mechanisms. *Psychological Bulletin, 111,* 127–155.

Kashani, J. H., Jones, M. R., Bumby, K. M., & Thomas, L. A. (1999). Youth violence: psychosocial risk factors, treatment, prevention, and recommendations. *Journal of Emotional and Behavioral Disorders, 7,* 200–210.

345

Kingery, P. M. (1998). The Adolescent Violence Survey: a Psychometric Analysis. *School Psychology International, 19*(1), 43–59.

Lutker, J. R. (2006). *Preventing violence research and evidence-based intervention strategies.* Washington, DC: American Psychological Association Press.

Mendel, R. A. (1995). *Prevention or pork: A hardheaded look at youth-oriented anti-crime programs.* Washington, DC: American Youth Policy Forum.

Phillips, L. H., Henry, J. D., Hosie, J. A., & Milne, A. B. (2006). Age, anger regulation and well-being. *Aging and Mental Health, 10*(3), 250–256.

Rovi, S., Chen, P., & Johnson, M. S. (2004). The economic burden of hospitalizations associated with child abuse and neglect. *American Journal of Public Health, 94,* 586–590.

Steinberg, L., & Scott, E. (2003). Less guilty by reason of adolescence. *American Psychologist, 58,* 1009–1018.

Weinstein, C. S., Tomlinson-Clarke, S., & Curran, M. (2004). Toward a conception of culturally responsive classroom management. *Journal of Teacher Education, 55,* 25–38.

Author Index

Subject Index